American Veterans on   r

"The truth of any myth, says Claude Lévi-Strauss, is the sum of all of
its versions. The same might well be said of any history, especially
that of war. There is never one war or one true history of it. Every
war is countless, in the lives it touches and in the stories it spawns;
and the truth of any war is finally 'out' and 'safe' only once all of its
stories have been told and listened to and preserved. Stories are a
matter of life and death for war veterans, a road to healing, a road to
be traveled by us all. Elise Forbes Tripp has done us all a great service by taking in and passing on to us the resonant voices and stories of
fifty-five men and women whose collective military service spans our
nation's major wars of the last seventy years. They cannot possibly
offer the whole truth, but they bring us closer to it. Every shard is
precious and indispensable."
—Robert Emmet Meagher, Professor of Humanities,
Hampshire College, and author of *Herakles Gone Mad:
Rethinking Heroism in an Age of Endless War*

"American Veterans on War *offers fresh and unforgettable
accounts as told by US veterans from World War II to Afghanistan
and Iraq. It's sensational. I'm also amazed by veterans like Don
Ryan who fought in multiple wars. We hear in these voices what it is
really like to serve in such different wars, and how veterans will
forever carry the imprint of war in their hearts.*"
—Andrew Carroll, editor of
the *New York Times* bestsellers *War Letters*,
Behind the Lines, and the National Endowment for the Arts'
Operation Homecoming

Praise for *Surviving Iraq: Soldiers' Stories*

"Surviving Iraq *is a valuable, indeed indispensable, addition to the
literature on the war, especially because it bypasses pretentious
analysis and gives us the voices of the soldiers."*
—Howard Zinn, author of
A People's History of the United States of America

"Engrossing reading that benefits from its simple format. . ."
—Kirkus Reviews

*"This fascinating collection of testimonies underscores the
universality of all war. . . . [A] shocking, moving and utterly heroic
portrait of young men and women in impossible situations. . ."*
—Ken Burns, director and producer,
The Civil War, The War (WW II)

*"[These] extraordinary stories and opinions range from the profound
and the patriotic to the humorous and the heartbreaking. Dr. Tripp
has done a masterful job of finding a diverse and thoughtful group of
individuals and of weaving their oral histories together in a way that
makes them, individually and collectively, unforgettable."*
—Andrew Carroll, editor of
War Letters and *Behind the Lines*

AMERICAN VETERANS ON WAR

Personal Stories from World War II to Afghanistan

Elise Forbes Tripp

OLIVE
BRANCH
PRESS

An imprint of Interlink Publishing Group, Inc.
www.interlinkbooks.com

First published in 2012 by

OLIVE BRANCH PRESS
An imprint of Interlink Publishing Group, Inc.
46 Crosby Street, Northampton, Massachusetts 01060
www.interlinkbooks.com

Library of Congress Cataloging-in-Publication Data

Tripp, Elise Forbes.
American veterans on war : personal stories from World War II to Afghanistan / by Elise Forbes Tripp. -- 1st American ed.
p. cm.
ISBN 978-1-56656-867-8 (pbk.)
1. United States--Armed Forces--Biography. 2. Veterans--United States--Biography. 3. Veterans--United States--Interviews. 4. Vietnam War, 1961-1975--Personal narratives, American. 5. World War, 1939-1945--Personal narratives, American. 6. United States--History, Military--20th century. 7. United States--History, Military--21st century. 8. Veterans--United States--Attitudes. 9. War--Public opinion--United States. 10. Public opinion--United States. I. Title.
U52.T77 2011
355.0092'273--dc23
2011023525

Printed and bound in the United States of America

Cover: Watercolor painting by Pennsylvania artist Tom Bostelle, 1977. Bostelle (1921–2005) served in the US Army, in both Europe and Occupied Japan during World War II. Permission to reproduce granted by the Bostelle Trust.

Book design by Pam Fontes-May

To request our catalog, please call us toll free at 1-800-238-LINK, visit our website at www.interlinkbooks.com, or write to
Interlink Publishing
46 Crosby Street, Northampton, MA 01060
e-mail: info@interlinkbooks.com

This book is dedicated to Leo J. Parent
Veterans' Services Officer for Central Franklin
County District, Massachusetts
For his 25-year commitment to providing support to all veterans
And his invaluable help to the author

CONTENTS

FOUR: IRAQ AND AFGHANISTAN: ENDLESS WARS

*Introduction: Fighting a Universe of "Bad Guys" on Their
    Own Turf*   346

Introduction

WHY WE FIGHT

This is a book of personal accounts of the wartime experiences of veterans of World War II, Korea, Vietnam, the Gulf War, and the unfinished wars in Afghanistan and Iraq. The narratives are entirely in the veterans' own words as I recorded them in 2009 and 2010. The interviews bring us face to face with the realities of combat and its never-ending aftershocks. The narrators revisit the reasons they were given to fight and what they believed in most while fighting. They also share their present perspective on the purposes, effects, and legacy of their and other US wars. The purpose of an oral history recorded from many individual perspectives is to give readers a varied text from which to draw their own conclusions. The juxtaposition of the living memories of different generations of soldiers adds insight and historical context to where we now find ourselves in Afghanistan and Iraq.

Military leaders often prepare for and fight the previous war, as the old saying goes. Because previous wars and their outcomes are the foundation on which each new generation of leaders, warriors, and citizens builds, I will briefly revisit the inheritance of US foreign wars waged before World War II, before these living veterans' spoken memories begin.

Naturally, our national rationales for war hark back to the earliest American colonies and the founding of the United States. US wars previous to World War II deposited layers of political and military antecedents and precedents, creating the geology of American thinking about what we should fight for in the world. These earlier military endeavors will always be a natural part of the story of who, why, when, how, and where the United States fights abroad. Earlier wars have left mental and sentimental habits in the national psyche that are part of the bedrock of our military experience and national beliefs.

For more than two centuries, we attacked, enslaved, killed, or expelled Native Americans who were considered a race apart, so as to occupy the territorial United States that we now live in. We also coveted and fought for lands held by European powers in the New World, and in defeating or buying them out, consolidated the continental United States. We believed in a manifest destiny that led to the west coast, our northern and southern borders, and many ports abroad. We engaged in conflicts that resulted in acquisitions from the Caribbean to the Pacific islands of Hawaii and the Philippines and became a colonial power.

In more recent memory, we became the imperial power that our size, wealth, and people made possible and probable. We developed an ambitious capitalism that has led us to global economic dominance. We have also become the preeminent military power of the world, leading to a ubiquitous military presence overseas that supports a strong and ambitious United States.

The development and use of US military force is as old as the founding father of our nation, George Washington:

> There is a rank due to the United States among nations which will be withheld, if not absolutely lost, by the reputation of weakness. If we desire to avoid insult, we must be able to repel it; if we desire to secure peace, one of the most powerful instruments of our rising prosperity, it must be known that we are at all times ready for war (*Fifth Annual Message to Congress, 3 December 1793*).

Another president and commander-in-chief, President Woodrow Wilson, left a key legacy for the 20th and 21st centuries in his vision of peace without victory during and after World War I. He spoke of the rights of people great and small to freedom and security, which he saw as a particularly American idea. He sent an expeditionary force to fight with our British and French allies, but also suggested that at the conclusion of World War I there be a "general association of nations" that would police the world to ensure against aggressors, a model that would become the League of Nations and later, the United Nations.

President Woodrow Wilson set out guidelines for both a permanent peace and a permanent global place for the United States. The first was based on the freedom to navigate the seas and to trade unimpeded, control of military armaments, and self-determination and resettlement of populations to encourage peaceful relations. The second was based on his hope that the US would, with its allies, police the world (assuming that someone had to) and enforce peace among nations. At the time, his vision failed in part because the US Congress wanted to insulate the country from further European wars (fearing being trapped in foreign adventures on behalf of others) and in part because our allies wanted retribution from the defeated countries.

After World War II, however, the US alone was best able and most committed to the role of keeper of the peace and has held on to it ever since. But policing is only one facet of our global role since 1945. We are also the preeminent salesman of both democracy and capitalism, the latter of which requires the acquisition of resources abroad, so traditionally the military has made safe passage for the growth of capital. Our resources have also been used to support weakened allies, secure friends in the Cold War, and help poor and afflicted countries.

The concerns of General Dwight D. Eisenhower, supreme commander of the Allied Expeditionary Force in Europe (1943–5) and a two-term US president (1952–60), remain of contemporary interest as they define a familiar mindset. He is often remembered for his warning about the military-industrial complex—its influence on both the level of peacetime armament, and its obvious investment in war. In his farewell address to the nation on January 17, 1961, he spoke to the period in which he served, which includes World War II, the Korean War, and the Cold War. In a prescient speech, he illuminated what no one would be able to control: our unleashed power. He considered that power a good thing if properly handled and so long as it stayed in American hands. He also saw its potential dangers:

> We now stand ten years past the midpoint of a century that has witnessed four major wars among great nations. Three of these involved our own country. Despite these holocausts, America is today the strongest, the most influential, and most productive nation in the world. Understandably proud of this preeminence, we yet realize that America's leadership and prestige depend, not merely upon our unmatched material progress, riches, and military strength, but on how we use our power in the interests of world peace and human betterment.
>
> Throughout America's adventure in free government, such basic purposes have been to keep the peace... and to

enhance liberty, dignity, and integrity among peoples and among nations. To strive for less would be unworthy of a free and religious people. Any failure traceable to arrogance, or our lack of comprehension, or readiness to sacrifice would inflict upon us grievous hurt, both at home and abroad.

Progress toward these noble goals is persistently threatened by the conflict now engulfing the world. It commands our whole attention, absorbs our very beings. We face a hostile ideology global in scope, atheistic in character, ruthless in purpose, and insidious in method. Unhappily the danger it poses promises to be of indefinite duration. To meet it successfully, there is called for, not so much the emotional and transitory sacrifices of crisis, but rather those which enable us to carry forward steadily, surely, and without complaint the burdens of a prolonged and complex struggle with liberty the stake. Only thus shall we remain, despite every provocation, on our charted course toward permanent peace and human betterment....

A vital element in keeping the peace is our military establishment. Our arms must be mighty, ready for instant action, so that no potential aggressor may be tempted to risk his own destruction....

Until the latest of our world conflicts, the United States had no armaments industry. ... We have been compelled to create a permanent armaments industry of vast proportions.... We annually spend on military security more than the net income of all United States corporations.

Now this conjunction of an immense military establishment and a large arms industry is new in the American experience. The total influence—economic, political, even spiritual—is felt in every city, every Statehouse, every office of the Federal government. We recognize the imperative need for this development. Yet, we must not fail to comprehend its grave implications. ...

In the councils of government, we must guard against the acquisition of unwarranted influence, whether sought or unsought, by the military-industrial complex. The potential for the disastrous rise of misplaced power exists and will persist. We must never let the weight of this combination endanger our liberties or democratic processes.... Only an alert and knowledgeable citizenry can compel the proper meshing of the huge industrial and military machinery of defense with our peaceful methods and goals, so that security and liberty may prosper together.

Eisenhower (who was a captain and temporary lieutenant colonel in World War I, training soldiers at Camp Colt in Gettysburg, but not serving in France) knew that the US government at every level, and an "alert citizenry," would have to set limits to the use of our power. While the horse is out of the barn, Eisenhower's warnings still resonate, and many of us know that his point remains valid and we are willing to accept that there are times when Americans need to "go home."

Starting our veterans' narratives with World War II, we find the mental bulwark that developed under earlier forms of US expansionism, colonialism, imperialism, militarism, commercialism, capitalism, and the resulting military-industrial complex. US soldiers continue to fight for our right to self-protection and security, our goodwill toward others, and our desire to share our national belief in life, liberty, and the pursuit of happiness as well as self-determination, democracy, and freedom. They are still taught that they fight in the tradition of the American Revolution.

The key word, the mantra for all of the above, is freedom. We fight to protect our own freedoms. We fight to both safeguard and export freedom to other peoples: freedom from dictatorships (even when we support them in our own interests), freedom from want, hunger, disease, and various ideologies. We fight for things we as a nation secured and immortalized in our founding documents (especially the Declaration of Independence and the Constitution) before and after our revolution against Great Britain, including the Bill of Rights guaranteeing freedom of speech, religion, assembly, due process, and the rule of law. Our flag flies over the land of the free and the home of the brave and we fight in the name of freedom when we fight abroad.

As the proverbial City on a Hill, we, like most other peoples, have an abiding faith in our own goodness. I found no veterans who had abandoned their belief in that goodness, even when some were skeptical about our country's intentions in foreign wars and the breadth of our military commitments. They also recognize the ambiguities of fighting, the confusion between friend and foe in Vietnam and recent wars, and what they see as the un-American excesses and aberrations of war, such as the My Lai massacre of civilians in Vietnam, and abuse of Iraqi prisoners in Abu Ghraib prison. Still, our soldiers believe that we are good, do good, or, at the very least, have good intentions.

This book appears at a time of national and international insecurity, when many are questioning what our global role should be. A surge of sagas of our national history have appeared, with the Founding Fathers playing a leading role, as if we are getting our moorings again. The foundation era is seen to flower in our leading role in World War II and the Cold War. What is striking is that we continue to recount, revisit, and even rely on World War II as our last best war. New fictionalized and documentary films and books on World War II are continuously being proffered to lend support to our belief in, and nostalgia for, our country's fundamentals.

September 11, 2001 has changed the US relationship to the Arab world, specifically to radical Islam, and to terrorism generally, and that has translated into two wars fought on foreign soil. The damage to the US psyche on September 11 was immeasurable, and in the near-term, irreparable. It tore off the protective barrier that US citizens had counted on to safeguard non-combatants in every war since the Civil War. We could always send our "boys," and now our men and women, across one or both of our oceans without fearing physical repercussions on our soil.

The United States has been armed and engaged in battle on and off since World War II, using its military strength to "make the world safe for democracy." The current wars in Iraq and Afghanistan bring into question where we place the outer edges of enforceable spheres of influence and self-protection between our own geographical borders and the entire globe. The new norm is frequent military engagements, a huge defense budget, and military bases around the world. I believe that the human and financial cost associated with this should come under public scrutiny and debate.

I have focused on wars alone, not the many US interventions, engagements, and peacekeeping operations undertaken to confront communism, radicalism, and terrorism. These latter include a long sequence of post-1945 interventions by our military and the Central Intelligence Agency (CIA). Any such list should include Greece, Germany, ex-Yugoslavia, China, Cambodia, Laos, Indonesia, the Philippines, Pakistan, Iran, Lebanon, Libya, Sudan, Somalia, Liberia, Angola, Cuba, the Dominican Republic, El

Salvador, Nicaragua, Grenada ("Operation Urgent Fury"), Panama ("Operation Just Cause"), Haiti ("Operation Restore Democracy"), and the UN-sanctioned 2011 NATO intervention in Libya ("Operation Odyssey Dawn").

Americans do not fold their tents and leave after each war. According to the Department of Defense (2005) Worldwide Manpower statistics (the most recent I could locate), we have a military presence ranging from a single military attaché to significant forces in 138 countries. In Germany, 66,418; Japan, 35,571; South Korea, 30,983; Italy, 11,841; UK, 10,752; Serbia and Kosovo, 1,801; Turkey, 1,780; Spain, 1,660; Bahrain, 1,641; Belgium, 1,366; Iceland, 1,270; and Guantanamo, Cuba, 950. This is remarkable testimony to the fact that the United States has been at war and maintaining the peace continuously since Pearl Harbor in 1941.

WRITING AN ORAL HISTORY OF WAR
Hearing what veterans think of their own war's benefits and costs to them and to their country, is key to this oral history. I hope readers will also listen to what older veterans think of recent and current American wars, whether a particular war should be fought rather than addressed through diplomacy, or should be left to others (including the principal parties in the country involved) to sort out themselves. In the case of Afghanistan, the question is how best to eliminate the threat of al-Qaeda short of sending large armies into such an inhospitable terrain.

Some narrators thought that the US was right to fight every war we have fought, including the ongoing ones. Others thought that we should only fight a war when actually threatened; others still, only if we could win. These differing opinions are not equally represented: there are fewer unilateral war-supporters than doubters. Clearly, my sample reflects local political views. In the population I interviewed, most veterans believed that some wars were necessary (such as World War II) and some were unnecessary (such as Vietnam, although there were different opinions of that); some were successful (World War II) and some were unsuccessful (Vietnam, although we showed we were serious there). I was truly surprised to find so few veterans who thought that the current wars in Afghanistan and Iraq were either necessary or likely to be successful.

Veterans are uniquely qualified to testify to the human costs of war and to question whether a new war is worth that cost. They also question whether it is effective to undertake a new engagement in countries whose actions and internecine fighting do not impact us directly (unless we believe that everything impacts us). Civilians do not often hear directly from veterans, yet our national policies are constantly creating new veterans, many of whom will have to fight battles with physical and emotional losses for the rest of their lives.

It needs to be reiterated that US armed forces fight wars that their political leaders decide to fight. The military in America neither picks its own fights nor sets the parameters for *how* to fight. Many veterans complained to me that every war since World War II was too "political." By this they meant "determined by the politicians," "conducted by the politicians in Washington, DC," or by "the military brass, in Washington or other safe places." They know they are employed to carry out political aims, but they want to fight effectively, for causes that inspire, and aims that can be achieved.

Most narrators in this book did not agree with the current US agenda in Iraq to install democracy and remake the government. They know that this is not what they are trained to do. The focus on societal and governmental change through elections is different from their assigned business—the winning of wars. They usually want a gloves-off war (but not a nuclear World War III) that can be *won*. Soldiers know that they are out of luck when it comes to fighting other countries' civil wars, wars against civilians, wars against insurgencies in which every single civilian (such as in Iraq or Afghanistan) can become an enemy fighter. These are wars for hearts and minds, not territory, and are especially hard to fight or win. Soldiers naturally want to see some benefit from their efforts. They often point out that even in bad wars American soldiers do some good while deployed, such as sharing goods received from home, building schools, and ministering to the medical needs of civilians. But how can this be their primary job?

War is designed, and always has been, to inflict maximum damage on the enemy. At the same time war also inflicts damage on all warriors. This latter cost has been acknowledged in all the great literature on war, and is being recognized increasingly by those who deal with the residue of war in veterans today. Governments have not always paid much attention to what falls in the "costs" rather than "benefits" column, yet we know that ignoring those human costs only compounds them.

The following veterans' stories of personal wartime experience include commentary on war in general and US wars in particular. Collectively, the stories raise important questions about recent US wars. Most published or otherwise preserved recorded oral histories of war are individual memoirs. Those that include a number of veterans almost always focus on one war. As noted earlier, I have chosen to present collectively, chronologically by war, the stories of generations of veterans. Their different wars are not continuous (although one war can beget another) but do form a continuum. I believe that the collection itself conveys more about recent US wars, similarities and differences, their cumulative character, as well as the lessons to be learned, than accounts of a single conflict can.

The reader should note that just as the term "veterans" applies to all branches of the service, I find it natural to use the collective term "soldiers" to refer to all who fought as army, airmen, Marines, and sailors. Their individual narratives identify the branch in which they served. In addition, I use both the "United States" and "America." The former is politically more accurate, but most veterans refer to America, as do many foreign nationals, so I let the context determine usage.

While I taped and transcribed all the oral histories in this volume in one-on-one interviews and met in person with almost all the World War II and Korean veterans and most of the recent veterans of the Gulf, Afghanistan, and Iraq wars, I conducted a number of the Vietnam interviews by telephone. One day, an interviewee told me he had known my cousin Bing Emerson, the only person I knew who had been killed in Vietnam. Word went out to his comrades who are scattered around the country, and they contacted me to tell his and their own stories. I devote a memorial chapter to this young Marine helicopter pilot as remembered by the aviators who flew with him until November 20, 1968, when he was shot down.

I primarily contacted individuals from the ranks, as their stories are much less frequently told and they better represent the US citizenry at large. Each veteran has contributed a portion of a lasting public record. Each soldier has vivid memories of what he saw and heard and what happened to him and his comrades. I never needed prepared questions. I learned (to try) to stay out of the way of the story, not to comment, asking for more, not different, information. The narratives are more than ample to make each story well worth reading. Their words ask us to hear and to see what they did.

Veterans know that they have engaged in an historic war and that passing on its lessons to younger generations and the public is worthwhile. They have talked with their war comrades and been tapped for memories by their families, although almost none of the ones I interviewed had made their narratives more public than that. I explicitly asked narrators to include only what they wanted to share with others, and to leave out what they did not. My experience interviewing thirty veterans in my earlier oral history of the war in Iraq (*Surviving Iraq: Soldiers' Stories*, 2008) taught me not to invade a narrator's privacy and sensitivities. (Please note that the Iraq section of this volume contains all new interviews.)

I set the stage at our meetings by explaining that I was an historian recording individual experience of war as well as soldiers' wider opinions and observations from the time they had served, to current wars. I left to the end the question, "What do you think of the Korean, Vietnam, Afghanistan, Iraq war?" A few let that question pass, most responded to it, and quite a few addressed the question themselves without prompting.

The narratives are edited to convey the narrators' character, experiences, opinions, feelings, and lessons learned. Taken together, the interviews are not militarily, geographically, sociologically, or ideologically balanced, as the selection of veterans was effectively random. I used those who work with veterans to make contact. I spoke with each person at length, so that the reader would hear enough of their experience to care what had happened to them, and to appreciate their views. I continued to interview veterans of a given war until I felt that the war itself had become "real" and its legacy to the United States made clear.

I included every person I interviewed without knowing anyone's views before I met and recorded them, and I pass on all of their opinions. There are, however, some similarities in outlook, especially among the World War II veterans. I chose to interview the people of the small towns and cities of Western Massachusetts, a stable population that came back from war to the place where they were born. Because I also live there, I could arrange to meet veterans in their homes, which was crucial especially in the case of the World War II and Korean veterans, who are elderly and have medical problems and appointments, and who welcomed multiple visits.

Most initial interviews lasted over two hours, with transcripts of 5,000 to 10,000 words, so the final versions contain only portions of the original text. While each contributor was treated equally, overlapping content between narratives, and the content of a given narrative, has made for varied length. Each narrator received a copy of the transcript to review before publication, and was encouraged to make corrections, deletions, or additions in a second interview or conversation. Quite a few edited their text without any prompting, in one case four times, with each better than the last.

From a corrected copy of the transcript, I sculpted the following narratives. I say "sculpted," because I took a block of text and kept paring it down, condensing the text but keeping it entirely in the narrator's words. Where helpful, I have elaborated on terms and references in brackets, and provided relevant background about events. I have left out frequently used filler words ("and," "so," "actually," "you know," "just") that did not qualify anything, and corrected some grammatical errors. I kept the narrative in both present and past tenses because people often tell parts of their stories (especially dialogue) in the present tense. When I rearranged the sequence of a narrative, it was to bring together comments on a certain event. I asked narrators to indicate a preferred first name for the short biography before their narrative (if different from their given name) and three asked me to call them "Sergeant."

My editor asked me to explain how I sequenced the different narratives. Naturally, I considered chronology, location, and what branch of the military the soldiers served in. I paired a few people: trench foot in France, being captured by the Germans—variations on similar experiences. I used both contrast and complementarity, in terms of experience, style, and character, to place the narratives. Some of the newer veterans have served in both Iraq and

Afghanistan, and with multiple deployments, chronology was a challenge. Among these most recent veterans, I tried to highlight the contrast in individual philosophies, which is still stark.

Oral history is more art than science. "Truth" and memory overlap but do not completely coincide. I have checked the facts that I could, and have evaluated stories based on what I found in historical sources. I selected vivid and detailed passages experienced firsthand, although in a few cases there are well-remembered secondhand accounts. This does not mean that I can be sure all memories are historically accurate, or that a reader might not be skeptical of an account of a particular event and I take responsibility for what I left undone or did not recognize as inaccurate.

A few personal comments are in order. I found that as a woman without military experience I was at an advantage in soliciting stories. Veterans willingly explained the technicalities of war (how to handle an M-1 or fly a helicopter) in order to educate me, which also benefits the civilian reader. Also, the two of us were not linked by nostalgia for our fighting days, nor were we competing over our exploits. I sensed that as a woman I was viewed as someone who would be empathic to suffering and hidden wounds, and veterans noted their fears, doubts, and disappointments. The many wives I met were gratefully acknowledged by their husbands as helpmates, and more often than not, sat supportively nearby during the interview. They seemed to welcome me as a fellow listener.

When asked why I chose the topic of war, I explained that as a college and graduate student during the Vietnam era I had been deeply affected by that war. My doctoral dissertation was a case study of patron-client relations in US foreign policy (Congo/Zaire). From 1983 to 1998, I worked as an international civil servant in an agency of the United Nations. This background reinforced my commitment to and belief in my own country and its enormous potential for good in the world, as well as a growing concern about the positive and negative impact of its global actions.

ONE
WORLD WAR II:
THE GOOD WAR

14,903,213	Served (1941–5)*
405,399	Died (1941–6)*
291,557	Killed in Action (KIA)*
670,846	Wounded in Action (WIA)*
74,074	Missing in Action (MIA)**

*Department of Defense (DOD) figures compiled by the Congressional Research Service, 26 February 2010. This figure always includes all soldiers who served during war time, even if they served outside the war arena.
**DOD Missing Personnel Office

Introduction

A TERRIBLE FIGHT BUT A GOOD WAR

Two great European memoirs of World War I, Robert Graves' *Goodbye to All That* and Erich Maria Remarque's *All Quiet on the Western Front*, are personal testimonies against wars that were fought with a belief in glorious death. World War I killed a generation of officers and enlisted men as if dying were the point of it all, as in ancient wars. Veterans of World War II make clear that in *their* war the great numbers expended were atoned for by the overriding purpose of defeating terrible enemy forces in battlefields across the globe.

For America, its allies and enemies, World War II is the defining war of the 20th century, and it was fought until it was won. The imperial Axis dictators did not ride the tide of history because, among other things, they took on the major political unit of the time: the nation state, which would not be obliterated by conquest. It became a worldwide face-off, a war that engulfed citizens and soldiers alike, leading to massive destruction and death. It also led to victory for the Allies who believed they faced an aberration, an evil that could, and would, be defeated.

World War II was the last war to engage our entire country and find a compelling role for civilians. Everyone who could, contributed, including those staying at home as civilian guards, children who hunted for foil gum wrappers, families who hung lined curtains to block the light along America's shores, and civilians who saved on gas and cut back on coffee and chocolate to save for the soldiers. Young women flooded into jobs they had not expected to perform and enjoyed new independence while waiting for the soldiers to come home.

The service of enlisted and drafted soldiers in World War II was vast—millions signed up when they were 17 or 18 years old. In many high school classes, students awaited their turn, sometimes skipping the chance to graduate. Brothers signed up one after the other, and many served at the same time. The carnage was wholesale but far away, and even in the darkest of hours, victory was assumed by most. The United States provisioned its allies well before Pearl Harbor, and afterwards sent forces overseas. Clearly, American soldiers helped turn the tide in favor of the Allies. Not only were they pivotal to the war, but the United States became the linchpin of the postwar world, emerging from that vast enterprise hale and hearty, and the father of the atomic bomb.

Tom Brokaw, in *The Greatest Generation* (1998), not only gave voice to World War II veterans, but by calling them the "greatest" renewed their pride. The theme of Brokaw's book is individual success following sacrifice. I interviewed veterans of the same war, a number of whom were encouraged to talk by *The Greatest Generation* and by the 1994 50th anniversary celebration of the Normandy landings. The veterans I spoke with measured their success by their lucky survival or lasting injuries, and by their swift return to normalcy, not by financial or professional success. They did not see themselves as historic figures, but as small figures in an historic war. They enlisted, or were drafted, as pawns, not knights, and remain, in their 80s, modestly proud of their role in the greatest of modern wars. We owe them thanks for their wholehearted fight, and for their sacrifices of mind and body to restore sanity and justice among nations, albeit imperfectly, as is always the case.

Meeting World War II veterans after all these years, the word that came to my mind was "gentlemen." They are gentlemen, and gracious, in some ways perhaps *made* gentle by the brutality they endured. Some personally witnessed the watchword moments such as the attack on Pearl Harbor, fighting under Patton, being a POW, or liberating a concentration camp—momentous in the public view and in their own eyes alike. All would say they are proud of their contribution to the war effort, but when they recount their experiences, they sound immune to the glories of war, and this immunity probably developed from what they had to do and what they witnessed done.

The following World War II veterans are citizens of a United States they believe in and of which they are proud. They returned home in order to forget war, marry fast, and have families. They decided to put the war behind them and look ahead. They are a generation of survivors of both the Depression and the war, and they are molded by the steel of their early years. They fear war, and some are critical of the more recent US wars that seem to be extending their country beyond its original shape and purpose. Even when critical of subsequent wars, they maintain their abiding belief in, and affection for, their country.

In accounts by the oldest of the veterans in this volume, readers will see that those who survived World War II lost not only friends and comrades, but their innocence. They could not dodge this bullet: they suffered trauma, but by keeping their experiences to themselves they hoped to spare their families a secondhand trauma. They generally revisit the realities of war alone or with comrades. They do not glorify war, or for that matter, even the leadership in war. It is important to note that in World War II, generals talked to soldiers and led the troops. Whatever you thought of General Patton or General Eisenhower, they were there.

Some groups of soldiers or auxiliaries are not properly represented in the following narratives. One important omission is of uniformed women who served as nurses and other staff. I located two WAVES (Women Accepted for Volunteer Emergency Service) but neither felt her story merited being included with war stories.

I wanted to make sure that, in the stories of this final segregated American war, the role of African Americans was recorded. Therefore, in addition to a narrative by an African-American army veteran, I solicited comments from other veterans. World War II had black army men, black airmen, and black sailors, although there were none in the Marines. Black servicemen were kept separate, except in the Navy, where their jobs were servile. In the Army they fought in their own groups, or served in ways only distantly related to armed combat. The general notion was that it was dangerous to arm black Americans. The Tuskegee Airmen program to train select African Americans to fly in wartime was a remarkable departure and success. The highest military and political echelons considered it best not to force integration on a segregated (de facto or by regulation) society at war. Truman desegregated the services in time for an integrated force in Korea, but it was not until Vietnam that black Americans served most fully, and in greatest numbers.

Many World War II soldiers looked forward to the adventure of war; after, older and wiser, they looked forward to coming home and having their own postwar family. They helped create and celebrate postwar America—our sentimental attachment to World War II is something that came later. Veterans were immediately rewarded by being told that they had discharged their duty to their country and to the world, and that their efforts and sacrifices were valued, necessary, and successful. They participated in the great festivities on V-E (Victory in Europe) and V-J (Victory in Japan) days, wherever they were.

When Studs Terkel published his oral history of World War II in 1984, he acknowledged that the war had become emblematic by putting the title "The Good War" in quotation marks. Its role in American history has not changed. The legacy of World War II has directly influenced every subsequent war. All generations alive today know that World War II and its outcome have defined the modern world. It gave absolute proof of US prestige, power, and domination and ended US isolationism. But our powerful nostalgia for that war can also cloud the view forward.

I suggested to veterans that they exercise an historical perspective on their own, and on subsequent (or previous) American wars. Those views, with which most of the narratives end, are important. Do veterans of a major global war believe that current US wars are worthy of this nation, and, more pragmatically, that they can be won?

1
ON LAND AND IN THE AIR:
ARMY AND ARMY AIR FORCES

Allen Jones, born in 1924 in Loone, has lived all his life in Tennessee. He finished high school in Bolivar, and went to the University of Tennessee Junior College in Martin for a year before he was drafted into the Army. He returned to college in 1946, but felt the time had passed, he had lost years, and got married. His story is about fighting through France under General Patton in the 3rd Army and being evacuated with trench foot. The interview was conducted by phone.

Before starting his World War II story, I include introductory words from his grandson Travis Jones, who was born in 1975 in Kentucky. Travis deployed to Iraq in 2004–5 and his story is in my previous book, Surviving Iraq: Soldiers' Stories. *In 2010 he deployed to Kuwait to facilitate the troop reduction in Iraq. He spoke to me about his grandfather:*

> There's this commonality between all wars, that no matter how times have changed, it's still combat. I talk more to my grandfather now, he and I share a common language having been in a war zone. He's stock-taking now, what he did, the guys he served with. We all knew he was a World War II veteran [but] if you walked in the house you would never have known anything, he never displayed anything. He really didn't mention much about it until after I came home. Not until the late '90s when *Saving Private Ryan* came out.
>
> Listening to him talk about what he did over there, he tried to find some sense of humor, some enjoyment, it was just so bad. He saw so much death and he saw so much hardship. He

was running up a snow bank with his battle buddy and having shots fired at him, and they both started laughing about it. He said he felt so crazy at the time, might as well just laugh because we can't think of anything else. It was horrible with death happening all the time. Hearing him talk about that, he was very honest and genuine. My grandfather might like to do one more interview just to put some stuff out.

Here is that interview.

They called all of us, warning us to get into the reserves, so we could get our education and not be affected by the draft. It didn't sound right to me, so I didn't get in the reserves. Within two weeks, they were calling up all of these fellows. So that made me gun-shy of anything the military had to say to me. I left college and came home knowing that I would be called up most any time. I chose the Army only because they were giving a 21-day furlough on the front end, because they were having a hard time getting people!

I was stationed at Myles Standish near Taunton, Massachusetts, about 30 miles from Boston, waiting to be shipped overseas. We were carried to the Chelsea Naval Base, loading supplies on ships. I realize now that it was because the stevedores were handling that work, and they spent a good portion of their time in the smoking rooms. It was taking a week to load up one of those ships with supplies. We old country boys, we didn't mind working. We began to load a ship a day. It was ammunition and of course the civilians didn't like to handle these big shells, they weren't sure how safe they were. It was a little bit of a conflict between the workers there, if they stuck their head into a boxcar where we were working and said anything, all we had to do was handle some of that ammunition!

I ran into that idea that war was good for the country. I was in one of the smoking rooms one day, they were talking about how good things were. "Man, this war is the best thing that happened to us in a long time." I said, "Man, what are you talking about, people are getting *killed*!" He said, "It's a good thing to have a little war going all the time, it lets the people have jobs, working well back here." I am not too sure but what some of the politicians now don't think the same way, because ever since World War II, they've kept some kind of war going, all the time. I think if the people who were making the decisions to go to war had to be involved in it, it would be a different story.

During the North African campaign, they were losing troops mighty fast over there. We left in July ['43] for basic training, Camp Hood, now Fort Hood, near Waco, Texas. I was sent to England after D-Day as a replacement in the 3rd Army, they had given Patton command. The 5th Division was an Army regular division, they were sent over into combat in the Rhine. It was a very sad situation because so many of those fellows never did get to return home. Their distinguishing mark was they had a red diamond stenciled on their helmet. So the first thing we did was put mud or something over that red diamond because it made a perfect target. The 5th Division was used by Patton as a spearhead division, so we were out in front in everything, all the time. The casualties were very heavy.

I was in the hedgerow country of France. The hedgerows had been there for years upon years to the extent that the ground for the hedgerows was approximately two feet higher in elevation than the fields they surrounded. They had been the fences for those fields. Those [Sherman] tanks could not get through because there were trees growing on top of those hedgerows, on those mounds of dirt. But one of the soldiers, an old country boy, he had been around a machine shop, and he says, "I can fix that." He went to work with a welder and he put a bulldozer blade on the front of those tanks. They could run into those hedgerows, cutting a path where tanks could roll right through. They brought in metal and made the blades for the front end of those tanks. The thing about those old country boys, they could improvise and mend most anything. That's the way they overcame the hedgerow problem in Normandy.

I was still in the replacement pool, we just followed the front. One morning I awoke to a terrible roar. I got out of my sleeping bag and pup tent. The sky was completely filled with planes as far as the eye could see. Most of them were up high enough that the bombers had a vapor trail, and this was the second wave to Saint-Lô. That's when they spent all day going back and forth. We were on a hill near Saint-Lô, and they were bombing and that was the beginning of what they called the Breakout. [Saint-Lô, 24–5 July

1944, was an important battle following D-Day that included the tragedy of US bombers killing US troops on the ground when red marker smoke drifted over their positions.]

They were American planes and it was a continuous roar all day long. The breakthrough came and the Germans were on the run. Patton was always in a big hurry, always in a hurry. What I mean is, I think he was probably a good general, but he lost about three times more men than the 1st or the 9th Army, either one. In any case, I was with the weapons battalion and I had two big bags of ammunition, in addition to my pack and my gun. I didn't weigh but about 130 pounds, and I was carrying two bags and each one of those rounds weighed eight pounds and there were six to a bag, so I had about a hundred pounds in addition to my rifle and my pack.

After this big breakthrough we traveled a lot of times by truck, but three fourths of the time we were traveling by foot. Patton didn't allow you to follow the roads, they were too vulnerable, so we were in the cross country through the railroads and streams, all the time, moving too fast. Our battles were pretty much from village to village. Sometimes we'd take two or three towns in a *day*. Of course, the Germans were fighting us. When they could stop, organize, they were very efficient with their equipment.

I will say the Germans had superior equipment than the Americans did, even in 1945. They had an artillery piece 88 millimeters, a breech gun. They would keep aiming those 88s directly at us, or they could use it in the regiment as an artillery piece. They had a .30-caliber gun, it was so fast, we called it a burp gun— that's about what it sounded like, spitting out bullets about three times faster than our .30-caliber machine guns. We lost a lot of people during that time; a lot of replacements came up.

When we were near the Moselle River, we were stopped. Of course, we were told we ran out of supplies. I'm not too sure. We were just too far out in front, because the 3rd Army was between the 1st and the 9th. Speaking of Metz, this outfit of ours wanted Metz. We had the Germans on the run but we had to back up because we were ordered to, we went back probably five miles. Then we fought for weeks to gain that back because it gave the Germans time to get a foothold. We were there for three weeks. That's when the Germans had a chance to regroup and kind of get stashed away. They didn't cut us any slack, that's for sure. The Germans would send out patrols at night, they were in the villages, with my glasses I could see them up walking around and maintaining their coverage. They didn't bed down out in the open like we were.

We are talking about the early fall of '44. That's when we were approaching Metz in October [the final battle for Metz was November 3–17]. It had begun to snow even then, the cold weather set in. The equipment we had wasn't for cold weather. In fact, I have found out since then that Eisenhower hadn't planned on a winter campaign. We had nothing but summer clothing. In fact, Patton made us turn in our overcoats because they were too heavy and we couldn't move fast enough, so we didn't even have overcoats. They didn't care, I don't think. I'm just telling you that's exactly what happened. The warmest thing I had was a field jacket that was taken off of a German, underneath my field jacket, it was quilted, and very superior to what we had. That was what I kept warm in.

The rear echelons grabbed the boots, so they never reached us. The shoes I had on were called split-cowhide shoes, and they wouldn't keep the water out, they didn't protect you. To make the leather go further, they split that leather, and it made for a thin piece of leather that was more like a sponge because my feet stayed wet all the time, the water just soaked through. I'm not sure I know myself what trench foot is. I don't think there's much difference between that and frostbite. Your feet would go wet for days, and you didn't even feel anything, they were so cold. I had never heard the word "trench foot," it was just a godsend that I found out what I had.

The job that we were doing, fighting from one hole to the next, you didn't pay any attention to the fact that your feet were cold, frozen. You never took your boots off. I had two pairs of socks to begin with, and I used to keep one on each side of my coat next to my body to dry during the day, and then I would switch them the next morning. I finally put both pair of socks on, trying to keep the feet warm. We didn't even take our shoes off at night because very seldom did we sleep with a roof over our heads. We just were out in a hole in the ground.

When we would stop, the Germans would stop and cover our area with machine gunfire and the shells and everything else. So for protection, the first thing I would do is dig a foxhole and keep my head down in, which saved me many a time because I could get part of my body down. If we didn't, men were being cut down in front with machine-gun fire; [the Germans] were raking that area with bullets after we stopped. You were on your own. It was left up to the individual as to whether he was going to expose himself or not.

Most everyone dug a hole. I'd break limbs off of pine trees and line the bottom of that hole so I could have a dry place to live. I had one of those shelter hats, one half of that pup tent I would use as a cover for my hole, and I would stay down in that hole if I felt it was safe enough to do that. Otherwise, if I didn't think it was safe, I would use my helmet, I wanted to be where I could get to my gun. Very little sleep did you get, maybe pass out. It was up early the next morning and on the move.

We lost a lot of people. I don't know why, but in combat when you went into an attack, you had the feeling whether you were going to succeed or whether you would have problems. We went into the woods and I didn't have a good feeling about the whole thing. We lost men down to one full company, consists of about 170 to 180 people. We never did have a full company, in fact we lost officers. Half the time we didn't have platoon leaders. Fortunately it was an extremely dark night. I have never seen it as dark. The Germans came back and they had really slaughtered our company that day and they were clearly looking for us, but we wouldn't fire because that would give away our position, we were really outnumbered.

But anyway, we wound up with about 28 people out of the whole entire company. We dug our holes, we stayed there. Then the next morning, we had the company radio, we were ordered to move over and protect the flank of our adjoining company as they went in to attack. What I had thought was, at least we'd get back to regroup and get a little rest. But there was no such thing in Patton's Army. No R & R—he was there until the war was over, or you were yourself.

We moved over toward the next company and in doing so we passed through a little village, we stopped to take break. I stood out in the doorway there, I looked up on the hill, and there was a medical aid station. I mentioned to the fellow, "I just bet we could get some dry socks." So I left all my gear, including my radio, gun and everything, and we walked up to the aid station and reported our position. They had a stove going and a fire there—boy, it was the first fire I had seen in a long time. I sat down and managed to pull my shoes off, and there was black all over my feet and toes. I began to try to warm my feet.

A doctor, or aide, came in and I said, "I bet you've got some dry socks back there somewhere, could you fix us up a bit?" He looked at us, looked at our feet. He didn't bring socks but he brought some tags with metal, with a wire on the end of it and began to fasten that on my clothes. I said, "What's this all about? All I want is a pair of socks!" He said, "Look at those feet!" "Yeah, they're dirty, aren't they?" I thought that was dirt, and he said, "Try washing it off!" They were black, there was gangrene all over the toes. So that was the end of my combat, they came and carried me back to a field hospital, from there they just kept carrying me back and back, around January ['45].

I was in Reims, France, in a hospital for quite a while. We never did get any medical treatment, all the medical treatment was on the injuries with bullets. We were then sent to England, from there I was sent back to the States in April, just before the end of the war. They sent us to what is now Fort Carson in Colorado. They wanted to get us into a dry climate where it would be more effective in the treatment. I couldn't walk, I was a litter patient. I didn't realize when I pulled my shoes off that I couldn't balance. Not only that, but the pain was such in your feet. But we got good treatment back at Carson. They saved my feet.

Matter of fact, every morning at 4 o'clock they would come in and select patients for surgery. Of course the Army didn't say any-thing, at least they didn't then. One day they came to my bunk, they were talking a little, they looked at my legs, left, and then they came back again. To my surprise, they left and didn't bother me. I never thought any more about it. The strange thing is when we came to be discharged from Carson I decided I wanted to see what was in that envelope. I opened it up and the first piece of paper I pulled out said, "Amputation ordered right leg upper two thirds." I didn't want to see any more. Then I realized why the doctors had been hovering around my bed making a decision. I say that the Lord was with me. It certainly wasn't anything they did or I did.

I got home two days before the president died—April 10, 1945. I had missed two Christmases away from home. It was a shock because it didn't seem humanly possible that we would survive, you had already prepared yourself for the fact. You just fought like hell while you were there. I was raised to work hard as a farmhand, my dad was a pretty rough taskmaster. In fact, I weighed 117 pounds when I went into the service. Of course, I grew up in the Depression, we didn't have any money. But we were never hungry—we'd cook livestock, we learned to survive.

Today I have been very guarded about what I went through, what war was really about. The closest thing to that is this movie *Saving Private Ryan*. There have been a few excerpts showing war, but until you are in it, you don't really know what's going on. John Wayne—that's Hollywood. I haven't gone into the grizzly parts of battles, I don't think it is really important because war is hell and there was never any good that could be gained by it.

I appreciate the work that you are doing. In church, a lady said, "I want to interview you about your experience," and I said, "I don't want to talk about it." I was a little annoyed, and I said, "Why do you want to stir this up?" She said, "Well, we have a generation that knows nothing about that and I want to record that," and I said, "Okay." It disturbs me to find that our educational system, especially in this part of the country, doesn't even touch on World War II in teaching history.

Larry Batley, born in 1925 in South Hadley, Massachusetts, was drafted at eighteen into the Army in 1943. He trained as a BAR (Browning Automatic Rifle) operator and was shipped to England with the 95th infantry division. He proceeded to France after D-Day where he was wounded in the battle for Metz, a city held by the retreating Germans. He also developed trench foot and was evacuated to recuperate in England, celebrating V-E Day there. Larry has saved many mementos of his service, and the narrative starts with his first letters home, with his original punctuation.

January 1944: Arrived at camp okay. Spent the day being fitted for clothing. My shoe size is now 12. At twelve noon we get a call over a speaker and we all march out and line up, then the sergeant takes us to the mess hall. For dinner we had liver and vegetables, pie for dessert. For supper we had hash, vegetables and bread pudding for dessert. It was good and plenty. I hope you don't feel too bad because I don't mind it at all. Went to the Post Exchange and bought this ink I'm writing with. Also a few post cards—just 24 for a dime and I sent 20 of them out. I think I may need a few references to be able to send you money, but I won't wait too long because I know you need some money. I was kind of blue the first night I was here, but I soon got over it. I guess I'm kind of getting used to everything and Ma, I don't mind it at all. I eat three good meals a day and I guess I'll be getting fat pretty soon.

February 1944: Two days ago we got a blood test, a typhoid shot that was only the first. We've got to get three more, I know that they will also give us some for Tetanus or lockjaw. We went by bus to a place about ten miles from camp. Had a good feed and sang quite a bit. We had a good time at the USO even though I don't dance. We had hamburger loaf for supper, beets, celery, piccalilli. Lots of nice young girls. I wish that I would get shipped out of here so I can get some mail and know what is going on, on the outside. Gee, when we left home, we thought we were getting into the War. Now, you think there isn't any war at all because no one talks about it. Dear Ma, don't worry about me because if you could see all the fellows coming in with over two and three kids, they got more problems than me.

[*Larry continued to tell his story, reading from an account he had written earlier.*] At Camp Myles Standish, one of the things that I will never forget was the day Paul Robeson came to entertain the troops. I remembered him from the movie *Show Boat*, in which he sang "Old Man River." This black entertainer really put on a great show for all of us. It was so hot, but Paul kept on singing. The GIs applauded him and wouldn't allow him to leave the stage. I remember him taking out a big handkerchief, and wiping the sweat off his brow. Finally, his time was limited and he had to leave.

Our ship sailed without an escort, zigzagging across the Atlantic Ocean. We were told the ship was fast enough, and with the zigzagging, no submarine could zero in. They allowed a certain amount of time for fresh water and the line for showers was as far as you could see. When I got into the shower, all soaped up, off went the fresh water, and on came the salt water. Believe me, I found out that salt water and soap did not mix. I was sticky for quite a few days.

On the afternoon of August 17, the *USS West Point* [AP-23] was sailing along the Irish coast. I remember how beautiful and green the grass was, with white cottages. We departed from Liverpool by train and were quartered at Camp Barton Stacey, approximately twelve miles from Winchester, England. Let me tell you about the double bunks we had. They were made out of two-by-fours. What they used for mattresses was heavy-duty canvas cloth filled with hay. By the time we got to use them the hay was like oatmeal and we had to shake and smooth it out so we could sleep on it. This mattress was laid on strips of one-inch banding material. The ground in the area was so hard it was like concrete. The Salvation Army club-mobile came around every day with coffee and donuts.

About the first week of September, our company traveled by truck to Southampton. I remember the busy harbor with all the high-flying barrage balloons above all the ships. We boarded a small ship and sailed over to Omaha Beach [a site of D-Day]. When we arrived there they threw a large cargo net over the side, we then climbed down into a landing craft and were taken to the beach. It was a beautiful warm summer day, not a cloud in the sky, and the beach and sand was nice and clean. And only a few months before such horror occurred on this same beach.

On the right side of the field was F Company, on the left, E Company. We had the large tent for serving meals. I remember those "delicious" meals. They served powdered eggs, shoe-leather pancakes, and lumpy oatmeal. This is where we set up our pup tents where it took two fellows to make one tent. After this came the latrine. The carpenters built a wooden box about 2 by 2 by 8 feet long, which I believe had five holes. Directly across the field, F Company had their latrines also. They were lucky, they had their own barber, he set up his shop by the latrine. I believe he figured he wouldn't miss anyone by being there. At the very end of the field was the tent for the PX. I still have my ration card.

The day finally arrived when we marched into a small village that had a train station and boarded the train. My platoon was lucky, we got a coach car. Most of the others had to go by 40 and 8s (that was 40 men or 8 horses, that is what it was called in WW I and they still called it that). I got a seat on the left-hand side of the car, when we went past Saint-Lô it was on my side. I remember only one large smokestack standing, the rest of the town was in rubbles. The trip took us four days. We would travel about ten miles an hour and at times had to stop and wait three or four hours. I guess they did that because supplies had to go first.

The next I remember, we marched to the side of a huge hill, with tall trees and large boulders. We were told to dig a slit trench and settle in for the night. It was here where reality started to sink in. In the not-too-far distance you could hear the thunder of artillery. On the following day, we marched out of our positions to relieve the GIs of the 5th Division. It was timed so it was done late in the day while it was getting dark. I remember crossing over the Moselle River on a bridge built by the engineers, made of wood. I know now, the 5th Division troops at this time were the only ones across the river. Our squad leader would take two GIs at a time and replace them with two others from the 5th Division. Our foxholes were on the side of a hill, on the very edge of a vineyard.

The Germans occupied the town in front of us. All there was in our area was a brickyard, a farmhouse, and a few other buildings. We were able to have a hot breakfast every day. The company cooks would bring our meals in thermos-type containers that had a hot water jacket around them that would keep the food warm. All foxholes were occupied by two GIs. One person at a time was able to go for breakfast. This is when I saw my first dead German soldier. Alongside a row of grapevines, there lay this dead German. He'd turned black and someone tossed some dirt on his body and face—I surely got scared. Found out later, they believed he was booby-trapped so no one disturbed him. I picked another row to go to chow after that.

In front of our foxholes the engineers had laid land mines. One night around 10 PM, one of the mines directly in front of us exploded. Not long after, another one went off. Then we could hear someone in great pain crying, "Matka, Matka." This went on all night, with more of the mines going off. When daylight came, the engineers cleared the field and the medics went out and picked up two soldiers in German uniforms. They were a mess. Word got back to us later, they were two young Polish boys, who the Germans issued rifles to during the day, and took them away at night. I knew that in Polish "Matka, Matka" meant "Mother, Mother." It all came together for me when they said they were Polish.

[*The battle of Metz*]. On November 13, we were told that on the following day we were going to attack the German lines. The next day, E and F Company, 2nd Battalion, assembled in a field behind our foxholes. About 4:30 AM we lined up behind one another Indian file, it was very dark, you could only see for about three feet. When I turned around, I could see in the dark two medics with the white circles and crosses on their helmets, and in-between them they had a folded portable stretcher. This was one thing that I did not want to see at this time. The attack was preceded by an intense artillery barrage right over the troops. What a scary feeling! I later found out that the barrage was less effective than hoped.

We began the attack at 5:45 AM. We no sooner got into the open field [than] the Germans lit up the sky with flares. We hit the ground, all hell broke loose. At first, about three machine guns were raking the area, then artillery fire, and finally mortars. My rifle jammed from the mud and wouldn't operate. As we moved through the field I was able to retrieve a carbine from a very badly wounded sergeant who was being attended by a medic. Not long after this, we ran into a machine gun firing from what looked like a cellar window. We tossed in a few hand grenades. It must have been close because they started tossing them back.

That is when I felt a burning feeling in my right leg. I knew it had to be a piece of shrapnel. I remember shouting, "I'm hit, I'm hit." I pulled up my pant leg to check it out and said, "I'm going to keep going." After we had taken out this machine gun, all the firing seemed to die down. It started to get light out; only about five GIs were there. As we moved forward, Lt. Crabb, from our company, was giving directions, telling us to go to our left down a ravine. We came upon some buildings, which we cleared out. One of the buildings must have been a meat market—the only thing in the store was two large hog heads hanging up in the window by meat hooks.

After clearing out all the houses on the street we started climbing up the side of a large hill. We sat down halfway up to rest, and to our right we saw P-47 bombing, strafing the town of Rozérieulles. When we reached the top of the hill, we were told this was our objective, dig in. While digging our foxhole, a fellow went by and was taking a head count and on his way back I asked him how many of us are here? He said, "As of now, 39." This, out of three companies? I recognized only one other GI from my company. Later, I found out that Pat Fitzgerald was wounded on this same hill on November 16. He was in F Company. He and I had left South Hadley together, and [were] wounded in the same battle.

About a half an hour after being on the hill, my squad leader, Staff Sergeant Olson, came over from the other end of our line. It made me feel so good to see him. He was my mentor. This is where

the sad story begins. Olson was looking for a rifle. He said a machine gun was raking that part of our line. He and two others were
going to go down to take it out. By this time I had cleaned my rifle
and he could have the carbine I had picked up. He took it and left.
Not too long later, I heard some machine-gun firing down the hill.
The two fellows came back but Olson didn't make it.

To my surprise, on the next hill, directly in front of us was Fort
Jeanne d'Arc, about one quarter of a mile away. We could see the
German soldiers going in and out of the fort. Before the day was
over, word got around the enemy had closed their lines to our rear.
All of us on the hill were trapped behind enemy lines. We were
without food, ammunition, and all I had was a full canteen of
water. We were lucky—we did have an artillery radio operator
with us. When we believed that the enemy might try to counterattack us, the radio observer would call in for artillery to box in
around the hill, and he did this for the five days we were there.

I remember the artillery observer along with a lieutenant,
lying down on the very crest of the hill. He asked for direct fire
from all 105 cannons. We saw no more movement after this barrage. I know now it was Martin Weiss who was directing this artillery, he was later mortally wounded by machine-gun fire. We
were finally located by our divisional artillery planes. They started
to fly in just treetop level, over our positions on the hill. I could
see the pilot open the right side door of the plane and kick out a
bundle of ten blankets; then another plane would drop D-ration
[field] bars. I remember some machine-gun ammunition belts
were hanging on branches of trees and GIs were shooting the
branches to retrieve them. Many of our soldiers were killed by
sniper fire. Others who went down into town looking for food and
water never came back. Finally, on the fifth day, around 11 AM, I
turned around—what a joyous feeling I had—coming up the hill
behind us was our relief column.

As we came down off the hill, they had a tent hospital already
set up. That afternoon I was operated on to remove the shrapnel
from my leg. It was here I was told I had trench foot. I was given
sodium pentothal. All the GIs but one was operated on that day.
One light was left on all night. I just can't explain what it was like
to be in this tent with all the pain these poor fellows had. [*He cries.*]
Sorry. One nurse just walked up and down and checked on every-

one all night long. The fellow next to me had a leg amputated just below his waist. The fellow across from my cot was in a cast from his neck down to his waist. The following morning they brought in a fellow with a cast from head to toe, a bar was in the cast between his knees, they had to pick him up and turn him sideways to get him into the tent.

Finally, it must have been about two weeks, I was put into an ambulance with three other GIs and taken to a hospital in Paris. The walls were painted light blue and seemed dirty with age. The lights were very dim, like 15-watt bulbs. I remember an accordion playing somewhere in one of the far corners of the ward. I was put in the left-hand corner of the ward with the trench foot patients. No one was allowed to get out of bed and had to stay off their feet. My feet were not as bad as some of the others. The fellow two beds down from me, his feet were black and his toes were like prunes.

Before I go any further, I would like to add something that General Omar Bradley [wrote]. I was under his command:

> The rifleman fights without promise of either reward or relief. Behind every river, there's another hill, and behind that hill, another river. After weeks or months, on the line, only a wound can offer him the comfort of safety, shelter, and a bed. Those who are left to fight, fight on evading death. But knowing that with each day of evasion, they have exhausted one more chance for survival. Sooner or later, unless victory comes, this chase must end on the litter or in the grave.

When I read this, it was as if he had written about me. After a short stay in Paris, I was taken to an airfield, put on a C-47, and arrived at the 124th General Hospital in southern England in a city called Torquay. I spent Christmas 1944 there. [*End of written text.*]

May 9, 1945

Dear Mom and Dad,

We are celebrating V-E Day and everyone is up to the square for the dance tonight. Boy, there were a lot of fireworks. They had a big baseball game in the front of the tent. It was between the enlisted men and the officers, but the enlisted men won six to two. There were lots of balloons with helium hanging up, and there were great big parachutes: one was red, one blue, one white. The beer is sure going fast. I stood at a parade this morning then went to church, ate dinner. We had a nice service for V-E Day. Well I guess I am going to close.

Your loving son, Larry

Bill Murray, born in 1923 in Holyoke, Massachusetts, enlisted in the Army in June 1942 when he was 19. He was severely wounded in the landing on Sicily in July 1943, and spent time in hospitals before being discharged in 1944. He then graduated from high school and went to Westfield Teachers' College and Holyoke Community College. He worked for 30 years for the Holyoke Transcript-Telegram *as a photo-grapher. He is active in youth groups such as the local Boys Scouts and has guided young men toward the military. In the following narrative, Bill describes his escape from death off the coast of Gela, Sicily.*

The war was on and I thought it was my duty to join the regular Army. My uncles were in the military, my mother's father was in the German army, he migrated before World War I. My mother was born in this country; her mother and father were German out of the area of Galicia. In World War II we had some relation of ours with a Panzer unit! But people always thought: "Oh well, they are Germans." The most patriotic people for the country were the Germans—this is the country they want, [and] this is the country they went for. I never questioned our loyalties.

When I was born, my grandfather said, "That's your soldier, Ella." My mother didn't know what he was talking about. He said it the day I was born, that he was sorry I would be involved in a great war. He could see it, when he was there, they were premilitary, very tactical. I was fortunate enough to make it come true.

We got over there the beginning of '43. I was sent up to Libya and into Tunisia, out by Lake Bizerte [near the northern tip of Tunisia]. The thing that impressed me was you could see all these ships that were sunk, stacks and spars. It looked like a swamp. You could see the German soldiers trying to quit and the German officers stood behind them and any man who tried, they would shoot him. You would see they were dropping back, they were trying to get out of there, but they couldn't—they were trapped. Even when you marched them out, they all marched just as though they were [in battle]. They obeyed their officers without any question.

The *H.F. Alexander,* she was a troop ship [a steamer used by the US Army in World Wars I and II], a convoy left New York. They told us we were going through Gibraltar and they were always afraid of submarines. So we were all ordered to stay off the deck and we were locked down below. You didn't have a chance to get out of there—[if a submarine came] we were done! Got into Oran all right and they disembarked and shipped you out right away. The next day you were gone.

When I joined the unit they had just finished in Algiers and we were moving into Tunis. I was a replacement. So when we finished in Tunisia, we came back to Oran where we were refitted with new equipment. These halftracks [front half with truck wheels, back half with tank tracks] became more modernized, armored, some plating around them. I think that's one of the things that saved us when I was on the LST [Landing Ship Tank] 313, which was hit—we were in the last row at the back of the ship. The vehicles were all gassed up, and when we got hit the explosion killed those in the immediate vicinity. I went off the fantail.

It was an aerial attack because we were going to the shore. Predominantly, when we were going to Sicily, they were telling us we were going to have all the air cover we needed, and we did—Germans! They were more prepared for us than we had thought. They announced when we were going in, what units were going! Maybe it was Axis Sally [a radio broadcaster] from Berlin, announcing for the Germans in American, "We know your unit's coming, we know that the 16th infantry is coming, we know the 1st Division—the Red One—is coming."

This month will be my 66th anniversary of July 10, 1943, when I got wounded in action. I survived, out of my platoon. Out of 30 men, 22 died that day as we were approaching the shore. I was on LST 313. I will never forget the number. We were offshore at midnight and we had just come through one of the worst storms that ever happened in the Mediterranean. They were getting ready to cancel the landing because so many of the soldiers were seasick.

The LSP [Landing Ship Personnel] was small—it looked like a little submarine, and that thing would go through the water. Well, I was on an LST with M15A1 armored halftrack tanks, because I was with an antiaircraft unit, the 105th, Battery D, Section 6. Each unit, they split them up among these LSTs, so a whole battery or a unit doesn't get wiped out if it happens. The only other one that survived with me was Sheldon S. Burch from Franklin, Louisiana.

Gela was one of the most disastrous times for our battalion in the whole war. You were in the well area and we got hit by a 500-pounder, from an ME109 [German Messerschmitt fighter plane]. Flew right over, missed the first one and got us. It blew the clothes off me, burnt me, and I was wounded with metal shrapnel. I couldn't use my arm, it was hanging on my right side, this hand was all crooked up, and I looked down and I could see the blood streaming down my chest. "Oh, gosh, what's my mother going to say?" Which is the truth, even the boys who are dying ask for their mother; that is why nurses became so helpful for these youngsters. Just like being born over, you didn't hear it, you didn't know it, it was quick.

Then the next thing I knew, I wanted to live, I didn't want to die. I heard some guys hollering, and on these LSTs between the well and the wall, the outside of the ship, there were gangways going up to the deck, so I went up to the fantail, the back of the ship, where they had dropped their cables to pull it off. The ship was burning, and these guys were, "Come on, come on, get out!" "I can't," I said. They picked me up and put me over one arm and I was sliding down the cable, and there was a Higgins [landing] boat near me, and the guy hollered: "Drop, drop, we'll get you," and that's the last I remember.

The next thing, I woke up on the beach, sitting on the front of a jeep, and the medic comes running over and hollers, "Get a stretcher," and they put me on the stretcher and give me morphine. The next thing I knew that night was that I was aboard the troop ship *USS Barnett* and they wrapped me with Vaseline and gauze because of the burns. The next day that ship gets hit, but it wasn't that serious. Later on that day they moved us out to the hospital ship *Acadia*. The nurse who was cleaning me saw a chip of steel in my eye and they took that out.

I didn't have my watch, my tags, my ID card, nothing. That 500-pounder goes off, it blows the clothes off you. It burnt many of the people, those that died, those fellows all burnt, kind of sad, they were all jammed in a spot and they couldn't get out. You were in the center there, in the middle. If you have ever been on an LST, you can visualize it. It's a big, long hallway this high, and all this heavy equipment is in there and you are bumper-to-bumper. Our equipment is not on deck because you have to get out down the ramp. You are holed up in there and those of us who did survive were blessed. Sheldon, now I didn't know he was in it until I saw the listing at the 45th General Hospital with me. He was the lateral tracker and I was the horizontal tracker.

We landed in Algiers and they took me overland, to the 180th station hospital, which was a Quonset hut—very hot. Then after we had been prepped up a little bit, they put us on a 40 and 8, the French had these boxcars [that carried] 40 men or 8 horses. Then they moved us across into Morocco, and we were in the 45th General Hospital in Rabat. It was a big school that they had taken over, all marble, and actually it was cooler. These are the tags that were on you. You usually had one on your toe so when they go through checking they knew from the tag who you were. It says, "Multiple wounds face." Face burn, the arm too. They picked the skin right off. No bones broken, but physically damaged all the way through.

Every man that was listed that day was from a different outfit: I have the list and it's four pages. We all got our Order of the Purple Hearts on August 5, 1943. Some were from March and April, I was injured in July. If I look at the names they were from the 505th parachute regiment, the 504th parachute regiment, the 180th Infantry, the 26th Infantry, 16th Infantry, home towns from Kansas, Texas, Ohio, Pennsylvania, Georgia, the Carolinas, Virginia, Wisconsin. [*Shows the documentation.*] The numbers after your name are your serial number. Mine is regular Army, 11070676.

I came back to the States, to Staten Island, and then they transferred us to Atlantic City, an Army general hospital on Main, the Army had taken over hotels to take care of the wounded. They were going to ship me to the Carolinas. I got upset about that. I said, "You know, I thought we were supposed to go closer to our home." The nurse said, "Yeah, but if they don't have an orthopedic surgeon, you're going to have to go there. I'll see what I can do." I didn't know her husband was a colonel on the JAG and he moved me to Fort Devens, where they had orthopedic surgeons, Lovell General Hospital, which no longer stands there. On the ground floor you had prisoners of war, German and Italian. They had to separate them because the Italians surrendered quicker than the Germans.

[*Did Americans have to fight the Korean War?*] In the sense of we had become the big brother. We have to take care of things and keep it in a proper order. I don't believe we should try and force our way of living on them, but I can see protecting them, getting them squared away, to keep South Korea free. We would have won if General MacArthur… he got a little carried away. He was a little too gung-ho. He said he wanted Eisenhower—how did he put it?—to cover the whole area with atomic waste along the border, and he says they will never cross here. That was his attitude. But he was a fine, smart general.

A stalemate. We are going to see what this 4th of July brings. [North Korea threatened to test launch missiles on July 4, 2009.] We're prepared for them. They can create chaos. Because this guy, Kim Jong-Il, I don't think he's got all his marbles. I don't see how these guys can control all these people, other than the fact that he has the military on his side, because if he didn't, he would have nothing.

Well, Vietnam, I think that was a waste of a lot of young men's lives. My son put his thirteen months in there. He wrote me and said, "Oh, Dad, in daylight, the A Shau Valley's ours, but the gooks own it at night." The thing there is we had the power, but the problem was too much politics was involved. Because we were ready to knock them off good, and the politicians wouldn't go for it.

Vietnam was a sad war because people here were so adamant against it, so many of these young ones didn't want to go. The reception that these fellows that served time over there got from these people caused a breach between the public and the soldier. When these National Guards out there at the college [Kent State] opened fire with ammunition, killed some of them, people started to realize that there's got to be something wrong. These guys were serving their country because they were told to serve their country. They were still drafting them then.

With all these young men from combat in Iraq, there were about 200,000 of them now that have been hospitalized and are being taken care of, lost limbs and such. People don't realize that the government owes these fellows because they paid the price. Had they got hit like that in our time, they'd have died. But this time with medicine being so fast they're able to do these savings, and that's what gets them out.

Your biggest problem right now in Iraq, in Iran, and all those places, Afghanistan, the fact that the British gave up on them a hundred years ago. They got out of there because first of all, they're all tribal. They don't want a central government, they want just their chief, and that's the way they go. Now they've got those mullahs, they control too much, their involvement, the religious thing. It is not for the good of the people, but for what *they* think.

Well, we're going to be kept there for a while. I don't think that we'll only be staying there to the end of 2010 because of the fact that these people, although they are trained, they don't have the stamina that our people do. Some of these were just naturally warrior people. There are sects: there are Sunnis and there are Shiites, as long as they have that, they don't have like we do here in this country. These people are just for their own little tribe. The only one that got to control them was Saddam, he had them under his thumb and that was the end of it. He made his biggest mistake when he went after the Kuwaiti. We could have annihilated them then. When those kids were coming back, I was at the base, I work with USO, and I said we were going back and sure enough as God made little apples, we went back there.

The young fellows could see that we were going to go back there because we didn't finish the job. Most of the soldiers felt he didn't go far enough. George Bush [senior] was a good man, but he didn't want to have a lot of casualties during Desert Storm. Then his son gets in there, he wants to rectify that. Well, it doesn't work. He wasn't—in my book—as good a president as his father. He was kind of wishy-washy, and he was influenced by Cheney and Rumsfeld, and they made the most money. All of a sudden, all these mess halls are controlled by contractors. We used to have our own do the cooking and now they have everybody doing it for them. Why was a man (Cheney) in that kind of position making that kind of money? He cost his government.

I thought we were wrong going in there, in one way. I don't think we could settle that thing. I thought if we just contained Saddam, we would have been better off, instead of going in there and pushing him. We beat them quick and fast, but there was no preparation there for what was going to happen afterwards. That was the big mistake, moving without having a plan of what you were going to do afterwards. And then they let them run ragged, let them all go, they're all gone with their tribes.

[*Can we win the war in Afghanistan?*] No, I don't think so, Russia couldn't beat them. They'll stay in the holes in the woods, in the mountains, you can never get them all out. We are spending tons and tons of money, just having young men get hurt for nothing. Our group [in the VFW] has dwindled now, the major portion was World War II. A few of them did join from the Korean War. But after that there was a pause where things were smooth, although we got involved in South America and the Panama Canal. If you go every ten years in the history of the United States, you'll find we had a conflict. Interventions, that's what it amounts to. We've been involved in Africa, the time when so many of our guys got killed, the Special Forces men [in Mogadishu, Somalia].

[*What was your reaction to the dropping of the atomic bomb?*] I thought it was a very, very good thing Truman did. He had more guts than people thought. It took a couple hundred thousand, but it saved millions. We brought them to their knees and that was it. Then we went back and fixed them all up and made them one of the richest countries in the world. So the consequence was the right thing because we would have lost millions of young men trying to get ashore. I think it was a necessity.

David Cohen, born in 1917 to a Jewish family in Brooklyn, New York, tried to volunteer for the Navy—before Pearl Harbor—because he had read Henri Barbusse's Under Fire *(1916) about the muddy trenches of World War I. Even with a Navy father-in-law, he was rejected because of his eyesight. He served instead in Patton's Army and was present for the liberation of two concentration camps, Ohrdruf and Buchenwald. After the war, David taught junior high school in New York. To this day, this ex-teacher gives talks in schools about his war experiences in the 4th Armored Division. His story sounds as if it happened yesterday.*

My mother became a citizen on my father's citizenship papers. They came from Latvia, which was part of Russia. My mother was illiterate, the voting meant so much. She would go to the store (my father was a glazier and carpenter), and practice how to write her name every September so she could go vote in November. And she would come back with her back straight, she was so proud to vote. They told her, "This is for the Democratic, this is for the Re-publican," and she says, "And where is the Socialist?"

We left from Boston, and it was a horrible experience. The motor broke down on our ship. It was a converted freighter from World War I. We called it the *HMS Rat Trap*. I got sick as a dog, I just wanted to die. I was hoping a submarine would sink us. But anyway we survived, got to England, landed in Cardiff, Wales. We were stationed in southern England, near Bath.

We were assigned to Patton's 3rd Army because our general, John S. Wood [commander of the 4th Armored Division] and Patton were buddies—they went to West Point together. General Wood (we were in Normandy at a breakthrough) was directing traffic himself! He crossed into the area held by the 7th Army led by "Bucking" Patch, a three-star General, and he had to leave our division. [Patton] was quite a character. He spoke to us. I am ashamed to mention the words he used. But anyway, we trained six months in England. After D-Day, July 14, we went all through France.

You hate war and you hate the idea of the army, the regimentation, but there's one thing you have—camaraderie. When I went to radio school, I met friends, they were marvelous. First of all, before you get into radio school, you had to have a decent IQ, so you got a lot of intelligent boys, not that a college degree makes you intelligent necessarily. [He laughs.] It was wonderful, in my outfit there was that camaraderie. Even today we have a division association and you have that feeling. There was no such thing as a Jew or an Italian, Catholic, or whatever.

We had a few instances, we had this hillbilly from Kentucky, he said, "The trouble with the Army is that there are too many Jews in it." Another time, we had a fellow from Astoria, Joel Tiger. He went into the latrine to shave and there were two guys talking, "This war is all caused by the Jews, you know." So he got their two heads and banged them together, he was a husky guy, and he says, "I am going to kill someone someday, I might as well start now." Anyway, our company commander got hold of it and we had a big meeting about this nonsense. We had many Jews, because most of our division came from New England, New York, Pennsylvania, so we were all mixed, Irish, Italian, Catholics, Jews, Polish.

In fact, our colonel came from Agawam [Massachusetts]— Abrams, he became a general. [Abrams] tanks are named after him. The Germans thought he was Jewish. We were on maneuvers in Tennessee, and I said (I think he was only a captain then), "Captain, I thought you were one of my boys when I first came in here." And he says, "The family came from England, there must have been a little Jew boy hanging around somewhere." I'd say 90-odd percent Abrams are Jews. The Germans hated him because he was no-nonsense, if they didn't give up, he'd burn the town down. "If it is going to save one soldier, burn the town down." He would give them [only] so much time to surrender.

But anyway, we went through France rather rapidly and a lot of good things happened. We were near Metz, France, when we got notice that we had to take all our insignias off and erase anything that was on the vehicles that showed our identification and division. We didn't know what was going on. We were told there was radio silence; that means the radios were off. It was a big secret. We moved up to Belgium—it was the Battle of the Bulge [16 December 1944–16 January 1945]. As we were going up, when it was radio silence, I would put on music. The best music would come from Berlin—Axis Sally. She would talk, "The Jews, they are not in the Army, they are home with your girlfriends and your wives." And then she'd play Benny Goodman playing a George Gershwin number! [*He laughs.*]

But I tell you, they had such spies all over. As we were going up, this was a big secret, [Axis Sally] says, "Fourth Armored Division, we know where you are. You are outside Longwy, France," and that's where we were. They must have had people telling them, and she was on the radio in Berlin telling us where we were! And here we had to take off all our patches. But anyway, we got to Belgium and it was cold, cloudy, and snowing, December '44. The German airplanes came out, our planes didn't come out, and that was kind of scary. I don't know if it's symbolic, but on Christmas Day, the sun came out, and the American planes came out. We relieved the 101st Airborne. Pretty rough, but I didn't have it that bad as a radio operator. I was in my halftrack, and where they had to go sleep outside, I could sleep in the halftrack. But it was cold and physically tough there.

After January, the Battle of the Bulge was completed for us. We jumped over to Germany. It was a funny feeling, you know. When you're in France you're still in a friendly territory, but when you're in Germany, you don't have any friends any more. Patton... he just *went*. One day, we went 50 miles, which is just unheard of in one day's advancement. It was radio silence, it was mostly secret, where we went... I'm not going to tell you too much about that.

We crossed the Rhine in April, near the end of the war now. Germans were surrendering by the tens of thousands, the roads were clogged with prisoners, they were giving up. Everybody knew the war was over but Hitler, he had to continue fighting.

That was April 5th. We got a message that they had to take a communication center, that it was a dangerous spot. This infantry battalion in our division went there and they radioed back that it wasn't a communication center—it was a concentration camp. They wanted all the doctors, the ambulances, nurses. We went in there hours later. I took pictures. When we got into the camp [Ohrdruf, a concentration camp associated with Buchenwald, was liberated on April 4], now this is a small camp, near Gotha, Germany. I remember the inscription on the Opera House that Germany was the home of Brahms, Goethe, and Beethoven, and when we got in there, there were about 50 to 60 bodies laying all around. [*Shows his pictures.*] These poor souls were alive just hours before we got there, but the Nazis, rather than let them live, clubbed them to death, you could see the blood, they shot 'em. And some of them they took on trucks and moved them further east to another camp where they gassed them, like Nordhausen [a sub-camp of the concentration camp Dora-Mittelbau] had a gas chamber.

This place was small, a labor camp. The bodies when we got there were warm. You could see the blood was caked in the mud. You see [*shows a picture*]—this is all blood. If [the striped pajamas] were blue, then they were Jewish. If they were gray, they were non-Jews. Not only Jews that he killed: eleven and a half million, six million were Jews, six million were non-Jews. Gays, of course, and mentally and physically disabled, Jehovah Witnesses. They killed Catholic priests and nuns if they helped a Jew or were dissidents of any kind.

This is where they lived. Rats, all kinds of vermin. No running water, no bathrooms of course, they just had pails. The twelve million that died, they were not all gassed or burned, they had dysentery, typhus, malaria, and malnutrition. Millions died of malnutrition. This is where they lived, just a straw mattress. And this is outside the camp, these fences were double-wire and they were electrified. One of the men told me that people would become despondent and they'd run over and jump on the fence and commit suicide. They weren't all Jews there, there were French and Yugoslavs, a lot of Polish and Russians because you know Hitler was out to exterminate the Slavic race too.

Well, we went back to our outfit, and there was a memorandum from Eisenhower that he wanted all available troops to see the camp. So we went back and came in with Eisenhower. He was there and that's [*showing a picture*] General Bradley. This is an inmate, a survivor, but Eisenhower looked at him and asked the interpreter to ask him a question—why he looked so healthy compared to the others? He said, "Well, I was a trusty, and they gave me extra food." Eisenhower was no fool. He looked at him and said, "I don't believe this son of a bitch. Lock him up."

Eisenhower turned green, shook his head, and said, "God, you have to have a strong stomach to take this." This is Bradley, the head general, and this is the interpreter telling him what I just told you about these people. Then all of a sudden, there was a commotion and a jeep pulls up with General Patton with his shiny helmet, his two pearl-handled guns, and he struts out and he looks into this place, and he came out and he heaves up. He started to scream at the top of his voice, "You should see what these sons of bitches did, see what these bastards did," and, with Eisenhower and Bradley standing next to him, "I don't want you to take a f——ing prisoner," he yelled.

Colonel Sears, he made the mayor and all the townspeople come in and see what was going on. The mayor and his two sons, they made them dig graves for these bodies. The mayor told Sears, "I didn't know what was going on," and Sears says, "You are a lying S.O.B. The smell alone will tell you what was going on." Let me tell you, the smell—never, never, if you were there, you will never forget the smell. It stays with you, it was awful. You smelled burning flesh, decaying bodies, and of course all the human waste and garbage altogether was God-awful. I don't know how they even survived. The people knew what was going on. Most of them couldn't do anything about it. Why didn't they? The Nazis would have killed them.

Eisenhower made a statement, "The waste, just think, any one of these children might have been a scientist (or doctor) to find a cure for cancer." We had a captain doctor, John Scotti, from Brooklyn, a real fine human being. He got so upset in Ohrdruf, he went in the middle of the street and he started to scream. "Now

I know how the Germans found a cure for malaria and typhus: they burn them and gas them and then burn them." You want to curse, if you ever had some of them Germans, you want to take your gun and shoot them. Scotti blew his stack and Patton, who was a big macho, he threw up, and Eisenhower turned green.

That's where they burned them. [*He show a photo.*] In Washington, DC, I gave the pictures to the Holocaust Museum. You could see the skulls here. They didn't have ovens, they didn't have gas chambers in this camp. Above the hill they had this place where they burned them. You see this in the back? That's not dirt, that's all human ashes. The reason it's white, they poured lime on it. You can see, there was still a body that was not completely burned.

We stayed there for a few days, we left and we went further east toward Weimar. We went into Buchenwald, a major camp. The 6th Armored Division got there a few hours before we did and it seems there were bodies laying all around there. In this camp there weren't just a few hundred. Buchenwald, that's where Elie Wiesel was, they had 50–60,000 there. We drove in there and we saw this body in the middle of the road, and the sergeant says, "Don't feel bad about it, he was the only Nazi guard left." One of the Polish inmates recognized him and took a gun from the American soldier and put three bullets in him and they just let him lay there. But you could see how fat he was, he was a Nazi guard, so there were no tears shed over him.

These bodies were all over the place, thousands and thousands. This is the graves registration. You can see the bungalows or sheds where all the people lived, the "hotels," there were 60,000 of them. Buchenwald, when we got there, they kissed our hands, our feet, crying. They wanted food and we were told not to give them any food. But I gave them crackers, and I had chocolate, my K-rations [combat rations], I gave them my cigarettes, they smoked, I didn't smoke. But the British had given them food—I think they had liberated Bergen-Belsen before—and naturally you are going to have compassion if they ask for food. They ate it so fast and stuffed it down, and their stomachs had shrunk so that it exploded, and many of them died. The irony of it all, they over-ate.

And this is the crematory. They would put them on a gurney, and they would slip them in the oven like they do pizza pies. Well, we knew that there was something. When we were in France, we picked up a Russian who had escaped a slave labor camp. He stayed with us a couple of nights, he explained to us that there were slave labor camps and how awful it was. That was the extent of it. We didn't know that went as far as extermination camps, how cruel it was.

A Polish diplomat [Jan Karski], he was put in the camp and he escaped and the Polish underground got him to England and he told Churchill. He also came to America to tell Roosevelt what was going on. This diplomat said that Felix Frankfurter was there and had said, "Don't make any waves." That was a period of anti-Semitism and Felix Frankfurter, which is *wrong*, said, "Don't make waves." You can't keep it quiet, that's why it *happens*.

That was April. From Germany, we went into Czechoslovakia, we ended up not far from Pilsen. The war was over, and the Russians were not far from us. People were so nice. They knitted shawls that I sent home to my wife and my mother-in-law and they gave us painted plates, a little town. Before we left Czechoslovakia to go back to Germany as occupation troops, we woke up around 4 o'clock in the morning, all the tanks, all the trucks, were covered with roses. This was the people, overnight this was their way of thanking us.

A lot of my buddies and myself went to the 16th Armored Division, they were in Marienbad, Czechoslovakia, ready to embark to go to France and go home. I see a kid in an American uniform, so I walk over to him and say, "Sprechen Sie Deutsch?" He looks at me and he says, "Ich sprech Yiddish echit," that means, "I speak Jewish too." So I start talking—the kid's name was Izzy, sixteen years old, he was taken from Poland when he was 12 years old. He went through three different camps, he was husky and a streetwise kid.

In the last camp, he was befriended by one of the German soldiers who used to give him extra bread. Izzy made friends with somebody, he called him his cousin, another kid from Poland. One day this German guard came over to Izzy and said, "They are going to move you tonight. If I were you, I would escape from the train. They are taking you to a camp where they are going to gas all of you." This was what they did. Rather than let them live, the war was practically over, but anyway, Izzy, he went on the train with this other kid, Morty.

This was the plan: they were going to jump out the window when the train went around the bend; there was a guard on top, he couldn't see them when they jumped out. They were picked up by a German farmer and slept in his barn, they told the farmer that they were two Polish kids that escaped. The farmer took them and gave them some food and gave them a shower. When he saw them in the shower he says, "You are going to have to leave, I can't keep you, you're Jewish." But he didn't turn them in—he just told them to leave.

They were picked up by an American artillery unit. There were two Jewish kids in the unit, both of the soldiers wrote to their parents to see if they could get these kids into America. The only way was if someone signed for them so they wouldn't be a burden on the state. They also met some major who said he knew somebody who could smuggle them into Marseilles and then into Palestine. So Izzy asks me, "Where should I go?" I said, "Izzy, if I were you, I would go to Palestine." I gave him my address and phone number. I got a call from Izzy, he was working for this kosher butcher [in Roxbury, Massachusetts], the father of one of the kids in the unit. This was 1948.

He tried to trace his family, his mother, father, three sisters, and two brothers—they were all killed in the camps. He was the only survivor, no relatives, nothing, that's why he adopted this other kid—they made themselves cousins. He got a job as a painter's apprentice in the Bronx. He calls me up one Friday, so I picked him up, brought him over to my house, my mother made a nice chicken Friday night dinner, and he stayed overnight. This is 1948–49.

Anyway, I lost his address, and he must have lost mine. I used to tell my wife, "I'll bet he went to Israel, fought in the war and got killed." I was always curious whatever happened to Izzy. About twelve years ago, this woman said, "You and your friend Donald Gosselin are doing a wonderful thing going around and telling the kids about the Holocaust. My brother and his friend in the Army took up two Jewish kids who escaped from camp." I told her about Izzy, he changed his name, she gave me a phone number and address, so I wrote a long letter.

One night I was out, my wife says, "Oh my God, you got a call from Izzy." He called up, he and his wife were crying, they finally met their cousin. Izzy put his name on the Internet, one day, Izzy gets a call from Antwerp, Belgium, a young fellow says I am your cousin. Izzy's mother had a brother that lived in Belgium. He was married and had a little girl, when the Nazis came in to Antwerp, they put the girl in a convent. The parents were sent to Auschwitz—they were killed, and the girl was brought up a Catholic. [*He laughs.*] She didn't know, she got married, had two children. One of them was an engineer and he wanted to know about his roots, so he was able to trace the name and he found out he was Jewish. He found out that he had a relative in America, he called Izzy up and he came to America. He was married to a Jewish girl in Belgium and Izzy and his wife went to the wedding in Antwerp, so he got to see a relative.

He opened up his own little market, a real entrepreneur. He was no dummy, a shrewd kid, a real survivor. In fact, he went to Israel when he was 72 to be bar mitzvahed—he had been taken into camp before he was thirteen. "You know, David, Hitler couldn't beat me, that cancer isn't going to." He died of cancer.

I believe there is a just war and a bad one. What we did to the Indians is certainly not a just war. A bad reason for going to war could be to take over an oil field, just for an oil company, was this President Bush's reason? Was he angry because they tried to kill his father? It seems ridiculous, but it could be true. Could he be that petty? The men he had around him, between the vice president, Wolfowitz, and those jokers, I just wonder if they believe in some form of imperialism. They want America to be shown as a powerful country. I would hope I am wrong, but that might be a theory.

Most of the fellows I was in the Army with felt there was some justification. That Hitler—forget the concentration camps—had taken over Czechoslovakia, Poland, France, so it was scary. These were all our allies. Like one guy said, "If he takes over England, he'll try to take over America. We'll all be speaking German." In other words, there was justification. There wasn't—like today with Iraq and Vietnam—that antiwar feeling. World War II, they felt that we were there for a reason, a good reason.

I think Obama is making a mistake if he goes into Afghanistan. One election in Iraq is going to be a panacea? The

Iraqis are probably sorry we invaded—at least they had some jobs and food when Hussein was there, it was negative, but at least they had something. My philosophy is: I believe in my country, they say right or wrong. I believe in my country, right. If it is wrong, I want to make it right! That's my belief.

Raymond Elliott, born in 1924 in Cambridge, Massachusetts, is an African American who served in World War II from December 1942 to 1946 as an engineer, building landing strips in the Pacific. His father served in World War I as a "Buffalo" soldier in the African American 92nd Regiment in France; his regiment was decorated by the French government with a Croix de Guerre, the highest military honor. Ray graduated from McGill University in Montreal as a chemist, worked testing for radioactivity, including the loop water on the Nautilus submarine. He later worked on heat shields for the Apollo space program. He still talks to students, especially about serving in a segregated army. Ray adopted the Bahá'í religion, which focuses on the oneness of the human family.

The time that I went into the service, in the North there was separatism, the blacks had their own grocery stores, their own doctors, and their own barbershops, partly because the blacks wanted separatism. The other reason, of course, was we weren't welcome into many situations. My attitude at the time: no just, equal opportunities were available for Blacks because there was institutionalized racism.

Now the institutionalized racism in the South was written laws, but in the North it was *de facto*. *De facto* segregation is a weird experience, there were reasons given for denying us different rights in the '40s when I was growing up. I was raised in a white community, I was never immersed in the black culture. I was sheltered from building a defense against being treated less than equal.

When I went into the service, it was a shock because I was going to immerse [myself] into an all-black culture, a black segregated Army. It was, in one way, a joyful thing, because I had always wanted to be amongst people who looked like me. Especially to *live* with them, I didn't have that experience. But I wasn't prepared for the treatment—without respect or dignity, or trying to take away my manhood by treating us like we were less than human, not equal.

It seemed that most of the white officers we had were young officers from the South who had gone through the 90-day wonder program of becoming an officer, and not well trained. They didn't seem to be that compassionate toward another human being, they just seemed like they enjoyed treating us in cruel ways. It was the human relationships that were the invisible wounds that we suffered in boot camp. There is a worry too, Blacks can sense when a person is a redneck, is prejudiced, has some hatred towards you. That was the most difficult thing, to be ready to fight and die for this country and be treated with such attitudes. When we deployed, it was worse. Apparently, the [officers] they put in charge of us were the bottom of the barrel.

The Army did not explain to us why we were segregated, why the Army was segregated. We had all kinds of thoughts. The government was afraid there would be riots if they put the Blacks together [with whites]. Many of the cities did not want black troops to be stationed within their areas. The government didn't want to confront the South, Jim Crow laws. In order to have unity in the Army, they had no choice. They should have had in place some social officers to share with us the reasoning—that would have made *such* a difference.

I didn't volunteer. I wanted to join ROTC at Northeastern University, in order to avoid going in. Mainly because of the way they had treated my dad when he came back from the First World War and he couldn't join the Veterans of Foreign Wars in Cambridge. I had [black] friends, "That's a white man's war, we are not going to fight, we should be fighting here in this country for justice." I knew that it was a segregated army, and I was tricked

into joining the service. I was walking downtown, and these recruiting officers called me over. I was eighteen years old, and I
said, "No, I am going to sign up in the ROTC, at school," and they
said, "You can sign up here for ROTC." I signed up and two
weeks later I got a telegram saying that I had to report to the
standing army.

I had a choice of what branch I wanted to serve in. Tuskegee
fighter pilot program, which was just beginning in [July] 1941, I
went in '42, I applied to be a fighter pilot. I was accepted for that
program and so they sent me to Biloxi, Mississippi where I was in
training. After being there a month or so, we would be interviewed by psychologists, and they'd ask us questions related to
how we would react if we were in a fighter plane. I went in to a
psychologist and he asked me if you ever fainted in your life before. I said, of course I fainted three or four times. I told him the
circumstances. I said, "But these were unusual circumstances."
And he looked at me and says, "Don't you think it's unusual circumstances if you are a mile up in the air in a fighter plane, a million dollar plane (he had to mention the million dollar plane)?"
So he says, "We are not going to be able to accept you into the program. But you do have a choice to be a bombardier."

I didn't like the idea of just dropping bombs so I signed up
for survey, map-making. Of all places, I was sent to Franklin
Technical Institute in Boston, back home, and not only that, but
Franklin Technical Institute is where my dad went.

I was in the combat engineers, in headquarters, the company
surveyor. They turned over dynamite every two months because
it becomes unstable, they lock you in this room and you have to
slowly turn them over. We used this dynamite to clear areas for
airstrips. We had to blow up obstacles in our path, tree stumps,
rocks, big boulders, and even small little hills had to be demolished. You're talking about almost a mile-long airstrip you would
be building, in the bush. Coral was perfect for a landing surface.
The main island where we were doing most of the work, which
was our final destination, was Okinawa.

We were prepared to invade Japan. The Marines were going
to go in first and secure the beachhead. Then we were going to
come in and lay the airstrips. A couple of months before they
dropped the A-bomb, we were being prepared to engage in that.

I'll never forget that because it made us think this is the beginning of a third world war, this is crazy! It was frightening. I was there before the bomb was dropped and afterwards. I was in the South Pacific from '43 to April of '46.

One of the things that was really discouraging to us was the USO was sending entertainers around the world and in this country, and never did we have them come to entertain us. A lot of them were black entertainers. In Hawaii we were at a camp but a segregated section. Overseas, we were never stationed near a large white army camp, and that's where the entertainers were going. We were stationed outside in black camps, bivouacked in tents away from the whites to avoid any conflict or riots, or disruption of unity in the army. The big point was to keep unity: if they were going to win, they had to be united in fighting [for] the cause.

But we kept our anger down. When we first went in, we were all young, we were fiery, we were ready to fight back against any kind of a derogatory attitude toward us. In the North, we were African Americans, but we mixed, we had some Southern Blacks, they were more passive. "You can't win. The white man, he's got his foot on your neck, he's going to keep you down," "When we get out, we're going to fight against racism." So we had that bonding from the beginning, to channel our anger rather than toward each officer (we used to joke about knocking them off when we got into battle) but to channel it toward a cause, a purpose, and that cause was when we got out, we were going to fight against racism.

We had a symbol, somebody got out of control, reacting like he is going to fight back, or curse out an officer and then end up in the brig, "Hey brother, remember…" and we would show the double V sign. [*He holds up both hands, each with two fingers forming a "V."*] Most of us were 18 or 19, when you have authority challenging you, reprimanding you for doing something which you feel crosses the line, without respect, you have a tendency to react. So when we saw this happening, when the officers were treating another black soldier without respect, we would get close, and [give the sign to] just cool it. We tried to calm each other down. The double "V" was reported in the black newspapers, but the rest of the media didn't pick it up.

I feel we planted the seeds of the civil rights movement. When we got back, we were going to take advantage of the GI Bill. Then we are going to organize with the NAACP and other organizations, and we are going to march on the South. Some of them had crazy ideas (these are young kids talking) we're going to confiscate some tanks from Ft. Devens and we're just going to move in on some of these areas where they had had so many bad experiences. They were trying to think of some way, now that they were trained how to fight, now that they are organized, that they could be militant. But that was only in their imagination.

My feeling was to educate the young folks, especially the young Blacks getting ready to be organized to go south and do boycotting. I'd experienced what it was like with insulting racism in the South, what it felt like to be chased by a mob, these experiences scared the daylights out of me. I became the NAACP youth advisor for Lawrence-Haverhill and Lowell, Merrimack Valley, over a hundred kids. We'd train them how to react when they are confronted with any kind of challenge, and to act with nonviolence.

The Blacks did channel their anger into joining the Black Muslims. I went when Malcolm X was visiting the mosque [on] Blue Hill Ave, Dorchester [Boston] to try to talk to him about not having this anger toward whites. He started talking, "The white man's heaven is the black man's hell," on and on. Finally, he called up his daughter, about seven years old, "Who's this?" and he showed her a picture of Marilyn Monroe. And she said, "Daddy, that's the devil." He went on and on brainwashing his own children. [But] the magazine [*Muhammad Speaks*] was incredible, all about little known facts about black history, the black Pharaohs, great civilizations, great inventors—we heard about Charles Drew. Then we heard stories about how white soldiers were refusing black blood, sacrificing their lives because of prejudices. We heard stories about a black bank of black blood for black soldiers.

I think about Obama. Many blacks think of him as a black Moses because he is trying to raise consciousness about human relations, how we relate to each other. Speak softly with a big stick is the way the United States always is, "We're the best, we're number one." "If your country doesn't do right we will come over there and we will straighten it out" rather than know about other peoples' situation, other peoples' government. I think Obama is going to encourage people to be more tolerant, more understanding of other civilizations, other peoples in the world. We are global, so we're going to have to deflect war, learn how to talk with each other rather than just threaten each other. I think what will help prevent future wars is for people to talk with people around the world.

The Buffalo Soldiers was a cavalry that was organized right after the Civil War in 1865. It was an all-black cavalry and they were commissioned to fight on the Western frontier against the Native Americans. [They were] called "Buffalo Soldiers" because the Native Americans thought that their hair was very similar to the hair on the buffalo—curly and dark brown. And they were vicious and very courageous fighters, Buffalos were. The legacy of the Buffalo Soldiers was passed down to the 92nd and the 93rd regiment, which were a standing army, a black regiment in the Army during and after the First World War.

My dad was a member of the 92nd Regiment that fought in France, and his regiment received the Croix de Guerre, the highest honor that the French government could give to any soldiers. The reason he fought under the French command is because no white [American] commander was willing to be in command of a black regiment. So the French government offered to have them fight side by side, truly integrated. They proved that they were not only valiant and courageous warriors, but that they could fight side by side with the whites without racial riots.

When my dad came back from the service after being honored by the French, he was not welcomed in the Veterans of Foreign Wars. He had a right, but you see there was *de facto* segregation in the North, and they had different ways of either demeaning your application, or not to accept you on some bogus reason. "To hell with this, we are not going to keep trying to become members, not welcomed, so we will form our own." Dad formed the first Black Veterans of Foreign Wars post in Cambridge, Massachusetts. He became the commander of that post and I have documents from their archives.

My father never talked about it, the only way I knew was when I saw the picture of him with the Buffalo Soldiers [insignia] on his sleeve. He never talked about the experience, none of them ever did. That left such a bitter taste in my mouth about fighting for our country. I was going to serve, but they didn't want to serve me. I wanted to carry on the legacy of my dad that history did not do. That's why I'm so excited about giving talks, to be able to pass this information on. It's part of American history and the young people—white and black—should know that.

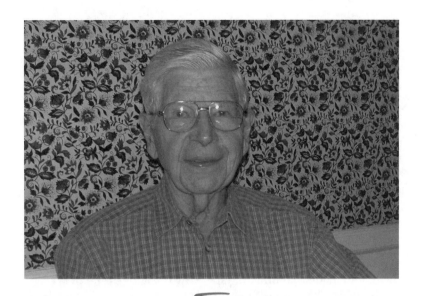

Bob Tyler was born in 1924 in Hartford, Connecticut, graduated from high school in 1942, and enrolled in the University of Michigan, planning to be a forest ranger. After a semester, he decided to enlist in the army, becoming an infantryman. He was offered officer training but turned it down because he had a low opinion of the lieutenants he observed as an enlisted man. He was a private, first class, all the way to Northern France, where he was made a staff sergeant. He was also briefly captured by the Germans and managed to escape back to his unit by hiding under grape leaves in a vineyard. He worked at Mass Mutual Insurance for 36 years after the war.

The Americans and British, French, and some of the Italians had pushed the Germans out of Africa, September of '43. We landed in Casablanca, Morocco, quite a coincidence because that was just the time that the film *Casablanca* came out. I actually saw it in Casablanca! I, as well as dozens of beginners who hadn't been in the front, crossed Northern Africa over to Tunisia by train, closer to Sicily.

A few days later, we got into Navy ships where I found the food was a lot better than what they gave us in the Army. We had C-rations, like a Campbell's soup can, you had little lighters, stove-like things you could put them on with a mug. Most men hated it, but I love food so much it didn't bother me at all. [C-rations: three 12-ounce cans, meat and beans, meat and potato hash, or meat and vegetable stew and three bread-and-dessert cans. In 1942, the Navy had color-coded K-rations: brown for breakfast, green for supper, and blue for dinner. Within these colored boxes was a plain tan box twice dipped in wax in order to keep the contents waterproof. A can opener, a wooden spoon, four cigarettes, chewing gum, sugar, and biscuits came with each meal. Breakfast: canned cheese product, canned meat product, compressed cereal bar, powdered coffee, fruit bar, water-purification tablets. Dinner: canned meat product, candy bar, powdered beverage, salt tablets, matches. Supper: bouillon powder, candy, powdered coffee, toilet paper.

By the time we crossed Africa and headed into Italy, the Americans, British, and French had driven the Germans out of Sicily, and made a landing in Italy. Near Pozzuoli, south of Naples, I joined the 3rd Infantry Division, and I was in the 15th Regiment, Company L. That division was just due for R&R, so I had ten days of not fighting. During that ten-day period I was able to get into Naples, it had all been bombed trying to drive the Germans out.

I was on the front lines, trying to push the Germans north out of Italy. It was front-line fighting, door-to-door fighting in cities in Italy, and sometimes it was in the farmlands. The Germans were in the towns defending themselves in different buildings. We would fire our rifles and of course there were artillery guns used from the back, and our airplanes were also bombing at the same time. In fact, that became a greater fear than the Germans—our being hurt by our own forces. Throughout the whole 30 months of my experience, from March of '43 to August of '45, 17 months were on the front line.

After a few months of trying to advance toward Rome, the whole 3rd Division was to make an amphibious landing in Anzio, 100 miles south of Rome. On the way up I developed hepatitis, yellow jaundice, which gave me a temperature of 106. That probably saved my life because I didn't make the Anzio landing until ten days later. When I did, most of my company's soldiers had been killed. The Germans didn't resist as hard as they might have on that day, but ten days later, they began to resist heavily. They were in the mountains over Anzio and they could shoot right down at us, and a lot of my buddies were lost there. They didn't wipe out the 3rd Division, but they wiped out several dozen soldiers that were part of it.

Three or four months after Anzio, the 3rd Division got into Rome. They didn't allow us to make the grand entrance that the conquerors of Rome had, only the upper echelons of soldiers got to go in at that time. Several days later, I went into the Vatican area, didn't see the Pope, but it was a beautiful, beautiful area that the Vatican had there in Rome. We had pushed the Germans far enough north of Rome so that I actually bought my mother a pocketbook, which she enjoyed very much after I got back. That was one city we purposely did not bomb, so there was no damage at all. The people were like our best friends. We were told not to go into their homes for food because the Germans supposedly had confiscated their food, [to] have enough for their army. The Italians—Mussolini did join Hitler as you probably recall—were friendly.

Then all the Americans regrouped and started going up the Rhône River valley. *The Day of the Panzer* was written by Jeff Danby, whose grandfather was killed on the thirteenth day. He was a tank commander, helping us move up north through southern France. Unfortunately, a hidden German tank caused an explosion that hit his tank and incinerated it. So his grandfather was gone, and that's why he wanted to write a story about how his grandfather died. I corresponded with Jeff from 2002 to 2008 when his book was published, telling him what I am telling you now, answering his questions. He quoted me in this book several times.

I forgot to mention that on the day that Jeff Danby's grandfather was killed I was captured. We had advanced too fast. The Germans made an entrapment (came in behind us), later I found that there were thirteen of us captured, but only three were in my company. We were put onto different vehicles that the Germans were using to make their retreat. About three days later, we were bombed heavily by the American artillery and the American bombers... [As it happens], my older brothers both were in the US Army Air Forces, one flew out of England and one flew out of Africa. I never knew which was which, but I waved [at] our P-42s or B-17s.

My capture was very, very scary. The three of us were in a vineyard, and when we realized that we had been surrounded by the Germans, we dropped our guns and held our hands up. When the Germans approached, we shouted that we were not going to fire. We were afraid to death, because you didn't know whether they were going to shoot us. We rode in different cars, because one car might be knocked out by one of our own bombs, then we would get into a different one and go further north, again in the Rhône River valley. I talked with the soldiers that had captured us, most of them were from Poland. Of course I asked them, "Why are you fighting for Hitler when he captured your country?" But as far as they were concerned, Hitler was good, so you see *all* the Polish people didn't resent being captured by the Germans.

In any event, about the third day we decided we were either going to be killed by our own bombs or by the captors if they got mad at us holding them up. The three of us made a break for it when we were all getting out of the vehicle because the artillery started. We ran from the highway through a grapevine field. In France, the grapevines leaves are much bigger than they are here, saved our life! The three of us hid under grapevine *leaves* because we escaped around noontime. We didn't want to be picked up again by the Germans, they were walking through this same vineyard, because it was safer in the field than on the road, the north-south railroad was being bombed too. We stayed there until it got dark. The Germans walked as close as you are to me [two feet]. They couldn't see us, we pulled the grapevine leaves down over us, and when it became dark we started to walk south again because we knew that's where our company would be. I was captured in a town called Allan [near Montélimar, Rhône-Alpes].

When we got back [August 30, 1944], we didn't know if the Americans would think that we were Germans. So we held our hands up, "We're Americans, we were captured three days ago, don't shoot." It worked. I went back to Company L, 15th Infantry Regiment, and proceeded up again north. It was later that I found out that more than three of us were captured, they didn't all get back. I don't know whether they were shot, or hit by our artillery. We continued advancing up north in France for another two or three months, fighting the Germans again. We went past Lyon.

One day three of us from L Company got into a barn that had ten huge wine tanks, twelve feet in diameter. They were full of bullet holes—and we hung our canteens to fill up with French wine. We were told not to go to the French homes because they wouldn't have enough food, not true in this case. A French couple invited me and two other soldiers to come to their home and have dinner. We did, even though it was against regulations at the time. In Europe, they don't have three courses, they have six courses and each is served individually. It was quite a feast and we didn't get court-martialed for it!

I went through Alsace-Lorraine. It was December of '44, standing in foxholes, with or without your shoes, did damage to your feet. We were never supposed to take our shoes off, but when they are soaking wet and you're standing in them, you take them off. [It] also happened the first winter—Anzio was in January of '44, and just before my feet froze. So I was back on a hospital ship. They wanted to amputate, but I said no, my toes weren't that blue. I still have all the toes. I have a 30-percent disability (in each foot) because of the frozen feet.

Then again in the winter of '44, after Christmas, I was cited for the Bronze Star, the Silver Star, and a Purple Heart. It was into January 1945 when my feet caused me to be evacuated. They brought me all the way from near the Rhine, through Paris (which I never saw because I was in an ambulance), over to a British hospital, outskirts of London. While my feet were recuperating, a couple of generals were going around different beds and awarding Purple Hearts. So I called one of the generals over and I said, "Does this qualify?" because I had been nicked by a bomb fragment at the same time my feet froze. He said, "Yes, it sure does." It doesn't show any scar now it was so minor, but it was at that time bloody enough to earn the Purple Heart, which I have.

They returned me in March '45 from London by ship, back home. By then my oldest brother, whom I mentioned earlier was a B-17 pilot out of England, had completed his 25 missions and was back in America. We were allowed to go home. It was an event of great emotion to say hi to my father and mother. I was still alive. My brother said, "How come you didn't tell us that you had the Silver Star or Bronze Star?" I said, "I didn't know I did." The only thing I know is what was written up in the award presentation [for action on December 26, Bronze Star, and December 27, Silver Star, 1944] that they gave me some time between March and August '45. I had no idea. In fact, I have very little recollection of why, except that it was pretty heavy fighting, both door-to-door in the French cities as well as in the fields.

That's pretty much the end of the story. I felt that with my two years of frozen feet I wouldn't make a very good ranger, so I started college again at Trinity College in Hartford, September '45, got married in '47. After discharge, I didn't join any of the military-type clubs, the American Legion where you stuck together with your buddies that you knew. I just tried to completely eliminate the war from whatever I was trying to do from then on.

I thought we should have gone after Hitler much sooner than we did. I didn't disagree with our going into Iraq either because I thought that Saddam Hussein might be another Hitler. That's why I think we went in and I still think the same. We should have tried to stop Hitler when he took over Poland and France, Austria and other places. The world did nothing to stop him. You don't want to be called a warmonger and people who said let's join England were called warmongers. It would have been a hard fight to get us to join earlier—there were enough people who disagreed with going into the war.

I don't think we were very much aware of al-Qaeda terrorists until very recently. I agree we should have gone into Afghanistan after Iraq because the terrorists there were very, very active against us. The Muslim religion, if you read about it, is as holy as Christianity, it's just that there must be a bunch of them that don't follow it, like a lot of Christians.

I think we ought to do our best in Afghanistan. The president was right in sending another 30,000 troops. Whether we will ever win or not remains to be seen. I think we should. Whether it can be done or not, conquer the terrorists or al-Qaeda, I still don't know what the difference is. I think we did the right thing in Vietnam. Too bad that so many people didn't think it was the right thing. That's really why we lost that war.

Rich Kells, born in 1922 in Greenfield, Massachusetts, lives a few doors from the house in which he grew up. He and four brothers all served in the army. He graduated from high school months before Pearl Harbor and worked at a mechanic shop. When he found out he was being deferred, he immediately went to the post office and signed up in 1943, and was deployed to Europe. He pursued the Germans up the Rhône Valley until he was captured. He spent the remainder of the war as a POW, and has a collection of the postcards and telegrams that radio-listeners sent his mother to tell her he was alive as announced by Axis Sally on German radio. After the war, he worked at the Boston and Maine Railroad as a yard conductor for 35 years.

We got on ship July '44, landed in Naples, Italy, just after the war in Sicily. Salerno, our camp, was on the battlefield. Who do I run into but my younger brother! He went in the service six months before me. We were at the depot, which is for any unit that had lost men and needed to bulk up their forces again. I finally wound up in the 45th. My brother wound up in the 3rd Division, which was a very big division in the war. I'm going to leave Italy now, and we are going to go to Southern France. We landed in Sainte Maxime, got all our gear, put on our hiking shoes, and we hiked for quite a distance. Eventually, we wound up near Grenoble, and this is where I started getting a taste of what the front line was.

We were going into combat, and some of the people were

coming back and were mentioning a couple of things I don't want to repeat. [*He consults a map.*] On August 15, we invaded southern France at Sainte Maxime. We were at Grenoble Falls August 23; we cleared Bourg [-en-Bresse] of snipers on September 4 and lost contact with the enemy. September 5, Lons-le-Saunier, Ornans, and Vercel [-Villedieu] were occupied without a fight. On September 7, the battle for Baume-les-Dames began and Baume fell to the 45th Division on November 26. I got captured some place up in here at Niederbronn [-les-Bains]. This is the route that the 45th Division "Thunderbirds" took.

Once we got into France, we walked and walked and walked. We went through towns, villages, and the people gave us apples and flowers, the only time I got any thank yous. I'm going hurriedly through this combat because I like to skip over that, I've never talked to anybody too much about some of the things that went on. We were fighting all the way up. We can probably skip over all my fighting and get into a week or two before my capture. The fighting is what every combat soldier goes through—basic things that anybody would recognize. I'm a foot soldier, rifleman. I had an M-1, one of the best rifles in the war.

I'm going to go right into my capture, if you don't mind. About a week, ten days before my capture, we were in a holding pattern and we knew the Germans were there, we could see them, so we moved up, we got our shovels and we dug slit trenches—not foxholes, which are down deep, just enough to protect my body. We made them nice and big and put logs over the top of them, keeping shrapnel from getting at us. We jumped in the German foxholes after we moved them out.

This is November, just before Thanksgiving. We were told they were going to pull us back because we had been on line and we hadn't had a rest for quite a while. We were going to have our Thanksgiving dinner in a nice secure hotel back of the line, *Hotel Cosmopolitan*. It's amazing that I am 87 and I am still coming up with this. They pulled us back and another division relieved us. Who gets left behind to tell these people (because they are fresh over from the United States) what the veterans know about? The next day I went back and gosh, it was a nice hotel, *fantastic*. We were able to shower and shave, first time in I don't know when.

Our bazooka team got blown away, so they needed to replace

the bazooka. This is how I got captured, incidentally. This friend of mine, Bill Banning from Boston (I tried to track him down after I got home and I never could find him), they set up a target, an old piece of junk a hundred yards away, they were looking for a bazooka team. You slip the ammunition in this tubular thing and then you hooked it up with batteries and it's mainly designed for knocking the treads off of tanks. We accidentally, and I mean *accidentally,* hit the target—so who's the next bazooka team? Bill Banning and me. My God, that was bad duty.

We're back in the hotel and word comes up that the unit that replaced us got in trouble and they were getting hammered on line. This is the day before Thanksgiving, the turkeys are on the *table* and we are going to have turkey and the whole fixings, they were *warm,* and we got orders to move out. God, we moved out back to the same general area and that was a bees' nest for Germans. We now had a field-made lieutenant, second lieutenant.

There was one building there that they were going to use as a command post, alongside a roadway. The lieutenant said to Banning and myself, "You go up a hundred yards, and dig in and hold." I said—I can remember this—"Well, where are the Germans?" "They're not anywhere around." This is the new lieutenant. So we moved out and dug in alongside of the road, there was a culvert and we moved into this hole with the bazooka. Carrying an M-1 rifle and the bazooka and ammunition, I could have lightened it up a bit if I had taken a pistol but I tried pistol target practice and I couldn't hit anything, so I kept my M-1 rifle.

As we were going up to dig in, I looked off about 150 yards and saw this person walking along on a ridge all by himself. I took it as a civilian and I didn't pay any attention to him. He was giving away our position, he could see us too—this is what I figured out before I got captured. We no more than got dug in than the Germans started coming in with artillery. We're veterans now, we've learned a lot from just being on line, and we know that they're keeping us down in our holes. You're not going to get up because you're going to get hit by shrapnel.

The squad of Germans (about eight to ten people) were shooting *away* from our hole, they knew exactly where we were, but the bullets were glancing off the road. They deliberately avoided killing us right then: they were trying to tell us, *We've got you pinned down.* So my partner noticed what was going on. I can re-member his saying, "You want to call it quits?" I answered, "Do we have a choice?" And we of course didn't. Now we're getting the signal "Kommen sie out mit the hands up." We understood that.

We got out, put our hands up, we walked up this little knoll where they were above us. They had complete control. We're now in the hands of the Germans and our troops are shooting furiously at the Germans *and* us. The troops behind me could see this action; we were in touch with one another. When the Germans started shooting at us that alerted the main part of our unit. Believe it or not, I was screaming and yelling to hold the fire and it got back, so whoever gave the order to fire gave the order to cease fire.

You won't believe this one—remember I said that we were in a holding pattern and the Germans were nowhere near? Over the knoll, down in a ravine, we were marched back to this building, fantastic, with all the typewriters and clerical people, you wouldn't *believe.* Not 200 yards away from where we were and nobody knew they were there. They were of course looking for informa-tion. We were being interrogated. Of course they weren't getting anything because you don't have to give anything but your name, rank, and serial number. Richard Kells, PFC. They were looking for information as to where the tanks were located, who my com-manding officer was. I can remember saying, "I'm not telling you." Well," he said, "I'm telling *you,* it's Captain Robinson." They had all that information anyway—they'd captured a lot more peo-ple than myself and Banning. We were eventually all gathered up en route to the main holding camp for POWs.

While we were there, we had a little postcard we could fill out to let our parents know that we were okay. I wrote my message down. By now my mother has already got the telegram that I'm missing in action. You know Axis Sally? She took all this infor-mation down that I had put on the postcard saying that I'm okay, and read it off the radio. Would you like to see some of those telegrams [and postcards] that my mother received? Axis Sally sent this over the airwaves, and all the ham radio operators from Canada and the United States picked up this message and my home address, wrote to my mother, sent telegrams, saying that I was okay. One post card from Ohio said the location was presumed to be Stalag 3A [this was correct], Luckenwalde. [*A sampling of postcards.*]

Providence, Rhode Island, January 24:

Dear Mrs. Kells: On a German short wave program from Berlin, this evening I heard a message for you. It was from PFC Richard W. Kells, serial number 31416714 saying, "Don't worry, I will send you an address soon. I am all right, all my love." I am sure you can write to and send packages through the Red Cross. Sincerely, yours, Teresa Lowenberg.

From Rochester, New York:

Dear Madam, last evening I picked up a German broadcast containing a message for you from your son, Private First Class Richard I. Kells, he is a prisoner of war, well and safe.

Another:

I received a message from your son PFC Irving Kell: "Dearest Mother: Don't worry. I am a prisoner of war in Germany. I am okay and no wounds. I am anxious to hear from you. Contact Red Cross for my writing address.

After they interrogated us, we walked and we walked and we walked, we finally wound up at a barn in a farmhouse where we bedded down, of course being guarded by several Germans. I'm still on this [west] side of the Rhine River. Now it's morning, we headed out again, walked to a small town that had a little POW holding camp and we were being interrogated again. It had a red cross on the roof of this building—from the air, you see the red cross and you don't bomb hospitals and POW camps.

When we got to this town, there was a bunch of German civilians there to greet us, not what I would consider a very cordial greeting. When I was back at the Hotel Cosmopolitan, I got new clothing and my field jacket had a 45th Division insignia on it. [The Germans] got two air raids, and they associated the 45th Division patch with the Air Corps [US Army Air Forces] because it was a golden eagle [a thunderbird], so they took me for being in the Air Corps. They were throwing stones (not rocks) at us, they were mad, needless to say, they just wanted to let their anger out at us.

There was a P-51 strafing emplacement in this little town, I could see it had a box bomb on it, a fast little plane. He came over and he was being shot at, I could see tracer bullets, and he spotted us, he tipped his wing over a little bit, and he waved his hand at us. I saw him, I saw the bomb come out of the plane and hit a building just beyond where I was. It tore the whole side of the building off but didn't start a fire. We were told to get out there and wave our jackets so that the pilot wouldn't strafe us—the German soldiers didn't want to get bombed either!

We were moved to some railroad station, put in boxcars heading back into Germany. We were moved to one of the main POW camps. When we got up there, I thought the whole United States Army was POWs, there were *tons* of them! It was around the Battle of the Bulge. We were housed in factory buildings, and they always kept the officers and enlisted men separate. We had French, Russians. That night, while we were sleeping, the RAF came over and they bombed that railroad station that we just left but they missed their target and they got a direct hit on our officers' building—unbelievable.

We still are not getting anything to eat. A little rutabaga soup, a grass soup, and cheese, the smell of it was so bad I couldn't even eat it, as hungry as I was. The rutabaga soup—you might find a little piece of rutabaga in some hot water. I'm not exaggerating, and the grass soup was so bad, and one slice of bread with some kind of jam on it. This is our diet for the whole length of time I was in prison, if you want to call them meals, maybe three meals a day. We always got our slice of bread. Some of it was dated, printed on the loaf itself, 1938. The bread was all buried in-ground and as they needed it they used to dig it up and feed it to us. The bread looked like it was rolled in sawdust. I remember the dates.

I'm going to backtrack again, if you don't mind. Another detail they had us do was to dig foxholes, or slit trenches for them, outside of the camp. This is January. The reason for that was the Germans got word that the paratroopers were going to parachute into this military camp. They flew over, the Americans weren't kidding, they dropped leaflets telling the Germans that if the war wasn't over by such and such a date, we're going to bomb your camp.

We were up near Berlin, the Americans did all the daylight bombing and strafing, and the RAF, the Royal Air Force, the British, did the night bombing. The Americans were awfully good about living up to the rules. The Americans bombed that military camp. They had incendiary bombs and they hit our compound, so when we came back [from work] there were a bunch of Germans, mad Germans now—they had hit warehouses full of canned cheese, Hershey's candy bars, anything that would keep. The next day our detail was to go clean up from the bombs. Because we were hungry, this guy bent over to get some candies, and a German guard kicked him in the head and on the body. But that, I've got to say, was the only act of brutality that I saw.

Now the war is really beginning to wind down. The Russians are coming in on one end of it, and the Americans were squeezing them. One more thing is the lice. They had built nests in any seam I had, crotch area, and in my head—they were taking over. I've got to mention the fact that all this time I was in prison, five or six months, I had the same clothing on that I got from the Hotel Cosmopolitan, same socks. The Germans were going to give us a pair of socks—you know what they were? They were a square piece of cloth. I used it to brush my teeth with, since I didn't have a toothbrush, none of that stuff that is necessary to keep yourself clean.

Then one day they said we are going to let you have a bath— the Red Cross is about to come in. The bath turned out to be a big, huge wooden vat. I don't know how many people had taken their bath in there before me, but it wasn't drained out. I don't remember going to the bathroom. We didn't get enough to eat to go to the bathroom. I stripped down, got in the tub, took my so-called bath, got out, put the same infected lice-ridden clothes on that I had had on for five months anyway, and then got back to the infested bed that I was assigned to. The lice are still with me.

Finally, the war is beginning to come to an end, and we are going to be moved one more time back to Luckenwalde (not "Buchenwald"), the name of the town where the main camp was. They had huge circus tents set up, the prisoners congregated from east, west, north and south. The Russians liberated us. They got there before the Americans did, and they lobbed a couple of artillery shells into the camp to let the Germans know to get out. There were Finns and Swedes, all kinds of prisoners. So now all we had to do was wait for the Americans to come in with the trucks. The gates were wide open.

Now we are not happy with the Russians at this stage of the game. The Cold War has already started. After a couple of days the Americans came, and in the meantime I went downtown a couple of times—we were still trying to get something to eat. The German civilians were begging us to stay with them, because now the Russians are taking everything they could from the Germans, and the Germans wanted us because if the Russians saw an American there, they wouldn't touch them. Of course, we didn't stay.

We were lucky. They were close to taking us back to Russia with them. Finally the Americans came, loaded us up on the trucks. I didn't know when Hitler killed himself, but I knew when Roosevelt died and Truman took over. I'm now in American hands, in a de-lousing building. The lice came out of my body in droves. Of course they had a pile as big as this house full of American clothing, burned it. We were stripped down and given all new and clean clothing. They didn't shave the head, they just put the powder on. They scampered out of there! [*He laughs.*]

This was in Hildesheim [near Hanover]. We were loaded onto C-47s headed for Le Havre, France, Camp Lucky Strike. Our pilot came in too fast and he started to climb up on the rear end of another plane that had landed just ahead of us, he went off the runway into a big gully. There we landed in a heap. [*He laughs again.*] My first plane ride, and we crash! Nobody got hurt other than bumps and bruises. They gave us something to eat. Unfortunately, it wasn't a lot. Our stomachs had shrunk so they were very careful. Then all of a sudden we could eat anything— chicken, pasta, eggs, [our] legs actually filling out, pasta, I guess that puts on weight.

[*Rich at first did not want me to relate the following story, which he had never before told, but later he left it up to my discretion.*]

The one thing that I didn't mention was this guy came back and he says, "I just shot a German medic." I didn't want to mention it because we were always drilled, any medic, anything with a red cross on it, you don't shoot. Why did he mention that to me? I don't know. You're the only person I have mentioned it to. That stuck with me all my life. He shot a German *medic*. Geez! He didn't say he *killed* him; he said he *shot* him, kind of bragging about it. He had the same information that I had, going into combat there are certain rules.

Of course in World War II we had no choice, they attacked us. We had to retaliate, we can't lay down and let them walk all over us. Unlike Iraq and Afghanistan, and Vietnam, and I don't know how we got mixed up in all those. I think what we're most afraid of right now, the weaponry that Iran has got and North Korea has got. They're close to having a [nuclear] bomb, the whole works, somebody's got to step up and stop these people who are aggressors. This country [US] I never figured was dealing for a fight, I always figured there was a reason for it. Apparently [in Iraq] there wasn't.

Ahmadinejad is not going to listen to Obama. He's well on his way to getting [a bomb]. If everybody has the bomb, good-bye earth. It was just Russia and United States for a long while, but now some of these small countries are getting in on it.

Colonel Don Ryan was born in 1920 in Minneapolis, Minnesota, and orphaned during the Depression when his mother left him with a couple she knew to "watch" him for $10 and never returned. Upon graduation from high school, he planned to attend the University of Minnesota and its medical school. Instead, at sixteen he joined the National Guard and volunteered for the Army before Pearl Harbor. He also fought in Korea, and became fast friends with a famous North Korean pilot who defected to the United States. Don flew SAC planes during the Cuban missile crisis, and was wing commander of Westover Air Force Base in Massachusetts before he retired. His story of meeting and marrying his wife is typical of the period.

We were overseas with the first American contingent to land in Europe in World War II on January 26, 1942. We were learning how to shoot the British 25-pounder cannon, and they called us all in to have an IQ test. Two weeks later I found myself back in the United States at Fort Benning, Georgia, in the infantry officers' school. I was a second lieutenant, and ended up as a first rifle platoon leader of K Company in the 65th Infantry Division, Camp Shelby, Mississippi.

While we were there, they took us over to an airport because the Army Air Corps [renamed Army Air Forces] was on a recruiting drive. [*He shows me framed pictures.*] I walked up to the pilot of the P-51 Mustang and I asked him, "How do you get to drive one of those things?" He said, "Sign here." One week later I was in the Army Air Corps. We had to go through the usual pre-flight primary, basic, advanced, and this is a picture of me in 1943. That was a PT-19 and that was my first solo flight in an airplane. I think that the reason they took the picture is in case we didn't show up again, they would have something to send home to our folks. Since that time, I have flown the C-45, C-46, C-47, C-123, B-17, B-25, B-26, B-29, B-36, B-52 airplanes, and I also flew fighters, an F-51, for seven years. I've flown 12,000 hours.

While I was in the 109th Fighter Squadron, there was a sign over the entrance to our briefing room: "Victory is in the mind of the pilot." So you've either got it or you haven't got it. I was the only one who survived [training] out of five. The reason my other fellow students washed out is they couldn't do the spins and stalls. I picked up a brand-new B-17 in Wichita, Kansas and I flew it over to England. That's me and my crew in Rushton, England in 1944. I was 24 years old at that time and my crew was anywhere from 19 to 23. After the war in Europe, I flew back to the States and said goodbye to my crew and I joined the Minnesota Air National Guard because I had always wanted to be a fighter pilot. That's a P-51 Mustang, the top fighter in the world at that time. I flew that for seven years, 1946–52.

While I was there, we were recalled to active duty. I was now a registered fighter pilot. The interesting thing about my National Guard duty after the war was that we had a lot of notable individuals in my unit. My squadron commander had sixteen airplanes to his credit in World War II. I was in the 109th Fighter Squadron, the 31st Air Division. One of the noteworthy individuals was Joe Foss, Congressional Medal of Honor, 28 airplanes to his credit in World War II, Marine pilot, front-page news all over the world. He was a squadron commander of the unit out in Sioux Falls, South Dakota. I was at Minneapolis, at the 109th.

Anyway, my squadron commander came up to me and he said, "Don, you always wanted to be Joe Foss." I admired him, I wanted to be a fighter pilot. I said, "Yeah." "You can join me." [So] I flew as the squadron commander's wing man out to Sioux Falls, South Dakota. We landed and said hello to Joe, had a cup of coffee with him. I was awestricken with this famous guy, and I said (we were going to fly with Joe up to Grand Forks, North Dakota),

"Joe, are you going to do a few whirligigs in the air?" and he said, "If you'd like." I said, "Just a little bit if you will." So he did that, and I stayed right on his tail. We landed at Grand Forks. When we got out of the airplane, Joe put his arm on my shoulder, and said, "Don, you should have been a fighter pilot." I consider that the greatest compliment I've ever had in my life.

When the war was over in Europe, I flew my B-17 back to Bradley Field, Connecticut and I turned it in. I said goodbye to my crew, and I was personally assigned to B-29s down in Laredo, Texas. In the middle of that training, the Japanese gave up. I like to feel that they knew I was in B-29s and gave up. That war was over.

When you came home on leave in World War II, the restaurants and everything were open 24 hours a day. With the war effort, everybody in the US workforce was on three shifts. If you're looking for a girl, go into any bar, any time of day or night, and they had just got off of work. [Marge Winship] was a telephone operator in Northern States Power Company, an 8-to-4 job. We were both 25 in 1945 when we met. She was quite a gal.

The war was over, tickertape parades all over Europe, Chicago, New York. My tickertape parade involved, "Hey, Ryan, you're discharged, see you in the next war, goodbye." I jumped on a train in Laredo, Texas and I rode it up to my hometown in Minneapolis. It was 11 o'clock at night, I went into the phone booth. "Hello?" It was her father. I said, "Could I speak to Marge?" "Who's this?" I said, "This is Don Ryan." "Just a minute." Pretty soon: "Hello?" "Is that you, Marge?" "Oh, is that you, Don?" I said, "Yeah, the war is over. I didn't get killed in either the European or the Pacific wars, so let's get married." This is Monday. She said, "Okay, when?" I said, "How about Friday?" I had met her a few times as a date. And we were married five days later.

I had no money, no job, five bucks in my pocket, no place to live. So I rode the bus over to her place, knocked on the door, and it was her father. "I'm Don Ryan, I'm going to marry your daughter." [He laughs.] It's a wonder he didn't set the dogs on me. We stood by a Christmas tree and said our vows. As we walked out the door her father said, "Have you got any money?" I said, "No," and he said, "Here's sixty bucks." What was sixty bucks in 1945—$300?

When I told Marge we were going to get married, she told her father that I didn't have any work. I'd been a bomber pilot in the war. He gave me a job with Otis Elevator Company as a mechanic's helper. "Pick up that tool box," and I would carry the toolbox around behind the mechanic. "Give me that 12-inch wrench," so I would give him a 12-inch wrench. I was there about a year, and then they made me a mechanic and I installed Otis elevators. I held that for about a year and then they made me a sales representative for five states—Minnesota, Wisconsin, North and South Dakota, and Iowa—and I sold elevators.

We were married 57 years. Everybody was getting married right away. I had enough brains to feel, even though I was madly in love with her, that I wouldn't do that to her because I was going back into combat. I could have been killed. Wouldn't that have been something, to marry a girl and live with her for a weekend and go to war and get killed, she's a widow? I was able to figure that out.

I had always envied the other kids in the neighborhood because they had a mother and father. I didn't. I was boarded out as a kid. In those days of the Depression such things happened. My mother left my father when I was a year old. She brought me over to a house in Minneapolis and she said, "Would you take care of my Don for a week, I'll give you ten bucks." She knew the people. She never showed up again and my father never showed up again. So these people kept me and when their son and daughter got married, they didn't have room for me in the house, so I slept on the screened porch in Minneapolis for two years. Thirty below zero, I would go to bed with all my clothes and shoes on. They were good to me but they didn't have any room for me.

I also earned all my own clothes. From the time I was about ten years old, I had a routine in the neighborhood. I would scrub floors, basement steps for the different wives, ten cents or twenty-five cents. I always had money. In the meantime, to make more money, I joined the Minnesota National Guard. I was sixteen, illegal. My National Guard outfit was called to active duty, by that time I was a staff sergeant, an enlisted man. After the war, I had to change my date of birth from 1918 to 1920. They commend you, they don't criticize you for that.

In regard to World War II, I think that was a worthwhile effort on the Allies' part. It was necessary. Hitler was obviously a crazy man. When he was developing a new Reich, he was imposing his will on Poland, he was berserk. He had gotten delusions of grandeur; he lost hold of common sense. World War II was a good, worthwhile effort on the Allies' part. All the other wars have had a political aspect.

2
AT SEA IN THE PACIFIC AND ATLANTIC: NAVY, NAVY ARMED GUARD, MARINE CORPS, AND MERCHANT MARINE

Ed Borucki was born in 1920 in Holyoke, Massachusetts, and enlisted in the Navy in July 1940 after working at the Springfield Armory as an apprentice machinist making M-1 rifles. He was assigned to the USS Helena, CL-50, a light cruiser. He was in Pearl Harbor when the Japanese attacked on December 7, 1941 and tells the story of what happened on his ship, where 33 men were killed. He now distributes literature at public events illustrating his involvement with the beginning of the war and the events of Pearl Harbor. He received a degree in education from Westfield State College, and taught business in the Chicopee high schools for 23 years.

I didn't go into the Navy for travel or adventure. [*He laughs.*] I am number four [in my family] and first to enlist in 1940. My mother was a widow with seven children. She had a very rough life. My father died when I was 11 and there was no help like we have nowadays for people like that. [Walter, my brother] enlisted in the Navy the next day after Pearl Harbor. He was killed when his ship was in a convoy, the *USS Ingraham* [DD-444] on August 22, 1942. He was nineteen. So I was a Gold Star brother and my mother was a Gold Star mother. That meant you lost a person in the war. There were four Borucki bothers, and we all served in the Navy in World War II. One served in Ft. Lauderdale, and another served in Sampson, New York. When the five Sullivan brothers were killed on ship, the Navy decided if you had someone killed to keep you on shore duty instead of exposing you to conflict.

[*Ed shows the letter to his mother concerning his brother's death and adds the information in brackets.*]

> Secretary of the Navy to Mrs. Anna Borucki, Holyoke, Mass:
>
> After full review of all available information, I am reluctantly forced to the conclusion that your son, Walter John Borucki, seaman second class, Navy, is deceased. Having been officially reported missing on 22 August 1942, he was a member of the crew and serving for the *USS Ingraham*. That vessel collided with another vessel [a big oil tanker] and sank in the North Atlantic as a result of poor visibility due to weather conditions. [Eleven were saved out of a couple of hundred]. According to section 5 of public law 490, 77th Congress as amended, your son's death is presumed to have occurred on 23 August 1943, which is the day following the day of expiration of an absence of twelve months.
>
> I extend to you my sincere sympathy in your great loss. You may find comfort in the knowledge that your son gave his life for his country, upholding the highest traditions of the Navy. The Navy shares in your sense of bereavement and will feel the loss of his service.
>
> Signed, Frank Knox, Secretary of the Navy

On the morning of December 6, 1941, the eve of the Pearl Harbor attack, we were in port in Pearl Harbor. The next day, at quarter to eight, I went to the engineering office to pass out liberty cards to the off-duty watch, and while I was doing that, the general alarm sounded. "Man your battle station, Jap planes attacking, break out service ammunition, this is no drill." I hesitated—nobody's going to bother us on Sunday morning. We dashed to battle station and I was knocked against the wall of the bulkhead by a torpedo, which hit just where I'd left. So I was saved by thirty seconds, and 33 of my shipmates were killed.

It was an aerial torpedo. The Japanese preferred using them. The torpedo blast killed a lot of people who were at the wrong spot at the time. It destroyed my office, which was just above the engine room. We shut off the valves and secured the watertight doors. We were on the first deck then, we weren't on top deck where we could see everything. After about two hours the all-clear sounded and we went on deck and carried out the dead and wounded. I remember the barber, at six foot two and 220 pounds, we had a hard time getting him up the ladder. He said, "I'm sorry I am causing you all this trouble."

On December 6, 1941 on the eve of the Pearl Harbor attack, my shipmate Salvatore Albanese from Flushing, New York, brought me a ham sandwich and on December 7 he was killed. The *Arizona* was burning. [Alongside] our ship was the *USS Oglala* (CM-4), a torpedo hit under them and hit us, it destroyed the *Oglala*, a wooden minesweeper. Of course they only had a few ambulances there. It was a nightmare. "I don't believe it, it's not happening. How could it happen?" We were peaceful there, big and strong, we never thought the Japanese would attack us. After the battle there, we wondered what would happen if they invaded. They announced on the public address system that Roosevelt had declared war. He said that the 7th of December would live in infamy.

[*He sings.*]

> Let's Remember Pearl Harbor
> As we go to meet the foe
> Let's remember Pearl Harbor,
> As we did the Alamo.
> We will always remember
> How they died for liberty.
> Let's remember Pearl Harbor
> And go on to victory.
> [© 1941, Lyrics: Don Reid, Sammy Kaye; Music: Don Reid]

I was transferred to the *USS Rockaway* [AVP-29], a seaplane tender, in Seattle, Washington, April of '43. I had been commissioned in October of '42. We served in the North Atlantic—went to Wales in the British Isles, the famous coal port. Of course we were on oil burners then. I got sent back to sea. I was on a troop transport bound for the invasion of Japan. The date for invading Japan was August 14, 1945. We were in Pearl Harbor when they announced the Japanese surrender. We still proceeded to the Philippines. I had enough points, [so] I was one of the first ones to be discharged, on October 15, 1945. I was a chief petty officer and chief yeoman in 1944. I felt anger about [Japan], but now I have a Japanese daughter-in-law and my [other] son is in Tokyo teaching at a Temple University branch—management. [*He laughs.*]

[On] our ship, the Blacks got the food, took care of the officer corps. If you were black that was the only thing you were allowed to do. They weren't allowed to shoot machine guns. They were restricted to taking care of the officers, feeding them. One of the black mess attendants, his captain was wounded and he took him aside and saved him and went to the machine gun and started shooting it. In '44, Truman started to eliminate segregation. I didn't see that because I wasn't involved after that.

There are only 5 to 10 percent of people who were at Pearl Harbor when it was attacked on December 7, '41 still alive. Most of them are gone now. I've been back seventeen times. My seven sons have been back. I took my three grandsons, my wife. [My] sons haven't served—they said Dad did enough service there. I lost 33 shipmates, I lost a brother. How many people have something like that? In our veterans' group, only two other Pearl Harbor survivors had brothers killed in World War II. I had all my friends killed there, so I was involved. We help to remember all these sacrifices, these lives. I would like to see more patriotism, more participation. Show the flag, love of country, participation in events, volunteer more, participate in ceremonies. Salute, stand up and hold your hand over your heart when a flag goes by, and when they play the "Star Spangled Banner." Join the American Legion and help them out there, offer scholarships, poppy drives. I had a sign that said, "If there wasn't a Pearl Harbor, there wouldn't be a Nagasaki and Hiroshima." It saved a half million Americans.

[If you were Truman, would you have used the bomb?] Yes.

George Bush, the money [for Iraq] was all off the balance sheet, he didn't ask anybody to sacrifice something. Some were involved, [some] weren't involved at all. It seemed far away. [Korea?] We weren't really prepared and that's the problem, they didn't have any equipment and supplies. We made a big mistake after World War II, with all the equipment and cutting everybody out, instead of keeping the Armed Forces big and strong as they are now. Korea was a police action instead of a war.

[What were your opinions about Vietnam?] I was against the war. We had a convention in New York City in '69, our group of Pearl Harbor veterans. We wanted a parade from our hotel to a veterans' memorial there to place a wreath and they wouldn't allow us, they were worried about disruptions with the antiwar people. [*Iraq, Afghanistan?*] I think we are sacrificing too many people. It shouldn't be this way. We were ready to go in there, as Paul [Wolfowitz] says, you have to get a swarm of people to go in there and the secretary of state [Madeleine Albright] says, "What's the army for [if not to fight]?" Bush had propaganda about the nuclear equipment and supplies there.

Charlie Sakowicz, born in 1926 in Whately, Massachusetts, was left holding on to a wooden plank miles from the coast of Japan after his aircraft carrier, the USS Franklin [CV-13], was bombed on March 19, 1945, losing more than 700 men and wounding 300. For days he drifted away from help, just holding on. Afraid of sharks and abandoned, he was finally saved by a ship and taken to Hawaii. He has never forgiven his captain calling those that abandoned ship cowards and traitors because, technically, the order to abandon ship had not been given, even though the ship was burning. The Franklin made it back under its own steam to New York harbor to a triumphal welcome.

I heard about so many friends going into the service, so of course I asked Mom, got a hard "no." Finally she said sure, so I joined—at that time, 17 was fine with the permission of your parents. I was assigned to the newly commissioned aircraft carrier, the *USS Franklin*. We used to call it Big Ben, [but] it wasn't named after Benjamin Franklin, it was named after the battle of Franklin [in Tennessee, in the Civil War].

I sailed off in '42. The aircraft carrier was the first Essex type, the biggest one at that time. I don't remember the first fight, but we had plenty. We've broken a lot of records, we've had more skirmishes, more fights, than anybody at that time. Went through the Panama Canal to the Pacific. After that, they found that they had to build a carrier or a ship only so wide—the *Franklin* had to take their gun mounts off because they couldn't get through. It took us about four weeks because every time you go through [a lock] you had to take the gun mounts off. They are five-inch guns, the mounts are like 40 by 40 feet.

Lots of times the bogeys (the Japanese aircraft), we would spot 20, 30, 40 of them. The fighters take off and an awful lot of times they'd fight for minutes and then they would skirmish and break up and take off. Then we were at Leyte, we had, God, thirteen real fights in Guam or in Saipan, which was just take off and bomb what you can, hope for the best. It was possible to fly over Guam and if the action was not severe (I was an aerial gunner, not pilot), dip yourself and you can see where thousands of poor Guam people were either pushed, or bulldozed by a Caterpillar, a lot were already dead, over the 972-foot stone cliffs [by the Japanese].

[*He shows pictures, taken on board the* Franklin, *of two Japanese captured when they ejected from their plane.*] The pilot was probably about 18. His Emperor was his God. They didn't hit the ship, [if] they were suicide, okay, they didn't make it. They flew in low, they got hit, because it was a bomber (they call it a "Betty") and these two Japanese went off into the water. They were picked up, everybody wanted to see them, touch them. The younger one was the pilot, the older one was the gunner who had more responsibility. He was supposed to drop [the bomb] when the pilot told him.

We found out one day that they both were dead. The walls of those compartments are rough—not cement, but a texture like that. These guys were watched by the cops, and I don't know if the police left them. They took a paintbrush and a toothbrush—they were sharp. They managed to slice themselves to commit suicide. I imagine the younger boy did it. If he was a kamikaze pilot, he would have hit the ship, not torpedoed it.

They informed us how close we were to Japan. I can never forget that, 27 miles [some accounts say 50 miles]. Captain Gehres was a John Wayne hero. In all the things we went through, he should have not been where he was. He wanted to get in there and fight, that's all there was to it. He got a big medal, he was honored and everything else. Up to the point where we got hit, islands by the dozens we bombed, and always hoped to get back to the carrier. I never had any problems, thank God.

[On March 19, 1945], the loudspeaker said we were in amongst a lot of Japanese planes and one of them was coming in lower than the carrier deck—we always thought he dropped a torpedo, a bomb that hit us midship that started it all. [*We take a break from this story while he composes himself.*] That morning of the attack I was having breakfast, it was around 6:30 AM and I could hear the ship's alarm, then we heard the bomb. Before the bomb, we started getting the hell out of the lower deck, I believe it was the 5th or 6th deck [below] there were four of us who hit the stairs at the same time to get up to the hanger deck and the flight deck while it was going on.

As we got up there, they were automatically closing the hatches. I was the second or third fellow, we couldn't make it, we were in that compartment, it started to fill up with water, the hatches were tight. I figured this was it. Another seaman, might have been an officer, maybe a group of firefighters, happened to come and open up the latch. From there we were right close to number five gun turret, which was ablaze.

I didn't go much further, five feet, and we knew what was going on [the ship] was listing so badly. This is when Captain Gehres got in trouble after he got back to the United States, for not sounding General Quarters, when everybody goes to their stations. They found out later he knew what was going on at the moment with the machinery and the ship, and he didn't have to do it, and he didn't do it. "Abandon ship" is another call, then you can leave. [Gehres did not make the call to abandon ship.]

We left because it was on so much of a tilt. I was scared, I said, "Let's get the hell out of here." Luckily I hit nothing in the water. A lot of them were killed because they hit planks. It's like this: here's the carrier, the gun mounts are here, that's when one of the bombs got through the steel hanger deck to the ammunition deck and blew up. There were mounds of torpedoes, and that's when I went off into the water.

When we got into the water, the cruiser [the *Santa Fe*] was alongside, picking up some of the guys, while everybody was fighting [the fire]. They didn't bother—that's bad, it's true—they didn't bother to pick us up there beside the boat, because [the current] was so strong, it was pushing us out, maybe a group of 500, 600, 800, pushing us out. We were still being not picked up from the water. They were being taken off the deck [instead].

We knew enough to get out of there. From where we were, midship, we're floating, we kept hitting the ship, people are sliding off. We started [drifting] away. The reason [Captain Gehres] didn't pick us up is because the tide was pushing us out. Frankly, if you read between the lines, [Gehres] was going to be demoted. He never was—he got promoted. At that point, I am out far enough and the cruiser is pulling away because of the currents, he couldn't do much for it, just stop the ship from burning.

In the meantime, we were holding on to anything we could. I had a plank from the flight deck, that's wood, I believe they are about ten inches wide and four or five inches thick. We had about eleven feet of that, and we held on. We were hoping that we were going to get picked up but the current was too quick. We're going out farther; the ship's pulling a lot of drowned sailors with them.

It never straightened out 'til the next day. I read this later: the captain got some of the mechanics, the firefighters got the [ship to] level off a little, and got a little power, so they straightened out a bit. When they pulled into New York City, they had a big tilt. They got [the *Franklin*] to run about five or six miles an hour. The ship under its own power and being towed by another ship, got into the Navy Yard in New York, and then to San Diego, and all the guys that were on it then got medals, some 500 of them.

In the water, we just floated, watched and watched and seeing death, maybe seven [on the same plank]. None of us were talking about the crew or the ship, just holding on. [*Could you see the ship?*] Oh, yes. We could still see it, you could see it just leaving us. It was dead in the water for a while. Then they started the engines, started to pull away. At that point, I think [the captain] in his mind thought, "You bastards, I never gave general orders to abandon ship, so as far as I'm concerned, all you that are out there are deserters." That came up in the court martial. But then they decided he was there, these admirals sitting in Washington didn't know what the hell was going on—he did. He got promoted too.

[*How long were you in the water?*] I told everyone seven days, but it was probably three or four days. All I remember is hoping that if [a shark] took a bite that was the only one. They brought a bunch of ships in to pick up what was around. After we got picked up, the guy came down and got us, they pulled you up, and bang, black, a towel in your eyes. [They] took that oil and grease away quickly. Take a damp alcohol cloth, and it will go.

From there I got to Hawaii. In the hospital is where I met Walter Lewandowski from West Street [in South Deerfield], too. He was fighting that night for the championship of the Hawaii boxing and they had bulletins, and he saw my name. He said, "Christ, that's Joe's kid." He called his wife and she called my folks. They were astonished because it could have been around the 25th that he told my parents.

There are 3,300 men on that carrier, but there were many that never made it. At least [the] 500 that stayed on the carrier all got medals. Gehres said all the guys that they didn't pick up but who were picked up by the tin cans, the cruisers or ships that were in the area, were bastards and he was going to see to it that they all were dishonorably discharged because they didn't get back on the carrier. He said they could have come back to the carrier. Horseshit. The ships alongside picked up who they could, figuring that the ship is going to go down. He said the ship was fine, didn't burn out, had power, Captain Gehres wanted those ships to bring back those men! He called them *traitors* because they wouldn't come back. He did save the ship, you've got to say that. Gehres retired from the Navy in 1948 with the rank of rear admiral.

[*What happened to you when you got home?*] I got back to Boston, checked in with the officer of the day, OD, and he said I have no assignment for you yet, but it will be posted tomorrow. So they posted it and I was to go out on a cruiser, that's about the third ship in the line of heavy ships. [The officer] looked down again, and he said, "You know, Charlie, you've got about 4,300 hundred points, yes, you do, son. You deserve them." And I said, "I need 2,600, right? I'm the hell out of here," and he let me go. If you had 2,600 points, you could be stationed in Hawaii for six months.

The colored pilots, their squadrons are just now receiving their rightful medals and honors. They were top pilots, Jesus, those guys were good. Truthfully, the African Americans on my ship, in *my* mind—a lot of jobs were done by them only because they were black and no one else wanted to do them. We had one guy who got so enraged with it, he was from Boston, he choked an officer and they flew him off. They weren't treated right, you know that. Thirty, forty years after the war, they are just giving praise to those guys who should have been getting recognition.

I don't understand why we're fighting in Afghanistan. Why doesn't someone say, "Hey listen, two countries tried to help them out, didn't work." [England and Russia.] I was upset that they had our troops there, and now it's not only 60,000, but 80,000. I say, if they want to kill themselves, for Christ's sake let them kill themselves. Who are we to tell Iran you can't develop a bomb? I don't understand it. Only because our man says, "Well if he's gets it, he's going to use it."

You're just killing our troops for nothing. If you want to help that country, fine. Go over there and flatten it. I may be all wrong, but I think America is too big. They stick their nose in everybody's business, they shouldn't. We've helped countries, Vietnam and other places. Right now, Afghanistan, but you know they're going to go back right to where they started. A lot of these countries don't want help. You got out of Vietnam, haven't you learned a lesson? [*Can America win a war in Afghanistan?*] Never, never. What have you won? Afghanistan, you can't stop the fighting.

Lionel Brindamour was born in 1925 in Chicopee, Massachusetts, and served in the Navy 1943–6. His ancestors came from Canada to the United States in 1847, with an earlier forebear immigrating to Canada from Chinon, France in 1756, and serving in General Montcalm's army in the French and Indian War against the British at Fort Ticonderoga and the Battle of the Plains. He asked me to incorporate a text he wrote about his wartime experiences into our oral interview, which he later edited. With his wife's encouragement, after they put their children through college, he got his GED and a diploma from Holyoke Community College in 1973.

I'm going back 66 years. I never really talked about it much. I never joined in the American Legion, Veterans of Foreign Wars. When they had the 50th anniversary of the Normandy invasion, it brought back a lot of memories. I watched Tom Brokaw, *The Greatest Generation.* So anyway, I joined the American Legion back about ten years ago.

I enlisted in the Navy April 14, 1943. I was 17. All of us took a train to Geneva, New York, to the Sampson Naval Training Station. We were asked what kind of ship we wanted to be on. I said, "I'd like to be on a battleship," but I didn't end up on a battleship. [*He laughs.*] Two or three hundred [of us] were put on a troop train bound for San Francisco. We left San Francisco about the middle of June 1943, going under the Golden Gate Bridge and going by

Alcatraz. We went on an LST—a Landing Ship, Tank. You've probably seen them in the Normandy invasion: they would hit the beach and lower their ramps, tanks or jeeps would drive out.

The voyage took about a month across the Pacific. We arrived at Noumea, New Caledonia. A few days later, five of us were assigned to the *USS Bobolink* [ATO-131]. From 1918 until World War II started, it was a minesweeper. When World War II started, it was converted to a seagoing tug, a big difference from a battleship! It was a small ship, crew of 65 to 75. I was promoted to Seaman 2nd Class; before I had been an apprentice seaman. As soon as we were aboard, the ship left bound for Guadalcanal, an island in the Solomon Islands.

By the time we reached Guadalcanal I was very sick and taken off the ship in a stretcher. I was told I was delirious, stayed in the hospital for about six weeks. I had spinal meningitis, probably caused by passing cigarettes from guy to guy on the ship. I was put in isolation, [and] I had a pharmacist's mate who took care of just me. I remember fierce headaches. The doctor told me what saved my life was penicillin. I assume that it was prioritized for the military, not widely used on civilians at that time. There were a lot of Marines and sailors that had been hurt in battle, especially the Marines. They had some horrific wounds.

The Solomon Islands were a chain of islands, going mostly north, up to Rabaul, the Japanese base on East New Britain Island, Papua, New Guinea. We used to bomb and strafe Rabaul a lot, naval battles and dogfights were fought. The Americans took one island at a time going toward Rabaul, Guadalcanal, Tulagi, Russell Island, Munda, Rendova, and a lot of other islands, like stepping stones. When I arrived, Guadalcanal had already been taken because that was in 1942 and I got there in 1943.

After I left the hospital, I had to get back to the ship. I went to the beach master [harbor master], "Can you tell me where the *USS Bobolink* is so I can get back to my ship?" I was told it was due in Tulagi, 20 miles away. "How do I get a ride over there?" He said, "We have a PT boat that is going over there." I got to Tulagi and asked the harbor master where the *Bobolink* was. I was told it had just left for Russell Island. Again, I asked for a ride. The harbor master said, "We have an LCI," a small amphibious ship, so I got a ride up to Russell Island and finally found my ship.

I didn't have any clothes in my sea bag or locker. I was told they were thrown overboard with my mattress by orders from the hospital, so I got all new clothes. I resumed my duties, and made Seaman 1st Class soon afterwards. The *USS Bobolink* did many jobs, such as towing barges for target practice for destroyers, and towing ships damaged in battle. At this time, October 1, the island of Vella Lavella had been invaded. The LST-448 had been dive-bombed by Jap planes and was damaged. The crew had been taken off, so we took it in tow back to New Caledonia. While en route it was discovered that the LST was sinking, so we cut the cable or rope and let it sink [October 5, 1943].

A couple of times while I was on board we went to a recreational island where the guys were given two cans of beer or soft-served ice cream. Once in a while, they used to let us go swimming in port near the ship. They had a sailor with a rifle on the bow, and a sailor with a rifle on the stern, watching out for sharks. If they saw any sharks they would fire a couple of shots to scare them away. Our ship went up and down the Solomon Islands, known as the "slot," many times.

I stood gun watch on the starboard 20-mm gun tub looking for Jap planes, ships, or submarines. Sometimes I stood a wheel watch, steering the course given to you by the officer on watch or the quartermaster. While waiting for transportation back to the States, myself and other sailors were assigned to storing bombs and ammunition in a big cave supervised by an Australian officer. I left New Caledonia around December 1943. I was a passenger with many other sailors on a French luxury liner converted to a troop ship. The ship was called the *USS Rochambeau* (AP-63), captured from the Vichy government by the Americans [April 1942].

I arrived in San Francisco sometime in January 1944. I left on a Union Pacific train bound for Springfield, home and family, and arrived four and a half days later—changed in Chicago to the New York Central. I had 21 days' leave, which I enjoyed very much. I needed home cooking, peace of mind, and relaxation. Being on the train for almost five days, there was a lot of soot and dirt, [so] I got in the tub when I got home. My father came into the bathroom—he wanted to check if I was all in one piece, if I had any wounds. [*He laughs.*] I said, "I am still here, all in one piece."

Fifty of us were sent by a Navy transport ship to the island of Abemama, a small atoll in the Gilbert Islands. Abemama had not been damaged by shells, so the island looked pristine, lush, and beautiful, like a Dorothy Lamour movie—like *South Pacific*. In our time off we fished in a beautiful lagoon like you see in the movies. The only problem was it was filled with sharks and barracudas—the native guys used to come fishing with us and they would take the hook out of the barracuda's mouth. If we wanted coconuts, the natives would shimmy up the tree and get them for us. I was in Abemama about four months. The Jack Benny USO show came to the island. Jack Benny, Rochester [played by Eddie Anderson], I can't remember if Mary Livingston was there, and his radio gang. It was nice to hear his jokes, see girls sing and dance. About a mile away from our camp, there was a native village that was out of bounds to the sailors. Once in a while, we would see a native woman walk on a road near our camp—they wore nothing but grass skirts. For a bunch of guys 17 and 18, seeing native women with their breasts exposed—we were not used to seeing that.

Around July 1944, the base was closed. We were taken off the island by an LCI to Tarawa and we flew back on C-47 Army transport planes. In July 1944, I was assigned to Waipio Amphibious Base in Pearl Harbor, another shore base. Some of the other guys were assigned to ships (my luck!). By this time I had been promoted to coxswain, a third-class petty officer. Our duties were the ships coming in the lock, to keep them from going too fast, not to make waves, making the water rough. I spent a lot of time in Honolulu; my only problem was I was always running out of money.

I was stationed there for about five months and became bored and asked for a transfer, hopefully to a ship. The war was passing me up and I wasn't going to see anything. Two weeks later, I got my wish. The date was now late January 1945. About a thousand sailors were put on a navy transport ship and left for the Philippines. We were sent to the island of Samar. It was a hellhole there. Mosquitoes, scorpions, bugs, and snakes were all over the place. You had to empty your shoes out in the morning. All around the base they had a big round fence, eight or nine feet high, because a lot of the Filipinos had elephantiasis, all kinds of diseases. At night, after supper, we used to take the extra food from supper and give it to the natives. I wished I was back in Pearl Harbor. I said to myself, "You dummy!"

Around March 15, a hundred of us were told to pack our gear. We were being assigned to the *USS Epping Forest* LSD-4, a big amphibious ship. Three officers and a hundred men were assigned to the ship as a permanent boat group. I had a crew of four, myself as coxswain, a fireman to take care of the two diesel engines, two seamen to take care of the lines. From Samar we sailed to Leyte in the Philippines and our boats picked up eighteen General Sherman tanks and their crews.

On March 27, the largest invasion force in the Pacific left Leyte and other bases with 1,500 ships bound for Okinawa. Endless ships. Our boats from the *Epping Forest* were in the first wave to hit the beaches with tanks, soldiers, Marines, and supplies. Before we hit the beach, the boat officer talked to the crews, giving us advice to unload our tanks and back off as soon as possible. Being out in the Pacific didn't mean we knew what had happened elsewhere. I hadn't heard about Iwo Jima, how horrific the landing was.

On April 1, 1945, all our boats on the *Epping Forest* hit the beach with our General Sherman tanks. No fire from the shore except our ships shelling the beaches. As I was driving to shore in my boat, I went astern of the *USS Texas* (BB-35), a big battleship, her guns firing, my ears were ringing. Battleships, cruisers, and destroyers were shelling the beaches, rocket ships were launching rockets. As my boat approached the beach, I expected it would be blown out of the water. But, as we hit the beach, nothing happened. There was no resistance. The Japanese didn't want to expend their troops fighting on the beaches. They pulled back and fought later. We were lucky.

Air attacks continued throughout the morning. Late in the afternoon most ships in the group received orders to retire for the night. Almost as soon as the anchor was weighed three Jap planes appeared over the ships. They were met with heavy antiaircraft fire, but two managed to crash into ships nearby and the third crashed alongside a destroyer. My God, that was a Fourth of July celebration! All the ships were firing, 20 millimeters, 40 millimeters, and all antiaircraft guns, debris coming down, spent shells hitting the deck. I was wearing my steel helmet and life jacket, which helped.

For three months all our boats were assigned to unloading Liberty Ships, bringing in cargo of all sorts and unloading troops. The thing I remember the most was when our boat was assigned to unload an ammunition ship. They loaded our boat with 155-mm artillery shells (that's the biggest shell there was). A big storm came while being loaded. Our boat was smashing up against the ship. I thought for sure the shells would start exploding. It was scary. We couldn't unload our boat for almost a week, with a bunch of shells, so we were stuck with them, no ship would let us tie up to them so we could get a meal. We ate K-rations, once in a while we were able to get a can of Spam, or some boned chicken. I remember sleeping on the steel deck with no bedding. When it rained, we were exposed, no place to hide.

One morning, our boat was assigned to bringing in Marine casualties to hospital ships. I believe this was a big push at the Shuri Line (Japanese defenses on Okinawa). My boat had to go up a small river for about five miles, at the mouth of the river I picked up two Marines to direct us where to go. When we got there, there were a lot of casualties. They were taken to our boat by Navy corpsmen who were giving them plasma. A lot of them had bad wounds. We went back down the river and took them to hospital ships. We made two or three trips.

Another assignment our boat officer gave us was to pick up— I didn't care for this —dead Jap bodies. We were told to drag them to the outer edge of the anchorage, as far as we could. We got a boat hook and hooked it around their waist and then just dragged them along and brought them out further in the ocean so they wouldn't be in the way. We picked up one or two dead bodies. They had uniforms. I assumed they were kamikaze pilots. Their bodies were all swollen up, and they didn't smell too good. Fortunately, we never found any American bodies. I'll never forget that experience.

After we left Okinawa July 1, we headed for Guam. In my personal belief, after our ship was repaired, it would come back out to the Pacific for the invasion of Japan. I left for my leave August 1, 1945 and during my leave the two atomic bombs were dropped. I never expected in my wildest dreams that I would be home for V-J Day. It was really exciting, everybody celebrating, hugging each other. What a relief to know that I was to survive the war. The bomb was a surprise to me. I had never heard of the atomic bomb. We thought it was okay—saved us from the invasion of Japan. I learned later that the first phase of the invasion of Japan was code-named *Olympic* and was set for November 1, 1945 to invade southern Kyushu, Japan. I thought the war was going to pass me up, but it didn't.

I was in the naval reserve for four years after I got out of the Navy. My four years expired about two months before the Korean War started. The North Koreans had invaded South Korea. We were protecting Asia. We'd been pretty well brainwashed on communism. North Korea is hostile, just like they were 50 years ago, the same attitude. I kind of thought we shouldn't have gotten involved in the Vietnam War. I can understand the feeling of other people—we were defending the world against communism—the Chinese and Russians want to take over Asia, Vietnam. It was, I wouldn't say, a stalemate, because we had to evacuate. My wife and I were both against our invading Iraq. We thought it was none of our business. The possibility of getting killed or wounded, for what? I was surprised that Colin Powell was advocating the invasion; he wasn't like Bush and his crowd.

World War II was a necessary war, very patriotic. We were just defending our country, willing to die for it. In Okinawa, there were almost 5,000 killed, *just sailors*, and between Marines and Army, over 12,000. Tarawa wasn't a big battle but the landing troops really got slaughtered. When I was hitting the beach in Okinawa, I was thinking about Tarawa. But even on the Pacific, we were right there, and we didn't know what was going on. Guys only listened to Tokyo Rose for music, they disregarded everything else [propaganda]. Nobody believed what she said anyway. They had all the popular music. I had seen *Wake Island* (1942), and all these other movies. They inspired you to be patriotic. I believed that Hollywood stuff.

My neighbor next door, their son just joined the army and I just heard that he's ready to be sent to Iraq. I feel bad for him. The parents, the worry they are going to go through, the young man, all the hardships they are going to have in Iraq and Afghanistan. I imagine that my parents must have gone through agony with me. That's why I wasn't anxious for our participation in Vietnam and Iraq. I knew all the hardships that would come.

Charlie Allard, born in 1924 in Springfield, Massachusetts, served three years in the Navy on the USS Fayette, *APA-43, an Auxiliary Personnel Assault ship. He was a 3rd Class Pharmacist Mate, helping "beach parties" made up of a doctor and medics who evacuated the wounded from beaches in the South Pacific. Having been a boy scout, he said he knew something about first aid and was selected to go to Portsmouth, Virginia, for six weeks to train. His six invasions (1944– 5) were Kwajalein, the Marianas (Guam), Palau Islands (Peleliu), Leyte, Luzon (Lingayen Gulf), and Iwo Jima. When he returned home he drove an ambulance for the fire department for 31 years.*

We never expected Iwo Jima to be that bad [and] they say Okinawa was worse. We had a beach party with eight corpsmen and a doctor. They went in about the fifth wave, and they set up a tent where they come out of the line and get first aid on the beach. Whenever they get morphine you are supposed to mark it on their head when they had it, you're not supposed to give it [again] too soon. Some of them had already passed away. When they were getting the beach cleaned up, they sent them out to the ship instead of looking for a place to put the dead. If they started bleeding again bad, they'd put a tourniquet on. Or if they were in a lot of pain, "When did you have your last morphine?" Give them a shot of morphine before they could get back aboard ship. We had two operating rooms aboard ship.

You know what surprises me? You would think that some of the medical men over there in Afghanistan and Iraq, some of those doctors would have a nervous breakdown with seeing casualties that bad all the time. Dr. C., the one that was in the beach party, someone told me at one of the last reunions that he cracked up after Iwo Jima.

When you get 30 wounded there, you walk along a passageway along the whole side of the ship, ten or fifteen field stretchers, two wooden poles with canvas attached and a four-inch leg on each pole to keep it off the deck. We used to take blood from quite a few people before an invasion, because you never know how much you are going to use. [Blood type] is right on your dog tag, and everybody had their dog tags all the time.

All young guys—I went in when I was 17. Like this Marine, we could have saved his life, we cut his leg off because unfortunately, he stepped on a land mine, and it was just hanging. When they take a leg off, they cut it and sometimes you have to push the skin back up so you can cut the bone back another inch, and pull the skin down and turn it all over so it will heal back over the bone. Some can handle it and some can't. This one Marine was only 19. "I don't want to go back home this way." So we put the Thompson light splint on him. "I'm all done, I'm no good anymore." He pulled the splint off during the night when nobody was around and died because of shock. What the hell. When you have got a hundred casualties aboard ship, we only had about 30 corpsmen, some of them had to sleep some time.

Everyone was so damned disgusted about Pearl Harbor. As the war went on you heard about Midway and the Philippines, how the Japs were treating the prisoners over there. Just between you and me, I never did see a Jap prisoner. Some of them would blow themselves up before they would be taken prisoner. We used to have a ship's paper, Bataan death march. You know what they did on Tarawa, what the Japs did? They knew where we were going to invade the island, so they cut down palm trees and put anchors on them so when the boats went in they couldn't get to the beach, they hit the trees that were anchored out there. It was like a coral reef that they made, only out of wood.

Tokyo Rose—we'd turn the radio on, and she would say where the ships were. She'd say, "We know where you are going, you are going to Iwo Jima. But wait till you get there, you're in for a surprise." They wanted to scare you. After Iwo Jima, Okinawa was the last invasion. After that, we were ready to load troops, we were ready to hit Japan. And if they ever hit Japan— Oh my gosh, I don't know how many casualties, it would have been like D-Day over in Europe. [*The atomic bomb?*] Oh, were we glad to hear that!

I've read a few articles about the black Tuskegee pilots. That must have been a great outfit. They went through hell to begin with. When I first went in the Navy, we had Blacks aboard ship. They set up the officers' table when they ate and they cleaned the officers' rooms. That's all they did—waited on the officers, served them, it was like walking into a restaurant aboard ship. The deck officers, they sat down, and the black guys, all in white, white pants, and white jackets. But when it came time for me to get out, they were beginning to come aboard ship as gunners' mates and signalmen, they were regular shipmates.

After I left Portsmouth, Virginia, I went down to Camp Lejeune, North Carolina. One day, I got a bus going to town and the bus was pretty well filled up. There was a seat in back of the driver and I sat there. A few minutes later an older black woman came on and she's standing up there holding on to the seat, and I said, "Here, sit down." Boy, that bus driver stopped the bus, "Hey, sailor, get back there where you were. She knows she is supposed to be at the back of the bus!" I felt about that high because I wasn't brought up that way. In fact, we had black kids at school, in West Springfield, we treated them like anybody else.

[*The Korean War?*] I can't understand why we had to be over there. Put it this way: Pearl Harbor, there was a reason. Wasn't Pearl Harbor part of this country at that time? No? I think Guam is a territory too. Actually, I don't know that much about the Korean War. I often wonder, "Why are we over there?" We had a reason for [being] over in Europe. I never heard anyone say actually why we had to go over to Korea.

Afghanistan and Baghdad, they claim that we are over there because of those two planes in New York. But I think there's a lot that Uncle Sam won't tell us. [Obama] wants to send more troops over there again and he's going to bring some back in another couple of months. They say they want us out of there in another couple of years, but look at the car bombings that are going on over there all the time, they can't even control that now. Look at the civilians they are killing over there, my God, every time a car bomb goes off—50, 60 people.

Look at it: we've been there over six years now. I shouldn't say this, [but] are they better off now than they were then? I mean we're still fighting in the same area, aren't we? Whenever there's a war, the economy usually picks up. You don't read anything about the tanks and army vehicles that are going over there. Every now and then you will see that one of them burned up. They're mostly General Motors, aren't they? All you think of General Motors are cars, what about all the plants that make the military vehicles? They must be booming now.

Don Walker, born in 1925 in Springfield, Massachusetts, served in the Navy chasing U-boats in the Atlantic, and after the Japanese surrender, helping repatriate Japanese soldiers from the Pacific Islands that were bypassed by the advancing Americans. Don tells a story about a Japanese flag covered with writing that he took from a Japanese soldier, and how he returned it 31 years later. After the Japanese surrender, he taught local boys on a Pacific Island how to play baseball, and tells all his stories with great humor. After our interview, Don turned his narrative into a booklet for his family. He worked in the insurance business after the war. He died of cancer in December 2010.

The war was on and they had an entrance exam for naval officers' training. I took that in my high school senior year and I passed it, much to the surprise of my parents and myself. [*He laughs.*] Two weeks after graduation, I was in the Navy at Tufts College in Medford, Massachusetts, that's where I met Dottie, my wife, a graduate of Jackson College, the girls' college of Tufts. My officer's training lasted less than a year, because I flunked out! [*He laughs.*] There's my report card. That's an "F" for naval organization. That's because I missed that mandatory weekly orientation meeting. You know where I was? Visiting Dottie at her dorm! [*He laughs.*] The best part of going to school was *her.* Sixty-two years we've been married. I would have had a commission. I probably would have been dead, too.

I went to Newport, Rhode Island, where I went to fire control school. Electrical, mechanical operations, the guns, the directors, the electrical circuits that go into firing guns, antiaircraft, depth charges, and all that stuff, it has nothing to do with flames. Came out a third class petty officer, went to Norfolk, Virginia and picked up the ship for the first go-round out to the Atlantic Ocean. The DE destroyer escort 139, *USS Farquhar,* after an Admiral Farquhar [from the Civil War].

We were in what they called a "killer group," a protective shield around an aircraft carrier (we called them baby flat tops) with four other Destroyer Escorts (DEs). We were looking for trouble with the U-boats, because they had decimated shipping before the war and in the early part of the war, laying off the eastern seaboard looking for ships supplying England. The wolf packs were all over the place. The Germans had developed a submarine that was like a tanker, and they would rendezvous with the wolf packs and refuel them at sea, so they didn't have to go back all the way to Germany or Norway to refuel.

Some people have heard the name "wolf pack" but don't realize what it is. It's a group of submarines, U-boats we called them, and they operated in a pack, just like a wolf pack. The U-boats hunt together so they are more effective, more productive as a whole group. If they could get *us* (destroyer escorts) they would, but they were looking to slide by us and get the carrier. They had what they used to call the shoestring play. You know the old story of the guy saying, "Your shoe's untied" —when he looked down, he popped him and gave the guy quite a going over? They put a U-boat to the surface over here, and the idea was we'd attack it, but there would be another U-boat over here, submerged, and while we were concentrating on the one we could see, they would torpedo us from the side—a decoy system. They had a lot of tricks they pulled, but we got wise to them after a while.

You haven't lived until you have been in the North Atlantic. We had waves that were 40 to 50 feet high, on the flying bridge I was looking *up* at the crest of the wave. I guess it bothered some of the guys but for the most part we were pretty seaworthy people. I was 18—it was an adventure. In a sense, it wasn't a war for us. But as we became more accustomed to what was going on, we became a little more serious. Then we were concerned about getting home. The realization came: Maybe you don't get home, this is for real. [*He laughs.*]

By the time we had contact with a U-boat, we usually had a pretty good chance of sinking it. We had 24/7 sound gear that sent out a ping that when it hit something, echoed back. Then they got a direction and a range on it and the conning officer [the officer in charge of directing changes in course or speed] would direct the ship toward the U-boat. The first thing that happens when the soundman got a contact, they send a chemical alarm over the PA system on the ship. They call that a chemical alarm, but it was three buzzes, so you knew there was something brewing somewhere. Then the conning officers would begin to move the ship for the attack.

Depth charges were dropped off the fantail of the ship and we had passed over the target by the time we fired. The hedgehog was fired *ahead* of us and consisted of 24 depth-type charges. Most people think of depth charges as the tin cans that go off and blow up, but anything that goes off under the surface is a depth charge. In an ahead-thrown attack they only went off if they hit something because it had a fuse on the front that was armed by rotation. It went up in an ellipse and came down and the U-boat was theoretically in front of us. We destroyed a few whales.

Most of the time, there were no survivors on the U-boat. It usually cracked and blew up under water and when that happens, there's very little chance. By that time they were trying to escape the attack they would be down 3–400 feet. There was one that did surface and they captured it and towed it to Argentia, Newfoundland. The Americans went aboard and shut off all the valves. They saved it. They apparently had set the U-boat to be scuttled—that was a favorite trick by the Germans when they didn't want it captured. The crew would get into their boats or be in our boats, they had delayed bombs on them.

In fact, the one that we sunk, I fired the depth charges, it was set at 50 and 75 feet to go off. One of them set off almost as soon as it hit the water, which means it was in close proximity to a magnetic field. It blew our fantail ten or fifteen feet out of the water. We saw nothing. It wasn't until after the war when we got the German records that we found out we'd sunk it. Sometimes we put sonar boards in the water, and then had to shut everything off of all the ships that were in a certain area, and then we would listen if there were any sounds coming at all from underneath. At times you could hear banging and so forth.

The Allies broke the German code in World War II so we could intercept their messages and we knew what they were doing. We found out later Admiral Dönitz, who was in charge of all the U-boat operations, had ordered six of them just before the end of the war to come over to the East Coast and do whatever damage they could, in April of '45. That's why they shipped us to the North Atlantic.

After we got up there, we heard the rumor that the Germans had sent the U-boats and they had V-2 rockets like they were putting over England, and they were going to do a last-minute harassing of New York, Washington, a last gasp. We had heard the rumor, but we never heard that the Germans had anything to transport those rockets. As we talked with the Germans later, they never had any capability to do that, but it panicked the East Coast. It's like the country now that has a nuclear bomb, if they don't have a rocket to deliver it with, what are they going to do except plant it through terrorists?

So they sent four aircraft carriers, one of them was ours, and 42 DEs up to the North Atlantic. Our station was just below Iceland. They got one of our DEs, the *Frederick C. Davis,* DE-136, on April 24, 1945. Operation Teardrop. All of a sudden one night, one of the destroyer escorts caught the surfaced U-boat recharging the batteries. They tried to ram it but it was so rough that the waves pushed it off. They couldn't man the guns because they were taking on so much water. So the U-boat submerged and one of the other DEs got U-880 later with depth charges. U-1235 and U-518 were also sunk. Three down, and three to go. Later, U-546 was sunk, with 32 survivors taken aboard one of the DEs. Four down, and two to go.

The final part of this is we had to go into Argentia to refuel and when we went back out again, on May 4th or 5th, we got a contact early in the morning, about four or five o'clock. I happened to be on watch that morning on the flying bridge, and the U-boat had got inside the screen of the carrier. The DEs made a semicircle in front of the carrier, and she was in the middle. They didn't care about us—they wanted that carrier. They got in on our starboard beam and we picked them up and we made an immediate right turn, and I personally fired the thirteen-depth charge attack. The charges went off very shallow. We saw U-boat 881, the last one of the six that left Norway. That was two days before the war ended. I always felt kind of bad for the guys in that U-boat.

The sequel to that was, years later, one of our torpedo men with his wife was over in Germany, I think it was Berlin, and they were going out to dinner, and they stopped at a bar to have a beer. They got talking with a German girl there about the war, and it turned out her brother was on that U-boat, U-881, that we sunk. She went home and got the list of all the crew that were on that U-boat.

We were anchored in Pearl Harbor when the war with Japan ended, on the beach watching a movie. They stopped the movie. It was typical of the movies in the Navy, it was used so many times and passed through so many ships, that the film was brittle and frequently broke going through all the sprockets in the camera. When it stopped, everybody was cheering, another busted movie. Well, the guy came on the microphone and said, "We have to inform you that the war with Japan is officially over. It is now V-J Day." Nobody said a word, it was so quiet, it was eerie. We thought it was a ruse of some sort, then he came on again and reiterated what he had said. We said, "Wow, this is it."

I liked the Navy, I didn't have anything to run away from. I just thought it would be nice to be home for a change, but we didn't go home. We headed for Eniwetok in the Marshall Islands and we took on 7,000 pounds of rice to feed the Japanese soldiers in the Caroline Islands, and took the surrender of the Japanese there. The American forces bypassed a whole bunch of islands out in the Pacific. We hoped the Japanese on these islands knew the war was over; they had radio contact I am sure. [But] when we went into the harbor at Ponape their dual guns were trained on us, we were afraid to death we were going to hit a mine or they were going to shoot at us. We weren't *sure* they knew the war was over.

We went right in to Ponape harbor, and sent a landing party on the island, and the Japanese surrendered. We were with another ship, the *USS Hyman* DD-732 destroyer. It was bigger all-around than a destroyer escort. The Japanese came aboard that ship, took down the Rising Sun flag and replaced it with the Stars and Stripes. The formal surrender papers were signed aboard the *Hyman* by officers of the Japanese Army.

We had time to get off the ship. We went on the island and we started playing softball. Of course the native kids in the village wanted to get in the game but they didn't know quite what to do. So we decided that we'd teach them how to play baseball. We sorted them out by size, made teams of them, and we made a diamond that we played on but we shortened it up a little because they were little kids. We had a regular Little League going on over there, and we were coaches, batting practice, pitchers, and everything else. We had these kids playing *baseball* like you wouldn't believe. They were so adaptable! They were terrific.

I was there six months. We were under orders to take all the Japanese Army off the island, put them on their own ships, and send them back to Japan. But you know, the Japanese Navy didn't have many ships, and sometimes it would be two or three weeks. Our job was to see that they got out to their ships and didn't have any weapons on them.

An interesting thing happened. While I was on board one of the transports standing watch, this Japanese soldier came aboard with a knapsack. He had a Japanese flag sticking out the top of it and I thought it would be nice to have for a souvenir. So, I just pulled it out of his knapsack. He was *upset* and was he mad! I had a Thompson submachine gun, so I just prodded him with it. He was jabbering away something awful when he left. I said, well, I got a nice souvenir, one of these big flags with the rising sun, all kinds of writing coming out from it. I kept the thing and it went home in a sea bag, and I never knew what the writing on it was.

One day I got a call from our home office. They had several Japanese insurance people over from Tokyo. I invited one of them (Ichiro Moji was his name), an assistant to the president of the Meiji Mutual Life Insurance Agency of Tokyo, to the house for dinner. This was in 1977. We played pool, darts, and had a couple of American beers. I think Dottie said to me when we were down there, this guy must know what that thing says. I had it in a plastic bag down cellar.

So I went and got it, spread it out on the pool table, and Mo looked at it, and he looked at me, and the tears started coming down his cheeks. I told him where I got it and what I did to get it. He said, "You have done this man a grave injustice. You have taken something very sacred from him. These names from the rising sun are all of his family and his friends who signed it and gave it to him before he went to battle, and wished him success in battle, and a safe return home." I said, "Oh, Wow. I'm in trouble now." [*He laughs.*] I felt badly, I really did.

So I thought about it for a minute and I said to him, "Mo, this is crazy, but why don't you take this flag back to Tokyo and see if you can find this guy." They found the guy, believe it or not. He was in Kobe, Japan. They ran an ad in the newspaper with a 6.4 million circulation, and the next morning this guy called. He took the bullet train in. His name was Jiro Ueda and he owned a liquor store. Thirty-one years later. That gave me a lot of personal satisfaction. I committed an act of piracy, if you really want to know, I stole something on the high seas at gunpoint. Little did I know when I took it how the ending would be. I thought it would just be a souvenir.

Vietnam was not a popular war, that's a problem… were we really threatened? I think that is where the real issue lies. In World War II we were threatened, you could see what happened in the Sudetenland, Czechoslovakia, Austria, France, you could see the creeping Nazism take over. Then the Axis was formed by Italy and Japan, and I think everybody felt this was it, so they got behind it. It took everybody at home to pitch in and do what they had to do. It wasn't always building arms but it was sacrificing at home for sugar and coffee, so *people* were in the war. Today we don't feel anything about a war, except maybe taxes, but that's in the aftermath usually. The people who lose a loved one know what's going on; for the rest of us, it's something we read about.

[*Korea?*] I was more concerned about Russia than I was Korea. Even though we weren't fighting Russia, they were communists and we were fighting the communists in North Korea. My concern was escalation, that Russia would enter the war [as] the Russians were training the North Korean pilots. So I had a great concern not about the Korean War itself but about what it might lead to. If Russia got involved, we thought we would be in World War III.

Vietnam was like the Korean War, it was far enough away so we didn't fear it spreading to our homeland. We were complacent. Most Americans thought, "Why get involved?" We seem to mind other peoples' business because [we] envisage a threat from a different culture and a different philosophy than we have as Americans. Most of it is human rights, as far as I can see. I support this because of the atrocities that some of these regimes put upon their people.

I think what's going on today is nothing but an outgrowth of what we've seen before in Vietnam and North Korea, and Hitler, Mussolini, Stalin, and others before them. I feel badly for the people who don't have the opportunities in life that the United States seems to give. Not to say we are perfect by any means, but we don't have to worry about what we say in the open like many of these people do. I feel that at the same time we are right, it costs us a price to be free and has throughout history. I think we need to continue to do that for our own freedom and for the freedom of our future people in the United States.

Iraq? We need their oil, human rights is just the mask, that appeals to more people. I think a lot of the problems that we have now are because of the materials that we need—oil, particularly. Human rights we use as a shield, but really, we're after something else usually. These people resort to violence to obtain what they want. They want to conquer us anyways, they don't like us, because of what we have done in the world. [He laughs.] Just looking at it from the outside in, I'd say that maybe we win the war, we leave there, and they go on fighting among themselves, and that's what's going to happen in Afghanistan, too. These people have their different cliques, they don't like each other, they don't know how to get along together.

Some guy like Hitler or Mussolini or Kim Jong-Il takes hold of the situation, that's where the atrocities start, to maintain power they have to kill people, that's where the human rights deal comes in. I think we're pulling out [of Iraq] now, we're going to turn it over to them. In Afghanistan the Russians had to leave because they couldn't get to the mountains. Look at what is happening in Iran—they can cause disruption.

I go on the assumption that nobody is a winner in a war. I pretty much stick to that, and I have for many, many years. I even thought that way before I went in the Navy. I think wars are inevitable because of the way people are taught to think. I just don't think that anybody wins a war. We've been fortunate in this country because we've never had the experience, after the Civil War anyway, of having been attacked and having the desecration and all the mess that occurs with dead bodies. We've been very fortunate in that respect. But I think if we were ever attacked, which we saw a little bit of in 9/11, that people would get a different viewpoint of who wins a war, and probably more so in today's world.

Regarding the larger impact of using the bombs, I was dead set to get those Japanese, they had killed so many and tortured so many going back to when they invaded China. And the Corregidor mess, the hundred mile march where they bayoneted so many of these people, that I was all for "let's get them." If I got killed, that's where I wanted to get killed, I wanted to die in the big field. I had no remorse whatsoever; I was delighted.

I guess at the time I was, but now I feel maybe it would have been better if they dropped it up on top of that volcano they've got over there, Fujiyama, to show them what would happen. It was tragic to see so many civilians killed by the bombs. The Japanese doctor we visited on the transport told us graphic stories of what he found after the blast at Hiroshima. But some of the Japanese officers that were in charge, they didn't want to surrender even after the second bomb went off.

In some recent times, it's hard to know who's the enemy. It happened in Vietnam too— they didn't know who was friend and foe. Complacency with today's situations can lead nowhere but to another disaster down the road. We must be vigilant and very alert to threats to our way of life. We must act quickly to safeguard what Americans have fought so hard to preserve. God Bless America!

Paul Seamans, born in 1923 in Malden, MA, served in the Navy reserve chasing submarines and blowing up mines, and retired from the Navy as a lieutenant commander. He attended Tufts University on a Navy ROTC scholarship. He served in the Pacific from the winter of 1943–4 until March of 1946. After his return he finished college, taught at the US Naval Academy, and later became the principal of an elementary school for 25 years. His is a typical story, starting with the Depression.

Dad went dead broke during the Depression. When the money began to be distributed, WPA, PWA, CCCs, he went to work on the sewer along with a bunch of World War I buddies. We used to put Shredded Wheat separators [the three layers of biscuits of Shredded Wheat were separated by a layer of cardboard] in our shoes and you cut them out as inner soles, because our shoe soles were worn out. We had a banana and Shredded Wheat for maybe five or six years. One of the cheapest things you could eat in those days was fish. Mom would send me down to the market, they would take out a codfish, which had been cleaned, and wrap it up in newspaper.

I went out to the Pacific Ocean where I started as the fourth officer on the SC-1363 [submarine chasers were not named], then the third, then I was the executive officer for not quite a year, then I was bumped up to be the commanding officer. I was the commanding officer for the better part of a year, brought the ship home, and decommissioned it in March of 1946. We were advanced on the basis of training, experience, and the recommendation of the commanding officer, who was leaving.

We spent more of our time shooting up mines than chasing submarines. By the time we got out there, there were submarines, one of them I think sank the *USS Indianapolis* (CA-35), that unfortunate boat that went west and didn't zigzag, and it was torpedoed. You may or may not remember that it was many days, if not weeks, before the Navy got the idea that it had a lost ship. At that time many of the crew had suffered [883 of the crew of 1,199 died, the largest single loss of the war]. There were Japanese submarines still extant, and that's what we were there for.

My ship was put in with a group of ships that made up a very large convoy, went to Guadalcanal. I often had the idea that they didn't really know what to do with us. The only island that I saw that had Japanese on it was Peleliu, and our ship was there on the invasion, this was in September of 1944. We ran within a hundred yards of the beach, if you can picture a horseshoe of ships, the ships in the middle were usually destroyers, metal craft and more important than we were. Our particular position was on the left-hand side. We were strictly a visual watch, and radar. Our participation was simply by way of 7 x 50 Bausch & Lomb binoculars.

About my ship. We had depth charges, port and starboard, and we had two K-guns. A K-gun actually looks like a "K." The depth charge is held on one side of the K with a cable, and on the other side a large cartridge is inserted. You fire a cartridge on the left side, and it kicks the many dozens of pounds of depth charge overboard. You drop a pattern—they are supposed to be dropped at such intervals that they form a diamond, to enclose the target down under the water. All I can tell you is that when these torpedoes go off, you think that *you've* been torpedoed because the rear end of the boat rears right up in the air. Your feet—it almost hurts because water doesn't compress, you *feel* it.

The mines that we shot at were floating mines that had been let go from their tether due to wind and waves over a period of time. Their only danger lay in the possibility that they might be run into by a boat, which happened. You'd be coasting along as part of a convoy and someone would announce, "There's a floating mine!" Then it was like a shooting gallery. They were all horned mines. First of all, the mine was always spherical. There were bumps on it that looked like tin cans. In order to explode the thing, you had to knock one of those cans off. That had a trigger, which initiated the major explosion of the sphere. I never saw one blow up expect by dint of our own shooting.

Every ship at that time was eligible for a black man, the officers were entitled to a steward who was to make their beds for them, see that they had clean sheets, polish their shoes, check their lockers to make sure their clothes were all hung up straight. It was crazy, because we were all college boys. We asked him, "What would you like to do?" He said, "I'd like a gun." We had two .50-caliber machine guns that had just been installed, so we gave him the one on the left hand side and he shot it a few times and he seemed to know what he was doing, so that was his duty for the rest of the war. He also helped in the galley. He had learned to cook opossums at his father's farm down south, O.B. Jordon, I think was his name.

A terrible typhoon hit Okinawa in the fall of 1945, October 9. The wind blew a record 205 miles an hour. Some of the crew and I put on our night-vision glasses, stayed up all night on the flying bridge watching this tremendous blow. The rain felt like BBs in our faces. When we went into Unten Ko at the north end of Okinawa, several of the boats were tied up to what were really telephone poles stuck in the mud. We tied up beside an Army supply ship, a smallish steel ship. We put our towing gear completely around their superstructure and where many, many ships went ashore. Our draft was less than that of the Army ship when it went into the mud; we still had two or three feet of water under us. We didn't go under.

We talked to the port authority to find out what was going to happen to us, we were supposed to go sweep mines in Japan. The port authority looked at us blokes and asked how long we had been away and said, "You'd better go home," so we got our marching orders. I was the captain. We got lost! We got out of Guam, and our gyrotropic counts went down, so all we had was the magnetic, which we never used. We were going to Kwajalein, and I think it was about a three-day trip and it rained. I could navigate well, the sky cleared the morning we were supposed to get in, and by God, I tell you, we must have been 30 or 40 miles off course.

There are seven stars in the big dipper. [*He names them.*] With all these wonderful names, you can't use them for navigation because they are too far down on the horizon, not bright enough. The North Star, which is due north, you can't use either because it isn't bright enough, you can't catch it in your sextant. The sextant is made of a split mirror; half of it looks at the horizon and the other half of it looks at a star. When you're navigating you have a slide on your sextant and you move it until you have the horizon touching the star. Then it will tell you how many minutes and degrees it is above the horizon. The positions of all of the stars are tabulated in Greenwich, the height of the star above the horizon, for every minute of every hour of every day. When you translate that at sea, you have to accommodate your navigation to the land difference between Greenwich and where you are. You have to have a Bowditch [navigation chart], which will explain to you the difference.

You use first-degree stars, like Vega. We had a star chart, we put it down on the deck, used a flashlight, covered over the front end of it with tin foil, made a little pin prick in the middle of it. We could shine the pin prick on the various stars, figure out what their name was. You need three stars for a triangle. After you've got your fix on three stars, you leave the deck and you go down to the chart house, and you pull out some tabulations, and running up and down there would drive you crazy until you learn how to do it—you can get your fix in fifteen minutes.

I went from Seattle, Washington, to Chicago, and I hadn't talked to my parents. The telephone operators had control of a bank of telephones, and I stepped to one of the girls, and she said, "You know, you young men are always in a great hurry!" I said to her, "You know, I haven't been home for two years." "Go take number five, right over there!" She knew right away, here was a Navy man who had to be patted on the back.

There is a very famous picture of a sailor man bending a lady over and kissing her in New York. I didn't get home to that, my ship didn't get decommissioned until March 1946. There was no great celebration when boys of my generation went home [although] we were certainly welcomed home with open arms to our families. I was in the little tiny community of Richmond, New

Hampshire, the people were all quiet, they were loving, and there's no question that they were appreciative.

When I went back to Tufts and we had our first class, three or four Jackson girls came in and took a look over the audience. They walked down the aisle and there was a little girl who sat down beside me, she never said a word to me and I never said a word to her. But it was so touching to have a warm-bodied girl, some of our boys hadn't seen a woman in over a year. So here was this darling little thing, came to sit beside me, and the warmth of it was really very touching.

[*Korea*] You will remember that that was called a police action, not a war. MacArthur got into trouble with Harry Truman because he wanted to dictate how things should go. Boy was he wrong! He was a braggart, he was a pompous sort of fellow, he was in the Pacific what Patton was in Europe, Patton who had the ivory-handled pistols. Do you know the Bonus March? [In 1932, desperate World War I veterans converged on Washington to demand their promised bonus wages. President Hoover called up the Army (led by MacArthur, and including both Eisenhower and Patton), to destroy their encampment and scatter the protesters.] He [MacArthur] was in charge of kicking them out of Washington, and his aide was Eisenhower, of all things. That was terrible.

Russell Brocklesby, born in 1915 in Greenfield, Massachusetts, served from March of 1944 to February 1946 as Navy mailman, 3rd class. Married before he enlisted, his pay was $150 a month, with $85 going to his wife Helen. He considered his ship, the USS Randolph, *a very lucky ship, as while undergoing repairs, the* USS Franklin *sailed in her place and was torpedoed with great loss of life. After the war, Russell was a lithographer in Minot's Printing and Bonding Company. His background was Scots-English; his father, a millwright, had immigrated from Liverpool. There were eight children in his family and nine in Helen's family, which was originally from Nova Scotia. Russell died in November 2010.*

When I got down to Turners Falls, [the recruiter] had me in the Army. I told one of the officers, "I was supposed to go in with the Navy." He said, "You have to go through this board" —there was an Army, Navy, and Marine officer. So when I went in with the army doctor, he said, "What's the matter with the Army?" I said, "Not a thing's the matter with the Army, but I enlisted in the Navy." We kept talking (my brother Earnest was in the Navy, and my youngest brother, Robert, was an officer in the Navy, he'd been in college). The Navy officer reached over, took the papers and said, "A good Navy man." [*He laughs.*] And that's what it was.

The officer was from [nearby] Northampton, and he said: "Russ, we have to have someone in the post office with the mail coming in for the boys." "Well, I don't know anything about a post office," and he said, "Besides, it is ten dollars more." "I'll take it." [*He laughs.*] I told an officer, "You know, I'm not really interested in saving stamps for Uncle Sam, I want to be top side." "Russ, you have got to have a G-Q [general quarters] station." "I know I do, I want to be on a gun, a military gun." He got me on a 20-mm, I was right where I could see the planes come in and run off, under any attack. It was two of us on it, one loading and one firing.

I was on the *USS Randolph*, CV-15. That ship was made in one year. Many aircraft carriers were brand new. Our ship carried one hundred planes, TBMs [Avenger], two different kinds. I was where I could see them come back from a raid, see them land and different ones crack up. That's where I lost a lot of my hearing, because our gun was right near the five-inch guns and they make a terrific roar. I talked to the [veterans'] agent years ago in Greenfield, and he said, "Well, you should have complained when you were in the Navy." "Well, I didn't because I wanted to get out after it was all over." So I did lose out there.

We never knew where we were going, because they didn't want anything that would leak. I always figured we had a very good ship and a very lucky ship. A bunch of their [Japanese] pilots (of course they were all doomed, they weren't supposed to come back), twenty of them flew from some base, coming in to bomb the ships in Ulithi, but very few of them made it. The one that made it was the one that came right into our fantail, under the flight deck [March 11, 1945]. It had a bomb and it blew up. We've got pictures of the damage. We were repaired right out there by a repair ship—they used to park right next to [us].

We could tell when the planes were coming in because the big guns on all the ships would start firing when the planes were miles away. The destroyers and escort ships would pick that up first and they would send messages back. The cruisers could fire the big guns; they had what we used to call the Buck Rogers Show. When it got close to a plane, it would explode. When they were firing, we were quite a ways away. Our loudspeaker would announce an attack, our guns were firing when they were diving on us. Our 20-mm guns (the 40-mm had more of a range), I couldn't say the actual range, but it would be close.

One plane, whatever hit it, the pilot of that ship came out in a parachute and landed right close to our ship. We were always told, "Don't shoot the pilot," because if they picked them up [alive], they gained information from them. They weren't supposed to parachute out, they were supposed to kamikaze, their duty.

We were getting prepared to go on a raid of the Philippines when the Japanese were there, but we couldn't go because we got hit by this kamikaze. So the ship that took our position was the *Franklin* [see narrative by Charles Sakowicz, page 73]. When they left they were in the position we would have been in, they got hit and there were 700 casualties [at least 724 were killed]. The ship came back [to New York], it was leaning, just like this. Like I say, we had a lucky ship and a good ship.

Our ship made one of the first raids on Tokyo, the first carrier in Tokyo Bay. We came from Ulithi [raids were conducted against Tokyo, February 16–25, 1945] on this maneuver. Then when they dropped the atomic bombs, we were getting ready to pull out of the area. The planes that bombed Hiroshima and Nagasaki were big heavy planes. They wanted all the [other] planes to get away, so when these big planes came in there would be nothing in the sky, they didn't want anything to interfere with that position.

We went to Europe a couple of times to pick up GIs to bring them home. On the hangar deck they put up rows and rows of cots. I was on the flight deck and I bumped into Charlie Moroz, who graduated in the same class in Greenfield. Half of our people aboard ship were given a 30-day leave, so there was a lot of room. This one night we're having steak for supper and I went to Charlie and I said, "Come on down tonight, we got steak for supper." He said, "No, I'm not going down, we are having *hot dogs*. If you knew how much I missed *Silver Arrow hotdogs*!"

We went to Naples, Italy—the Italian boys that were taken prisoner were all being taken back. I can remember them looking at Naples in the harbor, a lot of sunken ships saying, "Poor Napoli, Poor Napoli," so much damage in the harbor. They were happy going back. They were carrying the buckets and delivering the meals—they ate good! Rows and rows of cots, a lot of poker games.

Our soldiers that were taken captive by the Japanese, my God, the torture—they would make them march mile after mile, if they fell down, they would shoot them. I know a boy from Greenfield, he was shot, [on a] march into a prison camp. We've got pictures that our plane had taken with "prisoners of war" marked on top. Of course, we wouldn't bomb them. It's known that the Japanese had beaten some of the American boys. The American-[held] prisoners were always treated well, fed well.

"The Jolly Roger," was the name of the ship's paper. This is announcing the death of the president. There's a picture of a boxing match on board ship, a boxing ring, an African American and a white man. These fellows were sailors and they used to put these matches on, a lot of ships had boxing teams. The colored had their own quotas, they didn't treat them very good, a lot of them were in the post office.

Jim Duncan from Alabama, he worked at the post office. When we were getting ready to come home, I had a chance to get another rate, second class petty officer. Duncan enlisted for four years, had more time. I said, "Give him a chance," and he got second class. In the end, he was running the post office. He made out good, he was smart, too. Jim Duncan's mother baked us a pecan pie. We called it "pecan." She said, "'Pee can' is what you put under the bed! 'Pecun' is what you call the pie." [He laughs.]

We fought the Second World War because we had to. If we let them take over Hawaii, the Japanese would have taken charge of the whole Pacific—that would cut us all off from that part of the world. What they did to our boys, the ones that were destroyed there, my God, whole ships sunk, they bombed Pearl Harbor, just mutilated the whole area. All ships sunk, battleships with all the men aboard, and that's the way they left it.

[What about Germany?] Most people knew that eventually we'd have to get in there because they controlled whole countries over there. They had a very strong army. They trained for it for years and years and years. Listen to them talk, Hitler, you could see he was like a crazy man. All of those countries that had been run by the Nazis—France, they had to do as much to [try to] destroy the United States because we were very aggressive. Nobody stepped on our toes.

[Why did we fight in Korea?] That's a good question. Well, North Korea was going to take over South Korea. If they can do that, then they're going to go after something else to try to get control. I don't think the [US] soldiers in Korea had the training. It was very cold and they didn't have the right clothing for it. I don't think that the American people knew a lot. I think they were so sick of fighting in war, and they went back, they had kids, and they knew what they would have to go through. [*Vietnam?*] People were sick of wars. They had kids, they didn't want them to fight.

Edward Wells, born in 1926 in Montague, Massachusetts, speaks to school children about his experiences in World War II, surprising them that as a child he saw Civil War veterans marching in Memorial Day parades. He starts his narrative by repeating what he tells students, including his memories of post-atomic bomb Nagasaki and an Australian prisoner of war from Japan whom he helped repatriate. After the war, for three decades, he was a science teacher and a school principal in Braintree, Massachusetts.

I grew up in suburban Boston. You knew something was going to happen. It came to me quite vividly when the *Hindenburg*, the German dirigible, flew over the school, the fire drill was sounded, we went out and there was this beautiful, gothic *Queen Mary* floating in the sky, with a small biplane circling it. I was eleven years old, and I looked up and there were four bright red swastikas on the tail. At that time, all the newsreels and radio shows became concrete. Churchill had the personality and the vocabulary, brilliance, to do what people needed. He was the antithesis of Hitler. He could roll off a phrase and people believed him, and they didn't cower.

Falling asleep with my 15-cent earphones on, the radio stations, which were in the habit of signing off at dusk, came thundering on at one in the morning because Hitler's troops had invaded Poland, in September 1939. I did wake up the house. To me it was important—it was a sea change. In 1939, I was no longer eleven; I was thirteen. The English and the French had made clear to Hitler that if he invaded Poland they were at war with them. That did not slow Hitler down and he captured virtually all of Europe, at which point we knew we were committed.

I went to a Bruins game at the Boston Garden and they announced Pearl Harbor to an unbelieving, captive audience. I said to the children this morning, you had your own Pearl Harbor on 9/11. Coincidentally, the number killed was approximately the same in both incidents. You can remember where you were when you found out that New York had, in effect, been bombed, along with the Pentagon. I related going home from the Bruins game and my Dad said, "Well, you're fifteen now, this will probably be over [before you are eighteen]."

Two years almost to the day, I myself, aged 17, was in the Marines. I told the kids that I had a nice cruise in the Pacific with a few interruptions. There was nothing heroic about joining: we were at war, a world war. My graduating class in high school happened to have an even 100 men, virtually all of them ended up in the service. I decided on the Marine Corps. My total time was 31 months. I was at sea about a year.

My ship's name was *USS Cape Gloucester,* CVE-109, an Escort Aircraft Carrier built in Bremerton, Washington. I took a troop train to the West Coast, went out of San Diego. First landfall was Leyte Gulf, which was a staging area. The *USS Indianapolis*, CA-35, the [heavy] cruiser, 700 drowned [883 of the crew of 1,197 died, with 300 going down with the ship, and many more dying over the next five days before 317 were rescued], was sunk by a Japanese submarine [July 30, 1945, four days after delivering the first atomic bomb to Tinian]. They were supposedly controlled from Leyte Gulf, the messages were mixed up so they didn't send any help. Those men, those kids, because they *were* kids, they simply drowned.

In World War II, there was no feeling that we wouldn't win. The Atlantic is a moat on one side and the Pacific is a much bigger moat on the other side. In my opinion, recent immigrants [to the US] really understood that Hitler couldn't be mollified. I was in with a lot of the kids here who lived on lard and bread—that was the Depression, the kids of immigrants. They couldn't accept a Europe that was dominated by a man like Hitler.

Then I go on to say it was an interesting and exciting adventure, there were some bad spots in it, and I insist on saying I have only one combat star, a battle star, so they don't think I'm a decorated veteran. North of the Philippines, off Okinawa, by then the war was beginning to slow down. We had kamikazes, they hit the *USS Pennsylvania,* BB-38 [battleship], which was moored next to us, we witnessed a bridge or two flying off ships. I never considered myself even in danger. "Well, that's tough." That's a teenage kid talking.

We were north of the Philippines (this was in a ship's book that was sent out afterward), covering minesweepers, which were laying mines and clearing up Japanese mines so the Russians could come over from Kamchatka. If it had come to that, there would have been hell to pay. The mines were swept out of the way in the most primitive fashion: we had hillbillies up on the bridge popping off the mines [with guns]. Then putting down new mine fields that the Japanese wouldn't be familiar with, in effect, strangling them, so that the invasion by the Russians would be successful. The [atomic] bomb short-circuited that whole process.

My boat was an experimental escort carrier with Corsair F4 fighters—the Wildcats, the bomber. It was to cover the sweepers and let them do the job and clear the ocean safely, so from the Asian mainland the Russians could successfully invade Japan. By then, we were gathering troops for exactly the same purpose. Speculatively speaking, if the Russians had gone into Hokkaido, or northern Japan, they would have held on to more than the Kurile Islands, which they still hold, and we probably would have divided Japan up into Honshu and Hokkaido being one and Kyushu and Okinawa being the other. But the successes kept coming. MacArthur, who was so easy to dismiss, had a brilliant strategic thing—island hopping had never been done and he carried it right up to Japan.

I end up with a story about a young Australian who was drafted by his government to protect the empire, as I say rather sarcastically. He was from an impoverished place in an impoverished country, Perth, in the outback of the outback. He also weighed 65 pounds, because he had spent the last four years in Japanese prisons. He had been captured in Southeast Asia and his unit was loaded on four old rusty tubs and sent to Japan to work the factories. They were systematically starved although the Japanese themselves didn't have much food. I used to show a picture—he looked just like they did in the European concentration camps.

We were pulled up in Nagasaki Harbor, and he came aboard our ship. The man had to be deloused and cleaned up. We liberated quite a little food for him, and he entertained us with stories of the war, without any bitterness. Of course, he was lucky to be alive and he was glad to be alive, but he didn't blame his government, or the Crown, or the Americans who sank three of the four vessels as they went to the Philippines, or the Americans who had just wiped out an entire city [Nagasaki, 9 August 1945]. He didn't personalize his hate in any way, and was one of the more remarkable people I've met. He wasn't an educated man; he'd probably lived on a dirt-poor farm. He had a rather unhappy adventure, but survived it, even though he left half of himself physically in Japan.

I spent three days in Nagasaki, tied up. The water evaporators were tied down; they didn't try to distill water because the whole harbor was quite radioactive. All the fish were dead. There were no regular occupation forces, there were a couple of cowboy Marine outfits that were patrolling. The Japanese were very subservient under those circumstances. The prisoners were ecstatic to be picked up, fed, and deloused. We took them down to Okinawa, then they were divided up. I'm sure the most serious cases were given air flights.

Harry Truman had to make up his mind: do we drop this [bomb] or don't we? My first reaction as a still-teenage kid when it was dropped was, "Why didn't he drop it on Yokohama Bay instead of dropping it on a city?" I have apologized for a lifetime for us doing that, because I don't believe he would have done it to Caucasians. I have no way of proving that. I personally cannot justify wiping out a whole city. You had a semi-wrecked country, they had been firebombed, which can take out a whole city, too. They were a wrecked country, and they were trying to comply with a few international laws and get those people [POWs] out of there, get them back.

Even as a teenager, I couldn't believe we could bring ourselves to wipe out a city *twice*. When Hiroshima was bombed I was about 300 miles south in the Okinawa area. The bomb had gone off, people had flown in, and the defeated Japanese cooperated to the point where they put these men [POWs] on trains to go down to Nagasaki because the Allies insisted on it and the Japanese complied. Nagasaki happened to be one place where [my] small carrier went in and cleared the decks and gave accommodation to about 700 prisoners for a short trip down to Okinawa.

I got an official thing a few years ago from the Defense Department, if you were at an atomic bomb test or at Nagasaki you may apply for radioactive disability. Well, I was in my seventies then, I've lived this long, I didn't absorb too much radiation. [*He laughs.*] We were there roughly three days. We stayed out of the water, we had stored water, I didn't go on land, a few of the officers went on land, and they were at more risk. I know people who were granted radiation things.

But I was a little cynical about the VA. I think of all the people who didn't get much compensation for being killed. I'm not cynical about the whole thing, I think we did very well as a nation, we came together, we were unified. People ask me about how we handled integration in the Marine Corps, and I say it was very simple. When I went into the Marine Corps in 1943, there were no Blacks in the Marines. That's a bold statement—kids absorb that. That was the Marine Corps official policy. The Navy had stewards. I watched movies where they would put a black gunner on, but he's a *steward*. In general quarters, he's assigned to a gun, of course.

Truman began to change things—of course, he had the Tuskegee experiment. As late as Korea, and I have read this in print (that doesn't make it true) but Caucasian officers were reluctant to put rifles in black hands. Most of the black people say, "Oh yes, I worked in the construction battalion." That's from the Civil War onwards, you don't find Blacks. I was personally very pleased to see Obama get [elected] and I'm a registered Republican. I remember Massachusetts Republicans, they were the Congregationalists and abolitionists, the party of Lincoln. [As a child] I saw Civil War veterans in the Memorial Day parade.

The unsophisticated attitude of present-day America, people don't *want* to know about the Iraq war. They don't understand why we are there. A lot of mistakes were made by George W. Bush. We're repeating some of the imperial mistakes of Great Britain in trying to use our size and strength to control people.

The position we're in now—we have no way of analyzing what we've just done and where we're going. We are not out of Guantanamo, we are not out of Iraq, and we are not out of Pakistan, which is going to be the kicker. I'm sympathetic with the situation we've allowed ourselves to drift into, but I think it's a very bad mistake to look for villains. You can say George Bush did it, well, the administration, granted, acted stupidly. But this is a reason-less time. I don't see anybody willing to talk about Iraq. We are over there for our purposes. We haven't announced anything that people can endorse. I'm afraid that Obama's going to be sunk by it unless he can find a way around it.

Walter Kostanski was born in 1923 in Irving, Massachusetts. He was in the Navy Armed Guard protecting key shipping on privately-owned vessels during the war, serving for two years on the Esso Rochester. *After the war, he went to Franklin and Marshall College in Pennsylvania for a year, but his ambition was to play major league baseball (he tried out for the Chicago Cubs and the Brooklyn Dodgers), as he had been an MVP pitcher in the All-Western Massachusetts League. He served in the state legislature for 14 years and then was registrar of deeds for 24 years. He has worked hard to get recognition for the Armed Guard, a part of the wartime Navy not well recognized.*

We were forming convoy outside of New York in the North Atlantic, quite a number of ships. I should mention that we carried 150,000 barrels of high-octane gas, and then we had twelve P-38 airplanes tied down on deck, and had those delivered over to the Army. It was a new plane, and they were fighters, and they were going to escort bombers there.

I was a member of the United States Naval Armed Guard. Now, the Armed Guard, it was 150,000 of us that were gunners, signalmen, radiomen, assigned to the merchant ships. Our job was to try to deliver the supplies to Europe, in this case England. The Merchant Marine ran the ship, our task was to man the guns for protection. The Armed Guard was established on April 15, 1941, a part of the Navy that many people have never heard of. "We

Aim to Deliver," was our motto, and we *did* deliver. We felt very proud of that statement.

I emphasize the United States Navy Armed Guard because nobody knew about us! This is why they called us "the orphans of the sea." And yet, we were trying to get those supplies protected, because you had troops, you had all kinds of cargo that the Armed Guard was assigned to. On our ship, there were thirty of us Navy crew, with a Navy lieutenant that was assigned to us. About a hundred between the Merchant Marine and ourselves, the Merchant Marine ran the ship, the skipper was a Merchant Marine. When you got into the service, you learned responsibility and discipline. We were attacked at Pearl Harbor, the Germans were moving, they probably would have been in our back yard if we didn't move in.

Coming out of Manhattan, there were German submarines hanging out—there was quite a battle for the North Atlantic. A half hour out of New York, we had a German submarine attack, about twenty miles out, this is where your submarines would park themselves, starting from Nova Scotia, going right down to New York, and down to Florida. The submarines were so close they could see the lights of New York. Eventually, you had black-outs right along the whole coastline. This was my first trip, I was loading the 20-mm gun; there were two of us on a gun. The submarine, we never saw it, we did have a few escorts with us, destroyers and some Coast Guard that dropped depth charges to try to shake off the submarines. I think they probably scared them off. There was no surfacing of a submarine.

We journeyed on to Liverpool, England, where we left off the P-38s. Then we continued on up to Scotland, discharged the gasoline, came back to the United States, and then journeyed on to Aruba. That was an oil refinery, Dutch Oil. Then we took a load of Navy [diesel] fuel, we journeyed over to Dakar, Africa, you had the Free French there then, because the attack on Africa was in '42. We left off that load of Navy fuel, and then we came back and stopped at Curaçao, another refinery—you had Aruba, Curaçao, and Trinidad, all oil refineries. We loaded up, went through the Panama Canal, and headed out to the Pacific.

We stopped in New Guinea, Port Moresby, and discharged our fuel there. They shot us up to Aden, Persian Gulf, which is Iraq on one side, so we loaded up with fuel and we brought that back and let it off in Wellington, New Zealand. After Wellington, we came back though the Canal and loaded up again at Trinidad and then headed back out to the Pacific. We were supposed to go to New Guinea and discharge our oil, but in the meantime, they sent us up to Leyte Bay. That was November 11, 1944. MacArthur had arrived a few weeks before I got there on October 20, 1944. We hadn't gotten that news. A lot of what we got was scuttle-butt—you really only knew what *you* were doing.

The news we got was more of the Japanese, Tokyo Rose! When you are out at sea, the only thing you have is the radio. Recreation, if you want to call it that. Being in that vicinity, she played some good music, we appreciated that. Her propaganda we didn't pay too much heed to, we just let it fly off the top of our heads. In the meantime, they tell me that she was a Japanese-American. [Multiple broadcasters worked under the name "Tokyo Rose."] That was why we were tight-lipped, to make sure nobody got any information: "Loose lips sink ships." That was for our own protection that we were quiet. Whenever we went into port or anywhere, we didn't know where our destinations were until we had practically gone out to sea. Other than that, we were always in the dark.

The time we got up in Leyte, it was a real hot place, the kamikazes there were just being established, suicide bombers. Matter of fact, as we were going in, there was one that came down but missed us, thank God. It was nighttime when this happened, that's why we didn't open fire. What happened is that somebody among my shipmates had a port hole that was open—in the evening, you locked everything up, tighten up, make sure there's no light. The reason this suicide came down, he saw that light. He crashed on the tail end of our ship, but we never did have to shoot because we couldn't see it anyway.

That was quite a welcome there! Once we got inside Leyte Harbor, three times a day we'd have suicides come in and attack us, almost like a routine that they had, more so going toward the evening when it was tougher to spot them—they had the sun behind them. We had no radar. They even had a hospital ship known as the *Mercy* in the Bay, but there were many, many ships there that were hit by these suicides. [*You saw this?*] Oh, yeah.

Matter of fact, we were credited as a tanker for knocking out the Japanese bomber that was coming down—the United States

Navy recognized that was our hit. Being a tanker, at that time fuel was very, very valuable. Of course, to identify a tanker was a stack on the stern, other than tankers, your stack is in the middle of the ship. They were painting a lot of your ships grayish. We were a target: we would refuel into other ships—destroyers, other naval vessels. As I say, a target, more so that you have two ships hooked up to you to refuel—you're a *big* target, as a matter of fact.

Two years I was on the *Rochester*. Then they put me onto another tanker, the *Gulfcrest*, and then I had an Army transport, the *Belle Isle*. This was a trip that I was taking up to Greenland to take troops to relieve troops on the Army air base [Narsarssuak]. Of course there was a submarine nest within the Nova Scotia area. This was the same run that the four chaplains went down on, that ship was the *USS Dorchester* [February 3, 1943]. What the chaplains did was they gave their life jackets to the soldiers. We had that same run, no radar, but the Coast Guard, Navy did have radar, and they could pick out these submarines, depth charges also, that helped.

My dad was in World War I. He was in Poland, [and] he came over here to this country a young man. He worked in the coal mine, paper mill, but during World War I they had the Polish-American group that they organized, went up to Canada for their basic training, and then they shipped them over to France. That's where he fought, he told me.

To me, the bomb is very, very scary. You're not dealing with the A-bomb, you're dealing with the [H]-bomb, a thousand times more potent. The North Koreans now have, it is really scary. To me, you're just killing off people again such as we did on the A-bomb. We used it on the Japanese but it did save us from having a lot of our own boys getting killed. The Russians took over Poland and I don't think it should have happened, giving them Eastern Europe, Poland. Communism to me, you can't trust them. The North Koreans, the Russians, and the Chinese, they are killing us off economically. We are buying all their stuff, and I feel very strongly that in this country we should buy American. It's going to cost a little more, you've still got to appreciate this country and support it.

We went to war in Korea to protect the South Koreans, because they are our friends. The Chinese sent troops, they backed up to North Korea. We still have the guards over there. You try to have confidence in your leadership of your country. When they asked us to go in, we did. We had confidence in President Roosevelt and even President Truman. That was a tough decision to make to drop the bomb, but you've got to give these guys credit—Roosevelt and Harry Truman, for leadership.

I don't know about Vietnam. In regards to the leadership at that time, it was very confusing. It was a tough war, more so that you didn't come out a winner. A lot of lives lost, a lot of sacrifice. We didn't know that much about that country. There you go—depending on your leadership. We've got to follow no matter where you go, for your country. Everyone probably has ideas of what should have been done, what shouldn't have been done.

The whole world seems to be in turmoil. Since World War II, I don't think we have really settled down war-wise. There's a lot of bitterness in this world, dangerous world. [*Iraq/Afghanistan?*] I think I would go back to saying, your government, your CIA, you have got to depend on somebody for the information; these people put their lives on the line. I have the highest respect for the CIA. This is getting back to the Iraq war, who was right and who was wrong for us to go in there. I think if we didn't go up to Iraq, this Hussein, he was a vicious guy, he murdered close to a million Iranians [Iraq–Iran War, 1980–8]. He was on a move to really hurt people. [*Kuwait?*] That's right, we went in there. Here we [are] trying to help, but then you get yourself involved and you're trying to pull out, and it's tough.

World War II we knew that once we kill off our enemy, the war is over, period. This way here, like North Korea, we still continue to have guards. I think they need leadership too, the Iraqis. They are really poor people. When I was up in the Persian Gulf, we got fuel there. I could see the natives on the docks, and they're all eating out of one bowl, with their hands. And oh, the heat over there! To me, these poor soldiers that have got to fight over there; I have a real feeling for them. We thought that World War II was going to end all wars and it hasn't. It seems to be worse now than World War II.

Tom Herrick, born in 1927 in Lakewood, Ohio, graduated from high school in 1945 and with the draft still in force, took the entrance exams for the Merchant Marine, in which he served 1945–7. He became an economics professor after receiving a BA, MA, and Ph. D from the University of Chicago. His first interview focused on his experiences in the Philippines, South America, and the Caribbean in the Merchant Marine. His second interview is his account of American wars from World War II to the present, as follows.

World War II was a unique event, the civilized against the uncivilized. This is encapsulated in Churchill's famous speeches, and the good guys won. If you read Churchill's speeches, the two key ones in 1940 were "We shall fight them on the beaches..." at the time of Dunkirk and the Fall of France, then about two months later, as the Air Battle of Britain was coming in, "This will be their finest hour." This is the first time a major world leader [says] we are fighting to maintain civilization.

> I expect that the Battle of Britain is about to begin. Upon this battle depends the survival of Christian civilization.... Hitler knows that he will have to break us in this Island or lose the war. If we can stand up to him, all Europe may be free and the life of the world may move forward into broad, sunlit uplands. But if we fail, then the whole world, including the United States, including all that we have known and cared for, will sink

into the abyss of a new Dark Age…. Let us therefore brace ourselves to our duties, and so bear ourselves that… men will still
say, "This was their finest hour."—Winston Churchill, 18 June
1940

But World War II in turn created a situation in which we had
a falling out of the Allies. This is a very common situation, almost
axiomatic. You have a successful war where the allies work together and then shortly thereafter there is a falling out. Allies become enemies and this occurred almost immediately with the
Soviet Union after World War II.

So the problem as we go into the Korean War and then into
the Vietnam War, is to view that in terms of our relationship with
the Soviet Union, the Cold War enemies. The policy that was established after World War II when the Soviet Union and America
and its allies became enemies, was the containment policy. It hasn't
changed very much—it was developed by George Kennan, an official in the State Department. The idea was that because we could
not physically conquer the Soviet Union, or we *would* not conquer
the Soviet Union because we would have to use atom bombs to do
it, therefore we would *contain* the Soviet Union and the Soviet allies.

That led in turn to the Korean War and then the Vietnam
War, both hot wars on the periphery, the Soviet area of influence.
They were advertised as such. Particularly in the Vietnam War
the idea was that we were supposed to fight the communist North
Vietnamese, which were supposedly allies to the Soviets, and this
would be at the periphery. Also in the Korean War, North Korea
fell within the Soviet sphere of influence and became communist,
hence the fight at the periphery. You could see that these wars related back to the falling out of the Allies from World War II. The
fact that we interpreted that as an active threat is another question.

The Korean War was a war almost by mistake. The only reason that we could legally fight the Korean War on the side of the
South Koreans was through the UN, and that is the device that
we used, with a resolution that went through when the Soviet
Union had been AWOL on the Security Council of the UN.
There's a lot of speculation on that: did the Soviet Union intentionally absent itself during a period of several months, in early
'50? [The self-imposed boycott by the USSR of the Security Council was putatively an objection to the US recognizing Chiang

Kai-shek and Taiwan as the real China rather than Mao's mainland communist China.] Did the Soviet Union intentionally pull itself away, or was it a mistake on the part of the Soviet Union? What we know from the archives in the Soviet Union is that the Soviets did view [North] Korea as a rogue state.

That became a UN operation and the US was the major participant. The Korean War went back and forth, stopped roughly where they started. It was worth it because [it] was and is a manifestation of the containment policy. One of the problems [was] that South Korea was in the hands of a rather brutal dictatorship, Syngman Rhee. We were allies of Syngman Rhee; coming in to support a lousy government is somewhat parallel to the situation in Vietnam and currently parallel to the situation in Afghanistan.

The North Koreans felt that they could conquer South Korea because of the obvious weakness of the Syngman Rhee government. They were quite successful, they pushed us all the way down to the perimeter around Pusan and that was used as the base for the American troops push back. The Korean War was successful: it held the perimeter on the Soviet Union and the Soviet allies, the Cold War.

MacArthur was old, that was his last job. He was the peacetime director of that area of the world and all of a sudden he is put in this position as an active commander. He got a lot of brownie points by doing the Inchon attack that cut off the North Koreans. That of course led to the Chinese coming in and the possibility people were talking about, atom-bombing a corridor between Korea and China. Whether it was seriously considered or not, it was too dangerous, so we had the firing [of] MacArthur. Here was an isolated war on the periphery and it was touch and go whether you were fighting the Soviet Union.

The Cold War started as early as 1946, with Churchill's Iron Curtain speech. We actively fought the Soviet Union in a peaceful manner in Turkey and Greece, and we were successful there, holding these frontiers. World War III, the doctrine of mutually assured destruction, was very much talked about. The Soviets and their allies would not use their bombs because they would be assured of that, and we in turn established the Air Force Command (SAC) where 24/7 there were atom bomb planes and submarines going all around [the world] constantly.

Vietnam is a fascinating war because this was part of the containment policy and the perimeter war: the dominos, [if] South Vietnam was going to go communist, Thailand and all the others would presumably fall. A lot of aspects of it were completely phony. The war came about presumably because of the attack by the North Vietnamese on an American ship: the Gulf of Tonkin Resolution, which was pushed through the Congress, gave a blank check to support the war, very similar to what we did in Iraq. It came out that the Gulf of Tonkin attack was a lie by LBJ. Therefore the question—this was a tactical war, a war on the perimeter, a holdover—was it really necessary?

The fact that it became a hot war and did not go atomic is the good side of it. The fact that there's a lot of nastiness going on in the Vietnam War [is] the bad side of it. As you look years after the war, North Vietnam, a hardcore communist country, is doing everything it can to become capitalist to attract foreign investment, a "little China." You could argue the Korean War was very much in the cards because of North Korea ending up being an ally of the Soviets. It's quite possible if things had gone slightly differently in the case of the Korean War, they would never have gotten into the Vietnam War.

[Vietnam] was a complete mistake, a completely unnecessary war. As nasty as the North Vietnamese were, it was a Vietnamese civil war, north against south. I think a better policy would have been let them fight it out between themselves. China was not a lock-step ally of the Soviet Union in that operation, and that was being pointed out in the press at the time. The ordinary GI who was over there fighting might very well wonder, What am I doing here? The domino theory probably was baloney. World War II was an absolutely necessary war, a conflict between the civilized and the uncivilized... but the Vietnam War is basically a civil war, an unnecessary war [for us].

There are two Iraq wars. Bush senior's Iraq war, in '90, was quite successful. It shows the role of collective security, which was the idea behind the League of Nations and the UN. The diplomatic devices that were created at the end of these major, tragic wars (World War I, World War II) worked quite well. Iraq invaded Kuwait and Kuwait was part of our collective security. The Iraq I war is probably the most successful way that you should fight a war: you accomplish your aim, which was to free Kuwait, and in the process you destroy the army of Iraq. But we did not go all the way to occupy the capital and deal with Saddam Hussein.

Iraq II is the war that followed after 9/11. That was a completely phony war, manufactured by Bush II. One of the points oftentimes overlooked is that the Bush II policy of preventive war was actually established before 9/11 [and] 9/11 was used as an excuse to activate it against Iraq. The idea was in the neocons' view: if we bring democracy (whatever that is in the Middle East) to Iraq, that will have a spillover effect elsewhere in the Middle East. All of which will lead to a solution in Israel, which is a completely unbelievable concept, a national fantasy: if I do "A" (particularly in foreign policy) that somehow that will cause "B" to occur, which in turn will cause "C" to occur.

Bush II had in mind this civilizing role in the Near East as part of the foreign policy of America. The neocons coined the phrase the road to Jerusalem is through Baghdad, but they could have easily said the road to Jerusalem is through Saudi Arabia. They lost or we will lose, disastrously, Iraq, and it is only a matter of time before Iraq will go back to the way it was before.

The world is awash in oil. That Iraq happens to be sitting on the second or third most known reservoir of oil is completely irrelevant—there is oil everywhere. When Iraq was on good terms with the world, they were exporting something like six, seven, or eight million barrels a day out of their substantial reserves. Now all of a sudden the UN (American) resolution to boycott the export of oil out of Iraq, their exports were cut down to 4 million a day, even with the tightest of constraints. That argument does not hold water. The market for oil is fungible.

As you move into Afghanistan, the problem emerges: what are we doing there? It has been officially acknowledged that there are less than a hundred, less than fifty al-Qaeda in Afghanistan. If we really would be fighting in a country because we wanted to stop the expansion of al-Qaeda, logically we would be at war with Pakistan. When we talk about war on terror, terror is a *tactic*, so a war on terror is actually like a war on mosquitoes. It's a misuse of the term. It's obviously contrary to both domestic and international law. You could argue that you don't even have to have an act of war; you can just enforce the existing laws against that sort of activity.

That suggests that it is not a good idea to confuse that with a war against one country by another. The best tactic when you are up against foreign terrorists or terrorists who happen to be physically located in some foreign country is what we did shortly after 9/11 in Afghanistan when we went in there with a small contingent of CIA, Special Forces, and so on. We almost got Osama bin Laden! The idea of going in gangbusters with a declared war doesn't make much sense. The Afghan war will just boil down to [a] Special Forces sort of thing. This is what we are doing in Pakistan. Pakistan is an ally, we're not declaring war on Pakistan, but we do have various military activities to fight where we think al-Qaeda is, with the drone aircraft and all that. Our involvement with Afghanistan will simply fade but we will keep forces working *sub rosa*.

We get involved in Vietnam, now Afghanistan, and Iraq. If a controlling or an interested power is to have power overseeing the operation, the way to run the show is the way the Brits ran the show when they were colonial overlords in India and elsewhere. You make deals with opposing groups on the ground, tribes, the Sunnis, the Kurds in Iraq. The same thing in Afghanistan, you have different degrees of Taliban, and other groups there. So if you have an overlord position, the smart way to do it is to make deals. For six months you are making a deal with "A," maybe six months or a year later you are going to be dealing with "B," "A" is going to be your enemy. If we stay in Afghanistan, that's what we ultimately have to do.

TWO
KOREA:
THE FORGOTTEN WAR

5,720,000	Served 1950–3*
36,574	Died*
33,739	Killed in Action*
103,284	Wounded in Action*
8,025	Missing in Action**

Department of Defense (DOD) figures compiled by the Congressional Research Service, 26 February 2010
** DOD Missing Personnel Office figure

Introduction

FIGHTING THE COLDEST WAR

Victory in World War II erased the maps that the Axis dictators had so cavalierly redrawn and allowed the Allies to dictate to the conquered countries. The defeated were occupied and reformed to be either democratic (West Germany and Japan) or socialist (Eastern Europe). The Allies were aware that the USSR was going to claim its share of the postwar world, and thus the shared victory metamorphosed into the Cold War. New communist spheres of influence sprung up around the USSR and China, the "red menace" that inspired so much fear in America. At the same time, the US was building up its own spheres of influence.

Five years after a global victory, few Americans wanted to see another mobilization of armed forces and another draft. Korea began too soon after World War II to enjoy its popularity. Still, it was treated as a noble cause, this time defined as containing communism. Korea, however, was not a global war against the aggression of fascist dictators, but a war in which the US was fighting to protect a small but strategic ally in a far off country out of fear that the USSR and China might grab it from us. The two global giants (the US and the USSR) each resolved to hold on to the half of Korea it had liberated in 1945. Newly Communist China under Mao Zedong and North Korea, supported by the USSR with arms and MiGs, were pitched against the US and the five-year-old United Nations.

One half of Korea was fighting the other half. The UN peacekeeping effort relied on the overwhelming contribution of the US and South Korea, with much smaller contributions from the allied countries most concerned with what happened around the Pacific (Australia, New Zealand, and Britain, head of the global Commonwealth). That the Korean War resulted in a stalemate may have influenced the US to spend years seeking a victory in related circumstances in Vietnam.

If the Korean War diminished the euphoria of defeating Germany and Japan and restoring peace in 1945, it was also a continuation of that war. The US had suffered a major setback in 1949 when in a civil war, Mao Zedong defeated the Kuomintang led by World War II ally Chiang Kai-Shek, forcing him to flee the mainland for Taiwan. Believing that we had "lost" China, Senator Joseph McCarthy conducted a campaign to identify and blame domestic "communist sympathizers" in such unlikely places as the US State Department, the US Army, American universities, and even Hollywood. Now it appeared that the US might also "lose" South Korea.

The Korean War resulted in containment without victory or defeat: in 1953, the opposing armies returned to the starting line. Was it a success? What had it accomplished? It showed that Americans were willing to go anywhere and everywhere to fight the spread of communism. Each communist encroachment (at first in Eastern Europe, then globally) was considered a loss for the United States in the zero sum game of the Cold War. There was no way to win definitively against the new "evil," even if fighting for a good cause. The resolve to contain communism through collective security would reemerge in many locations in the next decades.

While the US was technically involved in a police action (a term introduced by President Truman) conducted by the UN, overwhelmingly the fighting was done by US soldiers and aviators with their South Korean (ROK) allies. At the landing at Inchon on September 15, 1950, of 300,000 UN troops, 86 percent were from the US. At the moment of the armistice, of 932,964 UN troops, 63 percent were South Korean, 32 percent were from the US, and 5 percent were from other countries. The stalemate in Korea continues sixty years later, and US and ROK forces remain there to guard against further aggression from the north.

The scope of Korean conflict expanded exponentially when the Chinese sent in masses of their own soldiers. A land war in Asia, Eisenhower had warned, should be avoided at almost any cost because, army to army, we could not win it. Post-World War II, in Korea, for the first but not last time, the US faced the realities of fighting somewhere on the vast Asian continent.

Could Korea also become the opening salvo of World War III? After General Douglas MacArthur liberated the Philippines and occupied Japan, he became supreme commander in Korea. He wanted to make the war atomic, and President Truman dismissed him. Truman did not want to flirt with World War III, especially as the USSR had exploded its first nuclear weapon in 1949. The Chinese exploded their first atomic bomb in 1964, and that may have set military limitations on the Vietnam War, again in order avoid an atomic World War III.

THE NARRATORS

The Korean veterans who recorded their experiences for this volume saw themselves as residuals to a world war in which their older brothers fought. When interviewing them, it soon became clear that they felt they were, and still are, forgotten. Korea is often referred to as the "forgotten war," sandwiched between the glorious World War II and the drawn-out conflict in Vietnam.

I found that if you had not fought in the first year, you were not sure you had fought in a real war. Holding the line defined the next two years of taking and losing territory. Still, the losses were staggering: over 34,000 US servicemen died (or are missing) in the war arena. In the small sample here, there is some cynicism about the military leadership. The military errors that occur in every war were more noticeable because of the near-rout of the UN forces and the intervention of the vast Chinese army.

This war did not have the sweep and movement of World War II, where advancing armies chased the enemy across country after country, and over the vast Pacific and its islands. The Atlantic crawled with submarines and ships, the skies of Europe were crisscrossed with thousands of airplanes, and its lands hosted untold numbers of soldiers. Yet Korea, fought in a microcosm, was successful in defeating and containing the US enemy, too.

3

FIGHTING THE "FORGOTTEN WAR"

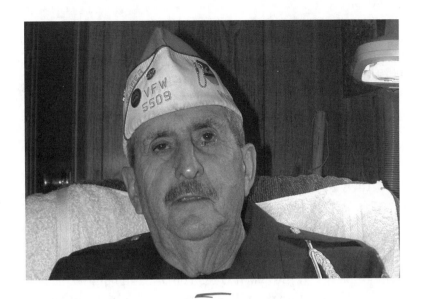

Al Hart was born in 1929 in Appleton, Maine, and enlisted in the army in Portland. He served in Korea for more than a year as a signal corps telephone installer. At first close to the front line, he could see the course of battle and recounts a story in which South Korean soldiers switched sides to the North Koreans (and back) when a UN base was overrun. Al has spoken about his experiences in a local middle school with Dennis Driscoll and Dave Hillbrook, whose narratives are in the section on Vietnam. He is a disabled veteran who earned two bronze service stars.

I went to Portland, Maine to try to get into the Air Force, took the test the first time and I got 100. That would qualify you for the Army, but to get into the Air Force, you had to get 110. I took it again in 24 hours and I got 103, but I couldn't get 110. So they said, "You are free to go home, sir." I said, "Well, I told all my friends I am going into the service, so I am going to join the Army." They said, "You'll have to go across the street." I went into the service in October 1949, Fort Dix, and after my basic I went to signal school for 21 weeks, Bell telephone, install and repair, Ft. Monmouth, New Jersey.

I was shipped out of California to Yokohama, Japan, on the *USS Weigel*, first of September. We got to Japan and I'd never seen so many GIs in my life. The next morning [I was told] you are on KP. I'd never seen so many dirty dishes, thousands and thousands of glasses. They said, "Why didn't you pay your dollar? If you'd have paid a dollar last night, you wouldn't have to be on KP because that dollar pays for Japanese help." The pots were so big—they had pea soup, okay? I had to go up a ladder to reach the top of the barrel and then back down in: after we drew the pea soup off, all of the ham bones had to be thrown out of there. This pot, without exaggeration, was deeper than I am tall, probably six feet deep.

A few days after that, we shipped out for Korea, headed for Pusan. As we were approaching Pusan it came on over the intercom, "The First Cav has lost almost all of their men, so all of you are going to be replacements. Tear off all your patches [the 2nd Infantry Division "Indianhead" patch] and throw them away, you will all be issued this patch here. You are all going to Inchon, Korea." We went up the Yellow Sea—on a clear day you can see clear down to the bottom. When the tide goes out at Inchon, it goes out one whole mile!

We were waiting to be assigned to different units. They picked fifteen guys to go to firing-batteries, I was the last one they picked. I told them I was signal and the officer said, "I am telling you to go, so you go." We traveled north all night 'til the next morning, through Seoul, up near the Chosin Reservoir. "What do you know about cannons?" I said, "The only time I've seen a cannon is in pictures." "Stick with me and I will use you to do communications." [The officer] showed me a truck that was loaded with thousands of dollars' worth of brand new telephone equipment.

So I stayed and I ran telephone lines to the three firing batteries. In each shell, in the casing, there were three bags of powder, if you put in all three bags, you would shoot a mile. They were throwing away two bags and half of the third one, they just wanted to get it up over the hill because the enemy was down on the other side. There was company fire every five minutes. Imagine the racket! I told him I was tired, and he said lay down here on the shells, the casements, in your sleeping bag and take a rest. It seemed as if I had just gone to sleep, and somebody kicked my feet and it was the same sergeant. "Either you've got nerves of steel or you are lying to me now." I said, "Sergeant, I'm not lying to you, I'm just tired." "Well, get up and get something to eat, and then I want you to start running wires to the rest of them." I stayed there and got all of that stuff in order.

One day, I was working at Captain Black's tent (I was in the First Cavalry Division, the headquarters), he said, "I have never had communication like this since I have been in Korea." I says, "Thank you, Sir." This team pulled up, had an officer in it, a major, and a driver. The officer got out of the jeep and he said to my captain, "Have you got a man here by the name of Hart?" He said yes. "We thought he was AWOL, because he's supposed to be running the switchboard. He didn't report, somebody said he got on the wrong truck and came up here to the firing battery. Tell him to get his gear together, we're taking him down to headquarters."

So Captain Black called me into the tent and said, "They've come to take you down to headquarters, to run their communication, but I'll vouch for you and I'll tell them that you don't want to go, you can stay here." "Sir," I said, "the officer who got out of that jeep, he outranks both of us, I think I'd better take orders from the top." "Well, you learn fast." I said, "I've been in a while and you have to respect the top man." But he said, "You can stay here, we'll take good care of you." I said, "You already have, but I think I'd better take orders from him."

I wanted to be polite in doing it—well, I was glad to go. Even though he was good, I was too close to the front. I don't like to tell war stories, but it was terrible. The battlefield was lit up at nighttime, we were back far enough so we could see it, and it was too close for me. My grandson used to say to me, "Grandpa, how many people did you kill?" I said, "I didn't kill nobody, actually nobody shot at me either. The infantry had to have communications. They took good care of us and they saw that we didn't get hurt."

A buddy of mine, they were bringing him back in a stretcher and blood was running out. He hollered for me, so I went over, and he said, "What did the chaplain give me last rites for, I feel all right!" I said, "That's his job," and I said to myself, I'll never see him again. When I went down to headquarters company, he came back to go up front again. His back was full of shrapnel, it was winter time, you could put your hand on his back and you could feel that iron, it was all cold.

Like I say, they took me down to headquarters company, I ran the switchboard down there. Korea in the winter was terrible cold, colder than Maine ever thought of being. One night, I was standing guard. It was snowing real hard, I could just see in the shadows somebody coming toward me. I loaded my rifle. Whoever was in the shadow said, "Don't shoot, it's me!" I said, "Who's me?" and he says, "I am your buddy from Hawaii." I said, "Come out into the light so I can see you," around headquarters it was all lit up. "What do you want? It's 20 below zero, why aren't you back sleeping?" He said, "I got permission to stand your guard, you can go back and go to sleep." I said, "You aren't pulling my leg are you?" and he said, "No, I want to tell you something. I am 21 years old and I have never seen it snow in my life. This is the most beautiful scenery I have ever seen, snowing like this and the light shining."

Another thing, to tell you how close we were, every night there would be this North Korean biplane flying over. We called it Big Chink Charlie, he didn't know for sure where we were, but when he flew over he must have had hundreds of shells, like fire crackers, he threw over probably a dozen of those, every night. We had this guy from Tennessee, "Al, I am sick and tired of him, I just get to sleep and he throws out those shells." They would burst before they ever hit the ground; it didn't hurt anybody, just harassment. He had his M-1 rifle, we all had our M-1s. "I'm going to shoot him down." So when he flew over the next night my buddy crawled out and he fired two or three shots. Boy, that plane took off. We stuck up for him; all of us in the signal unit took the blame for it. We knew that he would have gotten court-martialed because he gave away our position.

I've got a little story to tell you about the ROK. When I was up there to the front, the Republic of Korea troops, they were helping us. They were good as long as we were winning. The guys told me, "Al, you got the wrong impression. Wait 'til we start losing." Well, one night we were overrun. The ROK troops, they were with the North Koreans! We furnished them with all of their uniforms, all of their ammunition, we fed them and everything. Until they looked around, you'd swear that those are GIs, they're dressed the same. Then one night we got pinned down and the guy told me, "You see this outfit over here?" and I said, "The ROK troops, I'm in communication with them," and he says, "You're not now. They are fighting with the North Koreans. Tomorrow, if we start winning, they will be helping us."

You won't believe [this], either. When we were up there to the front, in the firing battery, let's say they brought in 150 rounds, okay? I said to the sergeant, "They're firing every five minutes, that's not going to last." He said, "You'll find out that this is a political war. That is our ration. If we get overrun and we're running out of ammunition, we've got to get out of here because we won't get another load of ammunition until tomorrow." That is why we know it's *political* because you had a ration, you didn't have a continuous supply. They give you [just] so many to use, it was scary. That's why they talk about the Forgotten War. It was cruel.

We had an interpreter in the signal corps, and our lines would be cut up. Let's say we run lines, we did them outside the road as much as we could, but if one tank passed another one, they would just chew it up. The North Koreans would take that same line that belonged to us and use it for their own communication. This line coming in to the switchboard, I'd say to my interpreter, "I don't understand what's going on." Then he'd pick up the phone and he'd say, "That's North Korean." "How do you know?" And he'd say a few words and the line would go dead. We would trace that line back and we would find out that it was all hooked up. As soon as he said those six words, the North Korean knew that we were on that line.

"I can tell you just where they are, what they are going to do, how much food they've got left." We would say we wanted to use that line, he'd say a few words and they would get off. "They are listening to us, too. They've got men working for them, same as I'm working for you." He didn't say it outright, but, "As long as you pay me, I'm your friend, and when you don't pay me, I'm not." He saved our life hundreds of times. We all gave him money, candy, anything he wanted. He said, "I've got clothes enough, *good* clothes, army issue, to last me if I live to be a hundred years old! If this war lasts another year, I'll be one of the richest men in South Korea."

When we were over there in Korea, we had a lot of English troops. We got a ration of 3.2 percent beer, more water than it was alcohol. They didn't get any beer, they were all issued gin. Until they got on to us, we would say, we'll give you a dozen cans of beer, [they'd] give you a pint of gin, their pint is half a liter, it was good gin. We could cut it with water, and it would make us a good drink. After a while they found out that they were getting the short end of the bargain and the only way we would get a pint of gin off them we'd have to give them a *whole case* of beer. It was Shaefer, made special for the army.

I shipped out of Korea and I went to Chitose, Hokkaido, Japan, Camp Crawford. They said, "We've got twelve transport planes that are going to fly out and you'll be home in four days. If you go back by boat, you'll go back to Yokohama, processing, and go by boat from there to California." I said, "I'd like to [fly], but they're losing some planes [C-124s]." I went from Hokkaido, to Yokohama, I got into the West Coast on New Year's Day of '53, I got on a troop train in Frisco, came clear across the States, got discharged January 12, 1953.

[His older brother, who served in World War II, told him] they would take hundreds of jeeps and trucks and they would chain them all together, put them on a ship, get out in the middle of the ocean, and run them off. Just dump them right into the ocean, thousands of them, tanks and everything. He said he could imagine what the bottom of the ocean looked like around there! What I understand (I read about that), when General Motors and Chrysler sell vehicles to the service, they sell them with the understanding that when they are through with them they will be destroyed. If they sent all of those back, they couldn't sell their vehicles. Whatever they sell, even uniforms, is sold to the government with the understanding when it is through being used, it will be destroyed.

[*Vietnam?*] This is my personal opinion, but it's discouraging because ever since Korea, all of the wars, Vietnam, they are all *political*. They will tell you we won down in Iraq and Afghanistan, they want to have the people to govern themselves. But the thing of it is, the only reason—and this will be disputed—we got down there is because millionaires have got too much interest there. We've got all the servicemen down there to protect the oil wells. It's *all* political, their investments.

China is the biggest problem we've got. If all the investments, all the money that we've borrowed from China, if they called in all of that, they'd own us. Now we've spent all this money for wind turbines, where did they build them? In China. Why didn't the

United States take a lesson from Russia? Russia tried for years to take over Afghanistan, and they found out that they couldn't do it, so they pulled out and left them alone. Here the United States, they drive the enemy out of Iraq, they go into Afghanistan—they're born for the guns and they die for the guns.

[*When Iraq started, what were your thoughts?*] I was thinking why not leave well enough alone? They were just fighting amongst themselves, why'd we go in there? They didn't want us in there. You talk to the GIs that have been over there, the Iraq people hate us but we're still forcing our rule onto them. They talk about how England forced their rule on the United States, well, it's the same thing. If England would get out of Ireland, the north and south would be all right. But England has got to keep their finger on them, and that's what causes the trouble.

[*Can we win the Iraq War?*] No. Because it's proved that they can't even govern themselves. [*Why are we still there?*] The United States is too good. They can't *police* the world; we can't *feed* the world; why should we try to *influence* the whole world? It's a crying shame. GIs are getting killed every day, for what? World War II was fighting for a cause. We didn't want them over *here*. Unless it is political, why are we sticking our nose into other peoples' business? It's terrible.

This is what made me feel good the other day. I got this letter from the Office of the President of Korea, signed by Lee Myung-Bak.

Dear Almond Hart:

On this, the 60th anniversary of the Korean War, we honor your sacrifice... We salute your courage in enduring the unimaginable horrors of war. We pay tribute to your commitment in protecting liberty and freedom. We Koreans made a promise to build a strong and prosperous country...so that the sacrifice you made would not have been in vain... We are today a democracy, with a robust economy, we are actively promoting peace and stability around the world... We are proud of what we managed to accomplish and we wish to dedicate these achievements to you. The Korean government has been inviting Korean veterans every year as part of its Revisit Korea program...This year we will be inviting 2,400 Korean veterans and their families. We Koreans and myself in particular, look forward to wel-

coming you. We hope you will see what you made possible…
what you did for us many years ago.

They gave us all a citation.

Ron Bassett was born in 1931 in Greenfield, MA. He was badly injured in practice jumping over Japan. He served in the 674th artillery of the 187th airborne and was in Korea from June 15 to July 1, then redeployed to Japan the next day, until October 19, 1951. He was discharged in February 1953. Ron worked for the Fuller Brush Company when he first came out of the service, got in under the GI bill as a printer, then worked in the post office for 31 years. His knees are still very painful and require medical attention.

I was in communications as a radio operator, and they kept asking for volunteers to go to Korea. They came out with a list that they needed to fill and everybody volunteered. I was the only shortwave radio operator in my outfit, so every time I would volunteer, the communications officer would cross my name off. Twice I volunteered, twice he took my name off. The third time, the communications officer said to me, "Aren't you going to put your name on that?" I said, "Before, you just crossed it off." I had a friend at Battalion Headquarters, so I called him, "Put my name on the list." When that lieutenant found out I was on the list to go, he could have court-martialed me he was so mad.

When we got to Seoul we went on a train, thirty-some hours. It was an old hokey train. [*He laughs.*] I'm telling you, they had big rods that ran the wheels, one of the rods came off and they had to stop and fix that. I was in North Korea, just prior was when they are pushing the United Nations troops back toward the ocean. MacArthur landed, that's when Truman pulled MacArthur out of command, because he wanted to go to Manchuria. MacArthur wanted to go right to the source—all the troops over there were ready to go with him. We were sick and tired of taking a hill, getting on top, taking a hill, getting on top. A lot of guys got killed that way.

I was in Korea less than a month. I was a forward observer, going up the hills. There was nothing there! Any vegetation was gone. We went up on a hill and we did a lot of digging and there was nothing but rocks! The enemy had embedded himself in the rocks, you couldn't get him out. You couldn't bypass them because they were right up on top of a hill directing fire at you. I got one bronze service star, but I was never in a battle. There were other guys who had been disabled, wounded, so I felt kind of low, we didn't deserve to be in the same category. [The bronze star can be awarded for valor and heroism, or awarded for meritorious service, as in Ron's case.]

Well, when we came up the Plungy Pass in the daytime, we came part way up on a rickety train, then we came the rest of the way up in daylight. When we left to go back to Japan, we left at night over that Plungy Pass and we just had slit lights, so you could see the next vehicle ahead of you, but you didn't know where it dropped off. It was really one lane, you could squeeze by another vehicle. It drops off about a thousand feet. We were carrying deuce-and-a-halfs with 105 howitzers trailing on the back and once in a while one of the howitzer's wheels would get off the road and the driver would have to speed it up to bring it back on. We had to drive along the road at night because snipers were in the area. Everybody had their weapons loaded and unlocked, that's how jumpy they were. A whole unit, roughly 4,000, they were lucky to have 3,000 fighting then.

They pulled us back to Japan, by Ashiya Air Base, so we could on short notice get back into combat. We'd fly around Japan, three hours and eighteen minutes, because that's how long it would take us to get back into enemy lines, they would get us used to flight time. If you're going into combat and jumping into enemy lines, anybody could shoot you, so you stick together real good. The guy behind you is looking for something wrong with your 'chute, you check your equipment, check the man in front of you, make sure everything is okay with the 'chutes. Then the last guy would check [in front of him] and turn around and the guy he just checked would check him.

There are bundles of supplies, maybe crates. They dump them out with parachutes before we could go. A crate full of supplies, not much food to start with because you wouldn't be hungry for a little while. They can take a [Howitzer] 105 or a ¾-ton or a 1½-ton truck, and parachute them in. A 2½-ton truck! They can parachute tanks in on a platform, and they have two or three big 'chutes and off they go. How do you think they are going to get their supplies behind enemy lines? In Korea a lot of 105s were being dropped into rice paddies and they couldn't get them back up because they had sunk so far in. You've got to realize: the six bundles go out first so anybody on the ground isn't going to get killed by a chute falling on top of you. Then you come out later.

It's a [monorail] system where the bundles are hooked up, they carry the bundles to the door and they automatically drop off. The bundles move that way, and we move this way. We have no monorail, we just walk to the door and jump out. We're hooked to a wire cable, they say "stand, hook up, check equipment." You get your orders and out you go. I think it's a fifteen-foot static line that pulls your 'chute out. The pack is over the 'chute, that pack has to come off for you to deploy. The pack is canvas hooked on with rubber bands, it stays up there, flapping in the breeze. Fifteen feet, that pack will pull off, it clips on the cable. You exit on the side by the back of the plane.

When I got hurt, you had nineteen men going out each of two doors, you have a DZ [drop zone] of twenty seconds, so from the time you can jump to when you are not supposed to jump, is twenty seconds. The jump master just pushes the button, we wait, then we go. When I was injured there were bundles but the monorail didn't work, that's what made us delayed. The jump master, instead of turning us around and making another pass because we were only practicing, pushed the monorail again and it still didn't work, so then he jumped us, and half of us are out over the ocean.

I was looking down, the fellow next to me (we were so close together, we could have spit on each other) said, "I don't see any boat," and I said, "I don't see any boat either." The boats would have been there to pick us up. I'm going to make for shore, with all that equipment, I can't swim. If you're jumping into the water, you're supposed to undo your 'chute 50 feet above the water to bail out and hope that you come up and your chute doesn't come down on you. You could drown.

You can steer a 'chute, you know. If I'm out here and I want to go there, you've got four risers, you've got twenty-eight suspension lines. The four risers are the bigger ones, I grab the two in front, pull them into my chest, but you have to be careful, if you pull them too close, it caves in like this, and you don't have a 'chute. You pull them in as close as you can, that slips the air out of your 'chute, you're making a fold that pushes you this way. But all the time you're pulling this way, you're going faster because the 'chute doesn't have all that air.

I made it to the breakwater into the rocks and my body kept on going, that's what snapped my knees. I believe that because we had such strong muscles, from the exercise we did, that that's the only thing that saved me from having them snap right off. I got up and fell down. Every time you are going to make a jump, they really look you over and I couldn't bend over.

At Normandy they jumped at 300 feet. It takes 300 feet for a chute to open. They didn't use a reserve, just the main chute, if it didn't work, too bad. During training we were jumping mostly at 1,000 feet. We had one engine in one of my jumps at Campbell that caught on fire, so they gave us an emergency bailout, no procedure, no nothing. We jumped that one with 450 feet. You're right on the other guy's back, in fact I had a chute come right up in my face. Because he hesitated, if you hesitate, jump out or push him out. They have to get out that door in a certain time, if they don't, they're in trouble.

I spent almost a year in the hospital. I was in the 118th station in Japan for five weeks, then the 141st General Hospital, and I was operated on in the Murphy Army Hospital [Waltham, MA]. They took cartilage and a cyst out, the ligaments and tendons were torn in both knees. This one I could bend, but this one even when I bend it now it would lock in place. They would put a hand on the knee, one under the ankle, and keep pulling and twisting until it popped in place. It hurts! I think they did more damage to it. [*He laughs.*]

When I got out, it was pretty near over in '53. I wouldn't trust the North Koreans, that's for sure. They've got something up their sleeve.

[*The wars we are in now?*] They're not going to succeed in Afghanistan. The Russians didn't. The hardest thing is you don't know whether you're talking to a friend or an enemy. The same thing in Korea: the South Koreans and the North Koreans, you couldn't tell them apart, the North Korean uniform wouldn't be any different from the Chinese. They had sandals with cloth wrapped all the way around their legs, the North Koreans in South Korea. It's like wearing a sneaker with a bunch of cloth wrapped all around it, tied up top. Funny looking thing, nothing you would really want to wear.

Art Miller, born in 1930 in Evanston, Illinois, graduated from high school in Skokie. He joined his father and brother in the family greenhouse business and was drafted to serve in Korea. He trained as a medic, and served in the vicinity of Panmunjom on the 38th parallel while a ceasefire was being negotiated. He remained until the following spring, because no one could be sure that the ceasefire of July 1953 would hold. Art continued in the greenhouse and landscape business in Wisconsin where he and his wife Joyce raised their family of ten children, including my daughter-in-law, Debbie Miller.

I got a notice in the mail from Uncle Sam, greetings and all that: now you are to report for duty. You just knew if you were of age you would be drafted unless you had some physical problem. Some of my friends were drafted into the Navy, but I would say that 99 percent of the people that were drafted went into the Army. I got out of high school, didn't get to go to college. I went straight to work in our business. I went in on July 18, 1952 and was discharged May 11, 1954.

When we went in we knew it was for the two years we were drafted. The only thing that changed that was if you were in combat, whatever they called a combat zone (we called it "went up on line"), you were on a point system, with so many days in combat you'd have so many points. I got out of there a couple of months early. May second or third [1953], from then on we were in a combat situation. The fighting stopped in July and I was there until the following March or April.

When we went over we were trained as infantry so we were quite sure that we would be ground troops. [*Did you volunteer to be a medic?*] One thing you learn in the army is you never volunteer for anything. They would say they wanted some volunteers and nobody would volunteer, so they would say, "You, you, and you." I got orders to go down to this other part of Japan to a school to become a medic. I had no idea where that came from, they needed some bodies in the medical corps. This is the way the army works, just like they needed bodies in the artillery, luck of the draw.

I got orders to go to Eta Jima [near Hiroshima City], a Jap submarine base during the Second World War. I was very lucky; it was very beautiful, nice and warm down there. We had six weeks of intensive, and I thought, very good, training. What I learned in six weeks I could have maybe learned in two and a half weeks, it was basically just first aid. Our job was, if somebody was wounded, to stop the bleeding, make them comfortable, give them morphine if they needed it, patch them up and ship them back to the battalion where the doctors were. I will say when I got out of that I felt competent, I felt I could handle situations.

We had a nice little first aid pouch, like a fanny pack, about eight or nine inches wide, and about ten inches long, it held a lot of morphine syrettes, bandages, certain pills maybe, an IV set-up. Every trooper had his own first aid pack on his belt, and we'd use that first. If you needed more, you had your supply bag. It had a shoulder strap or you could put it on your belt.

Then we had our orders to go over to Korea. We shipped out of Sasebo, a port city on the east side of Japan, from there to Korea is only a four- or five-hour ride. We went into Pusan, which is down in the southwest corner, the main port. Then they sent us on a train and we went I don't know where, and ended up in a re-placement depot, the "repple-depple," for a couple days until they figured out where everyone was supposed to go.

When the war broke out, they pushed us all the way back down to the Pusan area, we finally got some troops over there, and we pushed them back all the way up. But later on they came back down again after the Chinks entered the situation, it was up and down. When I got to Pusan it was very safe, we were back up at the 38th parallel. I went through Seoul at one point. It was all bombed out. We were near Panmunjom, that's the city I remember, the peace talks, you know. The 27th Regiment, 25th Division stretched on for miles and miles, whereas the 27th Regiment, where I was, we were up near Panmunjom. I saw the tent where they had the parallel right through the middle. The North Koreans sat on one side and the Americans on the other. There was a sign that we were in the demilitarized zone, police were in the area. Being a medic I had to go along with the troops, so we saw the tent city from a distance, where they were talking.

We had the ROK soldiers integrated with us. We must have had about 30 ROK soldiers in George Company alone. We had some screw-ups just like you would have with American GIs, but on the whole I thought they were very worthwhile guys. The young people we had with us were very grateful that we came over there and helped them out. Now, the fact that they were with the GIs, they were living high off the hog, eating, otherwise, they wouldn't have made it. They didn't have anything like a draft. The story was told, when the ROKs wanted to get some troops they went into a village and just rounded up every young guy that they saw and put them in the army. They were in it until the thing was over, and they had nothing to say about it either. So they were happy to be with us and it was good living for them. They had nice uniforms just like we did.

I would say that a good many of them could speak a little bit of English. They understood probably more than they let on. For example, they knew the word "chow." On the other hand when they heard "guard duty," they tried to tell you they didn't speak any English. They weren't dumb, but that's typical. We had a couple of Korean officers and they spoke pretty good English. They were integrated into the infantry, I don't think many Koreans went into the artillery because it was a little more complicated.

People ask about the Korean situation: they called it a "police action," they seem to forget it was a United Nations effort. It was the UN that sent us over there. It was of course the American force that was going, it was not just a United States deal, the communist threat was very prevalent at the time, so the UN had to act. I'm glad they did, otherwise it would have been a situation like the world war where the League of Nations did nothing. I think it was a big test for the UN, it helped them a lot.

When we were on line, we had a Turkish brigade just to the right of us, so I saw some of those Turkish soldiers. I would never want to fight the Turks. They are a tough bunch. They did themselves very proud, they handled it very well, quite a bunch of guys. The Canadians, the British, and the French, Belgians, all these countries sent troops over, not in big numbers, but they did send troops. Now they were under the command of the American forces, MacArthur was the top commander. There were other countries involved, and that was one nice thing about it: they showed up, trying to help. I guess everybody was under the 8th Army, under the American officers. Someone has to run the show; you can't have six different chiefs.

I was never a great fan of MacArthur's. [MacArthur always commuted from Japan, and never spent a night in Korea.] I think that what soured me on him was when the Marines went up to Chosin Reservoir back in late '50. They almost got annihilated because of the stupid orders that came out of Japan and MacArthur's crew. We were very fortunate at that point that the Marines had a Major General Smith [First Marine Division] who was in charge of them. He foresaw what was going to happen and saved them— it was like Dunkirk, they were able to load on ships out of there. That was the low point of MacArthur's career, and Harry Truman fired him. He was surrounded by a bunch of yes-men. You mentioned General Walker. We had another incompetent by the name of Almond, who was in charge of that particular phase of the war, and he was of this group, too. [Late November to early December 1950, troops under the command of Major General Edward Almond were encircled by Chinese troops. After finally breaking out, X Corps was evacuated from the port of Hungnam.]

The other thing was, [MacArthur] didn't, for some reason or other, believe the Chinese were up there. He kept telling the troops that there was nothing to worry about. Well, there were 250,000–300,000 Chinese troops and then they decided to make their move—we were very fortunate to get out of that situation. That, plus the weather: they had the coldest weather in history during that particular phase of the battle. It was sad. Some people were talking about [bombing North Korea], they kicked it around.

Maybe he had the right idea—but you never want to fight the Chinese, they'll outnumber you, no sense in that. He didn't think they were going to come into the war, that's what changed the whole thing, too. The North Koreans were completely useless until the Chinese came in. Without the Chinese, the thing would have been over.

A lot of them wore what we call tennis shoes. In the wintertime they had a padded uniform, like a down jacket, they had foot pads with the quilted jacket over the top. In the wintertime we lost a lot of boys from frostbite because they were not equipped for it. I know they said the Chinese would never beat a retreat, they would follow orders, go anywhere. I remember when we were stationed on one of the outposts, another smaller outpost was overrun in an attack by the Chinese. They were in waves, one, two, three, four waves, depending on how many bodies they figured they needed. The first wave would come in and the second wave would come in and pick up the weapons of the first wave. You could never get American GIs to do that without a weapon, but that's the way the Chinese just followed orders. If they turned around and ran the other way, their officers just shot them in the back.

You're dealing with a different breed of people, that's the way they operated. We were outnumbered. They lost a heck of a lot of men, those Chinese, they would take over a hill, and the next thing we would go up and take it back, then they would knock it off, you look at that as kind of silly, but that's the way the war was fought. You're better off with the high ground, so we'd decide we were going to take the hill rather than the big city. They had a number for the elevation: hill 839 was 839 feet to the top. "We're going to hit that one today," so troops went out and they got it, maybe took them two days to get up there. Then the Chinks would counterattack, they'd knock us back down, and somebody would decide we had to go back. We went back and forth on these hills. Remember Pork Chop Hill? There were terrific battles up on a number of those hills.

I do remember my first casualty that I worked on. We were out on a patrol one night and we got ambushed by the Chinese. One of the guys hurt was a very good friend of mine. The medics were always in the middle of the patrol, so the ambush came, my buddy got shot in the arm. Of course it was pitch-dark, [and] that was my first casualty. He was hurting but he was talking, kind of mad about the whole thing. There was a humorous side of it. I said to him, "You know where the bullet goes in, it's got to come out somewhere. It makes a bigger hole when it comes out." So I was kidding him about that, I said, "I can feel where it went in, I'll see around [the] back." And I said, "Well, *you* never could see well back there!" That was my first accident. It went through the arm and came out above his shoulder, I suppose he had his arm stretched out.

When a bullet went in, if it hit a bone it could go all over the place. Bullet wounds were the *least* of our worries—it was shrapnel that caused more deaths and injuries than bullets. [*How did you manage at night?*] You *felt*. He knew where it went in, you put your finger on it, [and] you could feel it, that's what they trained you for. It was Sergeant Bowen, I don't remember his first name. He located out before I left the war.

I was very fortunate; I didn't have a whole bunch of them. Sometimes when they overran and we lost quite a few guys, if the poor fellow was dead, you just moved on to another. The wounded, if they were able, walked back to the battalion aid station. The others were put on stretchers and they'd send up either a weapons carrier or jeep to transport them back. There were doctors at the aid station who would tend to them. The more serious ones were put on a helicopter and flown back to MASH. If really bad, they were flown to Japan. When the troops were on the offense, making a move, then people were getting shot, you were tending to a lot of bodies. Where we were it was running patrols every night. Some nights you had nothing. Sometimes you ran into those situations. We were running hot and cold.

When the ceasefire took place, we were very happy about it. There was some free time, and we were able to go down to the neighborhood bar to hoist a few. [*He laughs.*] It was a very happy time for everybody. The other thing, we hoped that it was going to last, they were stalling for a long time with the peace talks. One day it would look good, the next day, just the opposite. We would hope that's it, very relieved, that takes a lot of pressure off you. After the ceasefire, we were still holding our positions—anything could happen. What they did is fortify the positions up on the demilitarized zone, building bunkers. They called alerts to keep you on your toes; it wasn't as if after the ceasefire everyone went to sleep.

I never saw a prisoner. The only ones we saw were dead ones and wounded ones. When the fighting was going on there was an exchange of prisoners: we would catch them and they would catch our guys and we would exchange them. Matter of fact, a good friend of mine from my hometown was down in Koje-do, he spent a few months there. He told stories about how overcrowded it was. At one point they [prisoners] almost took the whole thing over. But they were very happy to be out of the fighting. That particular place was a big war camp. Everyone was waiting for the day when they could leave.

[*Communication with home?*] Letters only. Nowadays I understand you can e-mail back and forth. We wrote pretty regularly, the mail service was good. I think I satisfied my mother! My brother, at one point when he was in Japan they didn't hear from him for quite some days, and they contacted the Red Cross. Where he was stationed the old man [his officer] pulled him in and gave him hell because he didn't write his mother. He didn't want to be bothered by that! I wrote home at least once a week. I saved a little money—you got paid every month, you signed off on the check. You couldn't spend it anywhere, [so] my money was sent to my folks. I had a little nest egg built up. It helped me buy my first car, a '54 Mercury, it was a good model, the Mercury had a real good rep, a step above a Ford.

Going back, I start with the Korean War. I thought that was a good cause. The Vietnam War you might say that was the same but the situation never turned me on, the way it was handled. The war was fought from Washington, DC, which is never a good thing. There was too much politics involved. There was no way to fight a war over in that country when we were in a defensive position all the time. It went on for six years. When we pulled out, all the poor people who were on the American side were annihilated, apparently.

Then we get to the Desert War and Iraq. At the time Saddam was not the best guy, but we should have been over in Afghanistan where al-Qaeda was, with the 9/11 attacks. I think we got sidetracked in Iraq and we are paying for it now. We're still screwing around in Afghanistan. The old story, when you are in these countries there's the "Yankee Go Home" business. It always ticks me off. We try to bring the world over to our line of thinking, some of the countries don't want to do it that way. They have been fighting among themselves for thousands of years.

The difference between [North and South Korea] is just unbelievable. I feel sorry for the North Koreans; they have no say in the matter. But South Korea is a spectacular country now. When people say we have won a war, what is the price we have had to pay and what did you win? Matter of fact I just got my VFW magazine for this month and it is all about the Korean War. 60th anniversary. In the library there's not too much material out on Korea or even in the bookshops. For World War II there are thousands of books.

I personally felt that [the Korean] war was worth fighting for. The way it turned out I think it was worth it, but at the same time we ended up with a stalemate. The Korean War and the Vietnam War, a lot of people didn't want to go. I could see why they didn't. At the same time we had the Cold War going on. The Russians were quite chummy with the Chinese in the Korean War, they were all Communist nations. It didn't quite pan out, and that helped sever relations between the Russians and the Chinese.

Every once in a while the North Koreans start making all kinds of threats. I don't really feel they would get very far … Americans still have 28,000 troops there. The old people remember we saved their country, the young people are yelling "Yankee Go Home."

When you start reminiscing about it, you like to think of some of the humorous things, some of the other things you try to forget. We got shelled one night, and shrapnel hit someone quite bad in the face. Half of his jaw was hanging down, and I was working on that. But he had a wedding ring on his finger. It was surprising: he was in a state of shock but he was mumbling and I made out what he was saying, he kept saying his finger hurt. I could see it was swelling up. He had a ring, there was no way I could cut it off, but that was hurting. I was thinking, it's a good thing you don't know what your face looks like! I think he survived—he wasn't too bad off. I laugh about that now.

Bill Fellows, born in 1931 in Northfield, Massachusetts, told me when we were editing his text that he could tell I was ultra-liberal. I asked how he knew I was "ultra" and we laughed. Bill holds views that I might call "ultra" conservative, but the reader can decide. Bill worked in construction after his service and is disabled with PTSD. He wished he could have fought in World War II, but he was too young. He wanted to volunteer for Vietnam, but was not inducted. Bill did get to fight in Korea, and participated in some of the worst battles of that war.

I am a patriot and a warrior. I trained in 1947 specifically for a war, and when I was sixteen, they started a war for me! I didn't get to the Second World War. I felt so bad about it. When I went in the Army I lied about my age, of course. I went from being a farmer. I never had a hamburger in my life until I got in the army. I never had all new clothes, new boots, it was mine, I had a whole bag full. I wanted to stop working for nothing: I never got any money for [farming]. The army paid me $58 a month, and I didn't need anything. I didn't smoke cigarettes, I chewed tobacco, I got everything I wanted, good food, and they taught me how to live.

I just learned an awful lot about surviving, and every weapon they had, I learned. I could use explosives when they first came out with C-4. You can't be at war except *during* the war. In July 1950, I reenlisted for three years. I had signed up, I got my opening, and

I had experience [but] not a lot of rank…. I got there and I didn't go with the 82nd Airborne or the 1st, or the 24th Division, I didn't go with a unit, I got into a battalion they assigned me to, a division they assigned me to.

The first real whack I was on was Triangle Hill. I think we went up there seven times before we owned it. Goddamn Chinamen! They had infiltrated and taken our property, and they kept doing it. Bayonet, break their neck, anything, we killed so many they couldn't get rid of them. All of a sudden I realize that I'm killing kids. I'm killing little 60-pound people that didn't come up that hill with anything but ammunition. This was Mao Zedong's group.

Mao sent people in with sneakers in the middle of the winter. Most of them were frozen. They were his volunteers, fifteen years old, maybe not as old. After we found out what they were, it didn't feel good killing little kids. They had uniforms, quilted pajamas, all one color, grey-brown. That's all they had, sneakers, and their hands, holding ammunition in a case. They ran out of grenades, and *we* had none left.

Triangle Hill, that was in the Kumhwa Valley, in October [Operation Showdown, 1952]. I didn't know I was hit until I couldn't see anything. I was trying to get up a trench, and I couldn't see. I got hit with shrapnel mostly, they fixed my nose and they gave me new teeth. They pulled me back in a chopper, and they pulled a lot of the little pieces of shrapnel out of my face, gave me some shots, I slept I don't know how long. I didn't like it because a lot of my comrades were laying there dead and dying, so I went back and I couldn't find my outfit.

I got whacked again, but it didn't count because I didn't get to go to the hospital. They take care of you on line. They brought the Purple Hearts, I got one. I went to the Mobile Army Surgical Hospital (MASH) by helicopter. I had to steal a jeep to get back and find my outfit. The next day I was out of there, there were guys that needed that bed and were bleeding to death. I am there, nothing wrong with me, a couple scratches.

I loved recon because it usually takes a partner, you separate, you both get your communication. You don't use walkie-talkies, you make communications where you can see each other with your hands, let the other guy know what's going on. It gets cold, you've got to conceal yourself, you're going to be there maybe two-three days, you bring rations with you. You don't eat too much because you don't want to have to get rid of too much. Liquids are the big deal, [a] couple of canteens will last three days with no problem. [*How can you go three days on that?*] You've got little packages, two crackers, and a tin full of peanut butter.

If you could get your hands on beans, don't take them. We could smell them out—any beans at all, you would fart for a week. No mouthwash, chewing gum, alcohol, and cigarettes were only for an idle moment—the smell is dangerous. You don't wear clean clothes because the smell is identifiable. If it was below zero, you kept inside your field jacket your extra stockings. You always carried four pairs of stockings, you had to change stockings in the cold weather three times a day. Then you put the old stockings inside and you stink.

It was an experience. We walked Pork Chop Hill with our guys. We didn't have to go up on the first match, I was glad of that, I would have gotten killed. We watched that place, we walked it six times, six four-hour shifts, sometimes they go 36 hours. Then we make all the reports when we got back. They couldn't call, [the enemy] could hear. If you're down in the valley, you've got to cross the little river, you'd be in pine bush. You've got glasses [binoculars] and if you were careful you could use them [but] you've got to stay in the shade. You could see those bastards digging on the top of the hill.

Then all of a sudden there might be only two or three, and then you follow up the hill, and you see they're climbing, they place things on the top of the hill. A lot of dirt flying and you could tell they are laying out boobies [booby traps], the kind with wire you've got to go over. They're digging in. You get as close as you can at night, to test the wiring, get a close look. What they had done is they took a hand grenade, and they had it on strings, they pull the string. There were enough of them to go over the hill and trample us to death.

I was so glad I didn't go up on the first run. They lost 60 percent of two companies, over a hundred men in twelve hours. We were killing Chinamen. We had already gotten all the North Koreans, we killed them all, or put them on Koje-Do Island. You've heard of that? That was a prison we kept about 80,000 gooks on. They were soldiers, but they were rag-tag, they couldn't fight Americans.

November, I wasn't here, before Thanksgiving, November 19th in '50, my friend knew the Chinese were coming en masse, they attacked. He told me he could hear the bugles twelve hours before they came. They came on horses. Can you imagine you're standing there looking down the valley and that's what he told me he'd seen. That was the Yalu River, for twenty miles easy. "We had scopes," he said, "and the foliage changed from one day to the next, the scopes were not that good, the foliage was *people*. They moved 300,000 people in, overnight they did." They ran these poor bastards all the way to Pusan, Chosin [Reservoir], I wasn't there. Many, many of my friends, their spirits are still there.

Then we went to Old Baldy. These were totally worthless pieces of real estate. They overlooked nothing but some of the Kumhwa Valley. Right behind these two little knobs was a big mountain called Papasan. They came out of there, we kept watching at night when we are on recon, it looked like a parade. They had trenches dug, and that is on Old Baldy, and we are watching Pork Chop 2, and I couldn't believe it. I said Jesus, I hope they give us the atom bomb, but Truman wouldn't do that.

General MacArthur wanted the atom bomb and wanted to drop six of them in China, on every major city in China. He said with the proper hook-up we'll be on the doorstep of Mao's town in one year. I thought it was fantastic. They're Communist, hey! I'm now totally against communism, socialism likewise. Old Baldy, they must have lost three or four companies, maybe 800 men, and did you know there are still over 5,000 unknown missing American and UN soldiers from Korea? The North Koreans are not good, atom bomb them immediately. I wouldn't truck with them for two seconds. There would be an atom bomb in every major city in that country.

MacArthur was a god. He was everything I dreamed of, commanding this massive organization of people. Settling a whole nation [Japan], turning them into democracy. Another one of my other great heroes was General Eisenhower. He was the first person I voted for. My father disowned me because [Eisenhower] was a Republican. Don't mention "Republican" in *my* house. He did so much for America. You would have come up here on a dirt road if it wasn't for General Eisenhower. He planned the highway system, built the system, an architect, and a commander.

I went over in September or October 1952. The day of the ceasefire I walked down to the company command post, I had a knapsack on, a fatigue uniform, and I was the only one in the platoon who had a Siemens transoceanic radio. I got it off a guy who got killed; he told me I could have it if he got killed. I left it at the CP. Lieutenant Vara was going to take over the company, he was an ex-Marine. This was Shore's company, 31st Infantry [Regiment, 7th Infantry Division]. I was with them a lot, we got along good, and they had good patrols.

If there was no bruise, the medic might give you a whack of morphine. With no patrols, nothing going on, three or four guys would take a whack off of this little ampule. We had our guards, it wasn't out of the ordinary. When we'd done that, they used to have the heavy stuff. The golds [Dexedrine] that you could sniff, we'd make tea out of them. You've got no booze, the officers got all the booze.

[*Shows me his scrapbook*]. I earned three bronze stars. Alton Fellows, PFC, 31st regiment, 7th infantry division, Republic of Korea, 30 October 1953. I was discharged but I reenlisted. For wounds received as a result of hostile actions. They lost my other records in the fire in St. Louis, MO. [A 1973 fire at the National Personnel Records Center destroyed millions of official records of servicemen discharged from November 1, 1912 to January 1, 1960.] The bronze stars I believe signify Triangle, Pork Chop, and Old Baldy. FT 3, I was a third class specialist, honorable discharge, January 15, 1957. Total active service: five years.

The Korean War, I was glad when they finished because I had just done enough killing. It never bothered me until I quit construction. About a year after that, I'm waking up smelling dead bodies. This would go on for about a year and I used to go walk at night, but it wouldn't go away. I've been awake four days sometimes. I got the pacemaker in 2000, so probably this was 2002, 2003. I wasn't drinking any more. I went up to White River Junction— that was my hospital, when I came back from Korea, they just opened it up. I wasn't physically sick, I couldn't sleep. I joined the Greatest Generation Group. I went to see shrinks for three years, and [the Army] gave me 100 percent [disability], delayed PTSD.

We shouldn't be in Afghanistan, we should be in Pakistan. They're going to have their problems whether we like it or not, they don't want a democracy, they want to be like they are. Give them factories to build stuff in. We're wasting our money with them. In Vietnam we didn't lose the war—the politicians lost the war for us.

I'm afraid of what's happening now. We're getting beaten by a bunch of rag-tag bums. They are on a mission that they believe in. Muslims as a rule, they are radicals, and they don't believe the same way as we believe. They go to Allah, and he gives them 21 virgins. In Iraq, we pulled out too quick, they're going to have [a] revolution. You're not going to stop these people.

In '52, they sent us a whole bunch of inexperienced black soldiers in Korea, they were quite capable, but they had no experience, truck drivers… I had a squad of nine men, I got six black guys. And to top it off, they gave me three ROKs. They didn't know anything, and they couldn't speak English. The black guys were so scared… some of them had never fired an M-1. In Korea, mostly lieutenants running companies, that's 150 guys. Vietnam was the hairiest one, because they didn't know how to fight it. They dropped guys in jungles that couldn't read a compass. They had generals that could not command. Westmoreland was a total failure.

I never had a close friend from the war because I never knew anybody who lived. I lived. I was the longest in my company when I left. My whole platoon that I went into was gone in a week.

Not only did Colonel Donald Ryan fly in Europe (see his World War II account, page 62), then Korea, he also piloted the last mission of the Korean War in 1953. He later flew with the Strategic Air Command, including during the Cuban Missile Crisis. He holds strong opinions about America's wars since World War II. He was commander of two B-52 wings, one at Seymour Johnson and one at Westover Air Force Base. He also became a close friend of a well-known North Korean defector MiG-15 pilot who now lives in the United States.

I joined the Minnesota Air National Guard because I had always wanted to be a fighter pilot. [*Shows pictures on the wall.*] That's a P-51 Mustang, the top fighter in the world at that time, I flew that for seven years, 1946–52. And that's me on alert, I'm sitting on the wing of a P-51, see the guns there. We were recalled to active duty. I'd always dreamed of being a fighter ace, so I applied for F-86 jets in the Korean War. When I opened my big mouth and asked for fighters, they sent me to B-29s because I had flown four-engine in World War II. I flew combat missions on Okinawa, and I flew the last combat mission in the Korean War, a bombing mission.

They assigned me to an airplane, the *Command Decision*, a B-29. This is a picture of the *Command Decision* when we went out to fly on that last day of the war. They took a picture of the airplane because they planned that it would be in the Air Force Museum in Dayton, Ohio. After we flew it, they took it around the country and showed it off and that's a picture of it with the wings off in a bond drive after the war. "The crew that flew the last combat mission in this airplane is Captain Donald Ryan"—that's me and my crew.

We were called to the Air Force Museum and the Commanding General of Wright-Patterson [Air Force Base] pinned another medal—the Air Medal—on all of my crew. That's me as the pilot, [that's] the copilot, navigator, radar man, bombardier, engineer, radio operator, and these were all gunners. That was my top gunner, and that was my tail gunner. It's interesting to note, the tail gunner was nineteen years old at that time; after the war he became a banker.

[That same gunner] was at a convention one day, [and] he met a man that was a former enemy, a MiG-15 fighter pilot. The MiG pilot's [American] name is Ken Rowe and he has written this book, *A MiG-15 to Freedom: Memoir of the Wartime North Korean Defector Who First Delivered the Secret Fighter Jet to the Americans in 1953* by No Kum-Sok [his Korean name]. Here's an [inscription] that Ken wrote: "*To Colonel Don Ryan, Former B-29 pilot during the Korean War although we undoubtedly shared the same skies over the Yalu, I am grateful that we never met at that time. Please accept this book with my best wishes, Ken Rowe.*"

I value very much his inscription there. Ken came up to my birthday last year and we exchange visits a lot. We're very good friends. I own a home in Florida, too. This is a newspaper article on the visit last year: "Former Foes, Now Good Friends." Ken surrendered in South Korea. See, I flew the last mission on July 18, 1953, and it was in September that Ken [diverted his plane] to American sources. It was lucky he wasn't killed because it was an enemy airplane, and he landed at Seoul, Korea. There's quite a story there.

I can describe the last mission in Korea. We were in Okinawa, that's when they assigned me to *Command Decision*; each airplane had a name. I named mine *Margie*, in honor of my wife, but *Margie* was sick, so instead of flying *Margie* they assigned me to *Command Decision*. It was an old homestead airplane, been in the war since day one. It had been over the target 120 times. Because I was going to fly its 121st mission, it was potential newspaper business, that's why they took the pictures of it. It was at night, we were briefed about the target, and they said, "We don't expect many fighters at night but we do expect 185 guns over the target." It was MiG-15s, an airfield, Sinuiju.

The reason they wanted us to go up there is because the war was almost ending, that was July 18. We were still authorized for combat that day, but after the 18th nobody was allowed to bring any arms into Korea. They were in the process of negotiating and signed a cease-fire on July 27, 1953. The North Koreans were moving all the airplanes and equipment they could into North Korea, because when the negotiations began, there was no more input of weapons authorized, [so] they moved all these MiGs. That's why Ken Rowe, my friend, was on the ground, and said they were hauling them across the Yalu on boats to get them over to Sinuiju. They wanted to have as many arms as they could if the war went on. That gave them a chance to do that without being attacked.

We dropped fragmentation bombs, forty bundles of bombs, and each bundle would have about twenty fragmentation bombs. We carried 38 500-pounders and a photoflash in the front and a photoflash at the end. On a night mission, the photoflash would illuminate so our intelligence would be able to look at the pictures and estimate what the damage was. Once that thing left the bomb bay at about 300 feet it would disintegrate and it would become a cluster of bombs. Instead of dropping 40 500-pound bombs, we probably ended up dropping a thousand bombs when they were all disbursed. They would detonate 75 feet off the ground, *boom*, and they would destroy the MiGs, we would destroy them with ball-bearings. It was successful because we had about fifteen or eighteen B-29s that bombed that target. And that was the last mission of the war. We later found out that we had destroyed over forty MiGs.

We used to come from Okinawa, pass over an island just south of Korea called Cheju-Do, about 200 miles away. When we got over Cheju-Do, I could see the top of a round ball, and as we got closer, the ball rose above the horizon, and pretty soon there was a ball that we could see about a hundred miles away. It was about a mile in diameter, solid flak. That was over Sinuiju airfield on the southern bank of the Yalu River, which was our target.

We had to turn in and when we went right through that stuff, *boom*, *boom*, *boom*, we could read our checklists by the flak bursts around us. On the ground, they would anticipate where we were going to be, the enemy would have their antiaircraft guns. They sometimes had 150 antiaircraft guns around the target. It would just form a ball, a solid ball a mile in diameter that you fly right through. Any place you turned, a bomb burst, below you, above you, all over. That affected some people. In fact it scared the hell out of me. That was the heaviest flak I've ever seen in my life, anywhere. The target was there, and you're going right over the target. You couldn't say, "Well, they are shooting too much flak, I am going to drop the bomb somewhere else." When you're assigned to a target, you have what they call an IP, initial point, and from the initial point to the target, you do not deviate, that's the unwritten law. You fly right straight up to the target and release your bombs. But very few incidents are like that.

After that, I flew airborne alert for several years, from Griffith Air Force Base, Eglin Air Force Base, [and] Ramey Air Force Base in Puerto Rico. Two pilots, sitting in the seat for 35 hours, all over Europe, flying the circle of Russia, the perimeter of Russia, and we fly for 35 *hours*, wide awake. Have you ever been up for 35 hours? And have to be continuously, ultimately alert? If you had ever thought you were tired, you weren't tired. We'd do a night refueling, another refueling after we went around the Mediterranean, and get enough gas to come back.

That was secret and we had priority of the air, no commercial airplane ever flew around with us. They couldn't fly at our altitudes, it was restricted airspace. We would fly at 36,000 to 38,000 feet and we would start in Spain, fly around Israel, come back around the perimeter of Russia, meet another airplane over the Strait of Gibraltar, and fly from there home. Thirty-five hours. In the bomb bay of airborne alert, we would have four 1.2 megaton bombs. Now the bombs that were dropped on Nagasaki and Hiroshima were 25 kiloton—lady fingers! We had 1.2 *megaton* bombs, and each missile had a 1.2 megaton bomb. We would fly around and listen to SAC (Strategic Air Command) headquarters, and if they had told us to go…

In fact, during the Cuban Missile Crisis, my takeoff might be 3 o'clock in the morning. My wife always made breakfast for me, we'd have to pre-flight the airplane, and then they gave us a meal. We had steak, potatoes, and eggs regardless of what time of the day or night, a complete supper meal. We'd eat that and then we'd have our bellies full. My tail gunner would have to get out of the seat to put it into an electric oven, and we'd have about three flight lunches in flight.

[*What do you do about going to the bathroom?*] In the bathroom, in those days it was all men, we had a funnel that was vented to the outside, you had to be careful how far you stuck it in there, because it would suck, you pull it out, anyway. In 35 hours in the air, we never, if you will, pooped. We could in a great emergency, but nobody ever did. We've got coffee to keep awake.

On the day of the Cuban missile crisis, when Kennedy and Khrushchev were having their interchange back and forth, and on that day my target was Moscow. If we'd have dropped a 1.2 megaton bomb on Moscow, it would be wiped completely off the face of the earth. We had a go box, it was a locked box, the radar man, only he knew the combination, I had a lock and only I knew the combination. Nobody else did. If we ever had to go to war, we would go down in turn to that box and I'd unlock my lock and he'd unlock his lock, we would open it up and it would give us our target. It was top-secret crypto, as high as you can get in secrecy in the military. That's if we would have gone to war.

And what we would have done is we had what they called a suicide switch. If we were told to go to war and we'd start on our target, we'd flick on that suicide switch, so that if the airplane ever crashed, all the bombs would immediately detonate too. We never had to initiate it because we never went to war, but we were briefed on what to do in case we had to. We have post-strike bases in Europe. We would drop our bombs on Moscow, for example, then we would climb to 55,000 feet in the B-52 to save fuel to get to our destination. We would land in Arabia or somewhere like that.

It was a tense situation in the world. Here, all of a sudden Khrushchev had established missile stands in Cuba! They were within easy reach of any target in the United States. Luckily, a U-2 pilot identified that and reported it, then Kennedy and Khrushchev got back and forth. That day, Kennedy had told Khrushchev that any attack on any place in North or South America would be considered a direct attack on the United States with full retaliation. Full retaliation would be me and all the gang dropping the bombs on them.

We would have wiped Russia off the face of the earth. [*We could have received some of their bombs.*] Yeah, but all the B-52s were airborne at that time and they could fire all the missiles of the United States, nothing could stop us, the B-52s. We would have eliminated Russia. [*They would have bombed the United States.*] They both knew that. Khrushchev knew that—he gave up, it would have been the end of Russia and probably most of the United States. We would have been living like the Stone Age. We had sufficient bombs and targets to eliminate Russia. Period. Not just *bomb* Russia, *eliminate* it.

[*What was your view of MacArthur's desire to bomb North Korea and China?*] He was successful in going past the 38th parallel, we were having some success with our fighters, the F-86ers. I think that he did pretty well in eliminating the Japs in all the other islands, to end World War II, and then he got over-confident. I think Truman made a wise move in replacing him because we would have been beyond our capability, maybe. You couldn't occupy a land as vast as China, it's just too complex, too many people, too many areas, different languages. It would have been very difficult, if not impossible, to do it.

Vietnam was going on when I was wing commander. My KC-135 refueling tankers were supporting the Vietnam fighters. I think we overextended ourselves, I don't think it was well planned. I criticize McNamara and others for the use of the strategic weapons that we had. Had they gone in, well, I wasn't a general then to run the show, I would tell you what I would have done. I would have let everybody hide in the woods, in the trees as they did. Forget about them. I would have bombed the harbors, I would have bombed the roads, and I would have isolated that country completely. I would have cut them off from the outside world. They would have come out and given up. But as it is, we are fighting these people in the jungle—we're fighting *their* war, which they are highly skilled at doing.

I think we made a hell of a mistake by allowing the people in Washington to direct the tactical activity of the bombers. A friend of mine was a B-52 controller and he was in the command post on the ground. They'd get a report that a complete division of troops were being moved into an area, *a division*, that's a lot of men.

They'd call ahead and tell [Washington] about the movement of this division to the woods. It would take three days or four days to get approval to bomb it. In the meantime they are a hundred miles away, *now* we get authority to bomb the space they'd been in, and we did! Ineffective. I thought it was very poorly run. [*The Vietcong?*] I think that would have dissipated. They can't fight each other, or aid each other, leave them alone.

At one time when I was at Eglin, I was offered a chance to fly a C-46, a huge transport airplane. They called all of the pilots in to a top-secret briefing, *top secret*, there were guards at the door and when we walked in, they closed the door. We immediately raised our hand and were sworn to secrecy, we would never tell anything or anyone about that meeting, and we didn't. In that meeting, they had all of the B-52 pilots and copilots, and the CIA started to brief us. They briefed us on our ability to fly C-46s in Laos, and we would fly in supplies. They would open up the doors and drop supplies because they were being starved to death in Laos, the other side of Vietnam.

We would actually resign our commission, we would be civilians, so that if we ever got shot down, we wouldn't be caught as an enemy. Our family could stay at Eglin, in the house, we would get the same pay, plus $50,000 a year extra for going to Vietnam and flying C-46s. So we would have our Air Force pay and $50,000. I have two daughters, and that was a big deal. We went out, sworn to secrecy forever, 'til that mission was over. Two of my friends went over and they flew, that was 1971, because they were starving the poor people in Laos. I had an opportunity to do that but I wanted to fly B-52s and I wanted to be a general—I always had that in the back of my mind.

[*Why are we in Iraq, Afghanistan, and are they winnable?*] My thoughts are this: first of all, bad intelligence, Bush, Powell, they got bad advice. Now, Powell was honest because he interpreted the situation from the advice he received. I think Bush made a mistake, he over-extended himself *after* going in to get Saddam Hussein. When he toppled him, we should have withdrawn. The situation over there is so complex, good God, they have so many religions, beliefs, and everything, I don't think they will ever settle down. It keeps extending and extending and extending. They're talking about leaving in a winning way. Well, I think they ought to eat crow, get the people out of there, and forget about it, and let the Iraqis continue in their personal strife. That's my thought.

After we hung Saddam, I think that was enough. We should have said good-bye. Because they admitted at that time that there were no other weapons of mass destruction in there. Once they found that out, we should have gotten out of there because it is inevitable that it transitions into another problem. [*Iraq veterans?*] I think when they are interviewed they are loyal soldiers, military men. One thing you never, ever do as a military man is admit defeat or anything like that because you are there to support whatever your higher-ups direct you to do. When you do what you are told to do, you feel good about *that*. But you might not agree with the mission at hand.

I belong to a social club, we meet every week and have a discussion about the political aspects in this world. We discuss Iraq. It is generally agreed by all the members that it's a futile effort. You step on one bug and another comes out. It's inevitable, the failure, you'll never win. The suicide bombers, we can't understand that kind of philosophy. They feel if they kill themselves they will be rewarded with bunches of maidens. It's the new wrinkle.

[*What keeps us there?*] I think it's the continuation of an unknown because every time we say we received some success in one department over there, dang, we get another outbreak of another religious sect coming in. It's too complex! And they think much differently than you or I. Inevitable. If we can figure out a way to get out of there without embarrassing ourselves, I think we should get out regardless of how we do it.

[*If so many people know it may not be won, who doesn't know?*] I think you're talking about the desires of the generals to proceed and advance, just as I and any buck private want to be corporal and so forth. I think you're talking about generals having the same desires. We want to continue to advance, as a result, they don't want to be associated with a failure. They want to have a good rating from the boss above.

[*Does General Petraeus believe we can win this war?*] He's suspect along with the rest of them. He is worried about advancing, we all are, we're all selfish, he wants to get more and more. Maybe after he retires he wants to be the president. That's the motivation behind every human being, basically, anybody who gets promoted in rank and position, aspires to get to the next higher level. I don't care *who* you are, inwardly, that's your thoughts. That's what Petraeus is thinking about, I've always suspected that.

Any of those big shots want to go one step higher. "If I had only tried, I could have been"…the saddest words of all, what might have been. [*Afghanistan?*] I admire the Russians for having the courage to withdraw and say they made a mistake. I think that's what we ought to do there. Even with Obama, who said the troops are going to be out in such-and-such a time, he just authorized 30,000 more people to go in. He doesn't want to give up. I wonder why, what we *want* to win, win *what?* I've always wondered what we are over there winning for.

In regard to World War II, I think that was a worthwhile effort on the Allies' part. Hitler was obviously a crazy man. When he was developing a new Reich, he was imposing his will on Poland, he was berserk. He'd gotten delusions of grandeur, he lost hold of common sense. So it was necessary. World War II was a good, worthwhile effort on the Allies' part. Korea was not exactly a parallel to it, but I think we were trying to save a part of the country that was sensible, whereas the North was more driven by ideology. I think that they were imposing their will on the good people in the South. About Korea, I felt—not that I was really thinking politically, just as a soldier—when we accomplished [it] and the war was over, I felt that it was a job well done. All the other wars have a political aspect.

THREE
VIETNAM: THE LOST WAR

8,744,000	Served 1964–75*
58,220	Died 1964–73*
47,434	Killed in Action*
153,303	Wounded, hospitalized*
150,341	Wounded, not hospitalized*
1,713	Missing in Action**

*DOD figures compiled by the Congressional Research Service,
26 February 2010*
**DOD Missing Personnel Office*

Introduction

THE WAR AT THE END OF THE TUNNEL

The enveloping sound of the Vietnam War is the helicopter—Marines, Army, infantry, pilots, doctors, all hear the sound of the helicopter, hovering, transporting, inserting, extracting, evacuating, crashing, burning. Veterans never forget that sound. Over the helicopters are fixed-wing airplanes of all varieties, reconnaissance planes at the highest level, bombers, A-1s, many strata of flight that descend and ascend according to a choreographed plan that repeats itself again and again over the miles of sky and the kilometers of ground in Vietnam.

Beneath the helicopters are the land and people of Vietnam: a lush triple-canopied jungle, and also a brown, defoliated jungle. Under these dense trees or in these open plains, people move on the rivers, deltas, rice paddies, highlands. There are the villages of hooches with flammable straw roofs, farmers in conical hats and black pajama pants. These are the people of Vietnam trying to survive between aerial war, ground attacks, and intrusions from all sides into what used to be a hum of agricultural and commercial life. Intruders include the South Vietnamese government, its police, its armies, and the Vietcong, the old Vietminh, the insurrectionary combatants, the North Vietnamese Army, the South Vietnamese Army, many armies and many governments, domestic and foreign, whose political and military actions are ceaseless.

Clusters of humanity are also housed on military bases: rear bases, forward bases, landing zones, hospitals, hooches for Westerners, Quonset huts, and sand-bag bunkers. Here are the foreign intruders with their endless insertions, extractions, firepower, napalm, defoliants, flying aircraft that strafe, burn, sniff the jungle for human scent and traces, searching by day, pausing at night. There is no safety in Vietnam, no respite, no end to foreign occupation and endless internecine fighting.

The Ho Chi Minh Trail is a superhighway of war, a flowing river of materiel, men and women, new combatants, endlessly extending this war. The Trail attracts Army Special Forces, Asian mercenaries, trained dogs, pilots without identification. It lures American troops into the neighboring countries of Cambodia and Laos through whose (neutral) territory the Trail deviates on its way south. Some of the fighting around the Trail, therefore, is secret, unacknowledged, unrecorded, and Americans captured there have their own prisons.

The people of Vietnam are forced to accommodate the demands of the various players with guns. The allegiance of whole villages swings by day and night between the warring sides. The terrain can also be inhospitable: hilly and mountainous, it makes for difficult landings and takeoffs for the ubiquitous helicopters. Vietnam is often hot, humid, wet, with soggy rice fields and rivers. The area is saturated with war: about half the size of France, somewhat larger than Italy, it has absorbed more bombs than blanketed the whole arena of World War II.

Vietnam broke ranks with the wars of the 1940s and 1950s. It began in secrecy, and before anyone had been informed and fully appreciated what was happening, it was already established. A decade after Korea, a war against communism was again being fought in Asia (this time at the 17th rather than the 38th parallel), but it lacked the conviction of the two previous wars. Some veterans of Vietnam feel that suing for peace before we had exhausted ourselves further in the war effort was a sellout by the political leaders who had started the war in the first place. Negotiating for peace without victory underscored that the US fight had become futile. By then four American presidents had been involved, beginning with Eisenhower and Kennedy, through Johnson and Nixon. No president wanted to lose the war, so no president could abandon the effort while we still weren't winning it.

Vietnam was fought on both sides for the hearts and minds of the populace. Although the supporting cast was the same as in Korea (Communist China and the USSR vs. the US and its allies), it was less a war against communist foreign players (such as supported the North Korean army), as it was against local communists. The ideology was on the ground, mobile, spreading, so the fight was against a local communism that could cross borders throughout Indochina and prove the domino theory. The ideology was personified in Ho Chi Minh, who was clearly committed to a cause, be it communism or nationalism.

In Vietnam the US had as allies a series of leaders, and whatever our statesmen thought of them, we could not abandon them—and they could not abandon us. Diem did fall out of favor, and was assassinated and replaced, but then his replacements had to watch out on two fronts: danger came from both the US and in-country enemies. We came to accept, even laud, whomever we got in the serial South Vietnamese presidency. Our leadership felt we couldn't afford to have our war fail because it was a larger fight against communism and our global communist adversaries. We therefore couldn't allow the local leaders to negotiate a peace or compromise domestically, because that would undercut our larger mission.

The Vietnam War engendered a national debate but it remains mired in place, time, and a different generation of soldiers. Public opinion eventually moved the US government to abandon its ten-year effort. The reasons the war's opponents cited at the time included: the war's physical impact (such as Agent Orange) was overkill; killing civilians of both sexes and all ages was wrong; our ally was up to no good; we were not directly threatened by North Vietnam and its supporters; saturation bombing did not work; and we were not winning on the battlefield. While these were major arguments in the debate, they have faded with the end of the war. Vietnam remains, however, a pivotal war: it was a post-Korean effort to forestall communism, based on the outcome of World War II, but we did not win it.

THE NARRATIVES

Blaming Vietnam soldiers and veterans for the conduct of the war avoided the larger questions of the *official* conduct of the war. During the war, soldiers felt personally betrayed to have their country turn them into symbols of the conflict into which they were drafted. They were being accused of atrocities by the public, their own comrades, and by themselves, all of which was a cause of great suffering. Some veterans talk about having been spat on and accused of killing babies when they returned to military installations. Though the installations were actually closed to civilians, there were demonstrations to greet homeward-bound soldiers outside bases and airports on the West Coast. One could also take personally what happened to others. Discharged soldiers and those serving on bases often took off their uniforms in public. Some veterans became outspoken critics, while others protected themselves by not allowing their identity as Vietnam soldiers and veterans to surface in social situations or the work place.

A number of veterans note that it was demoralizing and downright scary when Robert Kennedy and Martin Luther King were both assassinated in 1968, the height of the war and the year of the Tet offensive. They watched as civilians came to blows at the Democratic convention in Chicago, also in 1968, and could barely believe that US cities were actually exploding in flames when Martin Luther King, Jr. was shot. Well-publicized draftees or potential draftees were moving to Canada and Sweden, and honorably discharged veterans were joining the antiwar movement. What was a deployed soldier to think?

Vietnam was also a war in which a soldier could not always recognize the enemy. North Vietnamese armed forces wore uniforms and acted like traditional foes, but the Vietcong were infiltrators, insurgents, inheritors of the Vietminh's liberation fight against the French colonials. This war "messed with the minds" of both sides. It also did not progress.

The soldiers and pilots almost all realized that they were doing the same thing over and over again, with the only "progress" made in the number of killed on both sides, even when it became clear that relative numbers of killed would not determine the outcome. Bombing North Vietnam did not stop their fight against South Vietnam, and the Vietcong did not slow down. Neither side stopped or paused meaningfully until it became clear that the time had come to negotiate a peace and abandon the effort and the sacrifice made by so many.

What the narrators focus on most is the core predicament of Vietnam: there was no overall military strategy of gaining, or even holding, land, which had in two world wars and Korea justified the massive loss of lives. There was also no local, on-the-ground, military or political strategy to win, in great part because the fight against communism was global. Our South Vietnamese ally was unsavory and incompetent in the eyes of our own men, who had to fight with and for them. If the local army, police, and government were not winning the domestic fight for hearts and minds (as the Buddhist resistance and Vietcong penetration indicated) how could our soldiers do so? Many, as we will see, tried hard, in the midst of the fighting, to do right by the local population.

In addition to deprivation, bravery, decency, and great losses, we see that soldiers continued to fight hard for their comrades, and for themselves, to survive. We also find out that alcohol and drugs were increasingly prevalent among all ranks, just as they were prevalent on the home front. With the military making alcohol available and inexpensive to officers, and the local Vietnamese population supplying cheap drugs to enlisted troops, one could literally zone out of the war zone when military tasks were done.

In this quandary, much of the rationale for the war turned to saving American military lives. The helicopter pilots you will hear from had as their business inserting troops, waiting, and then evacuating the wounded. They risked their lives daily to save the lives of other Americans. Many soldiers recognized that this important purpose was also a very short-term effort, and that the larger effort on behalf of the US government was failing. They knew that a failing war would earn them little gratitude or praise when they came home. This was a very hard war.

4

ON THE GROUND: ARMY, MARINE CORPS, SURGEON, AND RED CROSS

Dan Walsh was born in Springfield, Massachusetts in 1941 and recently retired as a veterans' services officer. A Marine, he was badly wounded in battle in 1966 a few months after he arrived, having fought almost continuously since his deployment. His son is a Marine Lieutenant Colonel: "29 years to the day that I got shot in Vietnam, he was commanding the same platoon I commanded, Lima Company, 2nd Platoon, 3rd Battalion, First Marines." Dan graduated from Providence College in business, and pursued a career in investments, and in a manufacturing company. His story starts with a meeting with the famous World War II, Korea, and Vietnam commander, General Jonas Platt, under whom he served.

I think you have to recognize that it took a very, very long time for Vietnam veterans to even talk about Vietnam. It was controversial, it had its detractors, and you just wanted to forget about it. Why should I tell my family the horrors that I saw and experienced? My platoon sergeant got killed, my runner got killed same day I got shot. There are some very strong memories of some great young men who didn't make it back. You say, why me? Why did I make it? Why did I turn just as he was pulling the trigger? Why did my runner kill a guy just on top of me? My platoon sergeant dies in my arms: why burden somebody with that? It's something I carry, it's within me; it will be there for the rest of my life.

See the picture up there on the wall? It's the Wellington Bar in Centerville, near Dulles Airport. That fellow there was our commanding officer at The Basic School (TBS). We were all fresh second lieutenants, his name was Jonas M. Platt. He was a colonel then. When we got to Vietnam, he was a brigadier general, the CO of Task Force Delta. I happened to have the distinction of being his reaction platoon for a couple of weeks. If anybody got in trouble in the whole Task Force Delta area, we went and got them out. So the four of us are sitting there at this bar, you could see the painting on the wall, the battle of Waterloo, and we talked about what we did. We were all wounded, we were all decorated, we had all seen some very difficult action, and he was our commander. This is two years before General Platt died in July 2000.

So I asked him, did he remember when this thing occurred and no, he didn't. I was very disappointed. Then, did you remember this? "No, I didn't, Walsh." How we had gone and rescued another platoon at night, we killed a lot of North Vietnamese, that to me was very significant. That night, coming in there and not losing anybody and having a real resounding success. And the other one was [Platt] was up in the air and he saw some Vietcong a couple of klicks away (a klick is a thousand meters). My platoon was the point of the battalion, we were in rice paddies, and I remember going along and all of a sudden I get a call from the company commander, "Hey, two (I had the second platoon, so I am "two") this is six, you are to proceed to the left, to the right," whatever his call sign was, he'd spotted some Vietcong, you're supposed to go in and get them out.

Okay, so off we go, you have two squads up and one back, we go through this village and all of a sudden I was all alone. My runner wasn't there, my radio man wasn't there, it was very thick brush, the hooches. Holy Jeepers, I took my pistol out and I put a round in the chamber, and we just kept moving through, and then I saw a couple more Marines. The sergeants and the corporals in my fire-teams and my squad leaders had all moved this thing perfectly, they came in and they got some of these VC and killed them. So this helicopter comes down, and [Platt] says, "Great job, lieutenant, you did an outstanding job." "But General, it wasn't really me, it was my sergeants and my corporals, my

Marines did this!" "Let me tell you something, Walsh, you take credit, and you take the blame. You're in charge." "Yes, sir. Aye, aye, sir." So I asked if him if remembered that.

He was a major in World War II, at Peleliu, he was at Chosin Reservoir as a lieutenant colonel, and he was now a brigadier general in Vietnam. He said, "I had a million of those occasions, every day we had something. You're talking about two things when you were there, and I was there for two years." So I was a little bit crestfallen. I said, that's unfortunate that you don't remember. It's indelible in my mind, I remember the lieutenant, we got out and were saved. You don't get any thanks, you aren't expecting it. Then you realized the bigger picture, this guy was commanding regiments and I had a reinforced platoon of Marines.

But we talked. The three of us had an awful lot of experience. Those two [men] were in the very first battle, Operation Starlite, in August '65. The big battle I got hit in was March '66, and we had landed in January. I only lasted three months before I got hit. But this was a great conversation. He told us all about his experiences and his awards, everything he did, and the man ended up a two-star general. I don't know why he didn't make lieutenant general. He was one of [Lewis] Walt's boys, a real warrior, we loved him, we thought the world of him.

I asked him, at the end of it, "You know, General, you fought in World War II, you fought in Korea, and you were here in charge here in Vietnam. Which one was the worst war?" Without a second's hesitation, he said, "Vietnam, and I am going to tell you why. You took the ground you stood on, and you had to take it over and over and over again. All those people around you, all those Vietnamese, you didn't know whether they were the enemy or they were friends. At night, did they change? Every day you fought. In the Second World War we had time, Iwo Jima was a year in preparation. Every day you people were shot at, your tension, your level of stress... and then, the way the soldier was treated when he came home." The three of us are, holy mackerel, here's a major general in the Marine Corps talking of the soldier. Soldier is all of us. Soldiering is a profession. It's an honorable profession, you have to be prepared for war all the time.

But it hit all of us. I thought that Korea would have been the worst—the cold, Chosin Reservoir, the incredible things that the

Marines accomplished there. It was 40 degrees below zero and your cheek would stick to your rifle. You would urinate and it would be frozen before it hit the ground. You have Mickey Mouse boots and 200,000 Chinese coming at you over the hills. Fox Company of the 7th Marines and the 5th Marines, the two regiments that were up there, and then our regiment, which was the 1st Marines. These men brought everybody out of Chosin Reservoir, they took all the dead, all the wounded, all the equipment. The poor Army that was on the other side, they grabbed them and took them along too after they had been decimated.

One of the wonderful things, the vehicles were laden with the dead. Not the living, so they relieved their difficulties in walking it off. They were walking to keep the circulation going too, but they carried the bodies out, eighty miles. They took every dead body—the reverence of taking every Marine out. Instead of piling them up on a big wagon, they were put on where they were number one. They brought everybody out on every piece of equipment, and they fought their way out against 200,000—more—Chinese. To me that was awful.

"No," Platt said, "Korea had its moments. The Inchon, when we landed... incidentally, the one landing you [speaking to Walsh] were at was the largest since Inchon when you landed for Operation Double Eagle." He was the head of that, he should know. "No, Korea was pretty static after that, it was a huge stalemate... And then it's World War II. All the time, we picked where we were going to fight, we picked Guadalcanal, we picked Tinian, we took Peleliu, we took Saipan, we took Guam, and Iwo Jima, we took Okinawa, but it was our choice. And we lost a lot of people, had a lot of tough situations." It was funny, he said afterwards, they had something like 40 days actual fighting in the Second World War. I was there [Vietnam] for over 40 days and we fought every day. Every day people got shot, people were wounded, you never had a chance to let your guard down.

[*Dan returns to his own Vietnam narrative about fighting the Vietcong.*] When I got shot I have no feeling in the leg. I found myself flying through the air, heard the shots afterwards. "My God, I have been shot, God damn it!" I heard myself say that. I was madder than hell. I knew the leg was hit, but there was no feeling.

"Hey, Lieutenant, how are you?". "Man, I am great now, Barth, just hearing you." So he rips my trousers, "How bad is it?" "You've got a small hole down here, oooh… some real big ones up here!" [*He laughs.*] So I say, "Okay, Patrick," he patched me all up, all the morphine was gone, I say, "How is it?" and he said, "It's bleeding there, but I stopped it."

They brought me back and the other lieutenant from the 3rd Platoon was wounded as well. His arm went up into the air, his helmet flew off, and I sat there and said, "Oh shit, you've been shot." I was watching him, I'm looking at him, it was almost like a slow motion, I still see it. The battle was so bad that it took three hours. They were shooting helicopters down. They finally got us out. Officers are always the last ones to be evacuated. I was very disturbed because I just left my men dead, ten of them were killed and twenty of us were wounded in this very intense battle.

We got on the helicopter. This big relief comes over you, but you are also thinking it's going to get shot down. All the enlisted guys had been flown out, and I'm looking at him, and it looked like he had stopped breathing and he was gray-blue. It was a good thing that I was on this side, so I leaned over, this was the bad leg, I started pumping his heart. I didn't know what I was doing but I figured CPR, got to keep that blood going.

We get to B-Med and they rush up, it's as clear as a bell, they grabbed me, I said, "No, not me, him," so they jump over me and they grab him out, and I'm thinking he's dead. All of a sudden, I hear this blood-curdling scream, I almost start crying for happiness. It was an incredible scream, that's Gene, if he could scream like that, he's going to be fine. He was. If he was seriously wounded he'd be on the hospital ship *Repose*. The next day I get a telegram, he's now in the hospital ship. It was Gene Cleaver.

Anyway, back to Vietnam: I'd been there two weeks. I was moving between my second and third squads, we were going down a highway—highway? a dirt road—troops on this side and I'm in the middle. As I'm walking, all of a sudden I caught someone looking at me. I look over and here is this woman, I don't know how old she was, she held my eyes, she wouldn't let my eyes go. As I looked at her she lifted up her left leg and she let out a stream of urine that just shocked me. Why would she do that with this terrible look on her face? Like "Get out of my country!" No men around, the women didn't trust us, you storm away, you still see her face, that betel nut, spitting and urinating.

We shouldn't have been there. It was a civil war. I saw that immediately, with that woman doing that, and the ineptitude of some of our leadership, and these people—why were they fighting, why were they so dedicated? There's Ho Chi Minh, they're fighting for something they truly, truly believe in. We're fighting and willing to give our lives because we signed a contract that said we'll do this and we'll give you our lives if you ask for it. I didn't care about Vietnam. In the Second World War, the Japs attacked us; attack them. In Afghanistan, get those goddamn Taliban, get those people that did this to us that cost us close to 3,300 lives, terrorism. Get them get them wherever they are, find them, kill them.

Vietnam, you did your job, you fought for the guys next to you, they're your brothers, you became very close. I never thought we were going to win in Vietnam. We won, but we didn't win. The politicians, LBJ, it drove him out of office. Vietnamization with Nixon, Watergate, all those things were intertwined. We won every major battle, but we lost. We won Tet, but we lost Tet. The government lied to us constantly, over and over. I didn't care. I'm a Marine, I'm leading my Marines. You give me a mission, I'm going to do it.

I liked the military, I was good at it too, I was one step ahead of the enemy, I could see things that other people couldn't see. You knew what was going to happen. It was kind of scary. January 28, 1966, I landed in Vietnam. Where I got hit was Quang Ngai, which was a couple of klicks south of the Song Tra Bong River. Thirty-seven days until I got hurt, every day we fought. It was Double Eagle and then Utah. And then, the flag of our battalion, 3rd Battalion, 1st Marines, I just delivered it up to the Springfield Museum. The first 90 days we were in seven major battles. I was only in three of them. Ninety days, major battles, two Presidential unit citations. We fought every day.

Jim Munroe was born in Boston in 1946 and is dean of Christ Church Cathedral in Springfield, Massachusetts. Jim served in the Marine Corps until he was severely injured in 1969 and evacuated. In 1984, Jim helped found a group of Vietnam veterans (now expanded to all wars and called the Veterans' Education Project) to meet and talk with each other. They also go in to middle and high schools and prisons to teach about the Vietnam War and about war more generally. He is still very active in sharing his personal story with audiences so that they can better understand the cost of war.

I was born and raised in a middle-to upper-middle class white sub-urban family. My dad went to work as treasurer of Phillips An-dover Academy. The struggle at Andover was to find acceptance somewhere. I wasn't quite smart enough, or good-looking enough, or rich enough, or popular enough, so I picked sports. That be-came my means of finding some identity and worth. I played soc-cer, hockey, and lacrosse. In 1964, just two years after Outward Bound started in the States, I went to the Colorado School and had a taste of that kind of experience, which spoke to my spirit.

Also, I was moving toward English as a focus, and in my sen-ior year I read *On the Road* by Jack Kerouac. That felt like a Bible for me; I was just gripped by it. I also was feeling that there was a call to something exciting in life and I was struggling with my studies. I wanted to go into the service. I was equating Jack

Kerouac's *On the Road*, with the Marine Corps! [*He laughs.*] I was somehow picturing the Marine Corps as a giant Outward Bound course and as a super-varsity soccer team.

I had no conception of defending my country against communist aggressors. I had no conception of being patriotic. I had no conception of issues of war and peace and it never occurred to me that I really would go to war. I just thought it would be exciting. I did my first year at Williams College. Vietnam was gearing up, this was '67, and the USMC was offering a two-year enlistment, so it seemed perfect. School seemed irrelevant and [I wanted] to do something exciting, and immediate, and full of adventure. So I enlisted.

I went to Parris Island. I can describe the first five minutes. It was July 23, 1967, at midnight, hot, hot, hot. The sign over the door said: *Through These Portals Pass Recruits for the Greatest Fighting Machine in the World*. I thought, oh, this is so cool! Out of the door walked a drill instructor who looked like the movies, twenty feet tall, shoulders twelve feet wide, Gold's Gym body, and Smokey the Bear hat tilted over his eyes. He got on the bus, and I remember what he said. "Welcome to Parris Island. If you are chewing gum you will swallow it. If you are smoking a cigarette you will extinguish it. You've got three seconds to get off this bus and two of them are up—now move."

We scrambled off the bus. There were yellow footprints painted on the ground, and we put our feet in them, which got us in four columns. Then, out of nowhere, four or five other drill instructors appeared, screaming and yelling. One of them got his nose a half-inch from my nose and screamed, and spit poured down my face. And somehow within thirty seconds I learned that those drill instructors had known about little Jim Munroe his entire life and had been spending years waiting for him to arrive because they understood that he was worthless, and the truth about Jim Munroe would be finally revealed.

Screaming and yelling, they ran us into a building and had us all stand with our backs to the wall. Then one drill instructor said, "Ready, strip," and we all took off all our clothes. So at 1 AM on a hot July night in South Carolina, fifty guys were standing at attention, naked. Nothing could make you feel more vulnerable and weak. They said don't move and they left. For several hours we stood there at attention, one guy fainted, and we just let him lie there. They came back at 5 o'clock and said, get dressed, and they herded us off to breakfast, and that was the beginning. Boot Camp was seven weeks. It had been thirteen weeks, but so many guys were getting killed in Vietnam that they shortened the training.

My military occupational specialty was artillery. I went out to California to Camp Pendleton training as a fire direction control person. There's a forward observer out in the field who sees some enemy. He gets on the phone and calls me up, miles away in a bunker, and gives me the map coordinates. Then I've got an ancient, very simple computer, plus charts and graphs, and I take his map coordinates and I change them into numbers that the howitzer can understand. Then I call up the howitzer, which is probably ten miles in another direction and give it those numbers. The howitzer shoots a shell twenty miles that lands somewhere near the enemy. The forward observer would call me up and say, 100 yards to the left, 50 yards closer in, and I change it again. Then I get on the telephone to give numbers to the guy at the howitzer who programs it.

I never in my underground bunker saw any enemy soldiers, and I also never saw the howitzer. I was isolated from that entire experience. There was a Doonesbury cartoon during Vietnam showing one of those big B-52s dropping 500-pound bombs, the huge ones, and it shows two guys in the cockpit and one of them says to the other as the bombs are dropping, "Hey, did you hear? The Knicks won by two last night." They're up there talking about basketball, having no experience of the devastation of those bombs hitting the ground. That was my experience for a while.

In Vietnam you went over all by yourself, and you came back all by yourself, and you joined a unit already in existence where people were constantly rotating out and in, so you made friends while you were there but there was no unit cohesiveness. My unit had been up in Khe Sanh, there were several people there who remembered that siege. There was a helicopter pad beside my hooch—all day long there was nothing but the sound of helicopters, but there was no war for me. Then along came Tet. I'd known about the previous year's Tet offensive, but it hadn't sunk in. Our unit got more vigilant during Tet, all over South Vietnam, attacks, not as big as Tet in '68, but still, really big.

I had gone to bed at midnight. At 2 AM on February 23, 1969, I woke up in my hooch to the sound of explosions. This is the moment in which the war stopped being an adventure. This is when it stopped being exciting. This is when everything changed. To some degree, my whole life has been shaped by that one night. Guys today are getting deployed to Iraq and Afghanistan three and four and five times. They're having an experience that I can't conceive of. I didn't have that. I just had that one night.

But the one night was horrific. I woke up and there were all these sounds, I didn't know what was going on. I remember looking up and seeing a little corner of the hooch missing and thinking, when I went to bed two hours ago that hole wasn't there. I could see stars through it. I had mosquito netting over my cot, there weren't mosquitoes, but there were rats and the netting would help keep them off. I rolled off my bunk and I got all tangled up in the mosquito netting. I felt stupid: John Wayne never got tangled up in mosquito netting. It was really hot, so I had just been sleeping in my shorts. I grabbed my gear in my arms and went outside.

Again, explosions everywhere, I didn't see anybody getting hurt, I didn't see any bad guys, just noise. There was a foxhole outside our hooch. I looked down in and there was a bunch of guys in it. They looked up and said, "Hi, Jim." I said, "Hi guys," and they said, "We're kind of full, so why don't you go to the next foxhole," and I said, "Okay". So I walked to the next foxhole, not knowing that within a little while two of those guys would be dead. I only learned that two years ago.

I got into the next foxhole and crouched down, there was one other guy in it. I put all my gear on. When I got everything on, I realized that I had forgotten two things. First of all, I had forgotten my rifle. A Marine never forgets his rifle. Not that I had any ammo—they hadn't issued any ammo. But still. In boot camp we had to pray every night, but it wasn't a prayer to God, it was for our rifle, a printed prayer "To Your Rifle." The second thing I had forgotten was my trousers. As I recall, John Wayne never forgot his trousers. So there I was in a helmet, T-shirt, flak jacket, underpants, and boots, feeling a little silly.

I started talking to this other guy who had been in Vietnam for thirteen months. He'd gone home but the Marine Corps had said to him, we've got this program if you volunteer to come back to Vietnam again for six months, then when the six months are up you can get out of the Marine Corps completely. So he'd gone home and had just come back. He'd gotten engaged while he was home and brought back pictures of his fiancée.

I don't know whether it was ten minutes or forty-five minutes, I just crouched there. I remember sensations. I remember flares going off and slowly coming down on little parachutes, creating light and flickering shadows. I was so unaccustomed to any of this, even the concept of flares during battle. I remember seeing little bits of paper floating in the air and I didn't know what that was about. I remember the smells of cordite or explosive powder, lots of yelling, explosions, and shots going off. At one point I peeked over the edge of the foxhole and couldn't see a thing.

Then, with absolutely no warning, no expectation of anything, there was in front of me in the foxhole an explosion. I learned later that a North Vietnamese soldier had thrown a grenade into the foxhole. I also learned that it was a Chi-Com grenade, a Chinese Communist grenade, a concussion grenade. It threw out some shrapnel, but was designed in an enclosed space to turn your brains into jelly. I was crouched when the explosion was in front of me.

At this point, I utterly fail to find adequate words to express that experience. The force of the explosion was so astronomically bigger than anything I'd been able to conceive of beforehand, and it was also evil in a way that's hard to describe. It's a little like if someone gets electrocuted—there's no physical pain per se in electrocution, but it's a force that's extraordinary, and it's bad, unbelievably bad. Another image that came to me later was of being a naked baby lying on a beach with a tidal wave of pure evil coming toward me and there is nothing the baby can do. The baby can't run away, the baby can't hide, the baby can't escape. There is nothing to do but just take it.

What I learned in that moment, but didn't know I learned until years later, was that I would spend the rest of my life making sure that I never made myself vulnerable like that again. I would guarantee myself not to be in a place where that could happen again. That was my way of learning to shut down and not take risks, to play it safe. When I talk with kids, we talk about the number one best way of dealing with that kind of trauma: suicide. Because then you're safe, nothing can hurt you. Drugs and alcohol are a good second best. I say to them that one of the ways I have picked is by being nice. Being nice can be a wonderful shield from being vulnerable, especially if you are a minister. It makes you look good. But it can be a hiding place as well.

Back to the experience. It didn't knock me out, I was dazed. It took some minutes for me to gain a sense of things. Presumably I was starting to go into shock. I remember feeling my arms and legs to see if they were there, and feeling that they were sticky, sensing that they were bleeding. It blew dirt under my eyelids, so it took me a little while to be able to see. The other guy had a little blood trickling out of his eye. I remember hearing someone yelling for help, and not going, and having the beginnings of guilt about that.

I yelled "Corpsman!" Somebody yelled, "Okay, here I come." This person jumped into the foxhole, when he hit the bottom of the foxhole it was like a trampoline, he just instantly jumped back out again. We were going to do something with this guy whose eye was bleeding. As I started to stand up for about a hundredth of a second, I had the momentary, fleeting, little impression out of the corner of my right eye, of something floating and then it exploded. That was the second grenade, presumably thrown by the same guy.

So it all happened again. What I learned later was that the second grenade killed the other guy. One report I read or heard was that he was decapitated by that second grenade. It's possible that his head was between me and the grenade and that his head saved my life. The grenade could have been a few inches one way or the other, and it would have killed me. I remember lying down on the floor of the foxhole, having no sense of a battle going on, just that I had been blown up. I thought I would play dead, putting my body in an odd shape thinking I would look dead, but then thinking, maybe I *am* going to die. Somebody yelled that it was okay to get out of the foxhole.

I crawled out of the foxhole in shock, and there was this dead guy lying on the ground, the first dead person I had ever seen. There was a lot of blood around his head. I didn't know we had that much blood in us. I crawled past him and I stood up, and this guy came running up to help me. He put some bandages on my legs, which instantly fell down to my ankles, and we both laughed about how ridiculous that was. I remember running, not knowing who I was running from or where I was going. Then this guy led me to the underground bunker where the fire direction control people were. I walked in and there were several people in the bunker who had been there during the entire firefight who looked at me, a *holy shit!* look.

They put me in a helicopter and flew me to the naval hospital in Da Nang. Because it was post-Tet offensive, everybody was pouring in and they were triaging. My ears were bleeding. At some point I was taken to a hospital ward, for not quite two weeks. The shock wore off some, and then I became afraid. I had not known real fear until that moment, then I learned that fear overrides everything else. With the fear came shame for being afraid, falling short of the image I had of myself. There was a ward down the hall of guys who weren't physically wounded but who had cracked up. I thought to myself that I could be there really easily.

I prayed, because before I went into the Marine Corps I had a Christian conversion experience, so Christianity had become tangible for me. I was praying for the fear to go away, and it didn't. I was praying for escape and there was no escape. One day a chaplain came and it turned out to be a chaplain that I had known at [the Marine Corps training center] at Twentynine Palms; the chances are one in a trillion of that happening. I saw that consciously as an answer to prayer. God was not saying, "I am going to take you out of this," but "I am going to stand with you in it. There will be a hand to hang onto in the midst of it, which will be enough. It will still be really hard, but it will be enough."

What happened to me was a fractured skull, which would be called in Iraq terms a TBI [traumatic brain injury], severe kind. When I got back to the hospital in the States they said they didn't see much evidence of a skull fracture but more of a concussion, also, punctured ear drums and shrapnel holes. I was thinking, if they're going to send me back to Vietnam, I don't know what I am going to do because I am so afraid. Only last year did I discover that there's a place where you can write and they'll send you all your military records, so I got them all in the mail about a year ago including a whole lot of medical stuff that I hadn't known about.

It was all over. I went back to college, I became a minister, and had my life. But of course, in some ways it hadn't even begun, all of the dynamics. Post-traumatic stress is really the issue in terms of the effects of war. By the way, I am on this crusade to drop the "D" and say that there is no such thing as PTSD, it's PTS. It's not a disorder to have stress after trauma. The disorder would be to have trauma and then not have stress. Stress is a really healthy response to trauma, it's a protective response.

In 1983, fourteen years after getting blown up, ordained at this point, I went with a group of clergy to East Africa. Our first night we got jumped by some Kenyan men, they stole purses and wallets, and a few people got hit and knocked down. It all happened really quickly and I didn't get hurt. The next morning we were walking and all of a sudden this fear welled up in me that was just overwhelming. It took me a little while to realize that I was feeling the fear of Vietnam. I was stunned to think that I'd been carrying it in me and not knowing it since 1969. With this little trigger, it was back as strong as before.

That afternoon we were going to visit a church outside of Nairobi. I remember sitting in the back seat making sure that there were people on each side of me because I couldn't even look out the window, a tidal wave of evil crushing in on me, and there was nowhere I could go. We got to a church and out of it came a women's group with beautiful dresses, singing, clapping, dancing, one woman in particular headed toward me. I just stood there as she got closer and closer, dancing and smiling. This is a very big woman, really tall, and ample in every way. She got closer and closer, and her arms went out, she came right up to me, and she embraced me. In her embrace I almost physically disappeared out of sight.

And just as I don't have words that can adequately describe the experience of being blown up, I also don't have words to describe what happened to me in the experience of that woman's embrace, except that as she embraced me I felt the fear falling away from me, like leaves falling off the trees here in New England in the fall. The fear was replaced with peace. It was an experience that came out of the blue, like a meteor invading our solar system. I hadn't asked for it, I hadn't expected it, I hadn't imagined anything like that could happen, it just happened to me as a gift. Nothing had changed on an earthly level, except that I was given peace. I can say that my prayer is that for all of us frozen in fear, this kind of embrace may be received and given to others.

There's the Veterans' Education Project. When I moved to Northampton someone contacted me in 1984 to say this new group had gotten started. I joined it in its early years, and it's one of the few things outside of church activities my heart is utterly convicted of. My conviction is that the reality of war is so obscene, so shockingly terrible, that it's one of the worst things in the world. Tim O'Brien in *The Things They Carried* has that chapter on how to tell a true war story, a paragraph where he says that if you hear a war story and there's anything redeeming in it at all, it's not a true war story.

Dennis Driscoll was born in Montague City, Massachusetts, in 1942 and graduated from college before enlisting. He identified his unit in the US Army as Recon/Scout Platoon, Delta Company, 1st Battalion, 50th Infantry, Vietnam 1967–8, 1st Air Cavalry, 173rd Airborne, Binh Dinh province, Phu My district. He was commissioned as second lieutenant in 1966 and honeymooned with his wife at Fort Benning while he attended jump school. His daughter was born a week before he left for Vietnam. While serving in Vietnam, Dennis was awarded the Silver Star, and earned the CIB (Combat Infantry Badge), and Purple Heart, 3rd Award. His commitment to the men he led is central to his story. Dennis enjoyed a career as a middle school social studies teacher after his return.

I was assigned to the recon scout as platoon leader. When we first arrived in Vietnam, the ship docked at Qui Nhon, north of Saigon. We all got aboard buses. All the windows have screens on them. There must be big mosquitoes! Sergeant Collins said to me, "No, Lieutenant, that's so they don't throw hand grenades into the bus." The reality set in. The next day we got our tracks, M113 (light armored track personnel carriers, mechanized infantry), we got our orders, and we moved north to our new landing zone, called Ichiban, "number one."

Our platoon's job was to scout, and make engagement or contact, search and find the enemy, find what trails they were using.

The area we were assigned to was just south of the Bong Son plain, a non-pacified area. The South Vietnamese military hadn't been in there effectively. The national police, whose nickname was the "white mice," conducted operations with us a couple of times. The second time I refused to take them because they started to manhandle some of the villagers, slap them, and I felt that wasn't the reason we were there. They interrogated people much too violently. They were little people, and they always had a white shirt, and we thought they were very mousy looking. That was a nickname that was used throughout Vietnam. They were manipulators and very corrupt, not all of them, but enough were.

We treated the villagers respectfully. When we went through, we tried to give some extra food, soap—the children had so many sores on them. They just wash, they never had soap. It made us realize how fortunate we are to live in the USA. Many Americans are so ignorant of how fortunate they are. If you talked to the boys from Iraq and Afghanistan they would probably relate the same thing. The Vietnamese were beautiful people—they had nothing to do with this war.

The recon platoon broke down into teams. We didn't use our tracks because of the noise they make, the enemy would obviously know you were coming. So we walked. We set up listening posts, ambush patrols, we'd stay out for a night or two, try to find where movement was, locations, and radio back in our coordinates. From the Ichiban firebase, the battalion moved to firebase LZ [landing zone] Uplift. That became the headquarters for the battalion while we performed our duties for seven or eight months. We shared [it] with the South Korean artillery unit, Ollie, on route 1, north of LZ Uplift. We operated from there and would go to the Nui Mieu mountains [and] the central highlands.

My platoon was outstanding. Many of the men were woodsmen, hunters, fishermen, experienced outdoorsmen; those that weren't learned very fast. It became a game of hide-and-seek with the enemy. We had to go slowly, very carefully. The environment itself was very taxing on these young men, some were eighteen or nineteen. I was an old man at 24. Some boys were from the Great Smokey Mountains and had never left the hills until they entered the Army. Some kids had never been outside the city, a real awakening. I tried to protect them as much as possible. I respected and loved them dearly, and still do. They were always good to me. They were wonderful—I would do anything for them.

We had an interpreter, whom we called Kit Carson (Kit Carson was the term we adopted because of Carson's experience with the Navajo Indians). He was usually a reformed (supposedly) Vietcong, or NVA. Nguyen Tram (the one we worked with), his family was all murdered by the VC, and he hated them with a passion. When you went into a village, he would be the interpreter, he could tell who was hiding what. Our mission was to find out whether the village was being used as a sanctuary. When someone comes into your village as we were, with weapons, they would do what you'd tell them. Then at night, the VC would come in.

These people were caught in an awful situation. You never knew 100 percent if a village was VC. They could be smiling at you one time and the next minute they are shooting at you. I hadn't experienced this, but some of my men had: when they were on missions there were children shooting at them. Of course the children are told by their parents if you don't do that they could be punished. We had to be very careful about booby traps, ambushes, and the environment itself. Those poor folks, all they wanted to do was work the rice fields, fish, and go home and sit by their fire and have their family with them and be left alone.

We had outstanding medics. One was Pablo Luna—please put his name in your book. What a good guy. We were going through this village. Pablo called on the radio and said a lady is having a baby and to send the lieutenant (me). What was I going to do? We assisted Pablo as the lady gave birth. We had to call the medevac to give her a little extra care. I believe the mother wanted to give Pablo her 14-year old daughter as a gift, a gesture of thank you for saving my child, almost like an arranged marriage. He said, "I can't bring her to Los Angeles—my mother would kill me!" We would go through that village a week later, we'd get all the [hand] waves. People really appreciated that side of the Americans, the vast majority of Americans were really wonderful men and women over there.

We had my mother and my wife send extra soap. Lava was the best, it didn't smell as much as Ivory soap. I don't think I showered for at least two months, when someone did, it was like they dumped perfume all over them. You needed to smell like the jungle. Before we went out on patrol, no one smoked or did anything that could cause smells that would stay with you. We were always in a hostile situation and a clean or smoking smell could alert the enemy.

Our senses were so heightened by the sounds and smells we developed a sixth sense. We spent a lot of time out on the trail. If you were running point on patrol, you sensed something, the hand was up, we all went down. We waited, no matter if you were a private, it was a decision to move forward or retrace one's steps. You have to really heighten your senses. If you are tired, you have to slow down. Talking with some of the boys who have come back from Iraq and Afghanistan, hurrying up is the worst thing you can do. Slow it down, make sure what you are doing is right.

Rear guard was also important. Your obligation is to the preservation of your men and to the mission. We had some bad days, really bad, some KIAs. You get exceptionally tired: that was one of my functions and of the NCOs, notice if the men are getting a little sloppy the way they walk on patrol, notice the way they carry their weapon. The next night, that troop doesn't go out, he needs some rest. You notice if they are not eating well, very common to have a lot of diarrhea because the water we would get out of the big Lyster [canvas] bags, didn't taste too good—KoolAid helped the taste. We would get dehydrated real quick.

When you're in charge in a combat situation, you have the power of life and death over your men, but you are not a God. There are situations where you don't have time to make a decision, you react. If you've worked with your men long enough, they begin to realize that your interest is for their preservation. Yes, the mission, but their preservation too. Having gone through a village five times and going through it a sixth time, something's wrong with this objective. I would trust the wisdom of my men, and listen to them. They would see and hear things I couldn't. When I did, that gave them reassurance that they weren't just in a meat grinder, turned into cannon fodder. They were making life-and-death decisions along with me!

God bless helicopter pilots! Today, when I hear a helicopter, it's a good feeling. Not cocky, but sure of themselves, "I'll be there," and by God, they were. We were always on missions where we used helicopters, I think ours were the 11th Cav—"Black Horse." My call sign was Silver Fox 1. We had a situation when we needed help, fast, "Silver Fox calling, we're in need of a mede-vac." "Silver Fox, we're on the way." We would get down, pop a smoke, let them know when and what color smoke so the enemy would not use it, which was a very common practice.

Many times we would go into an area where enemy were re-ported to be, but they were pre-warned. I think it's the same in Iraq. Many of our most successful operations were done either with vague language or misinformation, or our counterparts weren't informed at all. If the mission was secret, it was more likely to be successful. We'd call our counterparts, the Vietnamese artillery unit, the recon platoon is going to be in this area, but there's no reason the Vietcong and NVA couldn't be on the radio, listening to exactly what we are saying. Our radio transmissions were not secure.

There's a great amount of leakage of secrets, Catch-22, the in-digenous population is caught in the middle. If they don't do what we say they may be injured, but if they don't do what their evil counterparts say, we can't protect them. In Vietnam much of the government setup was similar to a medieval period where you had your fiefdoms. You would have a local landlord, maybe the village chief, then you would have a group of villages, like An Loc I, An Loc II, An Loc III—they're extended ancestral relatives. They held on to their very strong ancestral worship, their families, that's why Tet was so important, families come and gather and share, as we do for Christmas. The NVA [North Vietnamese Army] and VC [Vietcong] used Tet as a coordinated attack because many ARVN [Army of the Republic of Vietnam] troops were away from their units. Tet was a military disaster for the NVA and VC but a political victory.

We're a product of the '50s and '60s, communism and the domino theory, John Foster Dulles. You look back today and of course he's right. North Vietnam and South Vietnam, Cambodia and Laos are all communist. It was done violently. Of course, the [South] Vietnamese government didn't help much. They didn't care for those poor people out in the boondocks that really needed help. They took what they could from them. I believe the Thieu and Ky government was greedy with power and authority. I be-lieve that our government didn't really understand how the Viet-namese government was set up and how it struggled.

The Ugly American is a descriptive book about the lack of respect that our federally-appointed officials had for the local culture and local government. They're going to go in and tell people what to do? You don't do that. I think that troops that go to Iraq and Afghanistan today are aware of that culture much more than we were. You don't chase their women, you can have fun with the kids, but you've got to show that cultural and religious respect. I think for the most part, most of the American soldiers did. In Vietnam, because of Lieutenant Calley and the My Lai incident, many people characterized the American soldiers as baby-killers.

My Lai. It gets to a point that our men were frustrated and would take it out on the villagers, whether it's a lack of discipline on the part of the officer in charge, non-commissioned officers, [or] squad members. It's not just one person's responsibility [but] the officer-in-charge has ultimate responsibility. Captain Medina, the company commander [for the My Lai attack], was somewhere else, Calley was officer-in-charge. You've got to make sure your men are in control of their emotions at all times, and it's hard to do. These men had only sixteen weeks of basic training and AIT (advanced infantry training) before they went into combat.

Most of the young men in the platoon were and continue to be good Americans. They were never warmongers or baby-killers as described by some protestors. The American soldiers cared for the Vietnamese villagers. I still believe that we treated them better than many of the national police, Vietcong, and North Vietnamese Army. When we approached a village, we never knew what we would encounter. At times, the villagers were used as shields or decoys so VC or NVA could escape or catch us in an ambush. The men made good decisions to ensure the safety of the non-combatants.

Then December 2, we were at the rock pile just south of Bong Son, we got caught in an ambush. It didn't go too well, we lost two wonderful, wonderful guys—Tom Mitchell from Buffalo, New York, and Richard Holloway from Longview, Texas. I think that one of the hardest things we did was to put those boys in body bags. The third time was Tam Quan, the fifth or sixth biggest battle in Vietnam. A helicopter saw an antenna and they investigated. I was with one of my squads on the coast and they said you've got to come back, we have to head north with the rest of the platoon.

We ran into a NVA regiment. The first day our helicopters dropped gas on their regiment, but the wind shifted and blew on us, tear gas.

> December 2nd, Silver Star Citation: "For gallantry in action…
> First Lieutenant Driscoll distinguished himself by exceptionally
> valorous action… during a search and destroy mission near the
> Crescent Valley…. Lieutenant Driscoll exposed himself to the
> enemy fire as he moved through an open area to assist his fallen
> comrades. Upon reaching the mortally wounded soldiers, Lieu-
> tenant Driscoll marked their position with a smoke grenade
> and returned to his unit's perimeter. Though wounded during
> the engagement, Lieutenant Driscoll moved from position to
> position, directing his platoon's base of fire against the hostile
> emplacements. His gallant action is in keeping with the highest
> traditions of the military service, and reflects great credit upon
> himself, his unit, and the United States Army.

December 7 we got hit with artillery, I got hit in the shoulder, legs, hand, and hip. We were going through a cave complex, it was the end of the day, but we were alert, and something, someone just came right out of the ground and started firing. A few guys were wounded that day; I just squirted something on my wound to clean it out. We went on line again and we made heavy contact, we withdrew, and the artillery came in. We don't know if it was part of the NVA mortars, the short rounds, or the Vietnamese ar-tillery, but some of us were wounded pretty good.

A few years later I was swimming in a lake in Ashburnham, Massachusetts, and as I'm coming out of the water, this man on the beach said to me, "Hey, where'd you get those scars?" I said, "I fell down and had an accident." He said, "No, you didn't. You were in Vietnam." I said, "Yes, I was. My name is Dennis Driscoll, what's yours?" "My name's Joe Hill. I'm a doctor, a vascular surgeon. Were you in Vietnam December 7 in the 24th evac hospital in Qui Nhon?" I said, "Yes," and he said, "That's my work!" Honest to God.

Tet: militarily, the Vietcong and NVA were totally destroyed. Politically, I think the assassination of Kennedy and King—enough of this killing! You had two leaders, whatever their views of Viet-nam, they were assassinated, and this was going on in Vietnam. Are we going to be another Vietnam? Is this going to happen in this country? If so, let's get out, enough's enough. I think the military had just about won. We had gotten the sanctuaries, if we had done tactics a little differently at that point... but our country was fed up with the war.

The meaningful protesting didn't start until '66. I didn't have time to get into the pros and cons of the war. You go through this village one day, and you go through the village again and you get a couple of guys wounded. Wait a minute, what are we doing here? These people don't need to have their houses searched day in and day out. We'd go through the process of search and seize, search and destroy [but] we didn't burn down houses because someone had an extra bucket of rice.

I [applied for] two jobs [and was] turned down because I was a veteran. I know people thought, we don't need one of those "psychos." I respect those that protested—I truly do. I wish they had started earlier [*he laughs*] so we didn't have to go for such tragic losses. But what are you protesting here? Why did we attach ourselves to a government that they must have known was corrupt? The corruption was from the top to the bottom. Why didn't our government get that information? When our senators show up to these war zones, everything is going fine. That's a lie. That people are dying, it's not going right. Our government was blinded to that, or they wished to be blinded. Is there oil off the coast of Vietnam? Are we trying to get back to Vietnam today, as we *are,* because they are going to put in some oil rigs?

The vast majority of Americans are pretty good people in the eyes of the Vietnamese, willing to help the Vietnamese people to help themselves. [*Did we leave a positive image of America?*] I think so—taking care of orphans that were our own men's fault because they got it together with the Vietnamese women. [*Did we forestall communism?*] I believe that's a factor. It's the same in Korea: that the citizens of America are willing to take a stand.

As a nation, we weren't totally informed as to what really was going on. Why did we in 1954 all of a sudden get involved? The Geneva Convention, we wouldn't accept, did Diem have that much power? Who are these Department of State members that told Eisenhower we had to be in Vietnam because the next step is that they are going to take over Australia and New Zealand? How is a little Vietnamese guy going to take over these Aussies and New Zealanders?

What was our government's thinking—to make the French happy? What are we making them happy for? We just rescued them [in World War II] and are we now going to rescue them in Vietnam? It's not their country. Those that worked with Ho Chi Minh in the OSS in the 40s and 50s thought more highly of him than the Americans did. We need to reevaluate what we are doing. We are inflexible. All these colonels and lieutenant colonels are experts in the field about Iraq and Afghanistan? I've never seen so many experts in my life.

[*Shows pictures.*] This is Tommy Mitchell, God rest his soul, a black soldier. I don't know if it was Tom or another black soldier, when I said, "I hope you'll have a good time at home." "I won't. I'll go say hi to Mom and Dad. You know I'm a sergeant, I'm respected. Back home I'm a nigger." I have never, ever forgotten that. He was from Buffalo. Matter of fact, he came back early.

I was able to see many horrific wounds, suffering men, on both sides. It's so vivid in my mind how evil war is. I really felt Kennedy was going to have us out of Vietnam. Even Eisenhower said don't get involved with a land war in Asia, because you can't win. There's no separate boundary in Indochina. Korea was different, there's a separate peninsula. With Afghanistan, we have the same thing. But rules of engagement—when you engage your enemy, it should be quick, concise, and to the point.

No civilian deaths if possible. Before we could go into a village in Vietnam, as in Afghanistan, we let the local populace know we're coming. If you're a local Taliban or Vietcong chief, you can go in and terrorize those people, by the time the Americans come, it may be two or three days, and they're gone. Those people are caught in an awful situation.

You try to make the best out of every situation, but why go into situations that are not necessary? We went to Vietnam, we helped them out as a nation, and all of a sudden we pulled out completely and left these people who supported us to the mercy of the NVA. We're so involved throughout the world, in so many areas. Are we the only one that can defend individual countries against themselves? There are 195 nations, and how many are we in, 100+? I'm curious as to how many bases we have.

I can tell you what has been attributed to Edmund Burke, the great 18th-century British statesman: "The only thing necessary for the triumph of evil is for good men to do nothing." God bless all who gave the time to serve and the ultimate sacrifice. Thank you for reading my story and God bless you.

Pete Rogers was born in Utica, New York, in 1943 and grew up north of Boston. He was an army intelligence officer, a young captain. At nineteen, having left college, he enlisted rather than waiting to be drafted. When he returned from Vietnam, he worked in military intelligence until the end of his commitment and then completed his BA. He makes it clear how much he empathized with the Vietnamese people and how much he came to worry about the impact the Americans were having on their country. He had a career in human resources, often traveling overseas, and is an avid sailor. Now retired, he speaks to school classes about his experiences in Vietnam.

By enlisting, I was able to choose what I wanted to do as opposed to being drafted to become cannon fodder because you are going into the infantry. So at nineteen years old, I decided to choose military intelligence because it sounded exciting. I was apolitical. It was August of '63 when I joined the Army, went through basic training and intelligence training. I went to OCS in 1964 and got married right before OCS when I was 20.

Becoming an officer was the first time in my life that I had done something that I had succeeded at on my own. I reveled in that as a young 21 year old. After getting my commission, I went to jump school then went back into military intelligence to become a special agent. Back then, this is the 60s, it had a romantic quality—it was about learning how to cultivate and work with people who would give you intelligence information.

Berlin was the best place because there were large numbers of intelligence people on both sides, East and West, who were playing spy games with each other. They said no, we're going to send you to Vietnamese school and then to Vietnam. They created a separate language school just for Vietnamese in Fort Bliss, Texas. I had a Vietnamese interpreter with me in Vietnam just to make sure that I could catch the important things I might miss, but I could speak well enough so I could have a conversation with people, establish a relationship. That was the key thing about my time in Vietnam—I got to know Vietnamese people as *people*.

I got there shortly before the Tet offensive in 1968, on January 2. I was assigned to a combat unit, the 173rd Airborne Brigade, which had its own separate military intelligence detachment, the 172nd MI Detachment, to provide tactical intelligence information. We had our own commanding officer, and the funny part is that I was the most senior of three captains at 21. A major was the commanding officer—they were promoting very fast.

The 173rd was assigned to LZ English, north of Qui Nhon near the town of Bong Son in Binh Dinh province, which is in II Corps. We replaced a much bigger infantry unit, which had a much bigger intelligence detachment that had developed most of the sources. So I just inherited their sources, village chiefs mostly. The village in Vietnam was the lowest unit where there was a formal leader. Below the village was the hamlet, a group of hamlets made up a village, a group of villages made up the province.

There was no way I could establish loyalty other than based on the information that I was given by people. Did they give me false information that later turned out to be detrimental to our unit? I don't know that I ever got any really accurate intelligence information the whole time I was there. Our work was to get information that was going to be *tactically* important. Tactical intelligence is current information about North Vietnamese Army units or Vietcong operations, where they are and what their strength is. I was in charge of the counter-intelligence section of the 172nd.

I used to go to the river in Bong Son and get our jeep washed. In addition to the sources I inherited, the village chiefs, I also developed some of my own, the kids used to give me good information. They lived up the river, and they would come down during the day to wash jeeps and make money off the soldiers, and they would tell me what was going on up in their villages. I had chocolate that I used to give them. I loved the kids there; I spoke enough Vietnamese that I could talk with them. I had store owners that I used to go to, and prostitutes, and as many people as I could find that would talk to me. I really liked—loved—that part of my job. I liked the Vietnamese people.

The longer I stayed in Vietnam the more disaffected I became, the more I started turning against the American presence and started feeling anger for what I saw us doing to the Vietnamese people and the Vietnamese countryside. The thing that bothered me the most was how American soldiers talked about Vietnamese people, like they weren't people. That really hurt. I brought gifts and I paid them, and they invited me to their homes, they told me superficial things about their lives and I told them things about my life—we shared information about our children.

What we were doing to the people and the countryside felt out of balance, the amount of destruction we were causing and the amount of sadness that we were creating in the people felt too great for our purported purpose, which was to prevent Vietnam and other countries from falling like dominos. By then I was also realizing that the people in the countryside that I spoke with didn't give a damn about the government they had in South Vietnam. Matter of fact, they didn't like the Vietnamese military because they were brutal. If the Vietnamese Army went into a village that was suspected of being Vietcong sympathizers, they were awful to their own people, they would light their houses on fire, or treat them disrespectfully. That was very hard to see.

I think I also at some point started feeling that the Vietcong weren't so bad, that they weren't this awful terrorist enemy that we had been told they were. I'm looking back now and I think that was coming into my head. Many of the people were support-ing them, you see. They weren't doing the kind of awful things that the Taliban is doing in Pakistan, going and blowing up schools. Lots of people in the countryside were very much in favor of them. They were supporting the Vietcong, the Vietcong were South Vietnamese communists—the Vietminh, the Viet-cong. I came to that conclusion.

I remember seeing for the first time what Agent Orange could do to a forest and remembering how upset I was, the swath of brown dead trees the planes had flown over. They had this device that they hooked on to a Huey helicopter, and it could detect human beings, supposedly. It was an ammonia "sniffer." A soldier in the helicopter would read the device as the helicopter was flying over the jungle, and if he saw the needle jump a few times he would assume there were people. He would throw a smoke grenade out. Flying in back of our Huey were a couple of Cobra gunships who would then shoot rockets right through the jungle. We were killing baboons. [*He laughs.*] And even if we weren't killing baboons, it was remote killing, an early kind of a drone. The same kind of notion that you're shooting and firing and killing things you can't really see, from a distance. I don't remember being affected by that emotionally until afterwards.

I was really lucky because I developed a very close friendship with a sergeant who worked for me, and he was the only one who was saying, "My God what are we doing here, this is crazy!" Now, he was more anti-military than I was, and more political and sophisticated than I was. He was also an enlisted man so he was seeing our whole unit—the dynamics, the politics, within our little Army unit—from this totally separate way. I was an officer and also still quite naïve. I'd gone over to Vietnam basically supportive of our mission to help the Vietnamese people so that they didn't live under communism, and I bought that whole thing.

He was also irreverent, and funny, constantly making fun of the army, and it was refreshing to me. He was my age. He was stoned most of the time that he was there, I didn't even know that. I was very aware always of being squeaky clean, because part of intelligence training is when you have a top-secret clearance, you don't want to do anything that might make you susceptible to blackmail. So I didn't smoke any dope ever, not the whole time I was in Vietnam.

It turns out that he protected me quite a bit because he also became a whistle-blower when he realized there was a lot of torture going on in our unit. These prisoners who had been captured by our infantry were brought to our IPW [interrogation prisoners of war] section and we had fifteen or so American interrogators.

Working with Vietnamese interpreters, they were also Vietnamese linguists. They had a reputation for torturing people.

The most difficult thing of my whole Vietnam experience is when I walked in on a Vietnamese being waterboarded. I'd never seen it, I didn't know it was being done. It was being done by a particularly sadistic sergeant who'd been to Vietnam on many tours. I remember expressing something to him at the time about why are you doing this, I don't understand why you are treating him like this, and he just dismissed me. He was a lot older than I was, I had no authority over him, he wasn't in my section, he was in the IPW section, he had his own captain who was in charge.

I mentioned to my own boss, the commanding officer, about what I had seen and he basically dismissed it. I never addressed it again, and it has always weighed on me that I didn't do more. It turned out that my sergeant's hooch was quite close to the IPW area and he heard interrogations going on and was very disturbed by it. He got so upset that he talked to a bunch of the guys that were doing the interrogation and got it out that they were also very, very upset by what they were doing, by the practice. He got them all to write individual letters to deliver back in the States about the torture going on in the unit. A book came out a couple of years ago by Deborah Nelson, a Pulitzer Prize-winner and an investigative reporter with the *LA Times*. My sergeant is all through this book. [*The War Behind Me: Vietnam Veterans Confront the Truth about US War Crimes,* 2008.]

We were over there at the same time that My Lai happened, and My Lai was only fifty miles away from us. The army and the generals were getting crazy about this coming out in the public. Westmoreland actually commissioned a *massive* investigation into what level and extent of atrocities were going on in Vietnam. A huge number of CID [criminal investigative division] people had the goal of tracking down allegations of atrocities in Vietnam. Nine thousand pages that never saw the light of day until Deborah Nelson discovered it about three years ago. They were in the garage of a colonel who had been on the commission to investigate it, and when he retired, he kept them. She started pouring over these 9,000 pages, copied and copied and copied… She went back to corroborate and talk to the people whose stories she thought were most poignant and therefore relevant.

One of them was Bob Stemme, my sergeant. There was a lot of investigation around Stemme because he was the whistle-blower. He was articulate, and he named names, he named dates, he was very specific. There was a final report made to Westmoreland—it whitewashed all the conclusions. They basically discounted Bob Stemme's report about what he had seen. He had great data, as did the actual interrogators, yet the report that went to Westmoreland said "his information could not be corroborated, so should be discounted." You couldn't have gotten something much more corroborated than what he said. He was an eyewitness.

I googled his name and we just reconnected for the first time in 40 years. I asked him how come I didn't know about this, why didn't you tell me if we were such good friends. He just laughed and said there was a lot I didn't tell you, you were an officer. He also told me, "I also wanted to protect you." He said, "I loved you." That really shocked me.

I didn't know about My Lai until I came back and it happened only fifty miles away from me. Calley was the scapegoat. This book goes into quite a bit of detail about My Lai. [Medina] was the lieutenant colonel, the battalion commander's actual order to them was to not leave anybody alive in that village. But there was enough ambivalence in the way he said it that it could be taken either way. The people took it that he doesn't want any living thing in that village.

This was a wartime situation where the rules of humanity go out the door. That was another part of my role in Vietnam—the rules of humanity *didn't* go out the door. I was seeing this very different view from what a lot of soldiers were, I wasn't out there being threatened by Vietcong, I wasn't out there being attacked, being booby-trapped. I mean there was a war, they were fighting for their lives. I wasn't.

It wasn't until I had done more reading and talking to people that I came to realize that armies are trained to hate and to create an enemy that is dehumanized in order for them to be able to kill them easily and quickly. I didn't come to that until a lot later than my military career. Really, what I came back with was a sadness about what we do to other people in war. I didn't have a lot of compassion for the American soldiers at the time who were obviously being killed and wounded. I didn't have a lot of compassion for the South Vietnamese soldiers either, because I saw them being terrorists. I had just a lot of sadness for the little people, who are the ones that suffer most from wars.

In retrospect, we're very arrogant when we are overseas. It wasn't until we'd been in Iraq for a long time that we started realizing the complexity. It was a very simplistic operation. For several years, we didn't seem to understand the difference between the Sunni or the Kurds, we didn't seem to get how critical that was to understanding the situation. We get blinded by the mission, by what we think we *have* to do. In a way, we don't care. I think the only time we *care* is when we realize that it thwarts our ability to get the job done. We over-simplify. We pride ourselves in being efficient, and spending the least amount of money and the least amount of manpower in getting the job done, so it is all very quick. I don't think we *want* to know the complexities—[we think] everything is possible.

We don't really *get* the pain and the suffering that we create amongst the indigenous people. The collateral damage is written off as being critical to the mission, we may try to minimize it. I like to think that the military trainers now don't demonize the people as much, but I don't know what the training is like today. Someone talked about how they were going into Iraq and how his commander had told them they would be welcomed with open arms. On their way to invading Iraq, the guys in the turrets in the tanks were waving and smiling, the commander had infused in them before the invasion that we are going in to help these won- derful people. But as soon as they ran over an IED and two or three people got killed, it was like their brains and their hearts just switched over to being warriors.

That was how we went to Vietnam too, same message exactly. The communists were taking over. Back then the only thing you needed to hear was "communist"—by definition that was evil.

Ken Gregg was born in Boston in 1938 and is my and Bing Emerson's [see page 330] cousin, the only other relative I knew who served in the Vietnam War. An orthopedic surgeon, he signed up for the Army medical corps. I was struck by his statement that the evacuation hospitals where he served (all three of them) had never moved forward in the years before he arrived in 1971. While he was there, they were closing. His comment reinforced the impression of a war that never made lasting gains.

I trained as an orthopedic surgeon at the Tufts Medical School, then at the Dartmouth-Hitchcock Hospital, and also a year in Baltimore City Hospital. My military service was two years, the first year at Fort Dix, then three different evac hospitals in Vietnam, in 1971 and 1972. I started off in Chu Lai (91st evac) on the coast in about the middle of the northern half of Vietnam, then went up to a place very near Hue called Phu Bai (85th evac), and then after a short stay, down to Da Nang (95th evac). During that time these hospitals were closing behind me. My father had been in World War II and was also a doctor in evacuation hospitals. But they didn't have anything like the evacuation that we had with helicopters and multiple airfields that were close to the fighting area.

I received my orders to ship off to Vietnam. My wife Judy was very pregnant with our second child, so I took a very short week to be home to be on hand for the birth of my daughter, and the very next day, I left for Vietnam. We flew from McGuire Air Force Base to Anchorage, Alaska, to a military airport in Japan, then down to Tan Son Nhat airbase near Saigon.

I was traveling totally alone. On arriving there, I was twelve hours out of sync, a day ahead of schedule, quite disoriented. I got the treatment of somebody of high rank, someone who should know what he was doing. I was a major. There weren't a lot of instructions or guidance. I got my boots, my helmet, my jungle fatigues, and the appropriate insignia to put on my clothes. Then the colonel told me, "You're going to Chu Lai, you'll like it there." I said, "How do we get there?" I wondered about this business about traveling as an individual, landing in a totally strange place.

There were ham radio operators on the West Coast, and on the islands like Guam, to plug in phone calls from Vietnam to any place in the United States by land line. So I could talk to Judy and find out everything that was going on within a week of being there. That was comforting. I had many conversations with Judy, most of them on tape cassettes, which we mailed back and forth, so while I couldn't see my children, I got to hear them growing up. We could talk in the evening without worrying with these recordings. I did get a week in Hawaii with Judy in November '71 and another week at home in February '72. I finally got home at the end June of '72.

I spent about six months in Chu Lai and that's when we had our typhoon. [Typhoon "Hester," October 23, 1971.] It blasted off the roofs, it blew the kitchen and dining hall over the cliff, and we lost emergency power. We abandoned the hospital, moved out all the patients. A couple of us got some nails and picked up a lot of pieces of galvanized tin and put them back on the roof, and we spruced up the nurse's quarters and our quarters. A bunch of tough-looking Vietnamese ladies arrived wearing black pajamas and driving an old beat-up truck and were very happy to have us donate our unneeded roofs and excess plywood, something that they could see should not be wasted. I got a kick out of them.

After the typhoon, we were eating K-rations and C-rations, and we put out a bucket for rain. We read books in the evening by candlelight that was spitting and snapping and smoking. Local Vietnamese got candles and came up and sold them to us. During the typhoon, I only did one surgery with a hand-held flashlight. A piece of tin would come over flying at a hundred miles an hour, end over end from the roofs, and we had to transport the fellow from one building to another. When they didn't see something coming they would say, "Go!" and we dashed across the open space with the stretcher to put the patient we had operated on in the recovery room. He recovered.

After about a week, we had a convoy, two trucks and two jeeps, and we traveled north to Phu Bai, just south of Hue. Phu Bai was a horrible place to try to do surgery. The OR was very damp and had a very low ceiling, poor lighting, the first few cases I did there were infected. I was there for Christmas. I didn't know anybody, and it was quite lonely. I spent a lot of time (because I wasn't doing surgery) in clinics being a primary care physician. I used to sit up on the water tower and watch the airplanes come and go.

That's where Bingo's chopper in HMM-265 started from. They flew down to Da Nang and then flew inland to a hill southwest of Da Nang. I wondered, Where did he crash? So I went [to Vietnam] with that in mind. I would like to have gone there if I could and see where this happened. I wondered, was it on this hill up here? Are we that close? Bingo had a very humorous character, he was always quick and energetic.

After two months I left Phu Bai (that hospital was also abandoned), and went down to Da Nang. The hospital was large, the only American hospital left open in the north half of Vietnam, the other hospital was down in Saigon. We treated reporters, Navy people occasionally, say from a destroyer that didn't have a hospital on board. There had been a hospital ship, the *Sanctuary*, that left the year before we came because we weren't getting as many casualties in '72, as compared to the late 60s.

A fellow that I flew over with was a sergeant, we sat in seats next to each other all the way to Japan. I came back with him. He had septicemia, bacterial endocarditis as a result of injecting drugs. Sometimes the patient would be a little unstable, [and] they want to have a doctor on the airplane with him. There was nothing to do but watch the patient to make sure they were still breathing and conscious and alert. It was the damnedest experience to go with the same guy I came over with, taking him back to Okinawa.

Once you get to Okinawa, you see that he gets on the ambulance, tell them who he is and what's going on, then you're free. You can take off and do anything you want except they kind of expect you to come back. [*He laughs.*]

We did some interesting procedures on Vietnamese civilians, things we hadn't seen at home. I did a decompression of a tubercular abscess in a patient's spine. This was a Vietnamese farmer, there was rapidly progressing paralysis of his legs, he had terrible pain in his back. So I read the book on what to do, the general surgeon and I opened up his chest, pulled the blood vessels out of the way. We drained this big abscess and the fluid around his spine, and I took out one whole vertebrae and then about a half of two others. We took the rib that we removed to open up his chest and cut it to the right length to put it along the bone straight down his spine. Holding his chest and his pelvis, and someone else putting his knee in his back, we very gently straightened him out, placing the bone grafts we made in-between the vertebrae.

We tied the chest together again. The pain was gone, he was moving his legs and walking in a couple of days. We had him in a cast from his hips up to his collarbone. We printed in a waterproof envelope, glued to his cast, instructions as to how to treat him in French and in English and we gave him some bottles of streptomycin. We sent him off to his own hospital and doctor for follow-up care. We don't know whether it worked or not, but the cast was very impressive.

There was a very strict policy regarding the handling of American soldiers. One of the first rules was never close a wound with any possibility of contamination or foreign material. In World War II and prior to that someone with that kind of an injury would never have survived. In the Civil War days, one shot through the abdomen they couldn't treat, some people would survive and some would not. Amputations, if they were open and clean, they were much less likely to get infected.

They had to learn in World War II and the Korean War, and again in Vietnam, not to try to close a wound. These rules had been forgotten between wars. Between Vietnam and the current activities they didn't forget it. The fractures were stabilized in traction or splinting, the wounds were frequently checked. The primary concern was to make the patient healthy.

We did many amputations; we'd leave the stump open, tied up the bleeding with little knots. Sometimes we'd work all night and then in the morning when we were still half asleep, we'd look at it and we'd see all these little pieces of string and we'd say, "Oh, there's a piece of sock, cut it," and it was a knot you had just tied two hours before. I had people who lost both arms and legs. When you had a helmet and a flak jacket on, the arms and legs aren't protected and the body is. So the heart and the lungs and the head in many cases would stay intact, and everything else would be gone.

We had male nurses, and we had the lady nurses. The head nurse was a colonel. She was the one that I commented, "What beautiful boots, how did you get them so shiny?" She said, "I'll show you, so I gave her one of my boots and she polished it for me and then I handed her my other boot. She looked at me, "Major! What do you think I am!" [*He laughs.*] The nurses compared well with any other group. The male nurses tended to be more like Corpsmen, but they were working at the hospital and were well trained. Someone had to remember to remove the hand grenades before the surgery! We also had Vietnamese nurses and they were very helpful when we had Vietnamese patients in the hospital. My impression was that they were well trained.

I worked in three hospitals in Vietnam, and those hospitals never moved. They were stationary. I will say that within that first six months I got the sense that this was not a war that was going to be won. We didn't seem to be making any ground, it was just treading water. The fighting came and went, but you never had the sense that anything was being accomplished. I wasn't long in Vietnam before I had a sense that the war itself was insane, it didn't have any strategic activity, it was a stationary situation, the same things happening over and over again with no pattern of activity.

The feeling I had was the Vietcong had learned their lesson when they attacked in April of '72. They said, 'Okay, we're going to sit back to wait until those damned helicopter pilots are gone, then we will attack again.' We didn't really need to be concerned with these things because we had enough to do in the hospital. Personally, I think most everybody felt like they *were* doing a great job and they were appreciated for it. Our real concern was all these people that were coming in, that's all we really cared about. We didn't really worry about what was happening in the rest of the world—it's what's happening to my patient who lost his leg last night.

The one thing that I still regret to this day is not having a log of patients. I could have with some effort looked them up to find out where they were. I've never been near Walter Reed. We've been reading about places that are rather dingy-sounding where people have been going. Every time I read about someone who has been abandoned, and I know the kinds of injuries they had, it makes me annoyed that they are not getting the treatment they deserve.

[*He talks about Kenneth Kin, a Vietnamese doctor whom he knew in Vietnam.*] I think the last thing he needed was to have a lot of letters from the US when the commies came along and told him he needed his re-education. He came to visit us probably because he spoke good English and was an orthopedic surgeon. I really liked him, he was good, he knew his stuff. He practiced in Da Nang. My hope is that he went to camp for a few months and learned how to say "comrade" instead of "sir," and then he would have gone home because they would have needed him desperately, a competent orthopedic surgeon because they had all their own wounded to take care of. He was about my age, he could be seventy now, he had a young child who was the same age as mine. Dr. Kenneth Kin.

What were we doing there, what *could* we do there? Nothing. Did the Vietcong really think they could chase us out of there? No, but we left anyway, eventually. My impression was that, yes, it was insane. I think because we were in contact with the people for so long, and because both sides fought so hard, the North Vietnamese found out how many soldiers the US was willing to sacrifice, which was a huge number. I think other countries looked at us and said uh-oh, we'd better not get involved in a war like that. We may win it but how many North Vietnamese were killed, we don't know. We know 54,000 Americans were killed.

And look at us now—we're friends with the Vietnamese just like we're friends with the Japanese. It took a long, hard, war. More than anything else, I like to think that… [*He cries.*] Sorry… all the people that were sacrificed there didn't do *nothing* out there, because they showed what America is willing to do.

Don Chevannes was born in New York City's Harlem in 1951. A graduate of Seward High School in 1967, he received his AS at Plattsburg Community College in 1976 while serving a sentence in prison. He also attended Pace University in 1978–9. An army private in Vietnam, he worked as a lineman in 1971–2. Don was often homeless after his return and addicted to heroin dating from his time in Vietnam. He overcame his post-Vietnam difficulties and currently works at the Soldier On transitioning program at the VA facility in Leeds, Massachusetts, and is active in veterans' affairs. He also spends time with his two daughters and granddaughter.

Both my parents came out of Jamaica, so I was the first generation born here. I grew up in the middle of Harlem, 127th Street. I went to school at PS 68, and Junior High School at J. Fenimore Cooper. The teachers were always giving students advice on high schools they should go to. Miss Harris told me it would be better for me to go into a school that was considered well integrated. My perception of the world was that a person of color wasn't part of that world, because all the commercials on TV were white people. Anything good was never associated with somebody of color.

Chinatown, Little Italy, [and] you had an area of Jewish persuasion. We had the three melting pot areas and when you go into the school we would see this big map of the world, these were students from all parts of the country and the world, it was amazing.

I really enjoyed it because it was the first time I had a chance to mix with people of other persuasions. My neighborhood was strictly black. You had some Jewish people, they would own the stores; I never had a real one-on-one to get next to somebody with other than my skin color. It was a real good experience for me.

I got to Queensborough Community College, and the draft was on. One of the things that gets you out of the service, either you had a medical condition or you were in school, so I was in school. My grades weren't good at all, and somehow the draft board must have gotten wind of that or they must have been checking—I don't know how they did that. I got this letter, a token, and a meal ticket attached, the letter said you have to come down to the induction center. From the time I got the letter to the time I had to go, two days.

You had no excuse for not getting on the train because they supplied the subway token, and then you had to go to a certain restaurant with your meal ticket. Like the Last Supper, right? The induction center was Whitehall Street in lower Manhattan. I was thinking of ways to get out of the service. Friends would shave some soap and swallow it so by the time they got down to the induction center they were sick, throwing up, pupils dilated, blood pressure sky high, but I wasn't going to be eating soap.

So I thought when I take the test, why not just give them all the wrong answers, then they would say this guy is really too dumb to be in the service? That's what I did. When it came to the eye test, naturally I purposely failed that. After that this lady walked up to me and said, "Listen, you have a couple of choices here: either you take these tests over again or you are going to end up in jail." Jail was not an option for me, so I ended up taking the tests over and I couldn't figure out how she knew I was not being real. Then I thought about it. Gee, if you are just coming out of college, even though your grades aren't good, you can't be that dumb.

Fort Dix, New Jersey, April of 1971, out of 300 guys that went through this battery of tests, I scored the highest. They gave me a trophy. They wanted me to go to paratrooper school and I decided I'm not jumping out of a plane. They said we have three assignments: Germany, Korea, and Vietnam. They read off two names—they are going to Korea, one name, this person is going to Germany, everybody else is going to Vietnam. My stomach hit the floor. I was really scared when I was on the plane. The stewardess asked me did I want a pillow to sleep, and I was like, *sleep*? I looked around the plane and everybody is asleep but me.

When I went into Vietnam I was twenty. I compare it to what eighteen-year-olds do today: video games, skateboard, basketball, baseball. I've got a rifle and a grenade. [My mother] thought I was part of a greater good. Here I am in the ghetto, and all of a sudden now I'm in uniform, fighting for the country, part of the greater good.

They landed me in a place called Cam Ranh Bay. It was like a pizza oven. I ended up first going to Phu Bai, Camp Eagle. I was fortunate enough to have a front row seat for Bob Hope, Vida Blue (he was an Oakland A's pitcher), Jim Nabors, Dean Martin, the Golddiggers. He had the first black girl who became a Golddigger, Jayne Kennedy.

Long Binh was one of the biggest trading posts in Vietnam. I don't remember ever *getting* to the PX because me and my friend were heading to the Air Force base (because the Air Force guys lived really good) to have a drink. There was some machine gunfire, and we ended up splitting up. I hit the ground, I crawled, I even fell into a sewer and I stayed in the sewer. This went on for almost 35 minutes and I was in total shock. That freaked me out.

This particular day was either Christmas or Thanksgiving, a helicopter dropped dinners off and we could take as many plates as we could carry. I must have had about seven plates of food. Machine gunfire again, I didn't know what direction it was coming from, everybody's got their weapon pointing. Then, I am looking over the tall grass and I see this hat that the Vietnamese wear, so I am aiming my weapon in that area and I could start firing. I'm saying to myself, "Don't shoot, don't shoot," and finally a person emerges out of the grass. I know it's a Vietnamese starting to come toward me in a non-threatening posture.

The person came and sat down, got up, and walked a little closer, 30 yards away from me. I realized it was an elderly woman. She was making all kinds of hand gestures, and finally I realized that she was looking at my food. Right, I am saying to myself, well, she wants the food. I grabbed a few plates and I walked it toward her and I sat it on the grass, backed off. She walked forward and grabbed the plates, she started saying something to me and waving and I realized she had a little pocket knife that she wanted to give me for the food, she didn't want to just walk away. What I did was, I said okay because I think she really wanted me to have that pocket knife for giving her the food. I started thinking, "Oh, my God, I could have killed this old woman." All she wanted was the *food*.

I started using drugs in Vietnam. Heroin really, they had marijuana there, but I was using the heroin mostly. The Vietnamese would come and bring it in a very undercover way, but I found out there were a bunch of guys doing the same thing. Because the quality of it was much higher you could rub it on your skin, if you had a patch on, you could get high from that. I sniffed it, a lot of the guys would put it in their cigarette because when you smoke it you don't really taste it, and you don't really smell it either. It was 65 percent pure.

To give you an idea, if you had a teaspoon of pure heroin, you could probably make a quarter of a pound of heroin with a great street value—$100,000. The height of your highness would be about six hours, but your tolerance level starts to build like anything else if you're using drugs. Shooters, they may start off doing a little bit and really feel it, maybe throw up and feel sick, but after a while their tolerance builds. They need more and more and more and more and they get to the point of doing a whole lot more.

We were using piastres, French money, one dollar was equal to 500 piastres. Some people wouldn't make 500 piastres in a *year*, but what's a dollar to an American? Nothing. One maid, one Vietnamese woman, she may service thirty or forty guys: shining boots, wash and dry their clothes, press and starch their jungle fatigues, wash and fold the underwear, for *thirty guys every single day*, and she would get five dollars from each one of them. She was getting rich according to the Vietnamese standard. Americans spent like that.

So with drugs it was the same thing. [They would] find Americans who are on a convoy and little kids on a Vespa scooter, "GI, GI," and then they would offer you five dollars' worth of marijuana. You'd get a bag as big as a laundry bag, or a pillowcase full, but wrapped in a plastic bag. You would get a kilo, about two pounds of marijuana, for five bucks. They loved us there because we made a lot of them rich. Americans really uplifted the economy when they came over there.

We were on a convoy where these kids were trying to sell us drugs, to a place called Da Nang. The road was no wider than from [this] wall to [that] wall, and these guys are driving two and a half ton trucks. We're going up the mountain and we see the driver and the co-driver passing bottles of liquor back and forth, drinking, and you look down and see the cliff there. We ran across a Pepsi Cola truck on the side of the mountain turned upside down, people climbing with ropes, hanging on vines, the Vietnamese going down the side of the mountain to get to that Pepsi Cola.

So after Da Nang, you know every man wanted a woman, we took risks to do that. This is just one of the stories. This kid was telling us about his sisters, he has got all these sisters. I don't know if they were working for him or he was working for them, he was recruiting. I do remember going into a village in the back of a car. We were smuggled, the back seat connected with the trunk, so when we drive past any American military post and they look in that car, they wouldn't see us. Literally, [the Vietnamese] had these 1930s and 40s cars, they just kept putting pieces together to keep them running.

The girl that I slept with looked like she was four or five months pregnant. The parents, the family cleared everything out for me. I was telling them, "No, no, no, that's okay, you don't have to do that!" They are like, "No, no, no, that's okay, no problem." The girl took me to a well and she bathed me from head to toe. At the end of the night I think I gave her twenty dollars, *a lot* of money to them. To me it was just twenty dollars.

The biggest problem (which I didn't see coming) was when I got to California, and I saw this *resistance,* this kind of hatred for the military guys coming from Vietnam. There was an antiwar protest before I left, but it was so strong when I got back in June 1972. I got to the airport, I got a cab, I was so afraid to get out of the cab. All of a sudden it started raining, everybody was running for their house, now that was my break, so I paid him, ran upstairs, the first thing I did was take off my uniform. I never put it back on. I didn't want to tell anybody that I came from Vietnam because the war was unpopular. Most of us were like me, we went in there because we were told we had to go, or go to jail. For years I didn't tell anybody.

I got to the point where I was comfortable living in the street. Being drug-addicted, all I worried about was getting money for drugs. It took a while to snap out of it. The way that happened is I ended up coming up here [VA Hospital in Leeds, Massachusetts]. Didn't really want to, but I realized, gee whiz, all these years have gone by, what do you have to show, you aren't doing anything, what's going on with you? I'm starting to think why don't I have what other people have? Why is everybody comfortable, going to work and coming home? But I was thinking about drugs. When I came up here in 2005, I realized after a couple of weeks that my system was being cleaned out.

I started going into therapy for post-traumatic stress disorder (PTSD), I started group therapy for drug addiction, and I just kept going until I finally started learning something. I thought there was nothing I was going to learn, I've got to go through the motions in order for me to get to that next step. Then I realized it wasn't just me, there were a lot of guys that came out of war in the same situation, and even worse off. Wow, they don't realize the effects of being in the military, it wasn't all positive, especially when you are involved in a conflict. Because when I came back, we didn't have a debriefing, nothing like that, not like what they've got now.

But coming here made me see things differently. I realized that my family is a great gift. So now, as I'm getting older, I'm making all these contacts. Coming home and being rejected, and having these anxiety attacks, can't sleep, anger problems, drug addiction, isolation problems, the one thing that is curing me now is giving back. I'm off of drugs. I spend my every waking hour, just about, helping people, *every single day*. I leave my house at 6:30 in the morning, and I don't get home sometimes until 10 PM, but I enjoy what I'm doing. I don't mean this to be a commercial: "If you enjoy what you are doing, you'll never have to work another day in your life!"

That's exactly what's happening with me. I don't have to work another day in my life because I enjoy everything I'm doing. It's on my terms, I show more vigor than the people they pay. I don't get paid for anything up here [in] Soldier On, but I spend every day in the hospital volunteering. I received treatment in Ward 8 for combat veterans' post-traumatic stress. You go for a refresher (a lot of guys call it recharge), you get recharged, guys go every year, spend a week or two to get recharged. You never really graduate.

The Chairman of the Joint Chiefs [Admiral Mike Mullen] is coming down to receive an award [at Soldier On]. Fortunately, I get selected to pose for a statue, the guy who commissioned the sculpture said to me that he thought I was the perfect choice. "I wanted a person of color, and I also wanted someone who never asks for anything but only gives." Which is true, I don't really feel right asking for anything. I get my reward from helping people. I do that 24 hours a day.

[In Vietnam], black guys would have this thing where we would "dap," a form of hand gestures, almost like a dance routine with your hands. If you were black, if you meet another black soldier, you should know how to dap. Different places and everybody had different daps. If you didn't feel like dapping, you just want to sit down and eat instead of dapping with ten guys on a table—that was a big issue. I didn't feel like it. Give me a simple one, that's all I wanted. [*He illustrates.*] Don't give me this, and this, and that… [*He illustrates with a long routine.*] But if you didn't in some way you would be looked at as an outcast.

[*How did officers treat the different races?*] Were they treated equally? I would say, not really. The model soldier that they wanted was *white*. If you wanted someone to represent your platoon, it has to be a white guy who's a sharpshooter, who's physically fit, the model was white. That came crashing down where I was, because they had this one guy named Colin Dean. Dean was your poster guy. So during the last day of our training we have a battery of tests and the most you can do on these tests is 500. Shooting, obstacle course, physical fitness activities, multi-bars, crawling, running, jumping, and what happened was at the end of three days of activities they add the scores up.

I happened to walk into the office when they were adding the scores up and Dean got 465, the highest, and the lieutenant said, "This is our guy right here—Dean." They hadn't finished marking off all the cards, and then they said, "Uh-oh, Don, you got 485" (the highest in the whole battalion), so I beat Dean, they just took the highest score and that was me. So now the black guys were really happy, like an uplift for them.

Vietnam vets, disproportionate to the population, we have a high suicide rate, we've got a high drug addiction rate, we've got a high homeless rate, and we're only a minority in the United States military guys. Being in the war, coming home, not being diagnosed with these disorders, not being welcomed, not being recognized that there was something wrong, and not trying to find solutions or the proper help. For the military, the veterans' administration, to be coming around this thing slowly, and not quick enough, and they're still not fully equipped. There was no support.

Sergeant Gomez was born in Puerto Rico in 1948 and had a twenty-year career in the Army. He completed his education at Cambridge College in Springfield, Massachusetts, after his last tour. He heads the Bilingual Veterans Outreach Center of Western Massachusetts, serving the Spanish-speaking veteran community. Sergeant Gomez moved to New York at seventeen and noticed the number of young men in uniform and decided to enlist at age eighteen. He already had a brother in Vietnam, which could have led to a different posting for him, but as squad leader he decided to go with his men in December 1966.

I went to see the CO and volunteered to go to Vietnam with the rest of the guys. I met up with the 196th Light Infantry Brigade, 3rd Battalion, 21st Infantry, a wireman in the headquarters company. My job was to do switchboard operator at night, go out and check the wires on the bunker line to insure that the guards had communication between each other and the headquarters. I wanted to see action, I want to do some killing, I came here to fight a war! I [had] heard, back in the early fifties, about the Korean War. My godfather and my father served in the 65th Infantry Regiment in Korea, they used to come home, drink a couple of beers, and talk about the war. I guess I wanted to be like them, deep down.

There came an opportunity in January '67. I volunteered to become an RTO, radio transmitter operator. I became the radio operator for the company commander, meaning I went with the company to the field. When any of the platoons needed to borrow an RTO, I volunteered to go with them and this was going to give me the opportunity to get into the field as an infantryman. How stupid was I! That's how I got into the combat situation in Vietnam with the 3rd of the 21st Infantry. I was in III Corps, close to Saigon.

But that didn't last long because in May 1967 we got airlifted to Chu Lai, II Corps, and we replaced the First Marine Division because they went up north to Da Nang. We were the first Army unit to occupy so far north. We kept the sector south of Chu Lai about six to ten clicks, before that, we worked the area around Tay Ninh down at the Black Virgin [Mountain], what they call Nui Ba Den. It was about the tallest mountain there, on a big plain where you could see for ten miles. It was completely jungle, and I experienced my first combat there at the bottom of the mountain.

We had engineers that were making reinforced bunkers around the mountain because this mountain was packed with Vietcong. There was a big old cave in the center of the mountain, and they used that cave to come in and go out, it was said that the cave had columns all the way to the city of Tay Ninh. I came into contact for the first time with the VC as we were pulling guard one night. The engineers, once they finished their duties, they went to party that night, we took over the positions to guard them and to guard the area. Charlie (VC) slipped into the perimeter, and we didn't notice anything. They went straight to the engineers, threw a whole bunch of hand grenades into their tent—blew all of them up.

When we got up in the morning to retrieve our Claymores (anti-personnel mines), they were turned toward us. If we had engaged our Claymores…! Claymores are a half-moon instrument, about an inch thick, filled with 750 quarter-inch pellets and full of black powder inside. It has a blasting cap from the top and an electrical switch that you had at the bunker. If you blasted the blasting cap this will act like a shotgun, the pellets spread up to 60 meters in a half moon, left and right, and anything within 30 to 40 meters will be dead. We were going to get the blast if we detonated them. They [VC] went from bunker to bunker, turning the Claymores around. They killed thirteen engineers, and they slipped right back out. So that was my first experience with combat. Needless to say, I was very, very, very scared. Very quick, I didn't want to play no more. I heard the sounds, I saw the killing.

One afternoon I was on KP, kitchen police. There was this other kid peeling potatoes with me, this kid had been put to do KP permanently while he was in Vietnam because he lost it out there. He got so scared he started screaming, so the platoon sergeant pulled him out and didn't allow him to go back to the field. In about a week's time, his squad leader came to pick him up and told me he was going to be back right away. He had to take his replacement to show him how to set up a Claymore.

Fifteen minutes later, I heard an explosion, every one of us got into our trenches believing it was mortars coming in. We waited, nothing happened. I stuck up my head from the trench, scared, and I saw people running toward Alpha Company where the kid was. What had happened, while the kid was showing the other one how to set up the Claymore they put the blasting cap into the Claymore and started the electricity for the transistor radio and blew the Claymore. He was in front, he caught the full blast, he was cut to threads, and the other guy caught the back blast, lost both legs at the knees, both arms at the elbows. This was the first experience of seeing an atrocity like that. I always remember that kid, but no features, no name.

Another time, I was together with a group of Puerto Ricans because we seek each other out because of the language, the culture, the music, everything. That night we stayed up until midnight drinking whatever little beer we could get our hands on, and smoking whatever weed we had. Around midnight, the three Puerto Ricans from Alpha company (again, Alpha company, *Jesus Christ*), needed to go, because they had this patrol next morning.

About three o'clock that afternoon, we heard a firefight. That platoon where the three Puerto Ricans were, my friends, had gone up a trail and came back the same trail. Hernandez [*he cries*] and Torres and Rodriguez, they were part of the platoon. When we got there, they'd been part of that ambush, the whole platoon got killed. When we went out searching for the wounded... [*He cries.*] I found them, I found them. That was tough. It was really meaningful for me. When we were back in base camp we found out that Hernandez's wife had given birth to a son the same day he was killed. All of us were eighteen, nineteen, twenty years old, no more than that.

We had an impact area where we tested our weapons before we went out. I noticed in the impact area there were two kids collecting cooking wood. All of us knew there was a lot of unexploded ammunition in that area, especially for the M-79, which is a hand grenade shot through a weapon that looks more like a shotgun, about an inch round and about four inches long. I saw them out of the corner of my eye, paying no more attention to it, came back into the mess hall to have breakfast. A friend of mine named Torres was a cook, and Torres always in the morning prepared me a long, plain hamburger patty, because I was the only Hispanic sergeant, they always were doing little special things for me.

So I'd started eating. When I heard the explosion, right away I pictured the kids. I took off running to the impact area and there were the kids, laying. One of them was moving his mouth, his jaw, it looked like he was alive. The other one was gone, completely destroyed. So I picked up this kid with my arms to bring him out of the impact area, by that time others were coming, but I was the only fool to get into the impact area. When I picked up the kid I heard a strange sound like stuff coming loose from inside the kid. There was a big hole in his back and all his insides dropped right on my thighs as I picked him up. That was something that I blocked away for many, many years.

They were short of NCOs and every NCO they wanted to come back after a 30-day vacation. Come back to the unit, we'll promote you, and we'll keep you for another six months or another year. Of course, I say no, and I'm glad I said no, because later on that January, 1968, the company got wiped out in the Tet offensive. The first individual to be killed was the company commander and his RTO. If I'd been there, that'd have been me.

I reenlisted to lock myself in one job for another three years in Germany. By that time, I decided to make it my career. I ended up not going back to Vietnam until January 1990, with a group called the Full Circle, which University of Massachusetts put together, the William Joiner Center. The theory was that going back to where it started was good for your PTSD. We went for 21 days. I went to the Black Virgin Mountain, I was able to climb all the way to the top, and I pissed for every GI that was never able to make it up there. Then I turned my back and came right back down and never looked back.

We came into Saigon, and the first place we visited was Chu Lai and the tunnels. From Chu Lai we went to Tay Ninh, and all the way up to Hanoi, I was able to see Ho Chi Minh in his glass casket. I went to My Lai, where this guy did all the killing. They had a book there for you to write your thoughts about My Lai, and what I wrote in the book was, "Shit happens." The reason I did this is because it was not far from Chu Lai, and we got shot at from that village and of course we never did shoot back because we were not authorized. Calley, he's had enough, he did what he did. Many of us say if you didn't kill women and kids, well, they would kill you. Women, kids, old men, old ladies, they were going to kill you. It was so hard.

It came to a point that you wanted to come back to the war. It was one heck of an experience, a good experience, going back. Because right now, when I think about Vietnam, I think Vietnam is making it right. I call it the changing of the movie. I changed that movie that was always in my mind about the war, the destruction, the burning, the people suffering, I changed it with a Vietnam that is full of life, the people are at peace, the people are selling and buying, and eating. I change it with a Vietnam that is growing, that is green, beautiful. God, that country is so beautiful! The people in the south really took us in very well. They kept our culture, and anywhere you went you heard our music, you saw our programs on TV, and you saw them talking our language and asking for the green buck. [*He laughs.*]

When we got up north, it was like night and day. They were very cold to us, they treated us really bad; it was awful being in North Vietnam. But then, we have to understand the "whys" also, because of the bombing that we did. We were the first group to enter North Vietnam, [and] we were the first group collectively to go to Vietnam. We were meeting with different political officials, generals, veterans from the Vietcong, we exchanged our feelings, we exchanged our war experiences. We did a lot of exchanging. One thing that I noticed is that many of them were going through the same problems that we were going through.

In Saigon, they took us to a hospital where over a hundred women had given birth and their kids had been born with all kinds of defects because they themselves had Agent Orange. They were just waiting for this cancer to go up to their brains, and they are dead within a year's time. They took us to a room where they had 50, 60, 70 fetuses in big bottles. It was like you were looking at monsters because of Agent Orange. In 1990, even today, Agent Orange is in the area. These people are eating their fruits from the ground, they're drinking their cows' milk, cows eating the grass, and Agent Orange is coming right in them and that is why many, many of these women had cancer from Agent Orange. So it's not only us who suffered the atrocities in war, but *them*.

We Vietnam veterans open up the doors to ensure that not another generation of warriors will go through what we went through. We know where to send them, we know how to talk to them, how to massage them, and that will help them as long as they are looking for the help. Coming back, I was one of the lucky ones because I decided to stay in. I never received that rejection from the general public because we were alerted in the 70s not to go out of the base in uniform. Many of us did not ID ourselves as Vietnam veterans. From day one, we wanted to forget Vietnam. I picked up drinking more than what I was drinking already. I picked up the pot smoking, so I stayed numb. I picked up the dangerous jobs, the ones that kept me really going like a drill sergeant that was 24/7 teaching these kids what I have learned in Vietnam. I stayed intoxicated 24/7, numb, and very active. So I erased Vietnam.

When I was in Vietnam, I knew that it wasn't worth it. It wasn't worth a damn because we saw no progress in what we were doing. Firefight here, firefight over there, leave this area, come back the next week, occupy that area, fight here, move to another location, so there was no progress. There were skirmishes all around us, and nothing happening. And then when Tet came around that really pulled the plug on everything we'd done in the past. The thing that really pissed me off the most, and I had not been [back] to Vietnam yet, was when negotiations were opened for us to start exchanging with the communists, we opened up for the economy. That, for whatever reason, hit me, I got angry at that. Then I was thinking about it, well, why not?

It's like right now, the wars that we are fighting, Iraq, Afghanistan, all that is for the wrong purposes. For us that went to Vietnam, Afghanistan is another Vietnam. We'll never get out of there in victory and Afghanistan will continue to be

Afghanistan. There's no front, there's nothing there, it's for the wrong reasons. We're losing our young men, we're losing our resources, the only thing we're doing is keeping thousands of people in jobs, the jobs that we create to keep the [war] machinery. I believe that that's the only reason that we stay in that war, to keep the economy alive.

We did everything we were ordered to do. We were instructed to follow our commanders' orders. Don't blame the soldier, it's not his fault—he's following instructions. Their lives depend on what they do next, you can't stop and think. Am I going to fire, am I going to shoot or not shoot? While you are making that decision, somebody's going to shoot you. Whatever decision was a decision to save your life and save the lives of those around you. If it's the wrong decision, then we are human.

Joe Dougherty was born in Lynn, Massachusetts in 1943 and graduated from Brown University where he roomed with David Hillbrook and John Hartman, whose narratives are in this section. As his stories below illustrate, Joe is a great raconteur. He received his law degree from Boston University in 1967. His first draft notice came when he was a college senior, and, with the war still ongoing, a second notice came when he completed law school. He decided to enlist in the Army for a two-year tour and served in Vietnam in the 1st Air Cavalry. In addition to a career as an attorney, Joe bred and raced greyhounds for many years.

In Vietnam I was assigned to the 1st Air Cavalry, the little yellow patch with the black horse's head. We were at Bien Hoa, a big, big base. We got our supplies and uniforms, and there was a man in front of me, 6 foot 3 or 4, he was really broad-shouldered, big, solid. In those days he was an Indian, today he would be a Native American. You gave your name and he said: "Jimmy Two Babies." I assumed he was a big baby when he got born. The man behind the desk was giving him the supplies, and Jimmy said, "I will not take a firearm. I will not kill these people. I will drive, whatever you want, but I will not take a firearm." He didn't get a firearm. He got his supplies, his uniform, he walked out. Then I came up, I was the size of the sergeant, about 5' 5", and he said, "You don't know how hard it was for me not to hit him in the face." I started laughing, "Really?" I can imagine his hitting Jimmy Two Babies! [*He laughs.*]

They sent me to Camp Evans, about twenty miles south of the demilitarized zone [twelve miles northwest of Hue]. Then an event happened that really shook all of us. Bobby Kennedy had been shot. A lot of people felt that if Bobby Kennedy was elected president, he would end the war so people were really upset with his assassination. That was June ['68], the primary, that locks me in for the time I was at Camp Evans.

I finally got assigned to a radar unit and went to the village of Hai Lang, fifteen miles south of the border. We were set up across from the provincial capital, right on Route 1. For whatever reason, they dumped all the used oil, chemicals within 100 yards of us. It was like a black lagoon. The sun would shine on it, and at night it would stay as warm as it was in the daytime, it would keep us hot. We would spend 24 hours a day with the radar unit, and cover the area in all directions, watching the headquarters of the battalion two miles above us. Any projectile that got fired, we'd pick it up; the machine was good enough to tell you exactly where it came from. We'd call it in immediately to our units, and they could fire mortar rounds or shells [at] Vietcong or North Vietnamese.

A Vietnamese man and his boy had come up and were lobbing hand grenades at our guys. I have no idea why he did it. He might have believed the Americans were bad, they might have taken him and told him to do this, a suicide bomb, they might have said if you don't do this we are going to kill your family. People will do things they have to do.

[*Was he killed?*] [*A long pause.*] By you-know-who. Since I was on the other side, he had no idea I was over there, I had a clear view of them all the time. He could have been fifteen. He got hit with an RPG round, HI-69, it kind of blew him up, it's a high incendiary, when it hits, they're gone.

At this point they decided to relocate the 1st Air Cavalry to the south. My unit got sent to a place where they had Special Forces, Marine Tiger Troops. It was a hilly mountain area, and the headquarters for my unit was at Quan Loi [60 miles north of Saigon], red earth, they call it. We had an airstrip there. We got hit a lot out there with rockets, mortars. It was a busy time. We were at one place with the Army Rangers for about two weeks then they shipped us out to the mountain area.

Martha Raye [a comedienne who had entertained World War II troops] came at Christmastime and visited with the Special Forces. It's funny: you see people on TV, she just seemed bigger than life. She shook everybody's hand, "You're doing a great job." She was telling jokes. I'm talking about a place not even half the size of a football field on top of a hill. She played cards with them, and she was really good. She showed up in an open jeep, she was out there in a real combat area. I remember Johnny Cash had gone to Vietnam to perform at Long Binh Airbase and said how dangerous it was because rockets hit the place!

They started shooting the rockets from Cambodia in the Tay Ninh area, so they brought us over there. It's a big city on the eastern border. At that time there was political controversy about whether we should invade Cambodia. We got there around 6:30 at night and the mess hall was closing. We parked our truck, and the man was good enough to open up and give us a meal. I remember walking back and just as we were getting near the truck, looking back and the guy waved at us, and right then I saw a silver flash and a rocket hit the building, blew it right up. Fifteen seconds earlier I would have been where that man was. That man was blown to pieces. If he had said sorry, we're closed, he'd be alive today.

The thing is, I've always admired World War II people. You didn't enlist for [just] a year. You never knew if you were going to make it back or if this thing was ever going to end. You were always counting, every time you sent a letter home, you'd be chipper, things are going well, no matter how bad it was, you wanted them back home thinking everything was going well. [In Vietnam] I remember around Christmastime packages came in from a girls' college in South Carolina, sororities sent stuff to different units. I was very lucky, one of my law school friends was in a bar in Lynn and they sent me a hundred dollars at Christmastime. [*He laughs.*]

There was a lot of activity from the VC, Vietcong. The first NVA division was running around this area. After midnight on March 8, 1969, I was on duty, we had barbed wire all around the perimeter and trip flares started going off. That meant that the enemy was trying to get through the wires. Sappers were always a risk. There was gunfire, nobody was going to sleep, everybody was on edge. A rocket came in and hit the command post and killed the colonel [Lieutenant Colonel Peter L. Gorvad], and all power was shut off because the generators were there. So now there's no radar, no nothing.

There were two ways into the base. One way was where we went down to get the water. They hit the way we came with the water, and they broke through, and they overran the base. They claim they were regular North Vietnamese Army. The artillery piece was firing what is known as beehive rounds, tons of pellets in it, big projectile, shots spread out and just spray it. The enemy running on this side of me, running on that side of me, we're firing weapons, everybody's shooting like crazy, everything's in slow motion, it's absolutely unreal. They figured there were 600 dead enemy inside the perimeter. I think there were less than 100 of us, about 25 dead, but I don't know, all I know is that there were bodies all over the place.

It's all of fifteen, twenty minutes, it seemed like forever, early morning comes and the jet planes start showing up. The enemy is down on the river. They spotted them and they dropped napalm on them. You could hear them screaming, they were pounded good. After that, the helicopters brought in reinforcements. They had people working on the details with front-end loaders, they dug a big trench outside the perimeter and they would just bulldoze the enemy into it.

The general came right in, he was *angry,* ah, *angry*, the colonel is dead, the whole thing wiped out, the place is overrun. I saw the version of it in the VFW magazine. I read it, I remember laughing: "Attack on LZ Grant. The enemy was repulsed on the wire...The firing, the quads, .50-caliber guns roared, the beehive rounds, the main assault was destroyed on the perimeter wire... They were smothered by artillery concentration, the shattered remnants fled the battlefield only two hours after the attack commenced..." [*The First Cav in Vietnam:Anatomy of a Decision*, by Shelby Stanton.]

They began a program when I was up at the mountain with the Special Forces to give a little vacation time, maybe three days, two nights, to Vung Tau, a wonderful resort on the coast of Vietnam. The first night I went out with two guys and some guy was riding by with a horse and carriage and supposedly his daughter.

The guy from Nebraska decided he was going to bargain, he was happy, he disappeared. So the other guy and I went to a couple of bars, nursing drinks, and we were on the opposite side [of town] from where the hotel was. Suddenly, they started blaring on the loudspeaker that the city will be secured within five minutes, you must be indoors. We couldn't possibly get back to the place in five minutes.

We're standing there and this elderly woman said, "Come in here and spend the night. We've got two girls left." Jesus, what's this going to be? She wanted five dollars. Being a gentleman, I let the other guy pick, I have this other girl. They went one way, she sent me into a place and it was probably 30 feet long, 25 wide, divided down the middle, sheets or blankets on wire separating everything. There were beds in there. I had a good Catholic upbringing, I have no intention of… Everybody is moaning and groaning all over this place, I dozed off.

All of a sudden I hear noise, screaming, everybody yelling, running around. I jump out and look around and there's military police at the door. So everybody runs down, everybody is naked except me. Fifteen minutes later, the mama-san knocks on the door, "It's okay, they're gone now." Everybody got robbed! [*He laughs.*] Their wallets are sitting on the thing, they're all naked except me. All these naked guys looking around, they're all screaming and yelling, their money was taken. If you are going to have sex, it pays to keep your clothes on!

They had a program if you got back to American soil with less than five months in your tour of duty, you'll be immediately released. After June 10, I'm immediately discharged. I started my ride back to LZ Grant June 5, then I went down to the Bien Hoa base where you departed from Vietnam. I reported in to set up my transport back to America and they didn't have any record of me. They have to cut a whole new personnel file from St. Louis, which is the headquarters of their records, no e-mail, and ship it over there!

On the final night, I went over to sign out and the person at the quartermaster's desk for the supplies said, "It takes ten seconds, we don't process you until an hour before." "I'm leaving three hours from now, what's the difference if you process me now?" "That's the way we do it." It seemed strange. An hour before, I come walking in, let me put my gear in, and he says, "Where's your tent?" "What tent, you've got my file." "It says right here, it's checked off, you got a tent. It's $125, you can't leave until you pay." This is 1 o'clock at night. *"I can't leave, and you won't sign me out, because I don't have a tent?"* He said, "What can I do?" I said, "You know what? You give me a copy of that, I know a couple of guys that might give me some money." He gave me a copy.

[Then] "I remember, *I've* got a copy of what I signed! It's still in my wallet, let me give it to you." I get it out. "Look, there's no tent marked off of my copy." He went dead white, he looked at me, "You know what? Some rotten son-of-a-bitch must have had it in for you, but I am going to take care of this." *"Really?"* I think it was routine, you walk in and someone says you can't do it now, come back an hour before, it made no sense. I don't care if I was still over there today, *I was not going to give him a penny.* "Maybe I can get you off with $50–60 bucks." A lot of guys must have done something.

I got to a point over there, if I die, I die. I did crazy things. I watched *MASH* one time with the guys, walking around in a white tee-shirt, *I* used to sit on top of a bunker with a white tee-shirt and read and they never shot at me. If he shoots me, he shoots me. I got back, a lot more grateful for having gone through it and gotten out alive, devastated by some of the people I knew that died in it. I still remember that [Vietnamese] kid. I look back and I say, when you look at it geopolitically, if you're going to fight a war and have an enemy, you don't want to be in the enemy's territory. To put people in the situation we were in, where they could run over to Cambodia, Laos, go back over the border with impunity, you just put people in harm's way.

I majored in political science when I was at Brown. I'm sitting over there, I wasn't as negative about government as I later became. We've got to fight communism, we have to fight it over *there*, that's the theory we are all fighting with. You make it like Ho Chi Minh, because the communists backed him, was bad, so we backed the other choice. Deep down, when I look back, Ho Chi Minh probably could have won a national election, so we would have not given these people the right of self-determination.

The misguided thought that we could stop communism, and that Russia, China were really controlling him. [Eisenhower] inherits Korea from Truman, his experience is that Russia will do almost anything. In this case, China and Russia both were going to do Vietnam.

We've always had this international moral presence that we know what's right and wrong. The problem we run into when you look at it, it's about what's in the best interests of American corporations. I was watching a show on Iraq on TV, they are outside Fallujah, and the war's going on. The announcer is talking to a contractor, and he said, "What is it that you do?" "We're here to repair the water system." "When are you going to be able to start on it?" And the man says, on TV, and I'm listening, "They haven't blown it up yet." *What?* *"They haven't blown it up yet!"* Is Halliburton running wars to make money? Is that why we are over in the country?

[*Can we win in Afghanistan?*] Not a chance in hell. It's a tribal society. It's nice to talk about women's rights, but the people that you are going to tell it to? Everybody gets mad at me, but I believe this: Nancy Pelosi went over to the Middle East, she went to Jordan, she went here and there, Saudi Arabia. Hillary Clinton goes over there, Condoleezza Rice goes over. Their message to these countries like Saudi Arabia is that they should have more women in government. A tribal society, their history... this is how they *do* it!

I remember watching Sunday news, and President Bush, Jr. was sitting in an armchair. Someone asked him a question about why we are in Iraq. You know what he said? "That man tried to kill my father." And I said, 'Whoa, all these kids are dying over there because this guy tried to kill your father?' When his father was in [Kuwait, April 1993, to commemorate the Gulf War] there was supposedly a plot to kill him, and Saddam Hussein was behind the plot. I said to myself: Saddam Hussein was George Bush Sr.'s biggest booster because when he was going to be knocked out, when the Shiites were taking the country over, somebody said, "You've got Shiites over in Iraq, is this what you want, George?" So he took the "no-fly" restriction off Saddam's military, and [Saddam] took the country right back. Trust me, [Saddam] would never, never put a hit out on [President George W. Bush's] father.

The thing that bothers me most about America, the thing that

I think we need most, universal military service. What happened when you stopped the draft, people like me stop meeting farm boys from down there. You become a much more understanding person. I think also with universal military training when they want to go to war, in Afghanistan or Iraq, everybody's kid is at risk, not just the poor kid because he couldn't get a job. Everybody could lose a nephew... is this the war I want to send someone into? I'm thinking, a minimum of six months, a lottery draw gets you a year, a lottery draw once every other year gets you two years. I say people would be a lot more respectful of each other. In a wide-open free draft, I wouldn't mind [my son's] name going right in.

Al Cummings was born in Attleboro, Massachusetts, in 1948. He was wounded in Vietnam and his story illustrates the life-long impact of injuries. He enlisted in the Army in 1967 because he was unable to find a job and he expected to be drafted. While he made it home, his brother was killed in Vietnam on March 17, 1970, a gunner on a helicopter that crashed. Al is active in veterans' affairs, both locally and nationally, and his engagement with other veterans, from local Memorial Day ceremonies to reunions and recruitment of new veterans, is one of the main focuses of his life.

I landed in Vietnam, December 8, 1967. I was with the 25th Infantry, support with the 77th Artillery. We landed around midnight, so I didn't see anything until the next day. Actually, Vietnam was a gorgeous place, even with the killing and stuff. The convoy went from where I landed to Bien Hoa, on the coast, down south to where we were stationed in Dau Tieng. It was Saigon, Cu Chi, and Dau Tieng, my base camp and from there we did all our operations. We always towed the 105 [howitzer] on the back of the truck with us. I was a radio operator on the 105. People who were in firefights would call in for support and then I'd relay the coordinates that they were giving me to the people with a gun to fire off the 105. Another company was probably pinned down in a firefight and they needed support. It was during the Tet offensive.

We were like brothers. When I got over there, I was the oldest in the group. They welcomed us. They kept yelling something and I couldn't get what they were yelling, and then I found out that they kept yelling "short"—they had less time [left] than we did. We were over there for a year and some of these guys had been there six, eight months already. They were a great bunch of guys. We all banded together, they made you welcome. They kept an eye on you until you got into the swing of things.

Things were going good. Around April, we'd gone out on a mission and were coming back. We pulled over to the side of the road because it was getting dark to put up the camp. After the camp got set up I was going over to visit a friend in another bunker, and on the way I stopped and grabbed a couple of beers. I never made it to the bunker—I was hit. The first mortar came in and it was a dud. The second mortar came in and landed two feet in front of me, it just sprayed the whole front of me. They say that the reason my arm got the way it did is because, I guess instinct, I covered my face. I got a piece of shrapnel over on the side and I still take it out of me. I remember them putting me on a helicopter, the helicopter taking off and landing, going into the hospital.

Most of what I'm going to tell you was told to me, because I lost four days of my life when I was hurt in Vietnam. Hospital was in Bien Hoa Airbase. I was there from the 25th of April until I landed back at Hanscom Air Force Base on the 17th of May. I spent a year and a half between the hospital at Fort Devens and the Newington VA hospital in Connecticut before I was able to come home permanently. I had over two thousand stitches—they stopped counting when they were taking them out at Fort Devens. I have muscle and nerve damage in my right arm and hand. I've had seven operations on this over the years.

I had to learn to walk all over again. I got therapy on my legs so when I was able to finally walk, my mom came down, and I walked down the hall to meet her. They got me walking around August or September. Later, they had to go in and loosen the tendons up so the hand would open up again. Whatever they did the last time, it hasn't closed up since. It moves and everything, but I have no feeling from the wrist down to the fingertips, I have to be very careful. I can write with it and I can eat with it, as long as I am looking. If I go to pick something up, I can't feel it.

I've had therapy over the years. Two years ago my left knee was replaced; this December I had the right knee done. I worked up until I started having a problem with the knees. I play havoc at the airports. [*He laughs.*] Especially with the titanium knees! Years ago they used to give a card, but now with everything that is happening with 9/11, they won't let you have the card anymore. I tell them I can't go through the machine, two titanium knees, scrap metal, and they say, that's all right, don't worry. They put me off to the side and they wand me down.

I found out that they're having a second anniversary for our unit in October 2009. I was Company C, 6th Battalion, 77th Artillery. I've been corresponding with them, I have a list of the names, but I can't put faces with the names because I don't remember. I'm hoping that I'm going to be able to go in October to Chicago. I'm not sure because my wife and I live on a disability check.

[*Have you ever been back to Asia?*] No, don't want to go. I've had four or five different chances. I belong to the Vietnam Veterans of America, right now I am the region I director, I cover the six New England states. I'm also vice-chair of the national POW-MIA Committee. Our chairman goes to Vietnam because we have a subcommittee called the VI, Veterans' Incentive. They keep trying to get me to go and I just can't go. They understand. They would never force somebody to go.

JPAC, the Department of Defense [Joint POW/MIA Accounting Command], we talk to Vietnamese to find out where the graves are. JPAC goes over and excavates, finds the bones, brings them back and identifies them so we can bury our brothers back home. The Vietnamese are very forthcoming, they've helped a lot. There are five guys that go over all the time, so they've got a rapport with the Vietnamese. They're helping them locate crash sites so they can excavate and find some remains.

I have a brother killed in Vietnam, March 17, 1970. He was a gunner in a helicopter. From the report we got, they were taking off, something happened to the rudder, it stopped, and they crashed. They found my brother's body ten feet from the crash site. They figured he jumped before it crashed. His body was recovered and sent back to us. He was only eighteen. He's buried in Hadley, along with my dad, in the cemetery on Maple Street off the side of the road, white picket fence. Charles Henry. He's on the wall of Vietnam, in Washington, and he's on the wall in Lee, Massachusetts, that's where he was living when he went in, that's where he went to school. The school planted a tree, put a marker on it in his name. I think there are three or four trees from guys killed in Vietnam.

It's only been twelve years since I started admitting that I'm a Vietnam vet. I didn't want people to know because I didn't want to go through what my fellow brothers and sisters went through. What brought me back is when I got involved in the Vietnam Veterans of America—we have almost 60,000 members across the United States, Puerto Rico, Hawaii, Alaska, and that's when I found out that there were actually other people like me. Being with them, the camaraderie, it brought it right out and I have been able to talk about it ever since. It was the best thing that could ever happen. I'm a life member of the Vietnam Veterans of America, I'm a life member for the VFW, I'm a life member of the DAV, Disabled Veterans of America. I can't work so I've got to keep busy helping my fellow veterans, past, present, and future. It doesn't matter which war, we are all veterans. We are all brothers.

Herb Voudren was born in 1945 in Springfield, Massachusetts, and served in the Navy. His involvement in Vietnam focused on the Montagnards, who cooperated with the American military. Because of the nature of the tasks he undertook, he focused his narrative on issues affecting the people of Vietnam and left out some of his own activities. He made the point that one needs to understand the local people, their culture and history, and is critical of those who made political decisions in Washington without regard to the realities on the ground.

[The French] wanted to control the people first, then they could control natural resources, the raw materials these countries still had. Why do you think the French wanted to get right back in there after the Second World War? "It's French Indochina, it's ours, we're going back in." The British controlled that area after the Second World War ended. Now [there's] hatred for the British and the French and even Americans, because they didn't work with the people.

Read the history. When Eisenhower was in, Ho Chi Minh petitioned the United States government with the actual paper work consistent with the Constitution of the United States. Eisenhower went, "We are supporting the French. Let's not even get involved with this guy." Then it got into communism, flat turned him down. Communism, and what do we do? We sent war materiel to the French. The Vietminh, they beat the French there, before we go in there, because they wanted their freedom.

When the Vietnam War comes, we know what they have for raw materials. We'll make deals with the Diem government, we'll get the oil out of here, and that's what happened in Vietnam. Send troops in and pull them out, as soon as we're leaving you can watch the enemy walk in. I used to get so aggravated when I listened to the news when I got back. "Well, the people don't know whether they want to be communist or want to have a democracy." That was bull. They weren't telling the American people that these people didn't want communism—they wanted freedom. How come six million of them when we pulled out got on boats that were sinking? They went into Thailand because they knew they had no more freedom.

They knew what the communists would do to them and we just said, "Oh, we're not going to give you any more money. We're pulling all our troops out, too bad." So we abandoned not only those people, but our troops that were there. Most guys in Vietnam, I would say 90 percent, would say they were doing something for the country and helping these people. We didn't hate the Vietnamese. We just hated the way the war was being run and how they were lying to us about it. Restricted fire zone? Free fire zone? Get out of here! They didn't support the *people*, they let a regime take over and they supported it. Diem and all those guys [we supported] because he was Catholic, it has nothing to do with the people. That was a political thing, nothing to do with us on the ground.

The South Vietnamese government was corrupt, but who made it corrupt? Their government and our government, we allowed it to happen because we didn't put restrictions on what we sent there and what they were going to use. We didn't want to *offend* the government. But then you had generals who knew this was going on, smart people, what the hell are they doing, they're fighting a war from the Pentagon? Let them fight it from *here*. In the military you can't be politically involved in anything, it's against regulations.

They talk about suicide bombings [now], it happened in Vietnam, roadside bombs, kids walking up to you with satchels on them, blowing themselves up, killing Marines, army. The communists would take people that they could indoctrinate, they would put bombs in these little bikes that sold soda. They had a system within Vietnam of hardcore communist indoctrinates that would teach these kids, and if they didn't, they would subject their family to certain things. I had knowledge of this. They would put a bomb under a bike, mines on roads, they blew up American troops. But now hear about Iraq, IEDs, same thing, it's a road mine. In Vietnam, we didn't call them terrorists. They were in villages where they could convert [people] in hardcore Marxist classes.

In Iraq what are our troops doing with the people? They're going out and meeting these people on patrols, they're saying this area needs a school, *they* are saying that, not the government. These officers-in-charge and the sergeants are saying this is a pretty rural area, let's go out there and build them a school. But that's not *news*. Same thing they did in Vietnam—how many people knew that our Marines built schools? Built up villages' defenses, how many orphans that we took care of, GIs used to keep them in the hooches.

There was no [understanding] of what we were actually doing, except that we were baby-killers. But no one said what the North Vietnamese were doing, like when they attacked Hue City, how many thousands of people they killed. Not hundreds, thousands. They were killing school teachers, politicians, people in town halls, city halls, anybody who had anything to do with the control of the government, or teaching, professors, and the whole family. Why? So they could control the people. That's what any dictatorial power does.

The reasons that were given to the people were given by the politicians, not by us. If they protested the war they should have protested the politicians. If you're going to have a war, let's have a war; if you're going over there to help the people, let's help the people. We were told before we got back not to wear a uniform in certain areas. In Washington, they're having protests. Well, why not? People have got right in my face and said we were killing the people in South Vietnam, that we were destroying a country, we were bombing North Vietnam, we were wiping out villages.

My Lai, that stuck in people's minds—these guys are just killing people. That wasn't the truth! My Lai was an order, but people that were involved didn't like it. Who caught the brunt of it? Lieutenant Calley. What did they do with him finally? They released him because he was under orders, and if you don't follow orders in the military you are in deep… That wasn't the only place that things like that happened. He was a dedicated person, he's an officer, he's following orders, and the people under him have to follow his orders. But it got to a point after a while where GIs are going, "Hey, you mean I can't say what is right and wrong here?"

You've got guys like McNamara sitting back in the Pentagon saying, "Oh, we were going to bomb here, we're not going to bomb there." Why didn't they come over and sit in Da Nang or Hue City and say we'll run a war from here? From the intelligence report that you get, you're going to bomb, you're two weeks late, they've already moved out. Generals on the ground, the officer corps, and enlisted people on the ground knew what was going on. We should make the decisions, no matter how cruel it was.

Tet '68: We beat the communist troops in that they actually couldn't fight us in a confrontation, they lost. They took over Hue City but we beat them out of there. But the thing of it was that we stopped, instead of going into smaller villages and making a post there and working among the people. "We're here, we're not leaving, you'll be safe, just let us know where the enemy is, we'll clean him up." A lot of them didn't like their own government. They weren't getting their freedom from either side. They may be rice farmers but they weren't *stupid*, they're smart. They didn't have the democratic process; we [Americans] can voice our opinion without getting our house burned down.

Iraq: you had the Sunni, the Shia, and the Kurds all bickering, they'd done that for hundreds of years. If I was going to go in a country like that and cause problems, I would get them all fighting against each other. Al-Qaeda is like, "Oh, we're dumb?" So they got the Shia to get pissed off at the Sunni and vice-versa and they're bombing each other and they're actually training these people to kill each other and then they can control the country. And if you do it in the name of Allah, you'll go to heaven. So here, strap this on you, this is called hardcore indoctrination. Just like the communists did in Vietnam.

[*What would you say the lesson of Vietnam is?*] It's not to get involved with something unless you're going to go in there, fight the enemy, help the people gain their independence. Whether it's socialism or communism, when it gets to the point they're coming into this country and blowing up stuff, and it's not just here, it's France, Germany, it's all over the place. Americans don't want to see a 9/11 again, or subway bombings, bus bombings.

I was assigned to be with the Montagnards in order to understand the area and see what was going on. They worked in and off the base, but I don't want to say too much. The Montagnards, you can't take them out of those jungles and put them in an enclave and say that's where you are going to live. They have no freedom there. Who made the pacification program? Not the GIs, the government, again, *not listening* to the people on the ground! They sent American GIs there in a war, and you have the final decision if you are going to kill someone or not. Who do you kill or who don't you kill? Who do you trust or who don't you trust? But after you're in an area for a while and you get to know the people, then you know who's who, and they'll tell you. At night if we're not in the villages, they come and kill them, so it was a tough situation with the people.

I knew the history, which gives you insight on how to approach these people. I got to meet Mo Va Du. He was 53 when I met him. I got to see the village and ask him questions. I was very impressed with his English—he learned it just by talking to the troops. I used to give him a book and he would write things down, whatever we said that he didn't understand. He never went to any kind of a school. How could persons in the United States, or [its] intelligence, [think] these people are backwards if they had that much incentive to learn something? They had a civilization before we even had a country.

The South Vietnamese government was saying these people are insignificant, second-class people. We don't want to deal with them. They were worried about their main industrial areas, their cities; we don't give a shit if the communists take them over. Here I am sent there to organize this alignment. But then when you meet the people, once you gain their confidence, they'll tell you who is who. "Number ten, number ten" means "really bad." The troops are doing their job, but the government of South Vietnam wasn't cooperating and our government was saying these people are backwards because the South Vietnamese government is saying that.

Once I got to know these [Montagnards], even though they were so "backwards," they built huts, but they built them the same for a thousand years, up off the ground. Guess what, because of the monsoons, not hard to figure out. So were they that backwards? But the bottom line is, once I got to know him, it got personal. The Hmongs, when they really like you, they walk hand in hand with you, that means they're really close to you. After we left, everything was pulled away from them, they had no backing, we didn't support them.

Mo Va Du knew all the rivers, all the trails. He could tell you where the enemy was moving—he lived there. When you bring him into an intelligence meeting and he changes things on the map—they *live* here. Mo Va Du would go to a cemetery and tell you who was buried there. Why wouldn't you get in there and find out what is going on? Why wouldn't you want to find out how they live, not change them? His first wife was killed, the VC came into his village when he was out. When I knew him, he was already remarried. He had a new son, nine years old. He wanted to give me his son, "You take my son, United States, make him go to school."

We incorporated some of the Hmongs into the national police. It was hard because they didn't really trust their government. But I explained to Mo Va Du that anything that got them to the schools that were set up, they had to do this so they would have some political clout with the government. But it was like a too-late thing, even the South Vietnamese Army, the ARVN, they wanted nothing to do with them. Any of the Hmong that were in the army when they were on a duty post, they had to have families with them in the bunkers, little kids running around, their wives would cook—closeness in their own tribe.

My grandparents were Cree and Seneca and my mother was Irish. We have a French name. As far back as I could trace it, I found out I was part Indian. The monks in Quebec province, when they first came over in the 1600s, converted some Indians to Catholicism. Joe Yellow Feather and Running Bear got married, they gave them a French Catholic name, and they documented them. But you could still keep your Indian name. On my father's side, Canadian, Cree, all the Iroquois Nations, my grandmother was a Seneca and she spoke Algonquin [Iroquois].

President Jackson really persecuted the Cherokee Nation,

because they actually swung toward the white man's way of doing things, they had enclaves, and they took some of the black people in. They called them "Buffalo people," that's where the word comes from. They saw they had towns, they were owning a lot of stuff, so they put them on the Trail of Tears. They gave them blankets that were infected with small pox and sent them out to the Oklahomas. They took all their land over. [Jackson] was an arrogant, dictatorial, presidential-type power.

Cherie Rankin was born in Dayton, Ohio, in 1946 and grew up in Florida. She went to Vietnam in 1970–1 in a Red Cross program entitled the Supplemental Recreation Activities Overseas Program (SRAO) designed to engage members of the US armed forces in games and conversation. A group of young female college graduates circulated among troops bringing a fresh face (and a more familiar look) to battle-weary soldiers. She was ferried from firebase to firebase and also conducted activities in recreation centers on the larger bases. An interview with Cherie appeared in In The Combat Zone: An Oral History of American Women in Vietnam, 1966–1975 *by Kathryn Marshall (1987).*

I grew up in a politically conservative family in southern Florida, a religiously fundamentalist family. My parents were divorced when I was quite young. We were ignorant about the wider world, what we learned about politics got preached from the pulpit. We grew up knowing "Thou shalt not kill"—unless it's for God and country. Our country was right, always, I believed, and there was no such thing as a leader who would lie to you. Everything that was done from our country's perspective was the right way and we were the best country in the world.

Two things happened around my senior year in college that started the wake-up process for me. The first was Kent State on May 4, 1970 when the National Guard was called on the campus in Ohio and ended up killing several protesting students, and this was a total shock to me and to our country. People could not believe that our kids were being killed on campus. So for the first time in my life I joined a protest. I put a black armband on and we marched on the capital at Tallahassee. I was terrified that some photographer would take my picture and I would be on the front page of our local paper and my mother would kill me.

The second thing was that my baby brother graduated from high school and joined the Marines. My later observation of people who joined the military or even the Red Cross were people who often came from dysfunctional families and were looking for something to supply what had been missing. Young recruits— what do they know about the Marines? They're the toughest group, right? So if you came from a fatherless home (in our case, my father was an active alcoholic then), young men were looking for a way to prove themselves and to get their male identity.

So when the Red Cross came recruiting on campus for women who wanted to go off to Vietnam, I decided this would be a good way for me to find out for myself what was going on, maybe get a chance to check in on my brother. Also it was one of the few ways I could serve the country. The Red Cross had been contracted by the United States' government since World War II to be auxiliary support services to the military. They operated the SRAO program in Vietnam for eight years, the "donut dolly" program from World War II, in Vietnam. The requirements were you had to be between 21 and 24, have a college degree, and be single.

We learned about how to conduct ourselves with decorum as proper, virtuous young women in a war zone. Women at that time stayed at home and took care of the kids. All the people who trained us were older women. They were thinking in that paternalistic way where men are in charge and women take care of them. We weren't supposed to smoke in public or smoke at all, we weren't supposed to be getting drunk or drinking, and we definitely were not supposed to be having any sex. We'd be sent home if they thought we were involved with a married man. My role, my little blue dress, standing up in front of hundreds of armed adolescent males, was to say: "Looky but not touchy." Here I am to remind you of home, and guess what I am going to do with you right now? No, not that. I am going to play a game with you! It was a set-up. And it was also part of our culture then—women were arm candy.

Basically, we were charged with troop morale. It was our job to make the guys pleased that they were there and to remind them who they were fighting for. We were representatives of their mother, their sister, and their girlfriend who they were allegedly fighting for. To give them an hour at a time of relief from their present circumstances, we [took] mobile recreation programs to the soldiers, audience participation games. We did research on subject matter that would appeal to guys like cars and sports, we designed competitive activities with them. They all had to be mobile because we had to be able to carry them in a 3x5 canvas bag on the road.

I knew my brother was outside of Da Nang, a Marine, a grunt, so I requested Da Nang. Now, no one in my family had told my brother that I was coming. Two days after I got to my duty station and the first day I was in the Red Cross Recreation Center in Da Nang on Freedom Hill (which we called "The Last Resort") we opened the doors and my brother walked in. [*She laughs.*] Whenever his unit needed resupply, his CO would allow him to be the one to come to the rear.

I recall that there was a huge difference between the average serviceman at Camp Baxter [east Da Nang], in terms of education, and the officers. In this particular base, they had a lot of black soldiers who were exclusively infantry. I don't recall meeting a black officer. I would be walking past a group of black soldiers, I could pick up hostility, not necessarily at me, [but] they would look at me with some anger or intimidation. During that time the black power movement made it to Vietnam, and black soldiers were finding their strength and their voices as a race. They would take shoelaces and weave them into crosses and wear them around their neck. They would do the handshake, the power shake, bonding with each other. Whatever it was boiled to the surface, and there was a race riot on the base. People are often shocked when I report that we actually had a race riot, Camp Baxter, Da Nang area, probably the end of 1970 or early 1971.

All I know is I was scared and that we were pushed into our billets and locked in. Then they put several armed *white* American soldiers inside with us, who do you think we were more afraid of at night? The armed adolescent males *inside*. Every night you were vulnerable, we had to lock our room doors, and shove something up against them. After that I looked at black guys a little differently, I became more aware of watching how they were treated by sergeants. They would not talk to me about it. It strikes me to this day that race really wasn't commonly talked about. I grew up in southern Florida and we were segregated.

We did our programs in recreation centers, Ping-Pong tables, pool tables, card tables, we would talk to the guys, serve coffee. We also spent time going into the MASH units, the hospital units, going bed to bed. We'd do whatever we could with the guys, whether that was holding their hand, writing a letter home, chatting, or playing checkers. However, a lot of the time we were flying out to forward firebases. We'd be taken by helicopter, get dropped off, then the copter would take off because it wasn't safe for a helicopter to stay on a firebase for long.

I liked working in the centers best because I knew the guys there wanted to be there. They expected to see American females, they came to us. One afternoon I was walking around chatting with guys and I came to a table with three guys. I could tell that they were not new in-country because their uniforms and their boots were muddy, torn, and dirty, not pristine like you see in the recruiting ads. They didn't have clean-shaven faces, their hair was longish, dirty, and grungy looking.

But the most significant way I could tell, in a war, was that they couldn't look me in the eye and smile any more. They have what we call the 10,000-mile stare. To look in their faces, if you can get eye contact, there is nobody home, there is a vacant, distant look. The effects of things they have seen and done have taken a piece of their soul and their humanity, and they can't relate in the way they used to relate. So I knew these guys were in-country for a little while.

I asked if I could join them. Two of the guys said okay and I pulled up a chair. The third guy never said anything and didn't look at me. I started my routine: "Hi, my name is Cherie, and I am from Florida and I have been in-country six weeks. Where are you from? What's your name?" That was the beginning rap. I could engage the two guys a little bit, they told me their names, where they were from, how long they'd been in-country. Then you went to what was their favorite thing at home, their car, but no girlfriend topics because by now that could have been over. We didn't ask them what they were doing in Vietnam. You can see we needed the games because there were very few safe topics.

This guy who's sitting to my right felt like a heavy, ominous cloud, he's not saying a word, I'm getting no response from him. Then at this point, the soldier reaches into his cami fatigue pocket and pulls out a white jewelry box. He slides it over in front of me without looking, he's not speaking to me. Now on the base was a PX where the soldiers could buy stereo equipment and jewelry. It would not be uncommon for a soldier to go buy his girlfriend or mother something, and show it to me. They'd proudly show us pictures of their prostitutes when they came back from R&R. There were no inhibitions—the backdrop of the war made for instant intimacy between us and the guys.

So, I thought, all right, he can't tell me but he does want to show me. I pick up the box and I lift off the lid. I close it immediately. There is not a piece of jewelry in there, what's in there is about three inches long, about half of an inch wide. It's black, it's wrinkled. I put the box down, I look at him. The other two guys are now looking from me to him. Finally he sort of cocks his head, and looks at me through the corner of his eye, and he says: "It's a finger! Took that off a gook, ma'am." I was in stunned silence, I can't believe this. This is an American soldier. He's got a war trophy body part in a jewelry box and he's seemingly not ashamed of it. I was thinking, "We're the good guys, right? This is what the enemy is supposed to do."

What happens when someone gets assigned to a war situation where all of the rules and mores of their culture are gone? You can't really break just one of those values, just one piece of value that you had, and not have the others fall by the wayside. I believe there are really no rules in war. You're led to think that people are going to behave in some sort of respectable, civilized fashion when the whole nature of war is uncivilized. I saw a guy leaning over a pool table and his dog tags fell out of his camies and they were loaded with ears, it was repulsive. I knew that they alone were not responsible for what was going on, but that it was going to forever change them. When I would see guys with strings of ears, I would just avoid them. I couldn't, "Hi, I'm Cherie—whose body did you take those ears off of?"

Another duty station I had was in Cam Ranh Bay. We did a little fashion show at our recreation center. It was called the "Step'n Groove" (in Phan Rang it was the "Du-Drop Inn"—[we] women named these centers!). The Generals got wind of this and decided we're going to have you do this for all of the men. They built a huge stage and gangplank, got a military band together, and we had to perform a huge fashion show at night, under flood lights, in front of thousands of American soldiers. I would use the word *horny* American soldiers.

Then we were supposed to go down and dance with them afterwards. I was terrified, I was outraged, and I felt we were as close to being gang-raped as we ever could have come. Even the soldiers, they're not stupid, after the first few clappings, wolf whistles started, calls came out, people started reaching up on stage. I think even the Red Cross at headquarters got upset and decided that it was never going to happen again.

My near-rape experience. We had several rapes of women in Vietnam. They were kept very quiet. On my off-duty hours I used to go to an orphanage run by French nuns on the famous China Beach on the South China Sea. Probably the greatest tragedy that I experienced in Vietnam was seeing the multitude of maimed, burned, orphaned kids, especially those kids who had been burned by white phosphorous and napalm, ears melted to the sides of their head. God, how could we do that to children?

Our only mode of transportation when we were off duty was hitchhiking, getting into a truck full of guys was normal, and most of the time they were very respectful. I would hitchhike and get dropped off at the road to the orphanage, which was about a mile long. It was a deserted road, at the very end was the orphanage. I was doing this one day and a two and a half ton truck started pulling into the road and going very slowly behind me. A little creepy, so I stopped and turned around thinking I'm going to get out of the way and they can have the road. The guys said, "You want a ride?" I said, "I think I need to walk today, thank you."

My job was always to be friendly to the soldiers, smile, engage them in conversation, this might be the first and only time they saw an American female while they were over there. So it was *not* normal for me to turn them down. But I got a bad vibe from these guys, probably because of what their intent actually turned out to be.

251

I delayed leaving the orphanage because these guys were still there, but I couldn't delay much longer because I couldn't be out after dark unless I was under escort. I started to walk back and sure enough, the truck started following me again, and this time when they asked me for a ride I thought, "All right, Cherie, just get this over with, say yes, talk a little bit with them." Instead of them scooting over and letting me get in, one guy got out and that meant I had to sit in the middle.

So I started doing my routine, "Hi, where are you guys from?" and pretty soon the guy on the right of me takes his hand and puts it on my thigh, and I look at him and I say, "No. Don't touch me." Then the driver has got his hand on me, and they say, "You do this all the time." Every woman who has ever been connected to a war, there's an assumption that she is a whore, or promiscuous, or is a lesbian. These guys believed the rumors of Red Cross women over there "giving it out." The driver is continuing to drive very slowly, or maybe he stops, but they've got their hands all over me and I try to fight them off.

The one guy was black and he made a comment like, "Oh, I guess you only do this for white guys." That really pissed me off and I slapped him, I said I didn't care if he was purple polka-dotted. Then I stopped being afraid and I got furious. "How *dare* you? Who do you think you are? Do you know I have a brother over here—he's a Marine too! How do you think he would feel if he finds out you've been molesting his sister?" So the guy who is driving takes his hand off me. He said to his buddy, "Maybe she *doesn't* do this."

The other guy has the zipper to my dress (our dresses were one piece zipper things) and I said, "How would you feel if this was your sister? Would you feel good about that? Or your wife? You married?" I see a wedding ring. "Your wife? Would you like a guy to be doing this to her? I remember your name here, you're going to be in trouble because I am going to report you. Do you want this on your record?" Whatever logic I was using, whatever attitude I had, stopped them.

They stopped the truck, but I had to climb over the guy to get out. I got picked up by a jeep full of guys, they dropped me back, but I was still very anxious. I only told one woman, my best friend. We decided to go to the judge advocate and tell him what happened and decide whether I should prosecute or not. In the end, we decided it was going to be very complicated and probably nothing would happen to those soldiers. Before I came to Vietnam, one of the Red Cross women had been murdered in her bed, stabbed to death by a GI. It was hushed up, the women from her unit were dispersed and sent to other units. I learned about it from the guy giving me my plague shot at the Air Force base, "You hear about the Red Cross girl who was just murdered?"

I think something that happens to everybody who survives in a war zone is you numb out, you repress, you deny. I think probably that's true for most soldiers. They come home and drink and drug because they can't live with their memories or that they survived. When I speak to women who served in my job in the 60s, before Tet, there weren't anywhere near the sexual issues, they only report being treated with utmost respect; they didn't have the drug issues then.

After Tet several things happened. The tide changed in the US, the draftees who were coming in now were demoralized, they weren't coming in with any gung-ho attitude any more, they were picking up on how everybody felt at home. They came in with a much more reluctant and anxious mindset because the morale of the troops in-country [was] based also on the morale of what was going on at home. Then it became not uncommon when I was in the Cam Ranh area, a rear area, to visit units with men who were high, sitting around smoking (if they were shooting heroin, I didn't see it). The military started having drug testing, they had to have a clear urine before they were sent home. If guys were testing positive, they were put in a drug rehab unit in-country.

War is an equalizer. And there is, in my experience, no clear good guys or bad guys. War makes everybody potentially into a bad guy, bad things happen, and you do things that you never recover from. The whole idea that somehow, because we think we have a righteous motive makes every act that we do or even the whole act of war righteous, to me is absurd. The other thing is the whole absurdity of war, period. It's impossible to have a positive outcome from war, if there ever has been, it's over. Once we got nuclear weapons, it was *over*. Once we have the kind of warfare we have now, it is *over*.

The wars we now have are unpredictable and the soldiers are citizens. Now citizens are the victims, are targeted, Iraqis are targeting their own citizens to make the most mass civilian casualties, Afghanistan, same kind of thing. At the time in Vietnam, I thought most civilian casualties were accidental, but I'm not sure that was actually true, it was what I believed. And the environment, these horrible chemicals that we all used, depleted uranium, Agent Orange. The effects of Agent Orange are still lasting, babies being born deformed. Several women that I know who served in the Red Cross had stillborn or deformed children, or couldn't have children. Soldiers are told when they come home not to try to have children for at least a year. When I went to Vietnam the first time in 1970, there were Agent Orange-defoliated jungles. When my husband and I went back with returning soldiers in 1990, we noticed: *there were no birds*! Can we afford to live in a small world contaminated like this?

The trouble is that we can't do the *first* thing. If we do the *first* thing, that's how it starts happening. "Well, we can't back out now. We owe it to these people. We have made this, we have done this." It's not okay to say we screwed up, maybe that's the male machismo kind of thing. What are you winning anyways? Occupy a whole country forever? Maybe if you want to fly in, kill Saddam Hussein and fly out, end of story.

We are occupiers, even for well-intentioned purposes. As long as you're an occupier, you will never succeed at what your stated goals are. Iraq is a tribal society. We don't like it, it isn't our way, we've got to stop believing that our way is the only and the right way. We have some ordained right? [What] if the right thing to do is to say we are in over our heads in Afghanistan, we cannot accomplish things the way we are doing it now, we need to change, we need to pull out, even if people think we're chicken? I don't think we have many people who have that kind of courage.

5

IN THE AIR: US MARINE CORPS, ARMY, AND AIR FORCE

Robert Basye was born in Washington, DC, in 1944 and grew up in Silver Spring, Maryland. He graduated from Western Maryland College (now McDaniel College) in economics. He signed up for the Marines after his sophomore year in college in 1964, and was a helicopter pilot flying CH-46s in Vietnam in HMM-265 in 1968. He left the service in 1970. As with many pilots, his taking to the air was unplanned: he was recruited to fly at a time when pilots were in great demand, and it seemed like an exciting thing to do; it was also a good way to spend time in training before deploying to Vietnam. He has been a small business owner in medical products and is currently a remodeling company sales manager.

I went down to the recruiter and I said, "Okay, I'm ready to join up, I want to be a Marine." He looks at me and says, "Okay, I'd love to have you, we've got one little problem. The ground program for the PLCs [Platoon Leaders Course] is full, have you ever thought about being a pilot?" And I said, "No, I haven't. What do I have to do?" "Well, you have to pass a tougher physical, and you've got to pass another test to make sure you are smart enough, if you are willing to do that, I can get you in. That's all that's available right now." I said, "Sure." That little word changed my life, it was the defining moment in my life. It might have been a ruse, this guy was a pilot himself!

I got there two days after Tet started, late January 1968. That's how we started our tour in Vietnam—no weapons, down in a bunker, watching the tracers, the war going on around us, smoking Luckys. We walked in on the war. The fighting in that period lasted probably a month or two, then it settled back into what it had *always* been, which was a sporadic conflict. You could fly for weeks without anybody shooting at you and then you would get what we called a "shit sandwich," which was a real bad situation, where they were trying to kill you as you're driving in and out of the landing zone. We lost five or six pilots over there, maybe more than that. We lost two on that one day [see Bing Emerson's story on pages 330–344]

There're three or four stories about Vietnam that I relate. An emergency recon extract means that a recon team is caught up with some bad guys, there's shooting going on, and they've got to get out right away. So we drive over, it's back in the jungle in a place called Happy Valley. We arrive on station and we see the firefight going on below us. You can see the green tracers (theirs) going one way and the red tracers (ours) going the other. On the other side of that little itty valley were some really high mountains.

We're orbiting, getting their zone brief, they're calling up, "We need to get out of here." We're doing a couple of turns and I'm literally getting sick to my stomach. I can see what's happening, and I know that this is *not* going to be fun. When the time comes, you locate your clearing, ask for pop-a-smoke. I'm looking at the smoke down there and it's going right toward this little valley, toward the Marines that I want to pick up. So I do my turn and a half coming down, high-speed turn, by this time I'm into the mission so I'm not worried any more. I made a really weird approach: in order to get into the wind, I had to fly over the bad guys, I wasn't about to do that. So I went clear around this mountain. Now if I'm on the Marine side, and I see this helicopter coming in to pick me up disappear behind the hill, I'm thinking what the heck is this nutcase doing?

I came all the way around and snuck in behind them. I have a rookie copilot with me, this guy probably hadn't been in-country a month. I come around the hill, I look at the firefight going on, the guns are blazing, the .50s [caliber guns] are firing, I look at this copilot and the only thing I could see was his nose and his knees. He had stuffed himself so far back in that armored seat, I just burst out laughing!

I drove into the landing zone laughing my ass off, got the helicopter on the ground, blazing, shooting, killing going on. I see this VC guy stand up, point a rifle at my face, *shoot the rifle*, I'm waiting for the bullet to hit me—he missed the entire aircraft. Somebody shoots him, we pick it up, I turn around, we leave, we got out of there and we got not a scratch! He was about a hundred yards away from me, I saw the muzzle flash—it looked like it was right between my eyes.

We picked up six or eight guys on a recon team, you throw the airplane down, the ramp has already been dropped in the back, and they start piling on. If you've ever seen an H-46 in combat, know that it has no windows. The reason it has no windows is that when you do this, they bust the windows out so they can shoot. It didn't take the Marines long to realize that when you send these helicopters to rehab, you don't put windows in them because they were getting punched out. There are four portholes on a side, they leave them open.

They immediately get inside, they stick their weapons out and start shooting. The whole aircraft is like hell. I picked the aircraft up, and instead of going into the wind, where I would have to fly over the enemy, I turned it around. When you take off downwind, you really wallow. I was staggering with eight guys in the back, it takes a lot to get the aircraft airborne. It ended up just being exciting! I figured I could get out of there safer by taking the more risky takeoff.

[*As a pilot do you evaluate the war more broadly?*] I see where you are heading with this. Here's the answer: I don't believe that there were very many Marines or any other branch of the service that left Vietnam and thought that there was a purpose to it. We all realized somewhere along the way we were doing the same thing over and over and over again and getting nowhere. That's the way I felt about it, day after day, there's no victory, there's no battles won. It was just a game: this mission's over, tomorrow we're going to do it over here. Then three months later, you'd be back at the same place, doing it all over again.

As aviators, we did have another perspective. I swear to God, I have nothing but *absolute respect* for those guys on the ground. I mean, I wouldn't do that, there would be no way. They felt we were like gods. Think about that. I go back to Marble Mountain where we have hot showers, an air-conditioned hooch. I come home late, maybe I'm tired and I go to the O [Officers'] Club, and do what I do every night, I get drunk. Then I go back to my rack and I get up at 5:30 in the morning, do it again. We *commuted* to the war as pilots.

I knew nothing of what was actually going on. We saw the whole thing from 1,500 feet and the only time I was in a village was when I was landing there to either bring Marines in to kill people or take out Marines that had been wounded. The only Vietnamese I knew were the people who worked on the base, my hooch maid, the staff who came in the morning. We were detached. From a pilot's perspective, I think we have kind of a macabre view of it. How many maimed pilots do you know? You could probably run across an awful lot of grunts with missing this and that, shot there, whacked here. How many pilots do you know like that? Nobody. You know what? We either came home, or we came home in a bag.

I have some haunting memories of the wounded. We did a lot of medevac. There were these hospital ships that used to sail around Da Nang Bay, *Repose* and *Sanctuary*. I remember landing and having wounded, transporting them from *Repose* to Da Nang so they could be sent home. This one guy that they brought out, he was just... it was just his torso and his head that they had on that stretcher. It was unbelievable! I can still *see* that guy on that stretcher, just a stump with a head. I'm thinking, what the fuck, what is this?

The traumatic brain injuries that they are saving now... I think what's *wrong* is that so many are getting TBIs and no one knows about it. I don't want to attach politics to this, but I think the Bush administration was adamant about not having anyone know the consequences of what's going on. All these wounded and dead people that are coming back, do you ever see them? You never see that.

I went to Vietnam, it was the first time I had ever been on a commercial airline. Here I am a naval aviator, got my wings, I'm qualified, I already had 400 hours of flying time! I'm in my greens, and I sit down in my seat which is an aisle seat, and I see this woman coming down the aisle looking for her seat. She's got the hippie look. When she saw me, she literally *recoiled* in horror. I saw the look on her face and I was polite and I let her sit down, she sat as far away from me as she could. Some time goes by and she looks at me and she says, "What are all those ribbons for?" I was wearing maybe three, my shooting badges. "How many babies are you going to kill?"

Here's the other side of the equation. When I came back, we were dumped from combat, shooting and killing, and the transition is instantaneous—you're home. There's no buffer, nothing. You see your wife, your family, and then you're off to your next duty station, probably training pilots, that's what most of us did. When you get out of the military, you go to your civilian job. People would find out that I was a Vietnam veteran, the question I would get, "Did you ever get shot at?" It's like kicking you in the nuts. There is so little awareness of what actually goes on when you have a war. I think it's the same way with these guys in Iraq and Afghanistan. Nobody knows what's going on over there. They don't *need* to know.

There's a lot of support for troops today, but it's mainly just posturing, I think. It's a lot better than it was for us. When we came back, we came back to a country that was totally divided. The support for the war was so weak, it was divisive. I think most of us just tried to stay out of everybody's way. It was really too bad. And now all of a sudden, people know you are a Vietnam veteran and everybody is falling all over you. [*Would you have ever publicly opposed the war, as John Kerry did?*] Never!

I do believe that Vietnam was an error. The cause was noble, but the methodology was pointless, we ended up there right back where we started. Anyone who can think past the end of their nose can't deny that. There's a lot of posturing to make it all worthwhile—"the Vietnamese have it better now"—I don't know where that comes from. The admission that the politicians drove that conflict for reasons other than the domino effect... that was what we were all there for, to stop the next... I actually believed that, I used to recite that line, let Vietnam fall, the rest of Southeast Asia will go with it. That was a lie. [The real issue was] nobody wants to be the guy that lost the war.

Johnson started sending advisors in, okay, fine, we help them out, we get them organized, we send troops because they needed something for the Vietnamese Army and so forth. All of a sudden it gets bigger and bigger and nobody is paying any attention. And then somebody dies. Americans died in the conflict, you cannot let that go. You spill the blood, now you have to atone for it. You cannot be the president who let those Americans die and go unanswered, that's how you get sucked in, inertia.

I've had this discussion over the last two or three years, and they say, "This [war] is not Vietnam." It *is* Vietnam. It *is* Vietnam. The only difference is that it's in a different area. The weapons are a little bit better, but Vietnam was a *civil* war. The Vietnamese didn't really care who was running the show, they didn't want the communists to be there, but the North Vietnamese, as far as the south was concerned, half the people down there just said, get someone in power and leave us alone.

Dick Warren was born in Burlington, Vermont, in 1942. He was a Marine captain in HMM-265, then HMM-161, 1967-8. He makes a number of points about how hard it is to fight an insurgency. He had a chance to talk with General Pace (recent Chairman of the Joint Chiefs of Staff) at a pilot reunion, and asked him about the political mistakes made in Iraq and in Vietnam. He graduated from UMass-Amherst. He was married with his first child when he served in Vietnam and had four children, including two adopted Korean sons. He trained as a nurse-anesthetist, a job he loved. He and his wife Lynette twice served with a Christian ministry in Cambodia teaching English-language medical terminology, and Dick was very active in his church and its outreach. Dick died at home in May 2011 after a battle with cancer.

I have my nine flags still out on the front lawn. These have the names of all nine pilots we lost that year, including Bingo Emerson and Jack Harrell. It's funny how your thoughts on war change. When young, the height of experience, excitement, and worth was in flying and fighting for this country. Now when I watch TV reviews of dog fights in previous wars, I'm saddened even over enemy aircraft shot down. It's such a waste and craziness. Yet overt evil needs to be confronted at times, even as a Christian.

Tet is a week-long celebration. We arrived in Da Nang in the middle of Tet, which is probably the worst timing you could have had, because our first brief, the next day, was some major [who] said, "You've got five NVA divisions around Da Nang. We're in danger and in probability of being overrun." A great message to hear when you are a new pilot and you don't even know what end is up. But that is how precarious it was.

I remember getting off the airplane at night, and it was funny. As we were going off, there are all the people returning to the States coming right by us, taking our seat and going out. I met one guy with red hair who was in my OCS class at Quantico who was a grunt and didn't have to go through flight training, so he had already gone to Vietnam. He was taking the trip home, and he said, "THANK YOU! I'm taking your place going home, Buddy!"

If you look at the average Marine, 95 percent of them were motivated by what I was motivated by: Can I handle myself in combat? Ever since I was a little kid I always wanted to do that— John Wayne hero movies in the '50s, with much less debate about it, much less controversy. Second World War, there wasn't a lot of controversy; there was over Korea. I still think that the average motivation of the Marine is I am trying to prove myself, can I handle this? Some people have that, and other people, the majority of people, don't have it. I won't say a warrior class, but it is a grouping of people that have that motivation to experience that and see if they can handle it. Because you don't get the average cerebral candidate in the Marine Corps, you get a person who is emotionally motivated to prove themselves. They don't judge the training, they're judging themselves.

The first flight was an emergency evacuation. Went out over the ocean, flew around, was copilot, FNG (a "freaking new guy,") coming into the country. [We] flew around in circles while jets strafed and bombed the tree line. This was a whole three miles from the base, they were overrunning it, that's how bad it was. They had killed something like 1,000 to 1,500 VC in the wire of the perimeter of Marble Mountain before we got over on the base; it was a precarious situation, to say the least.

We flew off and waited for the A-4s to come in. We had two birds and were evacuating everybody, we were in the second bird, the first bird went in and took half the people out. But you've got the other half there firing at the enemy. Second bird has a bad deal because all those people are now on board and there's nobody firing at the enemy. We came in and sat down, and I looked out to the tree line, a couple hundred yards away. I could see the leaves going pa-pa-pa-pa-pa. There's a guy with a machine gun over there shooting at [us]. I remember the HAC (Helicopter Aircraft Commander) grabbed me and pushed me back. "Put your freaking head back before you get it blown off!"

Ten days later, I didn't believe in God back then, but Lord Jesus was protecting me and others. We were hovering and making an emergency evacuation, hoisting people up with a cable that goes down on the side of the mountains, it was a hellhole. Hovering over the mountainside, wounded Marines, it was only ten miles from Da Nang. We were out there on the Laotian border, we used to fly right into Laos without even knowing it half the time, it was that close in the real skinny part of Vietnam.

Anyway, we were hovering around the side of the mountain at about 60–70 feet, I looked down through the bubble and I could see what I thought was leaves popping out, and a guy stitched us. They had thirteen rounds that stitched right down between the pilot and me. All the people were sitting in their seats, and it went straight down the middle, never hit anybody, blew out many of our gauges, so we thought that we were going to crash.

The pilot pickled the Marine halfway up (pickled means you just cut the cable, he falls where he falls), because he thought we were going to go down the mountain and he'd catch the cable on the tree. We were staggering, trying to fly down the mountain to get control of the aircraft. If we caught that cable and the pallet with a Marine on it, it would have obviously killed him. He may have died anyway. He got pickled about 30 or 40 feet up, and we staggered down the mountain. I'm scared to death. The HAC was trying to see if he could fly the aircraft, we lost the gauges, but does that mean we have lost the hydraulics and all? We ended up flying down, set it down a few miles away, got some other aircraft.

[*What happened to the Marine?*] Down in the jungle? Don't know. He was on a litter, he got pickled back in the jungle. Hopefully his people are down there and able to retrieve him, but I don't know. We never found out. When we were in the hover, and lost everything, the aircraft is gone, I guess you just said, pickle the litter right then. You have to figure that here are the wounded Marines at the back of the aircraft, and here's the machine gun shooting us down, it's 50 yards down the side of the mountain, there was not much distance at all between the NVA and where all those Marines were.

But that was a long day. Back to the O Club, a lot of shots and booze, it cost a dime. The basic thing on drugs and alcohol in Vietnam was the officers drank themselves into oblivion most of the time—I was probably drunk 80 percent of the nights I was there. The enlisted smoked pot or whatever they smoked down there. The Marine Corps made it so cheap to buy alcohol and it was the expected thing that everybody go to the O Club at night and get plowed. People drank until 2 or 3 o'clock in the morning and got up at 5 or 6. You can fly tired, you can fly hung over, you can probably fly inebriated. You might not do such a good job. I was always into alcohol. Before I gave my life to Christ, I used to drink all the time. I drank in college, football, in the Marine Corps, afterwards until I was about 35. It wasn't anything the Marine Corps did—I brought it with me.

My brother was a Navy doctor, and he was already on the *Repose*. I got a message to him and he said why don't you come out and spend a while. So I spent a couple of hours out there. It was the worst possible thing. He was in charge of burn patients and he brought me around in the burn ward, and said basically, this person is going to die. Helicopter pilots, most people died as a result of impact, but in the explosion they were also burned. They crash and burn.

You would bring [a wounded Marine] into the LZ11 medevac station, an initial check, stabilize the patient and all that. You just flew them in, and you never saw them again. There was a disconnect that was probably beneficial between the cockpit and what was going on in the back because we had people dying back there, we had blood all over the place. We had chu-hois (prisoners of war). We just haul them. That's probably why you don't have a lot of dreams and post-traumatic stress, because there's a disconnect, it was just hauling cargo, people, C-rats, or a recon unit. We didn't see a lot of body bags, we didn't see lot of deaths. When pilots would die I wanted to believe they were just transferred to another unit.

But picking up medevacs, taking your fellow Marines out, that was something you could latch on to and feel good about. I had one particular time—it was a bunch of Marines that were wounded on the side of this steep mountain. When they didn't have a place to land, they would take C-4 [explosive] and blow out the basic trees, try to open up a space so you wouldn't get your rotor blades [caught], you could hover in and try in this case to hoist these people up. Problem was, it was so small, and the mountain was so steep that you couldn't fly into it, you had to back into it, like you are backing into a garage. Obviously, you can't see what you are doing. The other problem was usually you look down through your bubble and to the side, and you can get some kind of reference over land. Well, this went down 2,000 feet to the valley below, there was absolutely no reference. Reference needs to be five or ten feet where you can see the aircraft moving in relation to this fixed thing—something 2,000 feet below is absolutely useless.

So I had to literally fly over and then try to back in, listening to the crew chief, "Back, back, back, stop, stop." We were taking fire from the side, according to the copilot. I got all three rotors in the back, the blades were chopped up and it was still flyable. So I just sat there, and we started hoisting people up. Somewhere along the line, to this day I don't know how I did it, I ended up getting all three blades in the front. We stayed there twenty minutes, which is a long time to hover, and got eleven, twelve people up. That was good. Flew back.

At one stage, our CO was really a jerk. He got all ticked off because I had gotten six blades, and chewed me out in front of all the pilots and enlisted people; you *never* chew out an officer in front of enlisted people to begin with. Then you've got to figure: there was an aircraft that went in before me, he got one person out and got a blade or two and had to leave. When I left I had eleven or twelve [evacuees] and it was at the point where my RPM was starting to go down because I couldn't lift any more, and I took off and there were two or three left so someone else came and got them, and they got their blades. All three of them got the blades. He proceeded to chew on *me* because I got all six blades. [*He laughs.*] I only got twelve or thirteen Marines out of there. I didn't say anything because I was so mad.

Certainly the VC was an insurgency. Terrorism now isn't any different in Iraq. We were used to large army conventional war.

That was a big change going into that insurgency—a small group of dedicated people can inflict a whole lot of damage on a nation. Look at terrorism: a country is terribly vulnerable, you can't protect all the US people abroad, you can't protect all your events and your football games, and your stadiums, and your subways. If you think about it, people willing to commit suicide inflict a whole lot of damage all out of proportion to their numbers. The cost since 9/11 to plug the holes is astronomical, just look at the cost involving airlines. So terrorism is a whole new ballgame.

Blowing yourself up has devastating effects, the cost and men that it ties down. A few men, with a little bit of equipment, not much money, can inflict horrendous losses on people if [they] are willing to be amoral and die in the process. This we were totally not prepared for. You look back at what has happened in the past, and that can end up tying you down, it takes a lot to break free of that. Tradition governs. Tradition in football, tradition in war. People look back, they're comfortable looking at what they've been doing; it worked in the past. It isn't a wrong motivation, but there has to be this idea, okay, there's something new going on here, it's got to be out of the box, and just following tradition isn't going to cut it.

In our [2009] reunion, we met in private with General Pace who was chairman of the Joint Chiefs. I came away from our meeting with a very high opinion of the man, and of course he was a Marine. First of all, he was very approachable, he came around and talked, 50 to 100 people there. He went out of his way to address us and our questions, and he talked to me. I said, [I was in Vietnam] Tet of '68, and he said, "Well, that was when I was there, February '68, that was a brown bar," which was a second lieutenant. I said, "Guess what, General, I actually outranked you at one point!" He didn't get huffy, he just laughed about it, and said, "How about that!"

I had some questions to ask him about Rumsfeld. I have no use for two people: McNamara or Rumsfeld. I had read *State of Denial* by Woodward about Paul Bremer and the horrendous decisions this man made in the first week he was in-country. It was General Garner that he replaced, and Garner tried to coach him concerning the Iraqi party and the Army, and also concerning the regional committees they were forming to draw up a constitution. Bremer, in his utter arrogance and stupidity wouldn't listen to him.

So I asked [General Pace] this question, "I read Bob Woodward's account, and there were three decisions made in the first week that set the piece on its tail, could I get your comment on it?" The questions are: "Baath Party—why didn't Paul Bremer have the sense to get rid of the top echelon and a couple of layers and keep the rest of the people, the only people that had any experience governing Iraq for 30 years? That made 50,000 people with weapons instant enemies. Same thing to the army, [he] didn't get rid of the colonels and generals and keep the rest. You had another 250,000 instant enemies who had plenty of artillery and plenty of AK-47s. So in one week he made 300,000 enemies, all with varied weapons and we're still seeing the IEDs, so this is going to go on forever."

[Gen. Pace] said there were three channels: "Condoleezza Rice was one channel of communication, Rumsfeld was another channel, and Hadley, the National Security Advisor, was a third channel. They were not together at all, some major mistakes were made." He came around to at least acknowledge how poorly the piece was handled.

McNamara had this idea of graduated response to the Russian aggression of sending over missiles [Cuban Missile Crisis]. Khrushchev blinked, we got away with the embargo, the ships turned around, and it worked. Well, even at the height of the attrition that US soldiers were causing on the Vietnamese they could still keep fielding an army by putting all their young men and many of their women into it, indefinitely. So that wasn't going to work. And Ho Chi Minh was in it for "this is in the country's best interest, we were fighting the French for two decades." It's struggle and it's war, and it's living on nothing—makes pretty good soldiers when you do that.

So gradual attrition never did anything, it just hamstrung US efforts. They couldn't bomb Haiphong, they couldn't bomb the SAM sites, they were all off-limits. You can do an ammo dump here, and a fuel dump here and a bridge here, unbelievably stupid. This gradual "Rolling Thunder" was just a death knell that resulted in tens of thousands of people [who] died who didn't need to die. Don't play a half game. That's what we were doing—we were playing a half game.

LBJ—it's because he didn't care about that war. He cared about his domestic agenda, the poverty, the 100 bills he wanted to pass. He looked upon [the war] as a total nuisance, he just wanted to keep the fires low and keep it out of the way. Not like his domestic agenda against poverty. It was great he was against poverty, and [in] civil rights he did a lot of good things, but he just sold that war down the river. McNamara actually, with that silly graduated response, sold it down the river too.

They went to the Paris peace talks, and that rattled around for two or three years. Everyone says, "Well, the domino affect didn't happen." I happen to think it happened. Cambodia became communist under Pol Pot, and many said we drove them to it when we went in and bombed the poor Cambodian people. But I disagree, because Pol Pot was already in the works, our going after the NVA did not create that situation. The Ho Chi Minh Trail came through Cambodia, one of its 500 different routes.

If you want to blame somebody, blame the NVA. First of all, you can't win an insurgency, like in Afghanistan, when you have neighboring countries that are totally open. The enemy just runs in there, gets sanctuary. People denounced Cambodia, and kept the Americans from going in. I'm sorry, the Ho Chi Minh Trail is coming down through there, and your soldiers and all your equipment are coming down through there, then that's where you're going to go.

We lived in Cambodia a year and a half. We were missionaries in Phnom Penh in '91 and in 2000–2001. Pol Pot took 14- and 15-year-old peasant kids with no education, and scared them into obeying him, or you get shot. Like child soldiers now in Africa, they say, "You either shoot this old man we got from the village who is an enemy or I am going to shoot you." Well, what's the average child going to do—he's going to shoot the guy. That's why Pol Pot killed people. If you wore glasses, you were a businessman, if you went to school, he didn't want education and a mind that he couldn't brainwash, he wanted you dead. That's why he killed one out of four.

It was Pol Pot and his influence from China, his Maoist deal. Granted, Lon Nol was the US-backed prime minister, and he was corrupt, and does that add to it? Sure. You never find ideal people to support. Karzai, these are the guys we've got to go with. I think we've learned that democracy, some people are ready for it and some people aren't, they have a tribal background for the last hundred years, and democracy is not going to work. We may have to live with that. Democracy is such a fragile thing.

I think Iraq and Afghanistan are different. Afghanistan is a mountainous country—if you don't seal the borders, you have easy sanctuary, very rough terrain, whereas Iraq is more of an open desert, much easier to have wars in. Afghanistan is even more tribal, the Pushtun area, if al-Qaeda comes in, they are my guest, and I have to treat them well. I have to protect them for some dog-gone reason, and I accept them in. It is this whole culture thing that I think is crazy.

When I first heard there were outreaches to the Taliban [in Afghanistan] I was hoping they were going to make some peace plans with some of the Taliban to turn against some of the other Taliban and al-Qaeda and get some of this homegrown backing. In Iraq, they decided to go with the Sunni groups, who then turned Anbar province into a fairly safe area. They paid some of the Sunni groups—to me we are dropping billions of dollars in the war effort, well, spending tens of thousands to get this group on our side. My hope was we could do the same thing with some of the Taliban. That didn't happen.

Petraeus made some wise decisions. He turned the Sunnis against the al-Qaeda, paid them off. I have no problem with paying some of the Taliban off to get them on our side. It's probably a lot cheaper than the war machine that we're using by far. Bribery, whatever you want to call it. They've got to have money to live. We already have mercenaries with our contractors. We have more contractors in Iraq and Afghanistan from the US, like Blackwater, than we ever had in any war.

To rebuild a country I think you have to have a healthy measure of security first or the endeavors you make are just going to get literally blown up. I think you have to give some level of security to the people who live there, some of the Taliban, and some of the tribes, and the army in order to get to the point where people can start trusting. And once they start trusting they won't have anything to do with the Taliban. People don't want to be fighting and dying all the time. They want to live and enjoy life. It's about control.

Why did we win the Second World War? I think one of the main reasons we won the Second World War was the Depression. The Depression was so hard it prepared people to withstand the rigors of war for four or five years. I think God used the Depression to prepare us for what was coming down the road. We'd have been in deep trouble to respond to the Japanese aggression with any kind of force if we hadn't gone through that, if we didn't have a background of people who were used to struggling on a farm.

I wanted nothing to do with Vietnam, or Vietnamese, or thinking about it, or Asia, nothing, until I had a rebirth. I gave my life to Christ. I was talking about it for three or four months, and I did that and my attitude changed. One of the first tests was in church, to talk about the boat people coming out of Vietnam and how we should be helping them. I had an empathy that came the first time.

[My wife and I] went from Cambodia over to Vietnam. I went back thinking it would be all kinds of déjà vu, but if you think about it, the only way I knew Vietnam was from the air, so the only déjà vu I had was when we flew into Da Nang and I saw all those rice paddies and rivers and they looked kind of familiar. The rest of the time we were running around on the streets. I couldn't get on the base and the base was obliterated anyway. It was good. The Vietnamese appear much more open and friendly than one might expect. They let bygones be bygones.

David Bressem was born in Ludlow, Massachusetts, in 1948. He grew up in Springfield, and decided not to go to college but enlist in the Army before he was drafted. He was an army helicopter pilot in the 1st Cavalry Division and was severely wounded when the helicopter he was in tried to rescue men from another helicopter that had crashed and was burning. After Vietnam he returned to college and trained as a social worker, and has for many years worked at the Vet Center in Springfield. He had a brother in the Marines, another brother in the Merchant Marine, his father served in the Navy reserve, and his uncle fought in World War II. His physical injuries are still apparent, and his empathy for other veterans is clear.

It was not an option for me *not* to go into the service. Going to Canada or trying to get out some other way just wasn't an option. Back in the mid-60s, I was as hippie as anybody else, long hair, love, peace. I remember this poster saying you could be a helicopter pilot. I said, that's cool; that would be a lot more fun than beating dirt and walking on the ground. I took and passed the test, so I enlisted into the helicopter pilot program, officer candidate program, in '66. We learned to fly Hueys and to do combat training. Got orders to go to Vietnam, March of '67.

I went right to An Khe, the base of the 1st Cav for the Central Highlands. The first day we were walking across the tarmac and I remember a C-130 was taking off down the other end of the field and just after it took off, it crashed. I believe that everybody died in the crash [March 12, 1967]. I have no idea what caused the crash. I remember thinking that that was a pretty terrible thing, not so much the loss of life, but these were people who had survived their 365 days and died on the way out, on their way home.

That first week they were describing the various units that had openings. It was my feeling that if I'm going to be there I might as well *be* there, if I'm going to be in a war, I might as well perform those functions. The 1st Cav was this new model of fighting warfare, the mobile model, and the 1st of the 9th was a unit that went out and found the enemy. So I thought that sounds interesting, it's not going to be boring, so I raised my hand. [*He laughs.*] I figured I either wanted to do that or be in dust-off (medical evacuations). I wanted to *do* something, I didn't just want to ferry cargo or soldiers around.

There weren't too many volunteers for this unit, so when I raised my hand, sure, you've got it, you're it. It turned out that was the helicopter unit in Vietnam that had the highest turnover of pilots, through death and losses. I wound up assigned to a gunship platoon, Huey gunships. The first day we went out they said all those things they taught us in flight school about flying safely, evasive action, how not to get shot out—forget it all. Your job here is to find the enemy, the easiest way to find the enemy is to have them shoot at you.

The first major event for me was my first mission. We got called out to go to a little hamlet, there were VC there supposedly. We always flew with two helicopters. Sure enough we started getting fire from this hamlet. Never saw the individuals, they don't want to get shot, they're firing from inside grass-leafed hooches. It's up in the Central Highlands, a small agrarian community, a little hamlet. So we started returning fire and the machine guns we were using all have tracers in them so you can see where you are firing. When they hit a hooch, they oftentimes set it on fire. We wound up burning one little hooch and then we started receiving fire from the next hooch. In the process of this little firefight, we wound up (it was a small little hamlet, maybe four or five little hooches) burning the place to the ground.

Eventually we stopped receiving fire, so we assumed that we killed them all, logical assumption. We were about to leave from that mission, and I noticed not too far off in the distance that the villagers were returning from the rice fields. I remember thinking just as we were leaving that we made more enemies today than we killed. We just burned the village totally down. I have no idea if the people shooting at us were from the village, but we just destroyed this whole village and these people's livelihood, their homes. That was my feeling and it changed my whole focus.

I don't know that I had one before. I wasn't overly patriotic, I didn't go there to defeat communism. I wasn't sure I really understood or believed the whole domino theory. But my country called me to duty, and I'm a good doobie as a boy scout, so I'm going to do what I'm supposed to do. It did change my focus a little bit: it seemed that this war doesn't make a whole lot of sense. I just did my job the best I could. People's lives depended on it. It was an interesting perspective to have from that point on.

I arrived in March, but I only lasted until September. I remember very specific instances, many of them are pleasant and humorous, a few are not, some places I don't want to go. I have a vague recollection of a cargo net full of bodies. I think they were ours, because I don't think there was any reason for us to put the enemy bodies in a cargo net and take them anywhere. It's on the fringe of my memory. I don't see a reason to go there.

I find in my work here [in the vet center], and it is certainly true for me, there comes a point (it doesn't matter whether you fired a weapon or didn't fire a weapon) the impact of the combat experience is still significant. There's a division. For those people who were actually engaged in fighting, there comes a time where there's a shift between doing your job and killing the enemy, and taking the lives of a fellow human being. There comes a point where you realize that the military professional distance that we were trained to do evaporates, and you realize that the person you just killed is a person.

Sometimes if I'm helping someone with a claim (the VA likes documentation of things) I ask if they have any pictures of them in Vietnam. That stuff is helpful. So I've seen lots of pictures. Actually, some really gruesome kinds of things, from many wars, all the way up to the current ones. They don't bother me—I'm a vet. One day somebody brought in a photo album, I opened it up, and I nearly closed it because it took me back. It was a gut-wrenching thing. I opened it up again, we looked at it, and talked about it.

He had three or four pages, a couple dozen pictures. They were pictures of Vietnamese children, and wives, and mothers, parents. They were small photographs. The man who brought them in was military police involved in collecting and interrogating prisoners. These were photos of VC or NVA soldiers' families. They were the pictures that the enemy had taken with them of their family members. It just struck me: these are all the families that lost their loved ones, one of the costs of war. They are just like us. The enemy is no different, they just happen to be on the other side of the rifle.

My own personal thing: I remember we were called out to support a unit that was under attack, happened to be on a hill, a little bit of a cliff that was exposed. Especially from a helicopter, sometimes you see them [our men], sometimes you don't. They pop a smoke to let us know where they are, and where the enemy is. We were doing a very classic thing, a daisy chain where (there were at least four helicopters involved in this), one helicopter would fly in and fire and then peel off and get out of the way, and another would come in right behind it. You do this circle so you can have pretty steady, continuous fire on a spot.

I'd just made my run and peeled off, and I remember the radio contact called up and said, "Oh wow, did you see that? That guy just fell off the cliff, just like out of a John Wayne movie." It just struck me to trivialize that person's death, to relate it to a movie... Now, I didn't even see the person, but I knew that I had killed him. It became not the enemy any more, but a real person. I've heard this often. Sometimes it's people seeing, sometimes it's hand-to-hand combat, sometimes it's "I heard a noise at night in a foxhole," and they fire into the jungle and the next morning, there's the body. It varies from person to person.

War is not a nice thing. Jimmy Carter, in his acceptance speech for the Nobel Prize [2002], said that war is sometimes a necessary evil, but it is always an evil act. I think that is very true. To me, war is an immoral act. It's one society trying to kill another society, or another people in that society. They are just like us. The military does a very good job in trying to dehumanize them. That's why in the Vietnamese war they were the "gooks," they were "VC," they were "enemy," they were "Charlie"—they weren't people.

When I was being trained in the military we didn't learn about the Vietnamese culture, we didn't learn about the history of Vietnam and how they had been invaded over the centuries by many, many nations. What I learned was that they fight dirty, they use excrement on punji sticks [sharpened stakes in booby traps], a lot of things to dehumanize them. That's true about every single war. I've got a poster somewhere about the Huns during World War I that shows a monstrous German with a pointed helmet, literally ripping a baby apart. There's always that propensity to make the other person less than you, to distance them so you can go kill that person. Because otherwise, why would you want to kill another human being?

There was a very interesting statistic I heard once. It was something like 85 percent of the US combatants in World War II when first fired upon, froze when they first faced the enemy. Now it didn't take them very long to learn to shoot back, but the first reaction was to freeze. It said, prior to World War II when you learned to fire a weapon, you shot at targets, you shot at bull's eyes, you're not shooting at something real. When I was trained, we shot at silhouettes, now I'm shooting at something that looks like a person. A lot of people from Vietnam had issues with shooting children and women, because again, the silhouettes used were of men. They now are training people with silhouettes of women and people of all sizes.

I can talk about how I was injured. I have retrograde amnesia from it, meaning it goes backward maybe a half hour prior to the event itself. What happened was this. We flew gunships but we had a variety of missions. One of those missions would to be the eyes and support for a unit on the ground that has to go from point A to point B, providing air coverage for them. From the air you are looking down, I can see where to go, but I don't know what the elephant grass is like, I don't know what the terrain is like. I thought it would be beneficial for me to go on a patrol, to be on the ground to get some sense of what it's like down there so I could do my job better up in the air.

I had spoken about this a couple of times to my commanding officer. He said, "No, you're crazy. The Government spent too much money teaching you how to fly a helicopter, we're not going to put you on the ground to get blown up or get shot at." We were in the Officers' Club, everybody's drinking, so I started pushing this point again. I don't know if he was a little looser because of the alcohol, or he was tired of hearing about it, but to shut me up he said there was a routine patrol going out around the base camp of An Khe, the perimeter thing. Relatively secure area, not too dangerous, he was going to let me go. Okay, great.

The last thing I remember specifically was being on the flight line, getting on the lift ship with the infantry unit that would actually do the patrol. The rest I don't remember, [I] just put together what people have told me, what's in the book [*Hunter-Killer Squadron: Aero-Weapons, Aero-Scouts, Aero-Rifles (Vietnam 1965–1972)* by Matthew Brennan], other sources. Whenever soldiers are being inserted into an area, there are always gunships on either side, we would prep the LZ to make sure there are no enemy there. In this case they were rocket ships, as well as the mini guns, and the door gunners, they had 48 rockets on there. One of them crashed. It is presumed it was a mechanical failure, not enemy. I was in the lead lift ship so we went in to the crash site, which had started to burn, to try to assist them. It's my understanding [we] had to jump out of the helicopter. Just as we made it up to the [other] helicopter, it exploded.

There were a fair number of us that were killed. The copilot survived, I actually met him back at Walter Reed when I was there. He was paralyzed from the neck down. Everybody else in the helicopter had died and a number of the other people that came up to the helicopter were also injured or killed. They sent me to 69th evac in Qui Nhon. I was unconscious for ten days. I had enough blood transfusions for three complete oil changes. They did a venous graft and I was able to save my leg. I was injured basically on the right side, perforated ear drums, I had thirteen operations on my ears, lost an eye. They were able to save the leg but it has nerve damage, muscle damage, bone damage.

Came to ten days later, then spent a little over a year at Walter Reed, back in '68 during the riots and the burnings. At that time it was getting to be the height of all the antiwar efforts and the mistaken focus on the soldier as opposed to the politics. There was a lot of that hatred, the spitting, the fighting. I didn't experience any of that personally because I literally came out of Japan in a basket, never got off the plane, went by ambulance to Walter Reed, which was a military compound, a much different transition for me back to civilian life.

I hope our society has recognized that however you feel about the politics of the war, the people who fight it need your support. I think that has been a big shift as a result of the yellow ribbon campaign in the first Iraq war. I don't know a single combat veteran that feels they are a hero and if they say they are it raises a whole lot of red flags for me. I have a certificate that says I am a hero: I got a "Soldier's Medal" for that incident in which I was wounded. It wasn't a *choice*, nobody was *not* going to do that. I didn't tell the pilot to turn around and don't land, I didn't refuse to jump out of the airplane ten to thirty feet up in the air, of course not. That's what anyone would do, I think all people are capable of that.

The flip side is interesting too. I've heard, "Oh, I couldn't fight a war, do the killing," and *anybody* can do that. The dark side, almost anyone is capable of carrying a weapon and shooting it, it doesn't take any particular kind of person to do that. I do think it's the dark side. I do think war is an immoral act. There are varying degrees, too, but how can somebody *not* consider that an immoral kind of behavior? I think all veterans have this familiarity with death that is different than the civilian world.

There are a couple of points that are important regarding PTSD. One is that it's a perfectly normal experience. I believe that everyone who is in a combat arena, not necessarily just as a combatant, is altered and changed by that experience. What is important for people who have been in that situation to understand is that first of all, it's normal, and second, how is it influencing *you*? The symptoms [are] individual and unique to each person, by degree or by type. So there's a great deal of communality to it, but also a great deal of individuality. It's a life experience that one needs to *understand* and *process* rather than an *illness* that one needs to *cure*. You can't cure it—it's part of who you are.

I'll give you a quiz. As you talk to veterans, ask them what happens when people make mistakes in the field. To a person, I'll bet the response will be, somebody makes a mistake, they die, someone dies. We have an entirely different way of looking at someone's making a mistake, [even] someone spilling a glass of milk, someone cutting you off. It has nothing to do with there's milk on the table; it's got to do with someone could die because you did something stupid. Once the veteran understands where that's coming from, it's a lot easier for him to adjust that. It's not like a switch. I like to use the metaphor of a radio knob: it's like turning it down. Sometimes you can turn it all the way off and it goes away, sometimes you just get it from a ten down to a three.

I remember being scared twice in Vietnam and it had nothing to do with the enemy. I was flying low one day, and you've got your eyes all over the place, you've got to watch your instruments, watch where you are flying, but you're also looking on the ground. I pick my eyes up and there is another helicopter coming straight at me. It was a split-second decision, I went up to the left, he went down to the right—we missed literally by inches. I was so scared I soiled myself. [*He laughs.*] We landed, and it was my chase helicopter had seen something, came down without telling me. He should have let me know so I would be aware of that. I went over and beat the crap out of the guy. [*He laughs.*]

The other time was with Major B. I got to be his first copilot. You want to fly as low as you can, but you have to not hit things. He had the habit of flying into the tops of trees, which is first of all dangerous; second of all, it upsets your guns and equipment. We would do rocket runs and he would fly through our own shrapnel. He was a little bit too careless and rambunctious. One day we are out doing a mission and he was flying so low that he hit a tree, and I don't know how we survived because the impact broke both of the chin bubbles, the Plexiglas down by our feet so you can see down.

Somehow it didn't crash, we went back and got another helicopter. We all got cut with flying Plexiglas, even the door gunner and the crew chief in the back. He said he was going to put us all in for Purple Hearts. We told him to go shove it. [*He laughs.*] That's not what a Purple Heart's for. We got another helicopter because we were in the middle of this battle, and as soon as he went down lower, I grabbed the controls because I was not going to have him kill me or my crew. He looked over and said, "What are you doing?" "I've got the controls, sir." When he got to a safe level, I let go. [*He laughs.*] I'm overriding my commanding officer. That lasted for a day or two and then he got another copilot.

Those are the two instances where I remember truly being scared. It altered my view and this is something that's related to

PTSD and how people deal with it. It changed how I deal with commanding officers, or my superiors, or my bosses now in the civilian world. They don't automatically get my respect. That's why I see a lot of veterans [who] have difficulty with command structures because people in command, if they make mistakes, people die. So we have to understand that and learn how to deal with that in the civilian world. If you don't do what you are supposed to do, people die. You talk to any veteran and they will tell you that without hesitation.

I don't want to belittle in any way the 9/11 World Trade Center, but from a military perspective, that was *one* battle, *two* incoming rounds. Anybody who fights in a war zone fights *many* battles, *many* incoming rounds. If they're not fighting, they know it can happen any day. The wars today, people walking into your office strapped to an explosive like the CIA bomber [December 30, 2009 at Forward Operating Base Chapman, Afghanistan]. Or you have a rocket coming in to the Green Zone [Baghdad]. You never know what's going to happen so you live in a state of not necessarily fear, but heightened anxiety, heightened apprehension. There is a biological, chemical process that happens along with that. So even for those people in the rear it affects who they are.

Rod Carlson was born in Duluth, MN in 1943. A Marine captain and helicopter pilot, he flew the CH-46 in HMM-265 and 261 in 1968. He received his MBA at the Darden School, University of Virginia in 1972, and has worked in advertising agency management, and as a creative marketing and business strategy consultant. He lived in Miami for many years, and currently lives in New York. He tells his stories with a laid-back humor, including meeting Major Chuck Robb (President Johnson's son-in-law) on Hill 12. He spoke frequently of his wife Barbara and, like many of the veterans I met, is very appreciative of her steadfast support.

I came from a real nice family, a lot of support, a lot of freedom, a lot of high expectations, and a real good upbringing. I graduated from high school in Duluth then went to Principia College in Elsah, Illinois. At Principia I met my first and only wife, Barbara, in a historiography class. We've always shared a love of history so it was like we were ushered together in that context.

It was the summer of '65 that the Marines went ashore in Da Nang. I had friends who'd been in the PLC (Platoon Leaders Course) program and I knew I wanted to be an officer because my dad had been in the Navy in World War II. I got in the car and I drove down to Minneapolis to talk to the Navy and the Coast Guard. I was coming out of the men's room and there was a man [who] said, "You look kind of bewildered." He was a Navy chief, assigned to the Marine Corps to do recruiting. "Let's have you take this test." It was about a three-question aptitude test that a chimpanzee could have passed and I passed it.

The next morning the chief took us upstairs into a long auditorium, and there was a line of guys standing in their underwear. The chief yelled out, Stand aside, two Marine Corps candidates, and everybody moved aside and we walked to the front of the line, had our physicals, passed, and I figured, you know, there is something about this that I don't dislike. Going through the breakfast line, I say, you know, I've been here 24 hours and it seems like I can't even remember my previous life, so different from anything else I had ever experienced. Frightening, terrifying, but it worked out. Then I went to officer basic school at Quantico to learn to become an infantry officer. Barbara and I were married in the chapel at Quantico.

By then I had realized that I had a decision to make. I could have been an infantry officer, but I knew that if I went to flight school, we'd have a year together before going overseas. I'd like to say I've always wanted to be a helicopter pilot, but basically I am a liberal arts major. Liberal arts majors have never wanted to do anything—that's why they end up as liberal arts majors! I made it to flight school and it was a wonderful year because we both liked sun and swimming and there were no parents. Then we drove to Santa Ana, California where I learned how to fly the CH-46. I suppose I knew I was going to Vietnam but I was in California, so what difference did it make? I think we were naïve. I don't think we realized what it was until we got there.

I went home and said goodbye to Barbara, left her in Duluth with my parents, and went off. I can remember one very, very poignant night as we were waiting for transportation to fly to Okinawa and Vietnam. The guys said excuse me and got up and went to the pay phones and called home. I looked across the bar at Don Lammers and he shook his head, and I shook my head, and we said, "We ain't calling home." That was the first indication that this was going to be a difficult experience.

April 1st, we end up getting off the airplane at Da Nang. We're all fat, everybody else is tan and thin because of the heat and being in a combat zone, and we all look like we've been living in the French Quarter, totally out of place. We report to our aircraft group at Marble Mountain. We had air-conditioned hooches, like Quonset huts. We moved to Phu Bai during the fall.

The president had ordered us, the military, to block the Ho Chi Minh Trail, so we were doing inserts into Laos. It was supposed to be hush-hush and nobody was supposed to talk or write about it. It wasn't that the Laos missions were excessively dangerous, because everything was dangerous. People might get shot down going just a few miles down the beach and resupplying the Republic of Korea's Marines down there. It involved flying over there with fairly large gaggles to insert troops and to take troops out, and to resupply troops from some of our bases along the DMZ like Camp Vandegrif. I never did that [but] I remember vividly that it was going on. Vietnam is skinny, Laos is skinny, and it's all very close. To me, Laos, Vietnam, what's the difference, it's not like there was a line. It's just all jungle and it's a mess in the first place.

I was over there a month [and] I'd gotten some news from the home front that Barbara was pregnant and that we were going to be having our first child in December. I lost a best friend, Don Lammers, in August, this pretty much changed my life—depending on what day it is, it can be to a little degree or it can be monumental. So the idea of now my having a wife and a child, and a good chance that my child was going to go through life saying that she'd never known her dad, was a sea change for me. I was looking for any way I could minimize the risk, so I became the safety officer to investigate accidents. I wrote to Barbara every day and Barbara wrote to me every day. I remember December 12, I was out running and somebody came out from the ready room and said that the Red Cross had just called and that I was the proud father of a baby girl and mother and daughter were doing fine.

I'm very interested in my experience over there and all of our experience over there, the *becoming* aspect. By that I mean you go over there and you are nothing, and you don't know anything, and everything is very difficult, and you say to yourself there's no way I'm ever going to be able to do this. Everything you've learned seems to be totally inappropriate, it's chaotic, and you can't even understand what's going on over the radios. We listen to two radios, a high-powered radio that was for aviation, UHF radio, and then we listened to an FM radio, that was the radio that we were in contact with the troops on the ground.

Very often, there were a dozen conversations going on, on one frequency. So if someone said something, you didn't even know who was talking to you. Not only that, the helicopter is loud so you can't even *hear*—the pilot would turn to you and say, "Did you hear that?" You go from that to by the time you leave, you can do it. Not only can you *do* it, you can do darn near what's impossible. You know the helicopter so well, you know what it can do, what you can do, what you can get away with, you can infer multiple things, if you do this, this is or isn't going to work. And in an instant, you will say to yourself yes or no. You won't even *say* that, you will *feel* yes or no. People *knew* who did it well, you could tell in yourself.

It was a time when one more day could have been the day. We didn't lose somebody every day, by any stretch of the imagination, but the group *did*. Every day you would go to dinner at the officer's mess, somebody was dead. *Every day.* There were five squadrons, helicopters, and if it wasn't that, you knew somebody up in 161 in Quang Tri and they had been killed. You have to keep in mind that 1968 was the worst year of the war, certainly in terms of helicopter casualties, followed by 1969. Your perspective is totally focused on your own survival and wellbeing. Even in '68 there was talk about pulling out. Certainly by '69 they were starting to shut down a lot of the pipelines for new pilots. So it was like, well why are we over here, what is this, this doesn't make any sense.

What we didn't really know was where the war was *really* going on, and that was back home. It was the year of Martin Luther King, [Robert] Kennedy and all the riots, and we would read about Detroit being burnt to the ground, it doesn't make any sense. Here we are, we left America, and now this is all happening. I think there was an incredulous sense of what was going on at home.

Any time I'm asked about near-death experiences, I refer to the day our squadron flew in support of Operation Meade River in the hotly contested lowlands south of Da Nang. I was flying copilot with an experienced pilot in a CH-46A Sea Knight twin tandem rotor helicopter. We flew with fifteen or twenty other 46s and Huey gunships to the airfield at An Hoa, approximately twenty miles southwest of Da Nang, shut down, climbed out of the helicopter and assembled with all the other pilots for the pre-mission briefing. We learned that we and the other transport helicopters were going to insert a large number of Marines who were going to sweep through a hostile, fortified village. There would be a blocking force on the other side of the village to contain the enemy, which if all went according to plan, would be captured or killed.

We landed without incident, lowered the ramp so that the Marines could quickly exit and get to safe cover. According to the brief, we were supposed to lift off, make a climbing left-hand turn to a specified altitude and return to An Hoa to pick up another load of Marines. We were no more than 100 feet off the ground when over the radio we heard someone say, "turn right." This was a comment that was not directed at us. It could have been made by someone talking on the radio miles way, yet the pilot turned to the right and flew over the village occupied by the enemy.

I look down and there they are, countless NVA soldiers in conical straw hats and they're shooting at me. I see muzzle flashes that look like flash bulbs and then I hear the sound of bullets hitting the aircraft. Then I hear over the intercom, "We're on fire." I look to the rear and the troop compartment is black with smoke pouring out of the windows and aft hatch. Just a couple of months earlier, my best friend Don Lammers had been shot down and killed in the ensuing crash.

Then I hear a calm voice, "Burning '46 continue ahead to Hill 12." Then there were a series of thunderous, violent explosions. I looked out my side window and saw the Huey gunship that had told us to keep going to Hill 12 using its rockets, then its machine guns, to clear our path of enemy resistance. We flew on for what seemed to be hours, but was probably only a few minutes and landed at Hill 12 helo pad and shut down the engines. The crew then extinguished the rest of the fire.

That's probably as close as I came to *knowing* that I was in big trouble, because I could see the guys shooting at me. It looks like you're flying over a town in the countryside in Ohio with all the farm lights blinking, but there are no electric lights over there. People are just shooting their guns hoping to hit a dark object that's flying in the sky. Just because it's a big sky, it's not big enough. You have all the lights off so there's nothing to see, sometimes they can see the exhaust. It's extremely dangerous, that's why the only missions launched at night would be emergency medevac, if somebody was going to die before morning, because very often, the crew that was sent out to get them would be in more danger than the person who was deemed to be the emergency medevac.

As grateful as I was to have survived, I was furious at having my life nearly snuffed out by stupidity, and went off by myself by a row of sandbags at the edge of the landing zone and sulked. After a while, the pilot, as ebullient as ever, comes up from the command bunker and enthusiastically tells me that Chuck Robb is in the bunker and I should come down and meet him. (Chuck Robb was a major in the Marines and President Johnson's son-in-law, and then was a US Senator and the Governor of Virginia.) I ignore the invitation and continue to wallow in my anger. After a while, someone approaches from my rear and asks, "Are you okay?" I turn around and see a major wearing a nametag that says "Robb." I said, "Not really." He nods and walks away.

Later on after it's all over, I go to the graduate business school at the University of Virginia. I'm with my classmates, sitting in the student union, "Hey, look, there's the president's son-in-law, Chuck Robb." And I say, "Oh really, I know Chuck Robb." So I get up and I went over, Chuck Robb is meanwhile at the law school. I say, "Excuse me, I don't mean to bother you, honest, I'm not on an autograph hunt, but I met you one time, it was at Hill 12, and I was just shot down in a helicopter." And he looks at me and says, "Oh, yeah, I remember that." And I say, "Well, why don't you bring your food and come over and sit down and have lunch with us." So he comes over and the whole thing was perfectly normal.

[Robb] was probably the operations officer, a ground guy, Hill 12 was probably where they had a regimental or battalion headquarters. I think they were trying to downplay his relationship to the president and just let the guy do his tour. But on the other hand, I don't think they were doing too much to put him at excessive risk. To us he was a celebrity, but probably to all the other guys on Hill 12 he was just Major Robb. Of course, in the Marine Corps somebody would say, "I order you guys to treat him not as the president's son-in-law, but as Major Robb." "Yes, sir, we'll do that." "We'll take it under advisement." "You got it."

I recently have gotten involved with the Veterans Administration, a vet center, and I go to a group session. Periodically we will be very troubled by something and will try to help people come to grips with it. One of the things that nobody does any more is say, "Forget about it and move on." Because in 40 years you don't forget about it, and everybody knows that, and moving on is your ability to cope with what you can't forget. I think people who lost friends like Bing and the others we lived with don't *want* to forget because that would be a huge tragedy, to forget. So everything that I have gotten since, Bing hasn't gotten. Think about the heap of stuff that wasn't on his plate, that wasn't in his basket. The older you get, the bigger the pile becomes that he has missed. Then, nobody could forget that the families were shattered permanently because of this.

Fred Guertin was born in Gardner, Massachusetts, in 1944. He enlisted from UMass-Amherst in his second year when a recruiter approached him with the question, "Do you want to fly?" A Marine captain and helicopter pilot with HMM-265 in 1967–8, he earned the Bronze Star for Valor and the Distinguished Flying Cross (DFC). He became a corporate pilot and later the manager of the Fitchburg (MA) Municipal Airport. Fred was very helpful in pointing the way to other pilots who had known my cousin Bing Emerson, making possible Bing's story (page 330).

It was west of Kham Duc in Quang Nam province. We were under attack by militarily superior hostile forces. It was the next day that Kham Duc fell, May 12, 1968. The Marines and the Air Force got all or most of the people out the next day. It was mostly my squadron that did that. This was after we'd been shot down. There was no more room in the landing zone, but the aircraft before me was hit with .50-caliber machine gunfire, and he couldn't fly any more. I was the SAR (search air rescue) guy, and he was behind me so when he got shot down, I went back in to pull him out, and pulled the crew out of there. Just as I was landing, I was hit with an RPG (rocket propelled grenade). It ripped up the side of my helicopter, wounded my crew chief and my gunner and blew up behind the copilot's seat (he wasn't hurt).

Later on that day, an Army helicopter came in. They would

hover on the side of the hill on the perimeter with one skid on, just enough to get the people on board. Meanwhile, we were getting mortared. Before he came in, we drew straws to see who was going to stay behind and who was supposed to go. I lost. The wounded were going, regardless. I don't remember who else went except Billy Cihac was there. Anyway, Bud Fleming (Horace H. Fleming III is his real name)… I'm going to interject something in here, talk about coincidences. Remember when the bracelets in the 70s were made for the missing in action? I put my hand in the bag, and who did I pull out but *Bud*. I put it back in the bag. Really, it was scary.

The problem is when we drew up the straws to see who was going to go and who was going to stay, Bud was not part of that lottery. He was on the other side of the perimeter so he didn't know that he wasn't supposed to go. When he saw the other crew members on the helicopter, he thought that was his out, and he ran for the helicopter. Of course they had to pull off the hill, with the mortars and stuff. A couple of the Montagnards and Bud too jumped for the helicopter and went on to the skids. When the helicopter pulled up they couldn't hang on, and they fell. I got the long straw, that's what kept me on the ground, it wasn't voluntary. Billy was trying to help Bud and he saw Bud fall off and he said all he could see was Bud's face, desperation, as he fell into the jungle. I have thought of that often.

To continue with the story. The good thing about being an American is that to save our butts, they—Marines, Air Force, and Navy—literally diverted every flight in Vietnam up there to help us out, they were close air support, fixed-wing. We did have Huey escorts out there, too. There were some already supporting us and then they brought in more. They literally bracketed us, bombed the napalm, and walked us through the jungle. They knocked out a couple of ambushes until they could pick us up. The North Vietnamese Army, they were all there.

I don't think there is another country that would do that to save just a couple of people. There were more than a couple of us with the Montagnards (mountain people who lived mainly in the western part of the country), there were probably 75 or more Montagnards. They were mercenaries, we were paying them to fight for us. They and the Vietnamese never really did get along and I guess they still don't. They were tribal people. All I remember was George Bunder (Bucky) and myself and the enlisted guy from the helicopter. From the time we got shot down, it took the whole day. They got us late, late, late that evening.

When we got to a suitable place to be picked up, we had to clear the zone, George and myself supervised that. A squadron came to rescue us. The first time the helicopter landed, we were supposed to be the first ones on, [but] the Montagnards panicked and rushed the helicopter to get on. There were so many on there they couldn't take off. Jeb White had to go aboard the helicopter with a machine gunner and force them all off. The second helicopter came in and when they lowered the gate, he got on the tailgate and shot off several rounds with his automatic weapon, kept all the Montagnards at bay trying to get us on first, and they got us out of there. They took control of that situation. We got them all out that day, we got the Montagnards off at Kham Duc. Then they flew us back to Marble Mountain.

The following day was the fall of Kham Duc; two C-130s were shot down with 150 souls on each one of them. An A-1 Skyraider was shot down and an Army CH-47 was shot down trying to evacuate the space. It probably gave me a sense of validation for what happened to me. This is a big deal, this is why I got shot down. We never thought we were going to get killed. If you thought about getting killed, you died, if someone got scared, they died. If you start worrying about getting hurt, then you're not thinking about what you need to do—too defensive maybe, and you can be scared afterwards.

I can remember going up to some recon camps that had been compromised, it was like bang, bang, bang one right after the other. We knew when we went to get them out we were going to get shot at. It was really difficult to extract them—we couldn't land. We had to pull them up one at a time with a wench. There were muzzle flashes all over the place. We backed into the edge, picking these guys up, the rotor blades are just nicking the top of the mountain. You could feel the movement every time we got too low, we needed more power, we're hanging out over the edge and we can't see anything. All we've got to go by is the crew chief telling us: "Back, back, up, up, back, right, right, left," to stay over these guys.

We had armored seats and we wore a ceramic vest, and we had two .50-caliber machine guns, one on either side. When we would go into a zone every gun in the world that could see us was shooting at us. We knew there was a $500 bounty for killing a pilot. We heard it was for "a head in the helmet." I don't know how true that was, but supposedly they would get $500 and two weeks in Hanoi, and to them that was a small fortune. The RPG did a pretty good job of bringing us down. We survived a lot of small arms fire, as fragile as a helicopter is, it could take a substantial amount of bullet holes. The Russian AK-47s, you'll know the sound. It is a very cheap, cheap, cheap thing, it's pressed metal.

There were a whole bunch of different things about this war. Remember the Arc Lights? A code name for the B-52 drops. Just before a drop would happen, you would get a broadcast: "Arc Light, Arc Light," and they would give you the coordinates, and you look over there and the whole world is exploding. That was the call when they were going to do strip bombing. B-52s coming, they are dropping ribbons of bombs a good quarter, half a mile long, a 500-pound bomb, a row of explosion after explosion. You can see the shock waves going out. I don't see how anybody could live after being hit with that. It was an incredible sight to see.

There were little villages, little hamlets, just to the left of our airfield and the Vietcong was holding townspeople in there as hostages. The Vietcong captured all the people, but the people in the church, we liberated them, just annihilated the NVA. The church we are talking about was here. [*He uses Google Earth to show me the actual church.*] During Tet, the North Vietnamese had rounded up everybody in the village, a Spooky [USAF gunship] came in, that night Spooky and Puff [another nickname, as in "Puff, the Magic Dragon"] were working out there. We went out the next day, and those straw hats that the North Vietnamese wore were scattered all over the place. There was a high body count on both sides. That scared a lot of people: where did these guys come from, how could they do that? That was a surprise for us.

Then along came Khe Sanh [January–April, 1968]. Khe Sanh was left out there, set up as a trap: "Come and get us." Later on, they brought C-130s in and dropped off big canisters of napalm out the back of these things because the North Vietnamese were digging trenches and the trench fighting up there was coming closer and closer. Well, we had to do a proof-of-theory flight and we had this big hill and we put jellied gasoline in the back of our helicopter, we would run up the hill, kick the canisters out, and then shoot the tracer until it lit the hill on fire.

Where we had large firebases it was pretty secure. Hill 55 was out in the boonies there, Hoi An, An Hoa were also out in the boonies. We had bases and firebases all around them, they all could cover each other and that's how we made sure we all stayed safe. But there was no line, no front like you had in the other wars. This was an insurgency from day one. You had a guy working out in a rice paddy today and tomorrow night or tonight he's lobbing rockets at your place, he'd be a Vietcong. You didn't know who the good guy was.

We tried to win the people over. I remember one mission, we went down south and we had an elephant that had been tranquilized, put on a pallet, and we flew it to the farmers and said, "Here!" I didn't do it, it was my friend Paul Moody brought it up there, they use them for logging. There was another time when we would shoot elephants and get secondary explosions because the Vietcong had rockets strapped to the belly of the elephant and they would roam around in the jungle. When they needed the rocket, they would go find the elephant, take the rocket from under his belly and shoot it at us. I never saw it.

If you were in the jungle, it was very difficult to spot your people. We popped smoke grenades to try to identify their positions. We would get them on the radio. I am told certain coordinates, I fly over there, I can't see a darned thing! So, pop a smoke so we can find you. Sometimes if you said pop a red smoke, you might see a red smoke over here and a red smoke over there because the Vietcong were listening too. So we would say "pop a smoke," and "what color is it?" and then we would know it's them.

Your time got shorter, and you could start to see the light at the end of the tunnel. We had a calendar we used to call "short time" calendars. Usually it was the figure of a woman broken up into several pieces. Mine was a 200-day calendar. [*He laughs.*] I had a block of days on the bottom and she was split up into the last 100 days. You color her in, like the paint-by-numbers thing. Every day you filled her in, once it got into her body, you knew you were getting short. You weren't as aggressive; you want to get home. I think I stopped flying the last two weeks in-country, hell or high water, I'm going to make it.

People ask me why the Marine Corps? I think that John Wayne was part of that decision because John Wayne, after the [Second World] War, played the part of the Marine Sergeant, and they glorified the Marine Corps. When we were kids, the Marine Corps was the best and the toughest. That's what I wanted to be. [*He laughs.*] John Wayne was a Marine pilot. Ted Williams influenced me too—he was a Marine fighter pilot.

Jane Fonda. [Jane Fonda, "Hanoi Jane," visited North Vietnam in 1972 and posed on an antiaircraft gun. She also made some broadcasts from Hanoi directed at US servicemen.] Look what happened, they used her for propaganda. Just by her doing that, it gave them hope that the American people are falling apart and all they've got to do is hang on. America, they're not going to support this war, they've had enough of it, they don't have the guts, all you have to do is hang on. What is an example? When are the Americans going to leave Iraq? You crazy? You put that date out there they will just sit back and wait.

I don't know if we've learned a lesson there, though. Keep the politics out of it. Let the military do their job. We've gotten very soft as a country. Look at the body counts in World War II in a single battle, or the Civil War. We had three people killed today. Freedom costs. We want to do the job, but the last thing we want to do is go to war or fight a war. Schwarzkopf [Gulf War] tried to make that clear when he went to war: you're going to have major casualties. We were lucky we didn't [then].

We're just beginning in Afghanistan. I think we have to wait until the Afghanistan government is in control before we can pull out, otherwise, it's all for naught. We need some help from Pakistan, too. Did you see on the news today that the Pakistanis are getting sick of the Taliban too? Afghanistan? The tribe culture is too imbedded. The Middle Eastern cultures hate Americans so much. [*Can we win any kind of war with the Taliban?*] Probably not without annihilating them. You have to protect your country, you've got to protect your people. How do you tell a good Muslim from a bad Muslim? You can't. So what do you do? Good question.

I interviewed for [a job]. That was around the time that Kent State happened. They almost didn't hire me because they thought

I was going to be the type that would be up in the church steeple, shooting up the village! They thought I was wacko, because [they] asked me, "What did you think of Vietnam?" I answered, "It's the most rewarding thing I have ever done." His thought was I was killing people and I was feeling good about it, but in reality I was saving people.

The Bronze Star was awarded for actions on May 10, 1968. We were reinforcing a Vietnamese outpost near Kham Duc [*Fred describes that action in the beginning of his narrative.*] Distinguished Flying Cross was awarded for actions on September 15, 1968. I was the flight leader of a flight of two CH-46s. We were assigned a mission to extract a seven-man reconnaissance team that had been compromised and was under heavy fire. We tried to get to them a couple of times, but the jungle made a pick-up impossible. We directed them to a better area where I could only put the loading ramp on the side of the mountain as we hung out over the edge. This was done under fire and by voice commands by my crew chief. We stayed there basically hovering off the side of a mountain under fire until all the team was aboard.

Subsequently we were dispatched again to another team in trouble to extract two wounded Marines. Again, the jungle would not allow us to land. The team was under constant fire. We were forced to extract the wounded by hoist one at a time under fire.

We were dispatched a third time for another emergency extraction of a nine-man reconnaissance team that was heavily engaged. We were able to get the team to a suitable spot to pick them up. We dumped all the unnecessary fuel to lighten the helicopter. We landed and waited for all nine Marines to get aboard. This was done with lots of shooting in both directions and under cover of close air support.

I guess that the pilots of the OV-10s that escorted us that day thought that we did something pretty incredible to run three missions in succession with so much fire and all of them emergency extractions. They are the ones who initiated the award. We saved eighteen Marines that day.

John Hartman was born in Washington, DC, in 1942 and grew up in Norwich, New York. As a boy he read Civil War and World War II histories and watched the Korean War on newsreels. He served as a helicopter pilot in Vietnam from 1967 to 1968 in HMM-165, stationed in Ky Ha Airbase. When asked for a photograph, he sent a picture of himself and his wife Carol. "We were a team back then as well as now, and her strength and support kept me going." Their son Douglas was a Marine lance corporal in Desert Storm. John practiced law in upstate New York and now lives in Maine.

Midway through Basic School, we were out in the field for several days of infantry exercises and it was rainy, muddy, and miserable. Our platoon leader asked if any of us would like to fly in the back seat of T-28 aircraft that were going to provide simulated air support the following day, and I raised my hand more for the opportunity to take a hot shower and put on clean clothes than from any interest in flying. I found myself automatically on the list of flight school candidates, and I took and passed the flight aptitude tests and physical examinations. I felt somewhat chagrined because some of my fellow officers who had wanted to fly from a young age failed the flight physical.

When I left the States, we had to land at the civilian airport in Honolulu to refuel. We were tempted to go AWOL for a few days and enjoy a good time in Hawaii. The standing punch line whenever we discussed possible consequences was, "What's the worst thing they can do to us? Make us helicopter pilots and send us to Vietnam!" In those days we had to wear our good uniforms on the flight over, not combat uniforms. Then in Okinawa they boxed up our uniforms and put them in storage so we could pick them up on the way home when our tours were completed. I have wondered what they did with all the unclaimed uniforms.

I remember the Hawks back in the States calling for us to be unleashed upon North Vietnam as a means of successfully concluding the war, but we were having trouble keeping our heads above water in I Corps, never mind "unleashing" us. Their idea was mobilize everybody in the country and invade North Vietnam. The Marines were responsible for all of I Corps and we had our work cut out for us. The Marines were supposed to be the preeminent amphibious assault force: Vietnam had this long coastline, and we could have been offshore running raids all up and down the coast, but instead we had to play Army. I think the Marine brass didn't like to be outdone by the Army. I also thought that the helicopter allowed us to hop, skip, and jump all over the country, whether it made any tactical sense or not. We'd assault an enemy position one month, leave it the next month, and assault it again three months after that.

The Marine Corps leadership in Da Nang insisted we were winning the war in I Corps, but this required them to willfully ignore certain facts with which we were more familiar at the squadron level. One example was the "There are no .50-cals in I Corps." One part of their argument that we were succeeding was that the North Vietnamese and Vietcong in I Corps were so ill equipped that they only had small caliber weapons, hand-me-downs from the Vietminh or captured from the French. The enemy couldn't possibly have .50-caliber weapons.

After each of our missions we were debriefed by a staff sergeant from our squadron intelligence shop. He would go over the flight with us and fill out a written standard report form that was sent to Wing headquarters. He'd ask us where we had been, what we'd encountered, what had happened, and if we'd been shot at, where, and by what. If we told him we'd been shot at by .50-caliber weapons, though, it was a problem for him. He wanted to know why we thought so, and we'd tell him: we could tell from the loudness of the shots, or from the sound they made when they hit the helicopter, or we'd show him the .50-caliber-sized bullet holes in our helicopter.

In response, the sergeant would smile and say (and we with him in unison), "Sorry, Sir, but *there are no .50-cals in I Corps.*" It seemed that whenever he turned in a report saying that fire from .50-caliber weapons had been taken, it was sent back to him with the notation that "There are no .50-cals in I Corps," so in the end he gave up and refused to put in the reports. Some people were deluding themselves. Having .50-caliber weapons would have been a sign that they were doing better than we wanted to believe.

Sometime in 1967, problems with the CH-46 started and the helicopters would self-destruct and come apart in the air, killing everyone on board. The 46 has two rotors at each end of the fuselage, and the aircraft were coming apart just forward of the aft pylon, on which were mounted the two turbine engines and the aft rotors and transmission. When helicopters were lost in these incidents, we'd be grounded for a time while the Marine and Boeing experts tried to figure out what was going on. While grounded, we were only assigned to fly emergency missions. That meant we had to fly a potentially bad helicopter on a patently dangerous mission.

From my perspective, the war was being conducted on a day-to-day, catch-as-catch-can basis. There must have been some overall strategy with tactics to fit, but it wasn't apparent at my level. We seemed to be running around putting out fires. The enemy seemed to be exercising the initiative while we reacted. When we did try to exercise the initiative, the enemy just melted away and wouldn't fight.

Our lives were not all darkness, drama, and angst, but I can say that because I came out of it all without any physical or psychological damage by virtue of good luck and pure chance. The war was not without its many comic aspects. Before being shipped to Vietnam we were told to take green underwear with us, so my wife dutifully dyed all my white underwear green. I guess this was for camouflage purposes, anyway, the green all washed out after a couple of washings. It occurred to me that if I was shot down and trying to escape and evade through the jungle in only my underwear, I was going to have more serious problems than the color of my skivies!

I don't know if you've been told the story of the unofficial Marine Corps hymn in Vietnam. We were entertained by traveling USO shows, small shows at the smaller bases. The musical groups always performed one particular song that they knew would get them a standing ovation. The only portion of the lyrics I knew was the chorus, which was, "We got to get out of this place, if it's the last thing we ever do/ We got to get out of this place to make a better life for me and you." When this song reached the chorus we'd all stand and loudly sing along, "We got to get out of this place…." ["We Gotta Get out of This Place," by Barry Mann and Cynthia Weil, recorded in 1965 by the Animals].

Morale was generally good among the pilots. If we were having personal problems, we kept them to ourselves. In our line of work, the dead and dying simply disappeared, never to be seen again. We might have disagreed with the war's purpose or its conduct, but that wasn't our business. The common saying was, "It isn't a good war, but it's the only one we've got." We were professional Marines and naval aviators doing the job we'd volunteered for, aspired to, and trained to do. We rarely flew at night. We didn't have the night vision equipment they have today, so we unwound in the evenings. We joked around a lot. I had a lot more laughs as a Marine than I've ever had as a lawyer. It was not all doom and gloom. I've maintained that had I been an infantry officer I might have turned out to be an abject coward, but as a helicopter pilot I was too preoccupied flying the damn thing to be concerned about much else.

I could tell you about my most memorable mission, which was into Laos. We had squadron helicopters deployed all over I Corps at any given time. When we'd get back together at Ky Ha after our deployments, we'd usually discuss where we'd been and what we'd done. But there was one particular deployment to northern I Corps that no one seemed to want to discuss when they returned, and I didn't know what was going on until I was assigned to one of these missions.

The Ho Chi Minh Trail, or one branch of it, ran along in Laos just over the border not far from the Marine base at Khe Sanh. What was happening was the Air Force would bomb the Trail with B-52s and some Army Special Forces people would run reconnaissance patrols into Laos to assess the damage done by the bombing.

The units doing this consisted of a few American Special Forces troopers along with a contingent of Asian troops. Nobody was really sure who the Asians were. Some thought they might be Chinese or Taiwanese mercenaries and others said they were South Vietnamese soldiers without their uniforms. Marine CH-46 helicopters were being used to insert and extract these units. Of course, the United States officially maintained it didn't send troops into Laos. So we went unofficially, I guess. If asked, we were to say we got lost.

I was on one of these missions in June 1967 as the copilot of the second helicopter in a flight of four. After getting the assignment but before leaving Ky Ha, other pilots told me that the mission involved illegal flights into Laos. They said these are the most dangerous missions they had been on, that several Marine helicopter crews had been lost on them, and that if shot down in Laos one might want to consider suicide as an option.

We flew to the Marine base at Khe Sanh, and were briefed by a Special Forces full colonel. We were to take a unit consisting of Special Forces advisors and their Asian troops and insert them right next to the Trail so they could assess the results of a bombing raid. We were landing in a zone where you could only get one aircraft in at a time, so we weren't going to surprise anybody. After the insertion, we'd return to Khe Sanh and wait for the call to extract the unit.

We picked up the troops at Lang Vei and then it was a short flight across the border to the Trail. The insertion was without incident, and the North Vietnamese certainly planned it that way. We weren't shot at and didn't see any enemy soldiers. The Trail, right next to the landing zone, was a wide two-lane dirt road. It should have been called the Ho Chi Minh Highway. Along the side of the road, trucks, graders, bulldozers, and other heavy equipment were parked. There was no evidence of bomb damage. We dropped the troops, and I thought this might not be so bad after all, although the apparently abandoned landing site seemed spooky. Back at Khe Sanh, as it was getting dark, the unit called in to say it was surrounded, under heavy attack, and hadn't been able to move out of the landing site. It was getting too dark for an extraction; we'd get them out the next morning.

In the morning the unit was still heavily engaged. As we were preparing to launch, the pilot of our third 46, a good friend of mine, said his UHF radio wasn't working. This was our primary means of communication among the aircraft. He said he could down his helicopter and not fly the mission, but if everyone would remember to keep in contact with him on our FM radios, which we seldom used to communicate among ourselves, he'd go ahead and fly the mission. We all assured him we would remember. When we arrived back over the landing zone, a full-scale battle was going on. We began taking fire including from World War II antiaircraft guns that the North Vietnamese had set up. The fixed-wing aircraft were doing bombing and strafing runs around the landing zone and the Special Forces unit was still under heavy fire.

In the middle of all this, our first helicopter made its approach and landed in the zone successfully. You've got all these troops on the ground and they can be pretty upset and it's hard to control them—everyone wants to rush the first helicopter that comes in and get the hell out of there. It could only take out one fourth of the force. As it lifted out of the zone overloaded, it was shot down and crashed into the jungle. The guys from that crash made it back, I think all of them, to the landing zone again, back in the defensive perimeter. Then it was our turn to go in, we miraculously got in and got out with about fifteen or sixteen of the troops, but took heavy fire and some hits in the process.

At this point, it was my friend's turn as the pilot of the third 46. But the airborne controller announced that the zone was just too hot to make another attempt. Of course no one remembered to tell the 46 pilot this on the FM radio, nobody remembered that he didn't have his UHF radio. My friend started his approach, the air controller and everybody else was telling him don't go in, because we want to bring in some more fixed-wing and try to suppress the fire to get in safely. So he went in, we could see him as he was trying to lift out, and he had people hanging on the wheels, and crashed as well.

At this point we called off the extraction. Even if our fourth aircraft made it into the zone and out successfully, it couldn't get out all the remaining personnel, and those still in the zone would have then been too few in number to defend themselves. So our two remaining aircraft departed and flew back to Khe Sanh where we dropped our passengers. While the crew and some of the passengers of the first of our 46s to crash made it back into the zone, the crew and troops on the second 46 to crash did not. Our fourth 46 had mechanical problems at this point and needed repairs so it was decided to continue the extraction the following day.

By the next day, the Special Forces had recruited nine South Vietnamese Air Force H-34s to use for the extraction. The 34 was a smaller helicopter than the 46 with a smaller payload, but being smaller it was more maneuverable and might have more success. So we, in our remaining 46, accompanied the nine 34s as backup and returned to Laos. Somehow the troops, including the crew of our first downed 46, had been very active in the night-long fight. Once again, we were taking fire that the fixed-wing aircraft were trying to suppress.

The South Vietnamese 34s then began their approaches. Of the nine, three made it in and out and six were shot down. (Two of the fixed-wing support aircraft were also shot down in this operation.) My opinion of the South Vietnamese soldiers was not very high, but these pilots were fearless and I give them high credit for their performance that day. At that point, the only people still in the zone were four or five Special Forces personnel. Everyone else had either been taken out or was killed or missing in action. So we went in to get them.

Getting the last of a unit out of a firefight was never a pleasant assignment. As our troops broke off engagement with the enemy to get on board, the enemy had a good opportunity to attack the helicopter unimpeded. We also wanted to be sure we didn't leave anyone behind in the confusion so there was always a delay while we tried to get an accurate head count. Our crew chief was wounded. Lifting out, I spotted an American on the ground in the trees waving at us and took control of the helicopter to make a couple of passes over him and transmit his position to the controller. The Special Forces was responsible for trying to rescue those left behind in Laos. They did get out the fellow I had spotted. Then we flew back to Khe Sanh, got our remaining crew members, and flew back to Ky Ha.

The crew of our third helicopter remained missing in action. Years later, my friend the pilot and his copilot were declared dead. Their gunner had been killed on approach to the zone, the pilots died on the ground. Their crew chief who survived spent nearly six years in a North Vietnamese prison. At a squadron reunion in September 2009, I had lunch with the crew chief, by then a retired postal worker, and he recounted his many ordeals, including the first three years of captivity in solitary confinement. [He] did say they gave him his back pay when he finally got home, but that apparently was the extent of his country's generosity.

I had also learned in reading a book called *Honor Bound: American Prisoners of War in Southeast Asia 1961–1973* [by Stuart I. Rochester and Frederick T. Kiley] that Americans captured in Laos were not reported by the North Vietnamese. They were kept in a separate prison away from Americans captured in North or South Vietnam, where their treatment was perhaps worse. According to the book, the North Vietnamese took the very logical position that because the United States said it didn't have troops in Laos and because the North Vietnamese maintained that *they* weren't in Laos either, they could not possibly have captured Americans in Laos. Those of us who survived the adventure in Laos were given medals, including the Navy Cross, a Silver Star, and a Bronze Star. Mine was a DCF. The medal citations didn't say where we had been.

This was still pre-Tet; the war was still just semi-organized chaos, we were running around in all directions. If there was any overall strategy, I don't know what it was. Except you would always hear the high level officers, military personnel, telling the politicians that we were doing just fine and we could see the light at the end of the tunnel. As the saying goes, we didn't even know where the tunnel was, much less the light at the end of it.

I'm proud of my service with the Marines, and while I consider the Vietnam War a national misadventure, if not a tragedy, I'm not ashamed of having served there either, and have never tried to deny or disclaim the fact. For me it was the personal adventure of a 24-year-old male. I've never encountered any animosity directed toward me personally because of my participation in the war, and if I had, I would simply have ignored it as beneath my response.

As for lessons of the Vietnam War, I subscribe to the obvious one that a military superpower is unlikely to prevail against a dedicated and committed third-world opponent fighting on its home terrain among its own people. (We weren't helped over there by the corruption and inefficiency of the South Vietnamese government.) When we put a reconnaissance team into the jungle and it became apparent that it could not succeed in its mission, we went back and extracted it. It's too bad we didn't use the same procedure with respect to our involvement in the war itself. I guess the main lesson from Vietnam is that the United States doesn't pay much attention to the lessons of its history—witness our present misadventures in Iraq and Afghanistan.

This business about the military being not only about the guys that go in and destroy the enemy but then turn around and reinvigorate, reinvent, and reestablish the structure and the politics and the culture and the society, to me is just bizarre. That the military should be in charge of reestablishing a country and a society and then democracy is going to break out in three weeks is just absurd. I don't think anything is going to be very long lasting in Iraq and Afghanistan. There was an article in the *Marine Corps Gazette* a while ago about Iraq titled, "Winning is not an Option." I don't think the military is disoriented. Just financially, I think these wars are ruinous to our economy. We might just as well come up with an exit. People criticize you for it, but so be it.

I live in Maine. According to the National Guard guys here, they went to Bosnia, they've been to Iraq, they've been to Afghanistan, they've had their houses foreclosed on because they can't pay their mortgages, their businesses are shut down because they can't run their small businesses. These guys have had it tougher than I ever did.

David Hillbrook was born in Concord, New Hampshire, in 1942. He volunteered to be a helicopter pilot in the Marine Corps and went on active duty in 1966. He served 1968–9 as a pilot in Huey gunships and then as a forward observer for Marine infantry. He is a graduate of Brown University and roomed with Joseph Dougherty and John Hartman. He remains very active in local veterans groups. Dave's background is Finnish, Swedish, and Yankee, with a great-great grandfather who was a captain of a whaling ship.

I went on active duty in 1966. The training was minimal. As a helicopter gunship pilot, the Marine Corps was short of men. They were building up for Vietnam at that time. My gunnery training was shooting one rocket into a pond down in Camp Lejeune, North Carolina. [*He laughs.*] When I went to Vietnam, I didn't even have enough hours to be a pilot-in-command. The Marine Corps has what they call the Basic School where second lieutenants go for six months to learn how to be an infantry officer. They were so desperate for pilots in those days we didn't go to the Basic School, we went directly to flight training.

End of July '68, I went to Vietnam. I flew for about seven months, helicopter gunships. I can't say that I regret going at all. I'm kind of proud that I was able to do it. I was 25 when I got to Vietnam, left when I was 26. The UH-1E—that's where "Huey" came from. The army had different models of Hueys, big and powerful, they could carry six, eight, ten troops. When you see a show of Vietnam it's usually army helicopters coming in, a whole bunch of them.

The Marine Corps didn't have those. The Hueys were not very powerful. We had two pilots and two door gunners, plus we had our rocket pods and machine guns. If we went back to reload and refuel, we couldn't take off with a full load of fuel because we would never get off the ground. Because of the density altitude and the engines being underpowered, we couldn't get enough lift, and would bounce down the runway. It's not altitude but the density of the air. You know, an aircraft on a hot day takes a lot longer to get off the ground than on a cold day because the air is less dense. It's aerodynamics.

I can remember going down a 3,000-foot runway at An Hoa and bouncing all the way. We couldn't get what they call translational lift; it turned out we had about a one-knot tail wind going down the runway, when I turned around and went the other way, we were able to get airborne. It's just like lifting up into a hover and trying to move forward a little bit, the RPM would droop, so you would go down and hit the ground and the RPM would go up and you could go a little bit further. Finally, if you did that enough times, you hit translational lift where you could actually fly. We didn't have any passengers on gunships.

We also had what they call the "sniffer" mission, where you had some kind of a contraption in the helicopter that would detect ammonia. We'd fly low over jungle with the one ship that had the detector on it, with a couple of gunships flying along as escorts, and if the aircraft with the detector on board detected ammonia, we'd have to mark it down on a map. They assumed there were enemy in the area—ammonia is produced by human sweat. In fact my hooch-mate was killed flying that mission.

Another mission we had was called "fire-fly." We'd put a big search light in the cabin area of the helicopter. Actually, the searchlight itself would be hung underneath, but with a monstrous box-like thing, it filled up the whole cabin of the Huey. On those missions we didn't have any door gunners because there was no room for them. We would fly at night, up and down the rivers, patrolling with a huge searchlight. There would be a couple of gunships alongside and if they saw any enemy, they could engage. That was exciting because if you were shot down there was probably no chance that you could survive if you crashed.

One day there was a Marine unit in heavy contact with the enemy so the controlling authority sent us out. We could see wounded or dead Marines lying in a dried rice paddy. I was flying wingman; there were two helicopters. I told the flight leader that I spotted the fire coming from the little village. I said, I think we need to take this village out. The controlling authority had been monitoring our radio transmissions and said, "Negative, that's a friendly village. You are not authorized to fire on that village." The point is we could see the fire coming from the village, and the wounded Marines lying in the rice paddies.

I felt that we had to suppress the fire. Let's say that we some-how didn't "understand" the message from the controlling author-ities, so we did suppress the fire, we eliminated that village. That's an example of how you don't know who your friends are and who your enemy is. You could fly over an area one day where Marines had gone through a village and pacified the village, and you could fly over it the next day and get shot at. There was no hard-and-fast rule about when and where you were going to be able to re-turn fire, you returned fire when you took fire.

I guess a lot of people didn't think we should have been in Vietnam, a lot of people didn't want to go. There were protests against the war. What was the saying? "Hell no, I won't go." It's an "internal matter" in a foreign country, it's "none of our busi-ness," "we shouldn't be there," that type of thing. You try to do your job and survive. In other wars, people ask what's your moti-vation, someone does something heroic, charging an enemy machine-gun nest, something like that, and they ask them are you doing it out of patriotism, love of country? No, that's not your mo-tivation. Your motivation is trying to do your job and helping save your fellow Marines and soldiers.

My hooch-mate was killed. He had a little tape recorder. I re-member the day before he was killed seeing him outside making a message to send to his wife back in the States. His name was William Voss. There were three of us [who] went over to Vietnam together, Rick Keller, myself, and Bill Voss. Bill Voss was killed in September '68. He was flying on that "sniffer" mission that I told you about, shot down and killed. Because they were flying so low, they crashed somewhere in the jungle.

A couple of memories that I have of probably the best things I got involved in. One night we got called out, early January '69, a recon patrol, under heavy contact with the NVA, I think there were twelve or thirteen guys, they were going to get overrun. There were two or three of them KIA, a couple others wounded, they only had seven or eight guys who were able to fight. It was this black, cold night, we were flying low level in and out of the scud layer (puffy little clouds low to the ground) 500, 600 feet. This was probably 20 to 30 miles southwest of Da Nang. I could see the tracers coming up, we'd fly over a village, they'd shoot at us.

We finally got out to the area, established contact with the radio operator. You could tell from his voice they were in deep trouble, he thought they weren't going to make it. We couldn't see the ground, it was a dark night, they dug a hole, put a strobe light in the ground so you could see it from the air, people on the ground couldn't see exactly where it was. The radio operator said we've got a perimeter of about fifteen meters around the light. You had the fire anywhere *outside* that perimeter, so that's how we were making our gun runs, walking the tracers in so close they could hear the rounds impacting the ground right out in front of their position. We figured we were close to the perimeter, as close as we could judge to where the light in the ground was. We were able to hold off the NVA from overrunning this patrol. When we had to go back and rearm and refuel, a Spooky gunship, a fixed-wing, stayed on the scene.

We went back out a second time, we continued making gun runs and eventually these Marines were able to move with their wounded and KIAs to an open area where a helicopter could land. The transport helicopter went in and got them all out of there. The best part about it, talking to the guy on the radio, they didn't think they were going to make it, but after we were there for a while, you could hear the confidence returning in his voice. I still remember that.

I was flying escort, March '69, a big operation southwest of An Hoa, a big firebase. Most places in Vietnam we were out of the range of small arms fire, you couldn't see the ground at all. On the way to An Hoa, we flew over this place called Liberty Bridge, we had to tell the controlling authority we were there. Was there any artillery firing in the area? When we checked in we got a call from an air liaison officer on the ground who'd been monitoring our frequency. Usually, if they had a medevac, they had to go up through the chain of command, but this guy was a helicopter pilot so he knew that any aircraft would be checking in. He was calling us directly because we were flying right over his position, instead of the delay of going through the chain of command. Said he had a critically wounded Marine, and could we come down and pick him up.

Well, we couldn't see the ground. The transport helicopter was with me because we were part of the medevac package, and I asked if he was willing to go down, and he hesitated for a minute. So I said, All right, I'm going to go down myself. Even though I didn't have a corpsmen. "Okay, I'll follow you down." So we dove down through the cloud layer, broke out the base of the cloud, maybe 400 feet above the ground. There's vegetation, tall trees, we had about 300 feet of actual vertical room to maneuver, which is not a lot.

The infantry guy did pop a smoke and we were actually right near the area, and the transport medevac helicopter went in to land and started taking heavy fire from the tree line, maybe about a klick away. My job was to try to suppress the fire, so I started making rocket runs and gun runs, they were shooting at him on the ground. It took the ground troops a while to get the medevac to the helicopter because they were taking so much fire. But finally, it seemed like a long time, but we were probably there a couple of minutes—that *is* a long time.

Eventually, they got the medevac on board, he took a lot of hits on the helicopter, nothing vital, and he was able to launch out and fly low level. We ended up scooting along the ground under the clouds, got to An Hoa where there was a medevac facility. Actually, I think we both got DFCs out of that mission. It was a risk—we didn't know what was down there. That area was called the Arizona territory, or Go Noi Island, somewhere between Da Nang and An Hoa. [*What happened to the wounded Marine?*] Once they get into the medical system, we had no idea.

They call World War II the "good" war—they had to defeat Nazism and the Japanese, so there's not too much controversy about that one. Korea was a UN action—1950, Truman sent the troops in. The Marine Corps had to fight their way down from the Chosin Reservoir, a pretty tough campaign there, the "Forgotten War." Tough going at first because the first troops we sent over there, I believe, were mainly garrison troops stationed in Japan. They were not really prepared for what they ran into. The North Koreans came way down to the Pusan perimeter. We finally held them off. South Korea is a democracy, and the North is a real basket case.

There was a nice little article in the *Wall Street Journal* a few days ago about Robert McNamara. Mistakes were made but the intent was the domino theory, to prevent the spread of communism. Some countries are able to preserve democracy, Thailand and countries like that, they might have been overrun if we hadn't gone into Vietnam. A lot of people think that Vietnam started in '65 when Johnson sent the troops. During the Kennedy years, there were Marine Corps helicopter units in Vietnam, by at least '62. There was one operation that they called "Shu Fly" [mid-April, 1962]. Eisenhower warned about not getting involved in a major land war in Asia. I think it never would have happened if he still had been president. He would have known that you really can't win there.

They say we lost the war in Vietnam, but we were never defeated in any major battles. We never lost the war. Kissinger went over for the Paris peace talks—we just finally decided that it was basically unwinnable. It was time to negotiate. Even though we negotiated, we knew that eventually the North would violate whatever terms were made and would try to take over the country anyway, which they did. My belief is that if you're going to fight a war you'd better go in to win, or else don't go in. We did in World War II. Even today, that would apply. If we're going to be in Afghanistan and those other places, you've got to go in to win.

Look what goes on in Iraq. If a couple of civilians get killed, which is unfortunate but inevitable in war, these people hide amongst the civilians. But then you look at the media, it goes berserk. Then you look at World War II, we killed hundreds of thousands in Germany, I'm not talking about the atomic bomb— the atomic bomb was necessary. Many cities in Germany got blown to pieces. Even in Japan, we killed more in firebomb raids in Tokyo than the atomic bombs ever killed. We almost condoned killing masses of civilians in World War II. I've heard some people say if you go on patrol in Iraq and you shoot somebody, you'd better have a lawyer. In World War II, the media was 100 percent behind the war, as it should have been.

But nowadays, they're looking for ways to discredit Bush, any little incident like friendly fire. In World War II, how many Americans were killed by friendly fire? And now, one or two... I mean it's unfortunate, nothing that you would want, like Tillman. [Pat Tillman, a pro football player, enlisted in the Army after 9/11 and was killed by friendly fire in Afghanistan. The Army initially blamed his death on the Taliban.] A very sad, unfortunate situation, but things like that happen in the fog of war. There are major incidents of friendly fire that most people don't know about. In Iraq, I'm not condoning it, but I'm saying that in World War II there were many, many incidents of friendly fire.

I don't think there were a lot of civilian casualties in Vietnam, maybe when they bombed the North. My Lai, okay, that was an aberration, I would say. We didn't go around killing civilians. When I was with the infantry battalion, they brought all kinds of medical supplies into the villages. I never saw, when I was with the 26th Marines, that they went out and killed civilians. The VC themselves killed all kinds of civilians, village leaders and so on, if they didn't support them. We never deliberately killed civilians.

I wasn't there at the end. We signed a truce with the NVA. There was no victory celebration. We were looking for a way to get out of it. All our combat troops left in 1973, and they didn't overrun the whole country until 1975. So it's not like we surrendered whole divisions or they captured battalions or regiments. They couldn't overrun the country until we left. If we still had had our combat troops there, they never could have done it. They could never defeat us.

Lee Hines was born in Troy, New York, in 1943. An African American who entered the Air Force in 1968 as a CH-53 pilot, he flew sorties from Thailand to Laos during the Vietnam War. Lee made a point of arranging a flight with an all-black crew in Thailand, just as Tuskegee Airman Colonel Blaylock had invited him to do in a KC-135 years before when he was training. He has a BA from Boston University and a MS from Bay Path College in non-profit management and philanthropy. When interviewed, he was interim head of Martin Luther King, Jr. Family Services, a community organization in Springfield, Massachusetts.

I spent the first couple of years flying a big tanker, a fixed-wing airplane, a KC-135 ("Stratotanker"). I went through OTS in San Antonio, and from there out to Laughlin Air Force Base in West Texas. It was in the early spring 1970 when I went for transition training in helicopters and combat training. Back then, and that was a key difference between then and now, you did *a* tour, for *a* year. Today, I can't imagine that I'd have to go back. I hear these guys serving three and four tours, it was hard enough a year away with my wife and baby at home. Back then communication was a little bit more spotty: you could use the MARS system [US Army Military Affiliate Radio System], maybe once a week. You could talk on the telephone to your folks back home, where today they have e-mail.

When I flew KC-135s and I was in the Strategic Air Command, the second in command of my squadron, Joe Blaylock, was a Tuskegee airman, Lieutenant Colonel Joe Blaylock. Joe made it his goal of flying a KC-135 with an all-black crew, and we did. I was his copilot, and he had a black navigator and a black boom operator. As far as I know, that was the only time it happened in a KC-135.

In the same tradition that I learned from Colonel Blaylock, in Vietnam I wanted the challenge of flying with an all-black crew. Tom Callahan, who went to the Air Force Academy, flew as my copilot, and we had two black flight engineers. It was an in-country flight, it wasn't a combat mission, but we did it. We landed and a guy comes up with his clipboard and he says: "Okay, where's the AC (Aircraft Commander)?" The FEs (flight engineers) kept gesturing "go see him" over their shoulder with a thumb, and the next guy would gesture "go see *him*," until he finally got to me. They were looking for the white guy! [*He laughs.*] Among us it was a real accomplishment, and I'll remember that.

All of my combat experience was in Laos. I was with the 21st SOS, Special Operations Squadron. You're in a bubble that is limited in terms of your understanding of the big, big picture. Much of our work was under contract to the Laotian government. If you remember back then, we weren't in Laos, we weren't there! [*He laughs.*] I was based in the northeast corner of Thailand. The name of the base was Nakhon Phanom (NKP, or RTAFB, which stood for the Royal Thai AFB).

[Operations] in the first six months of that ten months were what was called infil-exfil [infiltration-exfiltration]. Our job was to take what were former North Vietnamese soldiers who had been captured, and the Army Special Forces would retrain them and supervise them. They would dress them up in North Vietnamese uniforms and our job was to take them over to the Ho Chi Minh Trail and put them in ("infil") on the Trail. While they were on the ground they would try to find out what the traffic was, people, the number of trucks, and radio that information back. We used to call them "runners." They'd come into NKP at night in a black airplane, they'd keep them in a compound and the next morning they'd load them in the back. Most of the time we wouldn't look back there, because we didn't want to know in case *we* were captured.

Typically they would stay on the ground for ten days. The only reason they would call was if they were surrounded and being shot at and then it was an emergency to go get them. That mission was made obsolete when we started using electronic devices to listen and smell and everything else. These devices looked like bamboo shoots [and] were put next to the route trail. The signal would go up to an airplane that was orbiting really high, like at 22,000 feet, QU-22s would send signals back to computers at our Air Force base. The second half of the time I was there we didn't insert people but used sensors as part of an operation named "Igloo White."

So [at first] we did that infil-exfil work, and we'd take supplies to some of the remote outposts in Laos, to these places that weren't supposed to be there. [*He laughs.*] It's funny, I used to hear people tell stories about the Second World War and the guys that flew the bombers, how they would go fly the missions during the day, and then they'd come back to England in the evening—the contrast was so stark. In some ways, it was that way in Thailand. I mean we were right on the border, the Mekong River, and when you crossed the river into Laos you were into combat area, three miles away.

There were some C-130s that were flown in Laos by the CIA, Air America outfit, that was based... well, they were there. [*He laughs.*] I can remember in Laos landing at this remote airstrip. Air America used to fly a regular commercial run, a scheduled service. While we were there, they landed and people came out from everywhere [*he laughs*] to get on this airplane, with animals and things. We worked closely with them when we were surveying different landing areas. We'd have to put on civilian clothes, we couldn't have any identification, and we'd go up to a base just south of Vientiane. They'd point out, "Don't fly over there, because there is a gun, don't fly over *there* because there is a gun, but right there, there's a good space..." and they would be flying over these spaces that they were telling us not to go!

In fact, one of my pilot training classmates was featured in a book called *The Ravens* by Christopher Robbins and was a part of this outfit. In the book, one of my missions is described. It was big mission, called a gaggle, in the second half of the time I was there. We were moving Lao troops around in Laos, under contract. The

Navy was supposed to have softened the landing site by shooting it up before we got there but they couldn't because the clouds were too low. It was the top of two mountains that overlooked the town of Tchepone in southern Laos. So on our way there the first time we said, "Well, we can't do it so let's turn around and go back." Once we crossed the border we were our own bosses. We didn't have anyone telling us you've *got* to do it.

I was relieved that we didn't have to go into combat, and as we turned around we got a call from some folks on the ground. They said come back and get us, so that's when we had to go back in. What I learned that I didn't know that day was that there were actually two other Lao choppers that were there before we got there and both of them were shot down and four Americans lost their lives as a result.

That was an exciting day, but we didn't lose any of our choppers. We did land, we came under fire. These were Pathet Lao. The reason I know that we were being shot at was [as] we were coming close to the ground, I saw a number of people standing up with rifles actually shooting at us! Whether they lived through the end of the day, I don't know because the mini-guns we had that could put out 2,000 to 4,000 rounds a minute, they were really tough. We had a gunner on each side, plus the A-1s that were still with us.

You don't really understand the big picture. Now I look back on it, in southern Laos that war was different from the war in northern Laos. The war in southern Laos was connected very closely to the war in Vietnam because the Ho Chi Minh Trail as it got further south came into Laos before going back into Vietnam. So, looking at it in hindsight, the reason we wanted to take this hill area was because it overlooked a key transit point, the town of Tchepone on the Trail.

In the northern part of Laos it was a war of indigenous Lao folks against the North Vietnamese and the Pathet Lao, who were trying to drive them out of the Plain of Jars, a major geographical identification point. We were working with the Hmong primarily, to save their land, to help protect them from being overrun. It was in northern Laos where we had a lot of contact with Hmong. We went to their main base at Long Tieng, a major transit point— just about every time we went north we would stop at Long Tieng.

It was a wild place. [*He laughs.*] There was a runway, but one way in and one way out. Most runways you can take off going either way. This one you had to take off against traffic. At the end of the runway was this big karst, a steep limestone hill, and at the bottom of that hill was a crashed plane that they left there. It was run by the Lao troops although the CIA was there in force, and there was always traffic going in and out and supplies being dropped off and missions being run. Being a helicopter, we didn't have to deal directly with the runway; we would come in either side of it, sit and watch what was going on.

My call sign for my squadron was "Knife." I remember "Moonbeam," the nighttime command and control airplane, the C-130 that used to orbit over the combat area. Before you crossed the border you had to call, "Moonbeam" and say you're coming in. You do your thing and then you say I'm going out. "Moonbeam, this is Knife, crossing the fence," and then you would give the time. The "fence" was the river, the border. After your call sign there would be a number, which was personally assigned to you on every single mission so that if anything happened to you, you would not have a name on your person, but others would know where you were by your assigned number. Before you left, you took off all personal items like rings and only had dog tags and a Geneva Convention card in case you were shot down. You always tried to escape and evade capture.

Sometimes if there was a MiG call, they would relay it and say, "Bandits, bandits, coming down." They gave the MiGs' direction, air speed, location, and heading. We knew, based on the radar capability of orbiting planes and other surveillance that the US had monitoring North Vietnam, as soon as they took off from any one of their airfields in the north. You had about five different radios going on, but usually if you got a MiG call, you'd focus on that. They usually had a target in mind, a plane, a helicopter, they would come down, make a pass and then zip back home before anybody could do anything.

Now, when I hear that seven CIA officers were killed in Afghanistan, that reminds me of the situation in Laos. I see the parallels and a lot of the same techniques around pacification, although it seems like we have to learn the lessons all over again. The lesson: if you're going to work with the local population then you have to really spend the time, you can't just go in and leave. You have to be committed until you can build the trust and demonstrate to the folks. These are not dumb people. I think we sometimes go in there with our American attitudes and think that we know it all. We build resentment based on that. These are lessons that I thought that we had learned, but it seems that we have to learn them all over again.

Bruce Lake was born in Jacksonville, North Carolina, in 1947. He is the author of 1500 Feet over Vietnam *(1990) based on his letters and journal from his tour. He served as a Marine helicopter pilot in HMM-265, Marine Aircraft Group 36, 1st Marine Aircraft Wing and in December 1968, earned the Silver Star. On his return, he worked for the Department of Agriculture in forestry in New Hampshire and Maine. He grew up in Keene, New Hampshire, where he and his wife Kay met at age 13; they were married before he went to Vietnam.*

Personally—maybe that's just how I rationalize my experience in Vietnam—what was so important to me flying helicopters in Vietnam, I've always felt most comfortable when I'm helping other people. We were helping people by bringing them food and water, we were helping them by bringing replacements when they were needed, we removed men from the field when they were injured, got them medical attention, we removed men from the field when they were rotating back home to the United States. So every mission that we flew was a helpful mission. We had weapons on the aircraft but they were more for defensive purposes, not for offense.

I do remember going to two memorial services in Vietnam. One was for our sergeant major, whom we had just given flight status to as a crew member. That week he was in the aircraft when it rolled and burned on the aircraft carrier and was pushed off the carrier to prevent everything else from catching on fire. I went to a memorial service in Phu Bai for Jeff Rainaud and Billy Hale and their crew members [KIA, 11 October 1968]. Jeff Rainaud was another pilot from New England. He and I were so close, we'd gone through some enlisted training together, and we had competed against each other all through flight school, our ID numbers were only one digit apart. I drove him crazy over that: I outranked him because I got my commission one digit before he did.

I was in Vietnam for eleven months. When you're a senior pilot who has been over there for ten, eleven months, you're going home soon. Sometimes pilots were moved up from squadron headquarters to group headquarters, or wing headquarters, so they fly fewer hours. I had become qualified as a post-maintenance test pilot in the squadron, and I was also training all the new pilots because I was the NATOPS (Naval Air Training and Operating Procedures Standardization) officer. I made sure that they had their standardized flight procedures for the H-46, so I was very familiar with the aircraft. The last two months of my tour, I was in Japan flying and testing aircraft that had been damaged in combat and rebuilt by Kawasaki. If they qualified, we would buy them back and send them back to Vietnam.

I believe the Silver Star was in December '68, Operation Meade River. The mission was one where the Marines all day long had not been able to receive any supplies so they were running low on ammunition, and were very concerned that they wouldn't be able to make it through the night. They were in an oxbow, the river made a curving loop around them, and their attempt was to keep the enemy on the opposite side of the river. It was a pretty serious situation. By the time we got the gear on the aircraft and were ready to go in and resupply them, it was nightfall. That meant we had to go into the zone at night and the Marines in the air could not fire back at the enemy on the ground even though they could see the rounds coming in, because it was dark and the Marines were so close [to the enemy] they didn't want to hurt [other] Marines.

We actually were able to get the supplies into the zone (I shouldn't say landing zone because it was just an area in the field). En route, several Marines had taken very serious casualties. That changed the mission. We found out even before we got into our spiraling descent that there were injured people that we had to pick up—our primary mission now was to recover Marines. That's why we had to sit in the landing area and wait for those Marines to be brought to our aircraft. I don't want to exaggerate and say we were sitting there for five minutes. We were taking fire while we were there; we knew we had taken hits in the aircraft. We were checking the gauges and instruments as best we could, to make sure nothing else happened before we took off. Normally, if you are inserting troops into a field, you land, they run off the aircraft, that might take 30 seconds. This was much, much longer than that.

I had probably made three or four missions at night in Vietnam. You have a radar altimeter on the aircraft, you have somebody standing in the zone with a strobe light, you gauge your distance from the strobe light, how bright it is, how close it is. It wasn't normally a problem. Where it was a problem, on the mission when I earned the Silver Star, the light disappeared because there was a tree between where I was in the aircraft at 400 feet and where the man was standing on the ground. Because I saw the tree, I knew we couldn't fly over it with our cargo net underneath. The cargo net or the helicopter and the blades would have gotten snagged in the tree. We just dropped the cargo net and either flew around or over the tree to land nearby.

The Silver Star citation reads:

For conspicuous gallantry and intrepidity in action…in connection with operations against the enemy in the Republic of Vietnam. On 6 December 1968, First Lieutenant Lake launched as a Section Leader of a flight of CH-46 transport helicopters assigned to the emergency resupply of a combat-committed unit during Operation Meade River. Briefed while on the way to the designated area, he was informed that there was intense enemy fire in the vicinity but that, because of the unknown disposition of friendly forces, it would be impossible to utilize gunships during the operation. In addition, the Marines on the ground requested the medical evacuation of three seriously wounded men. Darkness fell as Lieutenant Lake orbited over the zone, awaiting arrival of the injured Marines, but, because of the critical situation facing the men on the ground, he elected to attempt the mission and fearlessly commenced his approach to the landing zone, guided only by a strobe light.

As he came to a hover, preparatory to dropping his external load of supplies, he came under a heavy volume of automatic weapons fire which, because of the darkness, the gunships were unable to suppress. After dropping the load, Lieutenant Lake set his helicopter down and, despite the hostile rounds impacting about him, thirteen of which penetrated his aircraft including two through his side of the cockpit, he resolutely maintained his dangerously exposed position until the casualties were safely embarked. Then, displaying superb airmanship, he applied full power and lifted off through increased fire, skillfully maneuvering the aircraft out of the hazardous location and directing it toward Da Nang. His heroic and timely actions inspired all who observed him and were instrumental in saving the lives of three Marines... [Cited from *1,500 Feet over Vietnam*, 280–1].

I remember being called near midnight, total darkness, to rescue a sentry dog from the field, which really surprised me. To me it's funny now, because the military always used phonetic language, we did not know what the mission was when we were launched, we just knew it was emergency medical evacuation. En route they said to me, we are going to pick up a DOG [Delta, Oscar, Golf]. I am thinking, whoa, that must be pretty serious. Then when everybody said, "That's just a dog," it was quite a shock. But you realize how important the dogs were to their handlers. He was as concerned about his dog as he would have been about anybody else. We were able to get the dog out of the zone.

I didn't realize there were sentry dogs until that experience. They might have been sniffing dogs. They might have been sentry dogs because they had more acute hearing than humans. I've heard since that there has been a tremendous amount of discussion about the military dogs that were left in Saigon when we left several years later. Apparently there was no way to get the sentry dogs to the top of the embassy building where the helicopters were last leaving Saigon.

I didn't feel that we were advancing our positions. We had established big airbases like Phu Bai and Da Nang where there were dozens of squadrons, there were people in and out every day. We even had Vietnamese employees on the base. In the field we had places like An Hoa where there was a metal runway, and there were hooches for the officers and the enlisted men. In the field there were smaller areas, for example Hill 55, where they had wooden buildings and metal roofs on the administrative buildings.

When I landed on Hill 55 during the day to get a briefing, I would comfortably walk from the aircraft to the admin building, or the operations building, or to an area to get a meal. Those people who lived there said that once the night fell that they were in a lot of danger. We never seemed to advance from those areas. Whoever was in command of our area put troops in operations like Allen Brooke and Meade River, and we would move through the area, but we always went back to the same area and did the same thing, and we never held those areas.

I guess it really hit me when they told us that technically, when someone shoots at you, you're supposed to ask permission from somebody before you fire back. We never did that. We felt, we're being fired on, we're going to protect ourselves. How can you have rules of engagement like that? The Vietnamese people were, during the day, working in their fields, then at night, maybe they're firing mortars at you. That's one of the reasons why they said don't fire back because we want to make sure that we know who it is you're firing on.

Where I live right now, there were two men who served with the Army of the Republic of Vietnam. After the US left Vietnam, because they had fought for the South Vietnamese, the North Vietnamese kept them in POW camps for six or seven years. The day that I gave the TV interview, I walked into the studio and there were several former South Vietnamese soldiers in uniform being interviewed. Every single one of them thanked me for what the Americans did over there. So yes, in a way, it was successful. But personally, I had the feeling after a few weeks that we weren't really going to win. You talk to people from Vietnam, they will tell you, yes, you did win. But it's hard to feel you win when you are running away from the top of an embassy building and leaving things behind.

It absolutely amazed me that at 2:30 in the morning when I got back to the United States and I am leaving the military base to catch a civilian flight home in California, at that hour to have dozens of people holding on to the chainlink fence, calling us baby-killers and all kinds of bad things. It just shocked me. So that's the way I came home. Even today if I see pictures of troops who have served in Iraq coming through an airport and people thanking them or applauding, it just brings tears to my eyes. I'm happy for them, but it brings back the turmoil that I experienced.

When I left for Vietnam, there were literally hundreds of people there to send us off, they treated us like friends and family. Thirteen months later the only people there were people calling us names, giving us a hard time, and spitting on us. I had to make six different flights to get back home to Keene. When I got to the bus station a taxi pulled up and I said that I was heading home, and he could see that I'd been in the military. "Where are you coming from?" and I said, "Vietnam." He said, "This ride is on me."

When I first got to Vietnam, we had a black-and-white TV and we watched movies of combat. We would see how World War II was fought. It was so different in Vietnam because we never did advance that line, there was a base here, an airfield here, a hospital here, but we never moved beyond those places. That's when all of a sudden I said what are we doing? We're not advancing our line, we're not advancing our positions. It's not like World War II was.

That's a mistaken notion that we have as Americans: we see our culture as the right culture. I think a lot of people have the false intention of changing the culture to our way—you can't do that. Our form of democracy is entirely different from what the Vietnamese people might want as democracy. So we cannot impose our values on them. I think that's part of the problem that we have.

Steven Sunderman was born in Bremerton, Washington, in 1943. He had two tours in Vietnam, first as a CH-46 helicopter pilot in HMM-265, and then as an A-4 jet pilot in 1972. He and his wife of over 45 years, Sherri, grew up in Long Beach, California, and he graduated from the University of Southern California. He spoke with pride about his 44-year-old daughter and 22-year-old granddaughter. He moved to Las Vegas from Southern California fifteen years ago, and works there as a golf pro.

We were assigned to Da Nang, Marble Mountain, which is a *huge* Marine vertical envelopment (helicopter) facility, right on the beach, in I Corps, the northernmost Corps up by the DMZ. I checked in on October 31, Halloween, 1967. It was funny. On Christmas day we had the crew chief dressed up as Santa Claus, completely surreal! We would be going into combat zones, guns a-blazing and being shot at, and one of the gunners had a Santa Claus suit on! A little bit of levity in a very serious situation.

We all lost 50–60 pounds at least. My wife says, "My God, you were so thin." I went over there at 180, I was down to 130. We'd eat in the airplane out of cans, our stomachs churning. You just couldn't keep any food down. You were scared shitless most of the time. All you have to do is look at the pictures, you'll see how thin and gaunt we were, hollow-faced. It's death—that's what it does to you. I'll never forget the first time I got into a chopper and we were getting ready to go into a tough situation and I looked back over my shoulder into the cabin. We had sixteen Marines that were getting ready to go into combat. I will never forget the expressions on these young Marines' faces—absolute *terror*.

You don't just fly into the zone, you get over it and you spiral down so you can stay within the perimeter you're going into so you don't get shot up, you don't go out beyond that perimeter. Sometimes we'd bring our choppers back peppered with bullet holes. We were pretty safe up above 5,000 feet from .50-cals and we'd be safe about 1,500 feet from anything at 7.62 [millimeter] bore, the caliber of weapons such as both the M-14 and AK-47, so we had to be real careful that we didn't get popped from below.

Our covert missions were called recon missions where we'd insert a ten-man recon team and a dog, a shepherd or a pinscher. They would imbed themselves and observe troop movement that moved toward the Da Nang Valley. Recon units were ten to twelve heavily armed and heavily packed teams that would go way back up in the mountains. Their mission was not to engage, but to observe troop movements and call on the radio and let the people down in head-quarters know. The dogs were beautifully trained—they never gave up positions. At night, especially, the dogs could tell whether the enemy is nearby, where the human sense couldn't pick it up.

So when we picked the recon teams up in helicopters, the dogs would always come up next to last. We would put them on the penetrator (a steel cable with a small seat that came out of the helicopter) that we would lower down on a winch and hoist them up externally. When we couldn't land, we'd hover at 200–300 feet, drop the penetrator down through the canopy, the last guy would put the dogs on the penetrator and they would come up into the helicopter. Then we'd send it down again and the last guy would come up. The dogs were magnificent. The dogs had to be placed, bungied, and strapped onto the penetrator. All the recon teams had them. At Cam Duc a lot of the dogs were left behind, that was a chaos deal.

Basically, the enemy was becoming stronger. You have to realize that the Vietnamese lost about 2–3 million people—our kill ratio was 60 to 1. There are veterans who have gone back to Vietnam and talked to them, and a whole swath of their population is gone, people 50 to 65 years old. Those people don't exist anymore.

They've been excised because they all were killed, so they paid an enormous cost. I just don't have any desire to go back.

We were dependent on each other. We knew if somebody went down, one of our guys would go down and pick us up, no matter how bad it was. We were just young kids and we weren't there because of the politics, we were there because we were men of honor. Above all, we were together and we all loved each other and we just knew we would be there for each other. That's the only thing that held us together, held our sanity together. One of the saddest things that we had to do was inventory the personal effects of our fallen mates, and that was just horrible, that was absolutely awful.

I've got PTSD and I'm disabled, for years had terrible nightmares. But [I've] been in counseling for three years. That has helped. It pretty much comes right after you get out of there, but it's lingering, and it never goes away. I had a second tour. My wife was dead set against it. Finally she relented. I went to Yuma to fly the A-4 Skyhawk. I went back to Vietnam again in '72, flying out of Bien Hoa Airbase, the dive-bomber for MAG-12. We crossed into Cambodia in the A-4 to dive bomb in 1972. We had two outfits there, VMA-211 and VMA-311.

I was an athlete and athletes do very well with pilot training. I really didn't have any problems until I got out and started thinking about all the stuff I did. I'd be driving down the street and all of a sudden I'd just black out. I wouldn't remember how I got where I was. I was always back in combat. Now I'm in a group online, we're very close, there are twenty guys on there. It helps, absolutely. Probably nobody else cares, but it's like the *Band of Brothers*. I will support those relationships to the end of my life, those and my immediate family. We were very, very lucky to survive.

[*The lesson of Vietnam?*] Again, a personal opinion: I think it was flawed policy, but I wasn't there because of any policy. I was there to support my fellow Marines in the air and on the ground. I look back on it now and it was by far the most important thing I have ever done in my life. It was incredible and I would do it again, I honestly would. It's only because you become so close to these people that you'll do anything for them, they'll do anything for you. I could talk hours and hours about this. It was the certainly the high point in my life, that's for sure.

Gordon Tubesing was born in Seattle, Washington, in 1942. He had two tours of duty in Vietnam as a helicopter pilot, 1967–8 and 1975, the latter during the fall of Saigon, which is the main focus of his narrative. He retired from the Marines in 1986 as a major and then became a commercial pilot with American Airlines. He received his BS from Southern Illinois University in 1979 and his MBA from National University in 1981. He revisited Vietnam in 1996.

Seven of us went over together and six of us came back. We started to participate in combat missions in direct support of units who were in contact with the enemy as a result of the Tet offensive. We started flying resupply missions, the occasional medevac. But we were a rapid reaction force to help units that were in trouble. We'd bring in reinforcing units to get rid of the bad guys. Most of our activity would be southwest of Da Nang, in the river area, the flat area.

We were awarded an air medal based on twenty flights into an unsecured zone. That was one of our copilot duties, to maintain count of how many zones we went into that were unsecured because every afternoon, evening, or morning when we came in from mission we had to fill out an After-Action Form. We had to write down every coordinate of every zone we went into, whether they were hot, cold, took enemy fire, or fired back. Especially in '68 we had escalated fighting, but the Marines were extremely conservative in their awarding for meritorious situations like the air medals. We would award each single mission before they went into a zone or did something relatively above the normal routine, heroic or not. They issued the single mission air medals instead of doing the twenty routine hot zones, [for] the regular air medal. I came home after 10, 11 months in the squadron with 36 air medals, no single mission air medals. I flew into 720 hot zones that were recorded, the first one of my group to make aircraft commander.

The H-46 had a history. There were two problems they had with the aircraft, manufacturer's problems that were enhanced by combat operations. One was the synchronization of the rotor blades. We had a fourteen-foot overlap in the rotor blades between the front and aft blades. The aft transmission had a drive line directly to the front transmission that maintained the synchronization between [them]. Normally, before you found out there was a problem, your rotor blades were beating themselves to death. We never had that problem in the squadron all the time I was there.

The other problem was a system on the aircraft called Hover Aft in which the forward rotor systems were programmed aft, they would turn the angle toward the ground and allowed the helicopter to land flatter. Well, when they first got into combat, the pilots were attempting to engage this system at relatively high speed—they could slow down and use that tilting of the rotor systems to provide an air brake. They found out that this was putting stress on the air frame, toward the back of the helicopter, air frame station 410. After a while the air frame became weakened by this type of maneuver. We were having helicopters stateside and overseas coming apart at this particular station, breaking right in half. We lost several air crews to this particular problem.

[I] went back overseas in '74 for the evacuation of Saigon and the fall of Vietnam. I was there on the last day and I got a little bit of the operation. We left Okinawa January of 1975 aboard the *Dubuque* (LPD-8), Amphibious Transport Dock. We went with a task force down toward Vietnam, and sat off shore for almost a month and a half, monitoring operations and eventually ended up just off of Saigon, in the Mekong River, a place called Vung Tau. There was an airfield there.

We didn't get actively involved in the operation until it became quite evident that the war was lost. They were going to have to evacuate the embassy, at which time we started to get briefed on handling refugees, handling the enemy, flying in and out of the country. My commanding officer was told to provide a security force down in an area between Vietnam and Thailand. The island was called Phu Quoc, a penal colony where a lot of political prisoners were held. People going out of Vietnam were going aboard ships and we were supposed to provide a security force for these refugee operations.

The LPD was a landing platform dock. It has a huge V at the aft end of the ship in which they put landing craft and other resupply vessels. They have a large deck on the aft section above the open area below, and there you can land two helicopters at a time. The first couple of days of the operation were quite chaotic, right there in Saigon. The Air Force announced that the main airfield would be taken over by the bad guys and everybody was trying to get out of there.

If you have ever seen that picture where this Vietnamese helicopter comes in and lands on the ship, unloads a family, a bunch of bikes, household equipment, and the pilot who was Vietnamese, he lifts the helicopter off, hovers over to the side of the ship, and jumps out into the water. The helicopter sits there for a little bit and then catches the tail and breaks up and it falls into the water. We picked him up in a boat. He was forced to get off the flight deck because I was coming in there with a commanding officer for the briefing for the operation. All the decks were full of transient helicopters and light fixed-wing aircraft on the aircraft carrier *Hancock*. There was no place for him to shut down and get the aircraft stowed so we could land, so they told him he had to just ditch it.

[*Fall of Saigon*]. It was pretty dramatic because we had put a lot of time, money, and effort into that operation. We all went with the idea that we had a duty to perform and we did it, but you just had to resolve yourself to the idea [of] what was going to take place. We were fighting an ideology, just like we are in the Middle East.

[Iraq] is almost a direct parallel with [Vietnam]. Number one, our casualties are being taken by the same situation: with IEDs in Iraq, where there were booby traps in Vietnam. Eighty-five percent of our casualties were due to booby traps and IEDs, so that's the same. It's the same thing—the insurgents, like we were fighting the VCs, the South Vietnamese, a different philosophy than we had. There are a lot of parallels. I got an e-mail last night, a reporter for the Marine Corps, talking about the effectiveness of certain weapons over there, and the operations. The same thing: the M-16 that we had in Vietnam did not perform very well, whereas the RPGs and AK-47s that the insurgents have are still the same effective weapon that they had in the Vietnam war.

I've been back to Vietnam since. I went back in '96 with my wife and spent two and a half weeks. It was very fulfilling, I enjoyed it. The people were wonderful, 70 percent of the people we were in contact with there had not been born when we left in 1975.

6

A VIETNAM PILOT REMEMBERED: WILLIAM "BING" EMERSON, 1941–68

William Emerson, "Bing" or "Bingo," was born in Boston in 1941 and was killed in action in Vietnam on November 20, 1968, when his helicopter was shot down on the opening day of Operation Meade River. I knew Bing growing up as a cousin. He was the only person I knew who died in Vietnam.

This is his story as recounted by six pilots and a crew member who served with him. The pilots' own stories appear in Chapter 5. Bing was emblematic of a war that used helicopters intensely and he and his loss left a lasting impression on those who flew with and survived him. To this day, there is talk about Bing whenever these pilots touch base with each other. Their pride in their service in the Marine Corps may have burnished their accounts of a fallen comrade, but they remain true to him.

ROBERT BASYE

Bing was a very unusual character, a carefree, devil-may-care guy who was very pleasant to be around. I've never heard a bad thing said about Bing Emerson. That was the unusual thing about Bing, that he did collect so many friends. No question about it, Bing was a people man. It's hard to describe his allure.

He was an awards officer, he fell into that job somewhere in the middle of the year. When you were nominated for a medal, a DFC [Distinguished Flying Cross] or whatever it is, somebody has to write up the account. Generally the guy is just some other Marine who happens to draw that duty. If you've ever read the nomination for a medal, it's all bravado, the whole idea is to sell it. So there is "withering fire," etc... Well, Bing turned out to be an *expert*. It became known if Bingo was writing up the citation, you had a pretty good chance of getting it because he could sell them like nobody could. As a consequence, the awards went up, none were turned down. It was a squadron joke—your award's with Bing, you're in for your Silver!

Bing was a Harvard graduate, English [sic: Government] major, he could have gone anywhere he wanted to go. I never could figure out why he became a Marine. Marines are about testosterone, duty, honor, country, *Semper Fi*, do or die, a very linear society that follows the rules, it's all about team work and being a warrior.

That wasn't Bing Emerson, in my opinion. He was much more relaxed, much more carefree. There's another thing I want to inject here about Bing being a Marine. Bing was not a defiant rebel, not like James Dean. Although many of the stories that you hear involve what appears to be rebelliousness or defiance of authority, I don't believe Bing defied authority. I think the rigidity of the Marines and the military got in his way and he just bypassed it, he marched to his own drummer, literally.

About a year after he died, there was a posthumous [Silver Star] award ceremony held at the Boston Naval Yard, so we put together a detail of about fifteen Marines that went up in strict formation for him and his wife and the Emerson family. In memorializing that, the Emersons gave each of us an inscribed copy of a book entitled *The Heart of Emerson's Journals* [Bing was a great-great grandson of Ralph Waldo Emerson] to express their appreciation for our showing up. I have owned this book for forty years.

I'm looking at Bing's solo picture. The solo picture is [a] ritual, you're standing in front of the aircraft in which you soloed, which in our case was a T-34, a modified Beechcraft Bonanza. You look like an aviator. I'm looking at Bing's picture and he's got the Bing Emerson smile, he's got his helmet in his left hand, he's leaning up against the aircraft hull, very casual. It's always amazed me how so many people tell so many stories about knowing Bing Emerson. You'll hear a lot of great Bing stories.

Each time you successfully complete a part of the syllabus you have a check ride with an instructor. One of the most boring of these is called the DRN check, daylight recognition navigation, basically a drive around the countryside. It's designed to show the instructor that you can read a map, you won't get lost if you are in an aircraft. You can recognize terrain features and point them out. It's about a two and a half hour flight, and you have about three hours' worth of gas aboard. It can be tedious as the day wears on.

I was actually flying my check with an instructor. So we go through our routine and the instructor said, "What's up with this buddy of yours, Emerson?" I said, "Well, sir, I don't know what you mean." "Well, we flew his check ride yesterday." "How did it turn out?" "Well, I'm not sure, I'm kind of concerned," he said. "We were driving along and he got through the emergency procedure okay, we were straight and level and a constant heading, and all of a sudden we started to swing a left-hand turn and lose altitude. I couldn't understand what had happened, and I looked over and he'd fallen asleep and was hanging in the straps!" [*He laughs.*]

I just burst out laughing when I heard that. This is a *check* ride, there's supposed to be tension involved, your career is part of this, you've got to pass this test. For Bing it just wasn't that important, so when he got through the hard part of the ride, he just dozed off! I said, "What did you do?" and the instructor said, "I didn't have the heart to wake him up, so I started flying, I straightened the aircraft. He finally woke up and said, 'I'm sorry,' and took over the controls." To have your pilot fall asleep on you!

"Well, what do you think?" I said, "Well, Bing is a carefree guy, marches to a different drummer, but the answer to your question is, I don't believe he's unsafe." And that was the question. Tension is not something that entered Bing's life. He was not so driven by the need to succeed at proving something, once he got through the basics, it was, "Oh, really?" He just had that sense of relaxation about him. How this could happen is beyond me—he's fallen asleep in a DRN check run flying the aircraft!

As you mature as a pilot, you transition to a helicopter second pilot, a copilot, your objective is to become a helicopter aircraft commander and you take on different responsibilities. I became the operations duty officer. What the operations duty officer does is plan the flight operations for the squadron for a particular day. The watch starts at six o'clock in the evening and ends at six o'clock the next night.

You get what we call mission fragments, or mission frags, the schedule for the following day's missions. Sometimes they come in nice and early like ten or twelve o'clock at night. That night they came in at two o'clock in the morning. I look at the mission list and there's the usual stuff, a couple of recon missions, a couple of resupplies, or drive around delivering what were called "heavies," field grade officers.

Then there was this big mission, a four-plane strike, an attack mission where they were to drive out to a staging area, pick up four helicopter loads of Marines, take them into the Arizona territory, which was a known Vietcong stronghold, and insert these troops so that they could support a unit that was on the ground. This was a "shit sandwich," this was something that you had to assign good pilots for.

I got the rest of the pilots signed up for missions and I picked the eight pilots that were going to fly that strike, and Bing was, as I recall, the aircraft commander of the fourth helicopter. For some reason I put working with him a guy who hadn't been there very long, his name was Harrell. So the eight pilots are gathered in their gear, getting their bullet bouncers, getting their side arms and their other weapons that they would carry in the cockpit with them, they are out the door.

Bing is hanging back for some reason, I'm not sure what it is. He's the last guy out, there's no one there but me and him and he looks at me and says, "Can I bum a smoke?" I just lit into him, "God damn it, buy your own fucking cigarettes," chewing his ass, and he looked at me and said, "You're not going to refuse a guy his last cigarette, are you?" He just smiled at me. I gave him two.

That was the last time I saw Bing Emerson. That was the day. That story has haunted me. That was the beginning of Meade River. Like I say, when these missions were assigned you could tell from the way it was being set up and what the requirements were, that this was going to be a dangerous mission. He was hanging back and he was the last guy out of the ready room, he's got his gear, he wants to bum a cigarette and I give him a razz at his head about it. And he says, "You're not going to refuse a guy his last cigarette, are you?"

ROD CARLSON

We got involved with HMM-265, and that's where I first encountered Bing. I remember he was nice to fly with, he wasn't a hard-ass. He wasn't trying to lord it over the copilot, being a martinet. That's always been a tradition that if you intimidate somebody they will grow faster and learn more. He was just straight across, he was a friend of *everyone*. He treated everybody in a very fair, even-handed, egalitarian way.

He never really enjoyed military discipline. I say that because all the troops, all the enlisted guys who are responsible for the miracle of flight, the crew chiefs and the maintenance guys, all referred to him as "Captain Bing." They didn't refer to "Captain Rod." I think that he'd done something to warrant their acceptance, it was real and it was palpable. Beyond that, everybody not only liked him, I think they looked upon him as a different kind of person. I don't know how you'd define royalty in that kind of a context, but I think he had that kind of cachet. There was something about him that was very caring but also very devil-may-care. Of course there was a feeling about him, too, about carelessness, he didn't seem intimidated by anything, individual or organization. I'm giving you everything from my standpoint, also stories that I have heard.

I think he had a *tremendous* amount of confidence. In Bing's character there was a lot of *"watch this."* He liked cars, and somebody mentioned that he was fond of motorcycles. He was a very sensual, sensuous, vital kind of a guy. Who, if there was a possibility of doing anything unusual or unique or exciting, wasn't going to pass up the opportunity. So when you say was Bing a daredevil or not, you'd say this is totally outrageous, nobody can do that.

But if you look at it from Bing's standpoint, he would have said, "Well, I knew I could do it." And if you would say, "Well *how* did you know you could do it?" it becomes such an accelerated, high-powered, forceful learning curve, almost like it goes into the DNA. Nobody understands it, and it's so subtle and so invisible, that nobody even *writes* about it. Basically, all you can say [is] after a while you get the hang of it. Physiologically, and psychologically, it's a mountain.

I had read that the traveling Vietnam Memorial Wall was out at the Miami fairgrounds. This was in 1984, so I, my son, my daughter, and Barbara drove out there. They had got it set up in a hangar and as you go in there's a card table and a young man was sitting at the card table. We approached and everyone was quiet because it was like a church, a somber thing, and he said very quietly to me, "If you will give me three names I will look them up and tell you where you can find the names on the wall." So I said, "Okay, Don Lammers, William Hale, and William Emerson." He says back to me, "Officer or enlisted?" I said, "Officer." And he said, "Bing Emerson?" and I said, "Yes." And he stood up and said, "I was the gunner in the helicopter Captain Emerson died in."

This [was] Bruce Johnson speaking, himself.

FRED GUERTIN

We kind of lived in a capsule. This particular squadron, 265, was very, very closely knit and Bing was part of that. Bing and I, how we were connected, if one of us was on the radio after we finished this mission, or we were working in the same area on the flight back, we'd hear the other guy talking, and we'd say, "Just like that!" That was the "in" thing, talking to each other.

Bingo was a bit of a rebel, certainly. He made captain while we were in Vietnam. He was a good guy, always had a smile on. He was a rebel in the Marine Corps, I think. We were all from Massachusetts, we all had that connection. We all had the idea that we should do something after this thing. Bing was one of those guys you would never know was a Harvard grad. There's not going to be one bad word said about Bingo. We loved him.

He and his copilot were both killed when, I think it was rifle fire hit the deck, I think it was small arms fire that got him. I have a picture of Bingo, his family had it made up and gave it to us. I remember that a bunch of us that knew Bing had a special plaque made for his grave with the wings on it. He was buried in Concord [MA]. He was a nice guy, a special guy. They all were.

STEVEN SUNDERMAN

I first ran into Bing at the 39th Officer Candidate School, January 1966. Roughly 250–300 college graduates starting the officer candidate school at Quantico, Virginia. We became good friends then, and after we were commissioned in mid-May, we were both slated to go aviation, and then we wound up in Pensacola, Florida. Most of us didn't want to go helicopter because all the Navy guys were going jets, but it was Navy guys going jets vs. Marines going jets, twenty helicopters to one jet for Marines. We knew that most of the combat for the Marines was in helicopters because of all the vertical movements of troops.

I don't remember that Bing had expressed any overt patriotism, but he was a very, very physical guy. He was a football player, he played at Harvard, it was an adventure to him. He just took everything in stride and nothing ever got him down. It wasn't that he wasn't committed to the war effort, he just looked at it as a big, huge, gigantic adventure, and he took to it like a duck to water. It was amazing. Most of us were scared as hell. He wasn't scared at all.

Once we were kicked into high gear, nothing could hold him back. I flew with him many times. He was virtually fearless to the point sometimes of being a little overconfident, but that's what it took. Virtually daily we had serious losses. He was able to overcome it with pure enthusiasm, just will to survive. Although you had the will to survive, there was no guarantee that you would. You could fall to death in a second. We were flying 8–12-hour missions of combat, day after day, never any time off, just unbelievable.

I went home after my thirteen months, and that's when I had found out that Bing was killed on a mission, Operation Meade River. The last time I saw him was when I left in late October, early November. He was a real water-walker, just one if a kind. For him to be plucked from life at such a young age was just a horrible miscarriage of justice. But there is no justice in war anyway. He was a real man's man. He would have stood out anywhere. If he had an enemy or anybody who didn't like him, nobody knew about it. Everybody just thought he was incredible.

DICK WARREN

Bingo was delightfully unassuming, not trying to impress anybody. He always had a lot to impress them with from his legacy, the family he came from, the fact he went to Harvard. He was an enigma. You wouldn't think of too many people coming out of Harvard at that particular point in time with the antiwar movement just starting, and Harvard would be a main player. He could have easily avoided Vietnam, [but] still elected to go in the Marines, knowing that he would go to Vietnam. That was one of the draws of going into the Marine Corps, you knew you were going to go to combat.

He would tell the story of [being] on base out of Santa Ana. Before he would check in at the main gate to get on board the base, he wanted to check the oil because to Bingo having a machine operate correctly and seeing that the oil was there was extremely important. So, not having any rag right available, he wiped the dip stick on his cover [his hat] to check the oil. He arrived at the main gate, and the enlisted personnel said basically, "Sir, you can't come on base with that huge smudge of oil on your cover." That epitomized Bingo. He respected his country, he respected the Marine Corps, but he didn't necessarily respect all the protocol that was involved in it. It was probably more important whether there was enough oil than whether he looked spiffy in his uniform.

The site [www.popasmoke.com] has 5,000 pictures including pictures and captions about Bingo. One of the captions I remember about Bingo is [where] one of the enlisted people said, "Bingo was like one of us." Of course in the military you want to establish your protocols, your position, so that when you're ordering somebody to do something, they do it. But Bingo had this way of connecting, pretty much treating officer and enlisted alike, but still had enough command presence to be able to tell an enlisted man what to do and they would do it most readily. The enlisted personnel especially had an extra amount of respect for Bingo.

We have a picture of him two hours before he died, with his crew just before they took off on Operation Meade River, really a pungent picture, he and his copilot that were killed. The crew chief [William (Bill) Hester] survived, the gunner [Bruce Johnson] survived, some of the troops died, but Bingo and his copilot died. It's taken *two hours* at the staging point before he was to die on November 20, 1968. Bingo and Jack Harrell, two hours before they died, a tear-jerker to say the least.

All the information is on a KIA report. All that is on popasmoke.com, names, dates, squadron they were with, unit they were with, at least the pilots and flight crews, it may not have all that with the passengers. It will have a short synopsis of what they know happened and who was on board. They were doing a troop insert, so I believe at that point they should have had troops on board. They are all CH-46s. They're still using them in Iraq right now.

We had about nine pilots die when I was there. I knew seven of them. We just heard that there were two CH-46s that got shot down on Meade River. It was really ill-conceived, wasted people, but they were the only ones that got killed. So, you know, if a bird doesn't come back, it's a big pile of ash out there. People had gone in and picked up the bodies, they were not recognizable evidently—we know he's dead but it's not official. Two days later they confirmed it. This was in November. We'd lost people in September, October, November. It was just getting kind of numb after a while.

I don't think there would be a whole lot of people who wouldn't have liked Bingo. He didn't talk about his family, I learned that afterwards. I heard someone say that he was Ralph Waldo Emerson's great-great (however many greats it is) grandson, but I never knew about his Boston influence, that never came up. No one would try to elevate themselves like that. At that time you would have thought that was very poor [to] try to make yourself look like you are somebody. You were flying in combat, people wouldn't know who you were anyways.

BRUCE LAKE

Bing Emerson and I were acquainted with each other in flight school, but he was an officer and I was a cadet. We became aware of each other big time when I was in Vietnam. We lived in the same hooch and we often flew together as pilot and copilot, we swapped during the missions. This was the Marine base in Phu Bai near the Hue citadel.

I think if we ever talk about Bing, the pilots when they get together in reunions, telephone calls, the main thing that keeps coming out about Bing was that he was magnetic. Everybody immediately liked him because he was a friend to everybody. We still talk about that today. That's the lasting impression I have always of Bing.

One evening we were all sharing photographs from home and he opened up a big album and showed me a picture of his wife. I knew right away that the photo was taken from the top of Mt.

Monadnock in southwestern New Hampshire. That mountain was just a few miles from my home. I felt an instant connection to Bing from that time on.

Bing was physically a very strong individual. I remember one time when he came back from a morning of flying he did a handstand against the inside wall of the hooch and proceeded to do several push-ups from a handstand position. You can imagine from this experience that he had very large arms. So large in fact that he actually cut most of the sleeve off of his green military uniform, which at that time we referred to as "utilities." He was the only one of all the people in the squadron with a short-sleeve utility shirt. The rest of us just rolled up our sleeves.

Bing also showed me a photograph of himself on a Triumph motorcycle, completely airborne. He and I often spoke of riding motorcycles, and I could almost experience the excitement and freedom of riding just from his stories. It was because of these great conversations that I purchased a motorcycle when I left the military. I rode my own motorcycles on and off for 32 years because it was so close to flying. I could wear the same flight boots, helmet, flight gloves and feel the wonderful freedom and power of controlling the motorcycle as I had controlled many different kinds of powerful military aircraft. Even though Bing died on a combat mission in Vietnam, I still thought a lot of him with a smile as I rode the motorcycle.

We got invited to the Emerson residence in Concord, Massachusetts. We spent all day together with several of the brothers and sisters and Bing's widow, and we even visited the gravesite at the Sleepy Hollow Cemetery in Concord. I still remember the conversation with his widow about the Corvette Bing had owned, a '68 Corvette. His mother laughed when she overheard us talking about the car because the last thing Bing had ever said to her before he left for Vietnam was, "Keep the RPM over 2800," because the engine had a tendency to stall—it was a very powerful engine. "Can't you picture me, a small woman, looking though the steering wheel in this big Corvette at a traffic light, revving up the engine!"

When he and I flew together sometimes he actually frightened me. The collective controls all the pitch on all the blades at the same time. As you dove from 1,500 feet in a circular pattern down to the landing zone, you lowered the collective at a certain rate so that you didn't disengage the spline clutch. Bing was always so into powerful engines that he pushed the collective all the way down very fast, which disengaged the spline clutch and that meant that the engine and the rotor blades mechanically were disengaged. When we got to the bottom of the spiral and went to land, we pulled the nose of the aircraft up with the cyclic and we pulled in the collective.

But the way Bing lowered the collective so quickly where the clutch disengaged, we never had engine power at the bottom of the spiral. We had to wait desperately for two or three seconds, maybe longer while the engine speed caught up to the rotor speed to give us enough power to make a gentle landing. Basically, what he was doing by lowering the collective so fast was an auto-rotation each time we landed. An auto-rotation is necessary when you lose the engines on a helicopter, the rotors spin freely like a bicycle wheel does. Without power serving the engine, you controlled the speed of the blades by pulling in the collective and pulling back on the cyclic, which is the control that brought the nose up. Because we had to wait for the engine speed to catch up, it was like doing a landing without the engines every time.

He also had a tendency to stay very low and very fast on take-off when we made landings in the jungle landing zones. Several times when I flew with him, the lower cockpit canopy would brush the tree top branches as we took off. He just liked to feel the sensation of speed.

There's one thing that has always bothered me with my experience with Bing. That was after he passed away in a combat flight. He and I lived in the same building about three cots away from each other. I was one of the two Marines selected to inventory his possessions after he died. How do you know what to send back to the family and what to discard? The two of us who were inventorying the gear packed up everything that we found that we thought was significant, and we talked about each item that we tossed.

One of the items that we tossed was an old, broken, yellow toothbrush. It seemed insignificant to us because only half of the handle was there, the bristles were worn, but apparently it had significance to the family. After they received the gear, they wrote a letter to the squadron commanding officer, asking about that toothbrush. There was of course no way we could retrieve it. After I talked to his father, it seems that Bing often took rides on his motorcycle and as a joke he would attach that toothbrush to the back of the motorcycle and say that was his overnight kit.

To me, Bing was the type of person who was going places, you just knew that he was going to be something special. I had flown in Operation Meade River but to this day I don't understand why I wasn't assigned to fly on that mission. I did hear that when Bing's aircraft was going in, he was flying with Jack Harrell, somebody heard on the radio, one of the two pilots (either Bing or Jack) said, "We need a replacement pilot." That's all the radio message was. Somebody else thought they heard something about injuries to the legs. Again, that's just hearsay. From what I heard, it appears that the aircraft was struck from the front with either small arms or automatic weapons fire that injured one or both pilots and the aircraft crashed.

The thing that amazed me is that two crew members in the back survived, but barely. Bruce Johnson and Bill Hester. I met both Johnson and Hester afterwards. The day after we lost Bing and Jack, I was assigned to go to An Hoa, which is one of the places they had picked up troops to take them into the combat area, Meade River, and interview people who knew anything about the flight. I talked to a Marine officer who actually had one of the weapons. I picked up the weapon to take it back to the squadron, and it had a broken handle on it. That meant to me that the aircraft had hit so hard that it broke the grip off the handle, a pretty violent crash.

The same officer handed me Bing's camera. Bing was very proud of his camera. I remember times he used to set his tripod up near China Beach and take pictures of the mist and the fog rising over the water on the island that we could see just off the shore. He'd shown me some of those pictures and they were great. So I had the camera in my hand and the weapon in my pocket and I went to the Da Nang hospital.

I went into the room where both of the surviving crew members were, there were stainless steel surgical tables in the room, Bruce Johnson was on one of them. The other crew member was the first I came to and I never would have recognized Bill Hester. He was lying there with a scar from his upper left shoulder, all the way across his torso, down to his right knee. This was a scar that was created during surgery. I asked the medical staff and they said during the crash he had had a ruptured spleen. They knew that something was wrong but they didn't know what it was, and the scar was from determining what was wrong internally.

I returned the pistol and the camera to the executive officer, and right in front of me, the executive officer said, "This was Bing's camera?" and I said, "Yes," and he held up the back of the camera, removed the film cartridge, and pulled it out, exposing all the film. That infuriated me. I knew what wonderful pictures Bing took and I knew there would not be any pictures bad or hard to look at. The fact that, without any consideration at all, the executive officer just stripped the film out of the camera made me furious, and I don't think I have gotten over that frustration to this day. I knew Bing's family would have enjoyed seeing those pictures.

BILL "HESS" HESTER
This eyewitness account by the crew chief was sent to Dick Warren and subsequently Bill gave me permission to include it here.

The best I can remember, it was cloudy but cleared as we approached the landing zone. I think it was twelve 46s that lifted off Phu Bai en route to An Hoa... Bing Emerson was the pilot and Harrell was the copilot. Bruce Johnson was assigned as the gunner. Upon arriving at An Hoa, everyone was briefed on Operation Meade River... We were to fly over a small tree line then land right on Route 4. All 46s approached the LZs in a left echelon. (During the briefing we were told to pop a red smoke if we started receiving enemy fire.)

As Bing flew toward the small tree line, we received automatic weapons fire at twelve o'clock position. I grabbed a red smoke and at the same time Bing, over the radio, said "Hess." He never got a chance to finish. It was as if the lights went out. No pain. It was over quickly. I later came to in Da Nang...

I received third-degree burns over 15 percent of my body, a through and through gunshot wound through the side of my chest, a ruptured spleen, a head injury, and a broken leg. I was informed that Bing and Harrell died instantly during the crash. We also lost three infantry men. I'm sorry for the loss of Bing and

Harrell. I often wonder why I was selected to live and Bing and Harrell were not.

FOUR
IRAQ AND AFGHANISTAN: ENDLESS WARS

The Gulf War (1990–1)

2,225,000	Served
383	Total deaths (236 other deaths)
147	KIA
467	WIA

Congressional Research Service, 2010, statistics from DOD

The war in Afghanistan 2001–11
(Operation Enduring Freedom-OEF))

365,000	Based on monthly averages if serving a year, of "boots on the ground"***
1,537	Total deaths (of which 263 non-hostile)**
1,274	KIA**
12,306	WIA**

**DOD Statistics as of 1 July 2011
***FY 2001-12 includes estimates, Congressional Research Study, 7/2009. Estimate could be low.

The war in Iraq 2003–11
(Operation Iraqi Freedom-OIF; Operation New Dawn-OND [Iraq War renamed 9/1/10]

1, 060, 300	Based on monthly averages if serving a year, of "boots on the ground"***
4,456	Total deaths (of which 948 non-hostile)**
3,508	KIA**
32,130	WIA**

**As of 1 July 2011
***FY 2001-12 includes estimates, Congressional Research Study, 7/2009. Estimate could be low.

Introduction

FIGHTING A UNIVERSE OF "BAD GUYS" ON THEIR OWN TURF

The United Nations Security Council was doing its job as defined in the UN Charter when it authorized the Gulf War of 1991 after Iraq invaded the sovereign (since 1961) country of Kuwait in 1990. UN sanctions imposed on Iraq paved the way to confrontation while the US built up its forces in the Gulf. Saddam Hussein ignored the January 15, 1991 deadline for his withdrawal from Kuwait, and the US Congress voted to allow force if necessary to expel the Iraqi forces. US General Norman Schwarzkopf led the invasion, called Desert Storm, with the American public following his field briefings on real-time television. A coalition of up to 36 countries responded, including the main force of 575,000 US troops, 100,000 from Saudi Arabia (a threatened neighbor of Iraq, and ally of the US), and 45,000 from the United Kingdom, with $53 billion contributed by a consortium of European powers.

The actual ground fighting lasted a hundred hours in February 1991, backed by an aerial war of almost 40 days. The result: the decimation and withdrawal of all Iraqi forces and an unqualified victory for the US and the coalition forces. Iraq had also sent scud missiles into Israel and briefly crossed into northern Saudi Arabia. Not surprisingly, the Gulf War, with its yellow ribbons on the home front, was generally popular in the United States, and also abroad.

Following his defeat, Saddam Hussein brutally suppressed a Shia revolt in the south and a Kurdish revolt in the north. As a result, the US and UK enforced no-fly zones to block any further retaliation, also conducting sorties against Iraq's military installations in subsequent years. Meanwhile, the UN began a special investigation into Iraq's nuclear capacity, and was still investigating it in the months before the 2003 US invasion of Iraq. Trade embargoes continued, although the UN instituted an oil-for-food (and medicine) program, which allowed Iraq to pay in oil income for its imports of non-military goods. Saddam Hussein was carefully monitored during the years between the Gulf War and the Iraq War.

President George H. W. Bush decided not to take the fight back into Iraq in 1991, so Saddam Hussein survived, making the Gulf War a precursor to the Iraq war. The invasion of Iraq launched by his son, President George W. Bush, "finished" the job of removing Saddam Hussein, whom he referred to on September 27, 2002, months before the invasion, as "the guy who tried to kill my dad."

Veterans and civilians alike understand the US attack on Afghanistan in 2001 as a response to the September 11, 2001 attacks on the World Trade Center and the Pentagon by a group of nineteen terrorists who commandeered US planes. Almost all were from Saudi Arabia (one each from Egypt and Lebanon and two from UAE); their leader, Osama bin Laden, had planned the attack from Afghanistan. A number of US soldiers enlisted in response to 9/11.

With air strikes by the US and UK, Operation Enduring Freedom (OEF) officially began on October 7, 2001, ten years ago; being at war there has become normal. That December, US Special Forces with Afghan forces conducted a search for Osama bin Laden in the Tora Bora cave complex, but he eluded them and was assumed to have fled to Pakistan. Almost ten years later, on May 1, 2011, bin Laden was killed by a US Navy SEAL force (Operation Neptune Spear) in his compound in Abbottabad, Pakistan, followed almost immediately by his burial at sea, presumably to avoid having a corpse to bury that would be widely mourned. Since 2006, NATO has had troops in Afghanistan facing al-Qaeda and the Taliban, in a terrain singularly difficult to penetrate, let alone dominate.

As the Afghanistan war has continued, its goals have become entangled with the politics of that country. Veterans often mention that Afghanistan resists any occupation—even the hardy Russians gave up after ten years (1979–89). In addition, while the 9/11 perpetrator was clearly Osama bin Laden and his al-Qaeda organization, attention is also on the Taliban, which protected al-Qaeda and ruled Afghanistan from 1996 to 2001, and which still operates (among other places) from there and Pakistan. Since 2001, the US has supported Afghan president Hamid Karzai first as interim president in 2002, and then as twice-elected president (2004, 2009). The relationship between the US and President Karzai is uneasy because we wish he were more democratic and less corrupt.

The war in Iraq, Operation Iraq Freedom (OIF)—renamed Operation New Dawn (OND) on September 1, 2010—was launched in response to Saddam's purported weapons of mass destruction, sanctioned by the UN and conducted by the US and a coalition of "the willing." Like the war in Afghanistan, the Iraq war is part of a Global War on Terrorism (GWOT) or "War on Terror" designated by President George W. Bush. This term applies to a global military, political, legal, and ideological struggle against terrorist organizations, regimes, and individuals who threaten the US and its allies. It also applies to domestic initiatives such as the Patriot Act, the Office of Homeland Security, the Transportation Security Administration (TSA), and the Guantanamo Bay prison.

On March 23, 2003, the US and coalition forces invaded Iraq from Kuwait with about 180,000 troops. The war in Iraq was undertaken in the context of 9/11, although no links were ever established. This was a preemptive war, justified by the need for peace in the Middle East, the threat of Saddam Hussein again attacking his neighbors, and weapons of mass destruction (WMD). The US Secretary of State, Colin Powell, testified before the UN Security Council that there was evidence of WMD while US Marines were in transit to Kuwait. Although WMD were never found, a huge stockpile of explosives in Iraq continues to stoke the insurgency. Official rationales for what has become a US occupation of Iraq have shifted from interdicting WMD, to ridding Iraq of a dictatorship, to installing democracy, which in turn requires stability and an effective police and armed forces that the US has been training, but whose effectiveness it cannot guarantee.

On May 1, 2003, President Bush landed on the *USS Lincoln* to announce the end of combat operations and the demise of the Iraqi regime. The actual invasion was fast and effective, Iraqi forces easily overrun, and Saddam captured, tried, and executed on December 30, 2006. The US authorities in Baghdad disbanded both the Iraqi army and the Ba'ath political party. What has continued is a US fight against all kinds of insurgents, many coming in from other Arab or Islamic states. At the same time, there are internecine killings between domestic factions, religious groups, and competing political leaders.

General Petraeus launched a counterinsurgency, the surge of

2007, with additional troops, in which the US also supplied money and arms to Sunni groups to police their own areas (the Sunni Awakening). Following presidential and parliamentary elections that put Shia in power and displaced the Sunni-dominated regime of Saddam Hussein, the Iraqi national government is considered legitimate internationally. The Kurdish population in the north primarily governs itself, while also having representation in the national government.

We should note that the roots of recent US anti-terrorism and military counterterrorism predate the present situation. After World War II, Presidents Eisenhower and Kennedy and their successors were hostile to formally communist and socialist governments, but also to other movements they thought were anti-American, including a variety of groups called extremists, guerillas, insurgents, radicals, terrorists, and subversives. These last were often fought secretively, using Special Forces and the Central Intelligence Agency (CIA), as in the Bay of Pigs attack on Castro's Cuba and coups against Chile's President Allende and Iran's Prime Minister Mossadegh, leaders deemed unfriendly to the US.

The Global War on Terror is of infinite geographical, political, and military scope. It is a quagmire (a word often applied to Vietnam) because exiting altogether or extracting troops will always appear to be an acknowledgment of defeat—a mission not accomplished. As we see today, when radical Islamists recruit across the globe, the supply of insurgents is limitless. The US soldier's complex battle gear (with supplies and other devices covering the uniform) is in great contrast to the armed insurgent in his or her civilian clothes and vehicles.

Meanwhile, the US public has found its own focus on the human dimension of war: soldiers being sent in harm's way (to use the standard phrase), their losses, the suffering of their families, and their needs upon return. The public first responded to the lack of adequate protection (up-armored Humvees, body armor), how troops died (improvised explosive devices [IEDs]), and the numbers lost (closely followed as they approached each thousand-mark). The destruction in Iraq and Afghanistan has never been a focus, although it makes improving security a very great challenge.

Unlike the earlier wars we have covered, the current wars in Afghanistan and Iraq do not dominate the print media in banner headlines, but are presented at the personal level with photographs of soldiers and civilians. TV news mentions events and deaths but does not provide a nightly screening as stations did during the Vietnam War; the government does not distribute newsreels the way it did for World War II and Korea. These two real-time wars are being videotaped and their images uploaded by soldiers with personal computers. We rarely see pictures of badly injured soldiers, except in recovery. Under President Bush (but not President Obama), photographing coffins arriving at Dover Air Force Base in Delaware was prohibited.

Politically, these wars have something in common with Vietnam, as a number of veterans in this volume attest. The US would prefer a host partner government that was either democratic, or could be democratized, or is elected, which is why we support elections that help legitimize both the regime and our intervention. But the actual host governments today are weak and corrupt, the lack of law and order is persistent, and the populace suffers at the hands of factions such as al-Qaeda, militant Sunni or Shia militia, and the Taliban. The end is still not in sight, even as US troops withdraw.

THE NARRATIVES

The narratives by recent veterans do not have the patina that stories by older generations of veterans have achieved over time and retelling. They are, however, told with great urgency, realism, and candor. The current military experience involves constant exposure to gunfights, rather than infrequent pitched battles. As in Vietnam, the confrontation with an insurgency is a daily routine, and a daily danger. The US struggle for hearts and minds is overwhelmed and undermined by the level of daily violence. Soldiers recognize, as they did in Vietnam, that the civilian population is caught in a bind between local and foreign forces.

Current wars with volunteers do not have the 12- or 13-month countdowns that Vietnam draftees had. Multiple deployments are routine, and apply to regular forces, reservists, and the National Guard. Enlistment without a draft makes the nature of service something closer to a job. Soldiers expect regular pay, benefits, health insurance, treatment for on-the-job injuries, and a college education; current enlistees are, in great part, economic recruits. Veterans receive compensation for a diagnosis of traumatic brain injury (TBI), post-traumatic stress disorder (PTSD), damage from exposure to toxic chemicals, and disabling physical injuries. These traumas of war also educate the public as to war's many costs.

Veterans back from Afghanistan and Iraq often comment that the press only covers the bad news of soldiers killed, and ignores the good news of reconstruction and democratic elections. Many soldiers have trained host country's police and armed forces, built schools and police stations, and improved the lives and security of civilians during war. Soldiers often express good faith, concern, empathy, and altruism toward the local population. Some also see their job in moral terms: eliminating tyranny and protecting civilians. They also blame the insurgents for much of the ongoing destruction, and local corruption for the political impasse and slow economic recovery.

In wars against insurgents, soldiers complain that the rules of engagement (ROE) restrict their ability to respond to, or anticipate, attacks, a concern shared by a number of Vietnam veterans. Along with that, they have learned from their Vietnam counterparts that they are not responsible and should not be blamed for the US government's political purposes in going to war; they are carrying out the job as ordered. They have also had their share of negative press for mistreating host country nationals, most obviously in the Abu Ghraib prison scandal.

A common perception among recent veterans is that the societies in which they are fighting are culturally very different, that the local population and the US soldier have different mindsets. This observation reflects their education about the host country's mores and norms, including the injunction on having anything thing to do with women in Islamic countries. An unintended consequence of their understanding of traditional political hierarchies in turn leads to skepticism about the mission of installing democracy. While soldiers recognize that there are problems with their treatment of civilians, they also know that many Afghans and Iraqis want Americans to stay to protect them.

Some Vietnam veterans are now "adopting" newer veterans. Both generations have noted that the ill-treatment and neglect of

Vietnam veterans has led to a reversal, so they *both* now experience public support and acceptance, even gratitude. Civilians are no longer conflating the soldier and their war as many did during Vietnam. Separating veterans from their war would, however, have been unthinkable during World War II and Korea. At the same time, quite a few World War II veterans chose to become active civilians and inactive veterans for decades, and we will see what this recent generation of veterans will do.

There are some new and striking aspects to the current wars. These include the voices of women: we will hear from a female (this is the military term) Army commander with three deployments to Iraq and a female Army National Guardsperson who served in both Afghanistan and Iraq searching women (who cannot be searched by male soldiers) and working with the local police. With no front lines, earlier prohibitions (now revised) on using women as combat troops cannot save them from the attacks on convoys and bases, so they too have sacrificed their lives. On June 23, 2011, the *New York Times* noted that 28 female US soldiers have died in Afghanistan (not necessarily in combat), and different sources (including informal individual counts posted on the Internet) estimate 113–118 female fatalities in Iraq and Afghanistan through late June 2011. Female soldiers can also be subjected to harassment as objects of desire or ridicule by local men, and are vulnerable to assault by their fellow US soldiers.

Another novel aspect of the current wars is that miniature Americas, lined with chain eateries like Baskin-Robbins and Subway, have grown up on military bases in hostile territory during wartime, often with sport gyms and movie theaters. Soldiers have electronic contact with their families and music from home: iPods, iTunes, computers, e-mails, and the Internet are literally taken into combat. Music plays a big part in soldiering today—it blares from the Humvees as they go to battle (the attacks need not be silent). It also blares from the loudspeaker system of captured mosques, replacing the call to prayer in a kind of cultural occupation.

Most significant in the narratives from the wars on terror is the ubiquitous use of the terms "bad guys" and "good guys" to describe the forces that are fighting each other in Afghanistan and Iraq. Military games, now mainly video games, always have good guys and bad guys. In my earlier book on Iraq veterans (recorded from 2005–7), US veterans often called Iraqis "Hajjis" in a pejorative sense. (A *hajji* is one who has made the pilgrimage to Mecca.) President Bush once referred to the invasion of Iraq as a crusade, causing an outcry among Middle Easterners who recognized the reference to efforts by Medieval European rulers to wrest the Christian Holy Land from "infidel" Muslims.

Only one of the narrators here (all interviewed in 2009–10), used the term "Hajji." The secular description "raghead" has also disappeared. It is simply "good guys" and "bad guys" now. The bad guys are those who kill and wound you and your comrades, and so the good guys take retribution. Both President Bush and President Obama have repeatedly said that the war is not against Islam and Arabs, but against insurgents, terrorists, al-Qaeda, the Taliban, and their allies. Those are the bad guys in the War on Terror.

7

THE GULF WAR AND
THE WARS ON TERROR AFTER 9/11

Erik Johnson was born in 1970, grew up, and now lives in the small town of Leyden, Massachusetts. He graduated from Pioneer Valley Regional School in 1988 and enlisted in 1989, in time for the Gulf War/Desert Storm. He was a corporal in 3rd Battalion, 3rd Marines, one of the first units to be deployed to Saudi Arabia when Saddam Hussein invaded Kuwait. During the fighting, his unit secured the Kuwait International Airport. He felt then, as he does now, that the job of ousting Saddam Hussein should have been executed in 1991. His story includes the large "what if": What if we had not had to go back to Iraq? Erik is concerned that the US government undertakes tasks halfway, "handcuffs" its soldiers, and therefore does not success-fully complete its mission.

GULF WAR/DESERT STORM

I didn't have a lot of direction in my life at that point. I thought [joining the Marines] would give me a little focus. Once we were done with infantry training, I was sent to Kaneohe Bay, Hawaii. I got to see a lot of the world that year. We went to Okinawa, came back to Hawaii. We were only there about a week and a half. Guys had gone home on leave, got as far as the airports at home, and had to turn around and come back. Our unit had been put on standby to go over to Saudi Arabia. It was a long flight, thirty-some hours, from Honolulu, California, East Coast, Ireland, I don't know if we stopped somewhere else, and then Saudi Arabia. Maybe we should have hovered for a while and let the planet rotate underneath us and come back down!

Saudi Arabia—desert. We started putting in defensive positions out in the desert. We didn't have a base—the weapons company (I was part of a mortar unit) set us up in a rock quarry. There wasn't a whole lot of sand, so we'd take our Humvee out, fill up sand bags, haul them back, and create our gun pits. A mortar is a high-angle fired weapon, when the round fires off, there's a tremendous amount of impact onto the ground. When it's on rocks the base plate will move and cause you to be inaccurate.

We have a gun pit around us, much the same as the front line has infantry fighting holes. We store our ammunition, and have a spot for us to move because we have to be able to shoot in most directions. July, early August [1990], we were one of the first Marine units. We heard that Iraq had invaded Kuwait. There was a lot of talk of scud missiles, the capability that they had, so we weren't really sure what we were up against. But we were as prepared as we could be. We were there to make sure they didn't come any further south than Kuwait where they had already invaded. We were there to help defend and stop further invasion, by invite of the Saudi prince.

There were a lot of things that we didn't have that a lot of the places have now. They would send out a truck so we could go take a shower—that was how primitive it was. In the middle of the desert check your boots for scorpions, make sure you didn't have any extra crawling critters with you. They'd bring in a water buffalo, a big tank on wheels, and we would fill our canteens from that. As far as food, MREs [meals ready to eat] two meals a day, and they tried to get a third meal that was hot from some base camp.

We were a full battalion, in the 800 range. You're spread out (not all in one big camp) in your defensive positions. You have your line companies, then you have your weapons companies like we were, set up behind. Your line companies would be the equivalent of your offensive line, and your mortars would be your fullback or your running back, where you hand the ball off to, and we could be one of the quarterbacks too. We had representatives that were embedded with each of the line companies that would come back and tell us if they needed rounds on a specific spot, or if they had spotted something that they weren't supposed to see out there.

Khafiji [battle in Saudi Arabia], that was our unit, not my platoon. In weapons company there's an 81mm-mortar platoon, then there's a heavy gun platoon, then there was an anti-tank missile that would fire with a string that would engage the armored vehicles. The heavy guns platoon was actually the one that got into a small skirmish with the advancing [Iraqis] when they started to come down through, and they met in Khafiji. We were just to the south of that. The Iraqis were stopped and they retreated.

We helped positions there until a week or less before the main invasion thrust. The battalion picked up and moved further inland, our task force all came together, and then we made our breech north, up to Kuwait International Airport. When we went through the oil wells that were on fire, [it was] just black. We'd cover up our faces and noses with a bandana, try to keep as much of the oil and soot out of our system as possible. Even so, any exposed skin would be black. There were several days when if you blew your nose you got little black chunks coming out from the oil.

When we moved over to be part of the strike force going north, we could hear the B-52s carpet bombing, bombing, and bombing. We could see the horizon where it was just getting pounded. You knew they were getting hammered, you knew something was coming. They were dropping a lot of bombs up to the north. We made the push north. They stopped their bombing, and we came into Kuwait International Airport. As we came in, the Iraqis were leaving. We didn't really come into a whole lot of resistance. Four days, then they said it was over. What do you mean it's over? We've been here six months and four days later it's over? We secured the airport, and the next instructions were head back to Saudi Arabia. Once they said that they had surrendered, because we had been there the longest, they were sending us back to Saudi Arabia to get ready to leave.

Even before we left the country when they told us it was over—four days, we were on the outskirts of Baghdad and they called it off—I said to the other guys, we'll be back. We didn't do what we needed to do. We didn't finish what we started. All you did was push them back across the border. This is a country and a leader... that's not going to teach him anything.

One of the big talks was if [we] had followed back into Baghdad, if we tried to take Baghdad, would we receive a lot of casualties, to the tune of a fight we had never seen before, every Iraqi would defend their country, or their city. To be honest, I don't know what would have happened if we'd gone in. I do know that we were there, and we had a lot of troops ready. But when you're in the military, you never know.

I was frustrated. We were that close, wishing maybe that if we'd finished the job we started the first time, maybe some of those other things wouldn't have happened. Maybe had we gone and made that push into Baghdad, yeah, we may have lost some soldiers, maybe even me, but maybe 9/11 never happened. Maybe this next war over in Iraq never happens. Maybe these 4,000 or 5,000 we have lost so far in Iraq and Afghanistan, maybe that never happens. That leaves you kind of troubled that you were there, you were on the doorstep, so that all they had to do was say, Let's finish the job.

A lot of the same things I thought back then—if we are going to put our men, our women, over there in harm's way—then we'd better be finishing the job before we start bringing everybody home. Because every time we do something halfway, we start over again. I'd rather see it done right once than have it tried two or three times in order to get it figured out.

[*What should we do now?*] In order to give you a real honest answer, I would have to be over there and see. I would hate to tell you that I think we should pull them out only to be really close to having viable defenses in place so they can take care of themselves but are not quite there. You can't pull the rug out from under them. If you're going to prop them up and you're going to go through all that trouble, all those months of rebuilding, you've got to make sure that they're ready.

[*Afghanistan?*] My knowledge of Afghanistan is minimal. I don't know if we have a clear mission and how we're going to achieve it. I do know that the terrain over there is some of the most miserable terrain you can deal with. I know that many other countries have gone there with the idea of "we're going to take over," and they've failed time and time again. I know that technically we are not there to take *over*—we are there to hunt down and eliminate the terror cells, and restore some peace to the area.

But I can only hope that they've got some plan in mind and they don't leave it half undone. I only hope that they have a clear idea of what they are going to do, have a clear mission, and ultimately, they need to make sure they have the supplies and the backing to carry out that mission. Meaning the manpower, the tools necessary, because if you send them over there, you've got to give them the tools to do what they need to do. You've got to give them the freedom to do what they need to do in order to get you to the end of your mission. You can't handcuff them too much.

[*What about Iraq?*] Well, if they're at a point where they can defend themselves and they're starting to put their government together, then obviously, reduce our troops, and keep a minimal advisory force there for training but all along trying to scale back, because at some point they've got to take over their own country. *They* don't want us there and *we* don't really want to be there. "You don't want us there, we don't really want to be here"—seems as though we should be able to come to some sort of compromise. "We'll be happy to leave when you're ready to defend yourself."

In my opinion, the government sits back down there in Washington, and says we spent X amount of billions of dollars over there, but these are half-finished projects, you stop funding it, the money was wasted. So now you've [got] a dozen or twenty projects that you've thrown some money at, but just throwing some money at them doesn't necessarily fix it, and doesn't put your infrastructure back together. You've got to follow through, you can't pop some cash at it.

It's a complicated question. I don't know which way we need to go. I just wish we'd figure out where we are, and for our country's sake I think we need to get this to an end, get them up on their own two feet, and stop spending the money over there. I caution how many more resources we should be putting in versus how many more resources they should be pulling out of their oil funds and their own assets in order to rebuild *their* country. I don't think that America should be necessarily funding the rebuilding of Iraq especially as we are seeing oil go back up to $80–90 a barrel and gas is cruising back up to $3 a gallon. It makes it hard to think that we should finance that on top of… but I do think that the money that was spent was spent poorly. I'm not saying the projects they were spending on were *chosen* badly, I'm just saying there's enough information coming back that there was a lot of misuse of money.

[*Security has made rebuilding difficult.*] My personal opinion on that, that comes from putting the handcuffs on our troops that have to defend it. You have to be fired on… so I have to wait for you to go and attack this [project]—okay, we built a new school and you decide you want to blow it up. Handcuffs on the military are very, very tight. Rules of engagement, you've got to be physically shot at and then you can return fire. I understand what the rules of engagement are, but when you handcuff your guys, you're really putting them at a disadvantage.

[*We disbanded the Iraqi army and Ba'ath Party.*] You wouldn't have had so many out there trying to destroy everything you were doing. Because every one of them that you've told can no longer be part of this government, you've just now given them the go-ahead to be your enemy, to do whatever they can to fight you. I understand that the ones that were causing the terrorism, and the corrupt officials, obviously you don't want those in charge, and it's going to be hard to weed them out. It makes you wonder if it was wise to eliminate everybody who was in the army and everybody in the Ba'ath party.

[*What about when you came home?*] It was very heartwarming and touching to have a great number of veterans who had fought in Vietnam and other wars make sure that when we came home we weren't treated the same as when they came home. When I came home there was a small parade, a welcome home up into Leyden. People came out on the side of the street and waved. They met us at the town line, they had the fire truck out, [and] we went up through the town. There were lots of yellow ribbons. It was nice to feel appreciated when you got home.

Make sure that you greet them when they come home. They're not in charge of the decisions that this government makes. They've only signed on to defend the freedoms that we all have and enjoy. It's a real shame to mistreat them based on the decisions that they had absolutely no control over. In Vietnam many of them were *drafted,* were *told* they were going there. It wasn't their decision. I would hope we remember going forward to welcome home our troops.

Jon Schnauber was born in 1971 in Watertown, New York. He served 1990–4 in the Air Force, including a deployment to Saudi Arabia during the aftermath of Desert Storm. In 2000 he joined the Army National Guard and served in the Afghanistan war while stationed in Pakistan. He became active in veterans' affairs as an undergraduate at UMass-Amherst, 2004–7, and is currently studying for a graduate degree in social work at Springfield College in Massachusetts.

GULF WAR/DESERT STORM/OPERATION SOUTHERN WATCH

I graduated from high school, didn't have a whole lot of career options—I wasn't on a college track. I signed up for the Air Force in January of my senior year. The Air Force treated people well, great standard of living. Back then we were called security policemen, now security forces, the same as an MP but for the Air Force. I went to basic training in August and we started Desert Shield that same time. All of my training was focused on fighting Saddam, fighting the Iraqis. I wound up in Grand Forks, North Dakota, during the Gulf War. I went to Saudi Arabia, served a tour over there at Al-Kharj Airbase.

We are sitting in the dorms the night that we started the air strikes for Desert Storm and we watched it on TV, just like the rest of America. I went over a couple of years after Desert Storm—I was part of Operation Southern Watch. After the fighting stopped and Iraqis had drawn back into Iraq from Kuwait, we set up no-fly zones in Northern and Southern Iraq, Operation Northern Watch and Operation Southern Watch. I was on a little base with only 70 Americans in Saudi Arabia and we were in charge of Al-Kharj Airbase, which became Prince Sultan Airbase at the beginning of this war, one of the largest military installations in southwest Asia.

When I was there, we had a couple of hangars, there was a blast wall, a lot of the foxholes were still there. We had the largest reconstitution area since Vietnam. They brought in all the vehicles, equipment that they used during the fighting, either tore it down for parts, or refurbished them to send them back out. I was told a story that we used vehicles that had been emplaced years ago. We had bunkers over there where we stored the equipment to fight and that was there for years. Our patrol vehicles were from the early 80s, but they had no miles on them, which led me to believe the stories were true.

I was there six months. We hit Baghdad with 21 tomahawk cruise missiles at one point. I was in-country for that. [There were missile strikes against Iraqi military installations during the no-fly operations.] We saw them on the news the next day, which was very disturbing. Shouldn't someone be telling us, You might want to look out! They were launched from a ship off the coast. Also, while I was over there, Mogadishu went down [August 28, 1992]. We were only three or four hundred miles from Mogadishu, we actually supported them with supplies—C-5s and C-130s would fly in, pick up supplies and fly back into Mogadishu. [December 9, 1992, Marines arrived at Mogadishu, Somalia for Operation Restore Hope.] I remember watching the footage of the Somalis dragging downed pilots through the streets [October 3, 1993].

AFGHANISTAN/PAKISTAN

August 2000, I joined the Massachusetts Army National Guard, the Military Police Corps. Just over a year, 9/11 happened. I [had] missed the camaraderie, I missed playing with the toys, and hanging out with everybody. I was good at it, I made rank pretty quick. I started out as an E-4, got my corporal quickly, I was a sergeant within a year and a couple months. There were eight deployments after 9/11, state-side and overseas. I volunteered to go with the 972nd Military Police out of Melrose, MA (I was with the 42nd MPs in Chicopee, MA, but the 972nd needed volunteers). It was August 2002 that we deployed to Uzbekistan. After several weeks, I went to Pakistan, PAF Shahbaz Airbase, a very small base right outside the city of Jacobabad, Pakistan. The Marines had gone in first during the invasion, the 82nd was there when we got there, and we took it over from them.

We had three or four C-130s, and we also had Predators that were used for surveillance. All our missions were up into Afghanistan. Predators are an unmanned aerial vehicle. They can load them with specific weapons, none of ours ever were, they were surveillance only. The Military Police also ran Raven missions, an Air Force term—close-in security on an aircraft going into hot zones. You're part of the air crew, you're security for the aircraft upon landing. How do they put it?—these are "uncompleted air fields within hostile territory." You're the first one off that aircraft when it lands, you secure the perimeter of the aircraft, you engage any hostilities coming toward the aircraft or towards its crew, they drop off people or supplies, and you're the last one on the aircraft prior to take-off.

We are based out of Shahbaz [Balochistan province, south-central Pakistan], but we had constant missions up into Afghanistan. The air crew would fly into one of the larger bases in Afghanistan, Kandahar, Kabul, then we'd pick up whatever we needed to pick up, and transport that up to the Forward Operating Bases [FOBs]. All our missions ended up at FOBs where Americans are, usually very small bases. Chapman was one we frequently went to. [On December 30, 2009, a Jordanian suicide bomber killed several members or employees of the CIA at FOB Chapman, an operations and surveillance center in the eastern province of Khost, near the Afghanistan–Pakistan border.]

At night, in Pakistan, quite often we watched gunfights in the city. We were told it was the religious factions fighting one another around election time, or it was bandits. We would literally sit there at night on our observation posts and watch the gunfire, automatic weapons fire, tracers ricocheting off into the sky, gun battles. Explosions would go off, coordinated along with the gunfights, then afterwards, you would hear all the people, the women and children, screaming. We were just third-party observers. We weren't allowed to go outside of our base. We worked with the Pakistani military in our control center. They would be like, "Oh, a truck blew a tire." We were like, "That's quite a shock wave for a blown tire!" The base is separated—there's an American section and a Pakistani section. You see these guys driving around on motorcycles. We were told by Air Force OSI [Office of Special Investigations] that those are the [Pakistani] intelligence people.

One of the surreal moments was [with] a Pakistani army guy, probably lower enlisted, outside of our gate at his little post. We went out one night to build a relationship and we were all talking to him, obviously not really understanding a lot. We had a laptop, and we were asking him, Do you know why we are here? He didn't seem to understand, so one of the guys pulls out his laptop, and plays the video of the planes crashing into the towers. He was just looking at it—he had no idea at all. This Pakistani member of the military had never seen it before. Obviously, we didn't *know* this because there is that language barrier, but you could see a very surprised, what-is-this expression on his face. Shortly after this, the Pakistanis stopped manning the post outside our gate.

In Afghanistan, one daytime mission to Chapman FOB, and I'd gotten off the aircraft standing there on the perimeter, just looking around. It hit me: I wasn't engaged in direct fighting, but I was still responsible. Being part of it all was the sense that came over me, to include the killing of other humans. That should be the same for someone who's sitting back home in their armchair. We're all part of this, whether we like it or not. Whether you're a soldier on the front lines or you're sitting at home watching a football game, this is our country that's involved in this, and this is our country that's killing other people.

I came home right when the invasion of Iraq was starting, and I thought that was wrong. Hearing the news, reading the news, seeing the news, it didn't seem to me that our country had used enough of its power, [and] that we should have done more prior to sending people in, more talking, more diplomacy. It didn't feel like the right time to go that next step. In hindsight, I certainly don't agree with it. It had a lot more to do with peoples' agendas rather than what was best for the country.

Every protest, what you see is we hate America, we hate Americans. It's never I hate this individual person (at times it's I hate George Bush), essentially, that's the country they're talking about. Afghanistan made perfect sense to me at the moment and even for the next couple of years. It doesn't make much sense to me now. Iraq doesn't make much sense to me now. We already had our military wrapped up in Afghanistan. We can't even engage another front at this point, and we are. Don't get me wrong, I'm not antiwar, it has its place, but I'm also pro-soldier. We're the ones that have to fight and die.

I spoke [to a group] last summer and I asked, "How's everybody enjoying World War III?" The media isn't calling it that, but if you look at it, we're fighting two major wars in a region of the globe and on top of that we're fighting in several other continents. We're fighting in Africa, we're fighting in Malaysia, all these terrorist groups that we are fighting against. Whether it's a military fight or a law-enforcement fight in the United States, it's still part of this war on terror, which is global. There are dozens of countries that are involved. This is literally a world war that is being fought right now. It's the longest war that we've ever been in, and it's taking up just as many resources if not more, has as many countries involved, if not more, than World War I or World War II.

[*Is it winnable?*] I don't think it is *supposed* to be winnable. It's much like the war on drugs—there's no end in sight. You're never going to win the war on drugs, it's built to just pour money into and have no end. These wars that we're fighting right now, we're fighting an enemy that can't be seen, that's global, that has so many different factions. You can't win it. There is no way to track down, there's no head of state, Osama bin Laden isn't the answer, there's no country that you're going to overthrow, or beat, that's going to come to a table and sign a peace treaty. It's never going to happen. *Ever*. Until someone says, Okay, we're done, it's not going to stop. And nobody at this point in history is ever going to say that we're done with this. I don't think we're going to see it in another ten years.

We've been hearing for several years now we're pulling out of Afghanistan, we're pulling out of Iraq, we're reducing our troop size. One of the things that happens is that when we say we reduce our troop size by 10,000 troops, we send 20,000 more in, but they don't tell you that. It's a revolving door, it just isn't built to stop. North Africa—it's going on there already against terrorist groups. Any group that does something that anyone can consider terrorism, they're going to be a target, and we'll take the fight to them. It doesn't have to be the Taliban. Al-Qaeda is in North Africa. Any country that aligns themselves with them, Yemen… There's always going to be a battleground for this war.

September 11 spurred it; obviously, 9/11 is our Pearl Harbor. I think one of the problems is that the American people are not involved in it. We have a society now where the people can sit back and not pay attention. The common citizen doesn't think about the billions of dollars that are going into this war, maybe two billion dollars a month. Where's this money coming from? It's coming from our federal, our state budgets, the states are fighting this war just as much as our federal government is. When we go federal in the National Guard, the federal government picks it up. Those are state resources that are being taken—the people that leave their jobs, their communities, it leaves a gap in our society. All this money is coming from all of us. It's being taken out of our schools. It's all being taken out of our community.

I was an undergrad at UMass-Amherst, and I was really not well. One day I realized there must be other guys here going through something similar. I started working with a couple of other veterans to organize the Veterans and Service Members Association [VASMA], which focused on veteran needs. We built three core principles with the group. One was community service: a lot of us feel disempowered, we feel we don't have a lot to offer because we're not doing that job that was of great importance [military service], so we could go out and use the skills that we had and become involved with our communities. The [second] aspect: advocacy for our own needs. The college and administration certainly weren't aware of what they could do to make our school experience that much more. The third core principle: networking with the administration, other colleges, or with the Student Veterans of America throughout the country.

We advocated for and got an administrative office, a drop-in center with computers, books, places to sit, X-Box 360, so guys can hang out and play video games, coffee machines, snacks. The certifying agents are there now; it's a one-stop center. They can ask questions about benefits and get directed to other administrative offices on campus, which now have points of contact specifically for veterans, like the VA, the Vet Center in Springfield, religious institutions. Two of us created a 14-week class for veterans focused on veteran integration into the university, writing college-level papers. VA representatives explain benefits, Veterans Education Project guys tell stories about their reintegration. The guy who teaches the writing class is an Afghanistan veteran.

It can be extremely isolated as a veteran. I got home and my whole world completely fell apart. My fiancée, whom I had been with for seven years, two kids and a home, two weeks later, our relationship was over. When you come home, it's never the same. Your family has learned to live on their own, your spouse has learned how to take care of everything in your absence. You're not needed. Doing the mundane tasks of shopping every day after being in an environment where everything you did had purpose, had meaning, was important. If you didn't do your job the right way, people could die.

I wasn't diagnosed with PTSD for seven years. I just recently was. It's listed as an anxiety disorder in the DSM-4, *Diagnostic and Statistical Manual of Mental Disorders*. The way I'm coming to understand it, it's based in fear, which is a really hard concept for people in the military. Anxiety can be around anything. Even now, a lot of my anxiety comes from relationships, standing in large crowds.

It's founded in fear and that's where the whole fight-or-flight mechanism kicks in. You're now living in a society where you're not in danger, you don't have to be looking around. But if you're standing in a crowd and your fight-or-flight kicks in automatically because that's what you are trained to do, you become very, very anxious and certain chemicals are released in the body and mind where you can't think clearly. You're looking for weapons, and if you start doing that in a crowd waiting to go into a movie, civilians would look at you. Wow, he's really messed up!

If you surround yourself with really positive support and provide yourself with a very stable environment, then you can live as if you don't have it at all. But if life just isn't good and you're not in a stable environment, that's all going to agitate it. Not a lot of people return to stability. The spouses and loved ones are the heroes, the ones that really hold everything together, during and after. Without them, I have no idea what would happen to the majority of our veterans.

Chris McGurk was born in Orange, New Jersey, in 1975 and graduated from high school in Washingtonville, New York. He speaks of "a McGurk family thing—service and pride." He served in both Afghanistan (2003–4) and Iraq (2005–6). He joined the army reserves in 1995, and served with the 10th Mountain Division, 1st Battalion, 87th infantry, retiring in 2006 after being a squad leader and a platoon sergeant. He gave testimony to Senator John Kerry's Senate Committee on Foreign Relations on April 23, 2009. He has dedicated himself to working with veterans, including in the IAVA (Iraq and Afghanistan Veterans of America) and the Massachusetts Veterans' Affairs SAVE program. He earned two Bronze Stars with "V" for valor, a Purple Heart, five Army Commendation medals, four Army Achievement medals, and three Army Good Conduct medals. Having served in the two ongoing wars, Chris offers suggestions on how to support the Afghan people, rather than diverting our efforts to a war in Iraq that does not have a clear rationale.

AFGHANISTAN

I was there from July of 2003 to May of 2004. To me it was a very humbling experience. Coming from a Western culture where you can wake up at any time in the middle of the night, walk into your bathroom, have running water, have electricity, to a culture that is basically in the Stone Age. Everything they rely on is by generator or battery. They heat their homes with firewood. Any time we went into a house while we were on patrol we were always welcomed in, they were always offering us chai. The average Afghan male is five-foot six, and the average American male is six-foot. We must have looked like giants walking around with all this body armor and equipment. They were very curious [about us], but it was a very cautious curiosity. It took them a while to feel comfortable enough to really talk with us.

The kids had no fear. "Mister, mister, Pepsi." Or they wanted a soccer ball. The only thing we had were pens. Something as simple as a pen would seem amazing to them. A good 80–90 percent of women wore burkas, they were completely covered, head to toe. We tried to stay respectful of the culture, we didn't approach a female if there was a male member of the family present—there was no need to have conversations with them. Especially when we were out on patrols, we were with village elders, who were males. If you did come into a household doing a search, the females would be ushered into another room.

For all the wonderful experiences I had in Afghanistan, I can for the most part truly separate the anger we felt for those who perpetrated 9/11 from the Afghan people. I was very struck by their resiliency, their fortitude. They get up every day and go about their lives in an environment and time that is very chaotic. They understood what happened on 9/11, shockingly enough, a lot of them did. [But] they were completely suspicious of who we were, why we were there. They asked us a bunch of questions. Those that had never seen a Westerner before fell in love with digital cameras. They thought it was the coolest thing in the world that we could take a picture and show it on the screen to them.

Two major events shaped my time in Afghanistan. The first one happened on September 29, 2003. Part of my company, Alpha Company, moved from Orgun-E to a firebase called Shkin [in Paktika province], four miles from the Pakistan border [South Waziristan]. All-over Taliban, one of the major crossing points from Pakistan. There was a tribe, the Waziris, they were along the Pakistan–Afghanistan border, a lot of them were Pakistani military who manned checkpoints right by Shkin firebase. At night, they were emplacing rockets that were launched at our firebase. During the day, these were the guards that we were working with. Every day we were getting into ambushes and firefights.

On September 29, one of my sister platoons was out along a place called Losano Ridge, named after an Air Force forward air patrol who was killed in 2002. The Losano Ridge was the main skirmish area between us and the insurgency. The one platoon that was patrolling started coming under active fire. This day the fire seemed a bit more intense—it seemed to not dissipate. After a while, normally, they would shoot and run. They were using mortars (they drop the munitions down the tubes) [so] they called back to the firebase and asked for backup. I was the first platoon, we rolled out, jumped in our Humvees and went out to the ridge line to help.

We went out with our company commander, Captain Worthan. I was an E-6, staff sergeant, the senior squad leader in the company, but I was also the senior squad leader in my platoon. I was in charge of dismounting, walking along the ground, getting into the area that the vehicles couldn't go. So this day, my company commander, and my platoon leader Craig Mullaney (the gentleman who wrote the book *The Unforgiving Minute: A Soldiers' Education* about our unit), said, "Sergeant McGurk, can you dismount, we're going to walk this ridge line and see if we can pinpoint where the enemy fire is coming from, and if not, we'll hop back on the vehicles and go back to the firebase." At this point, all the enemy small arms fire had stopped, so it was quiet, nothing going on.

We found a little compound where somebody had been the night before, fresh-brought firewood, fresh footprints, strings, and wrappers. I called that back to my company commander. We pushed forward a little bit further, one of the lead elements in my squad, Sergeant G., surprised three fighters that were hiding in a bush. He immediately opened fire and they returned the fire at him. If I remember correctly, he killed one, and wounded one of the others. As soon as that happened, pardon the French, all hell broke loose. We had actually triggered an enemy ambush.

There were eleven in my squad and we were being engaged by 60 to 100 ACMs, or anti-coalition militants, that's what we call them. We were pinned down. We were taking extreme enemy fire, RPGs, hand grenades. At the initial onslaught of the ambush, one of my soldiers in my lead team was shot three times by a sniper. It hit him below the body armor. When that happened, Sergeant G., the lead team leader, started yelling for a medic. The medic came running down a good quarter mile. I was EMT-certified at the time, and the two of us started working on Pfc. Evan O'Neill, from Haverhill, Massachusetts. [1st Battalion, 87th Infantry Regiment, 10th Mountain Division.] He was one of the first combat deaths from Massachusetts in Afghanistan. The doctors said even if he was shot and fell on an operating table, chances are he wouldn't have survived because one of the rounds hit his descending aorta, so it shot off.

I'm able to tell it, not with less emotion, but I manage to get through it. I have first responder training. We go out and tell stories and give training to police and teach them how to de-escalate a situation when working with veterans. One of the stories I used to tell is this, and I used to find it very difficult. I'd never lost a soldier in combat before. I was the last person with him, along with the medic, when he passed away.

His words—it wasn't like you see on TV, people screaming for their mother, this very dramatic scene. It was almost serene and peaceful. He was more worried about the fact that he'd let the squad down, if the other guys in the squad were okay. Not once was he worried about himself. He was a nineteen-year-old kid dying and making sure that the rest of the squad was okay. That's something that stays with me forever. After that, being a leader, you start questioning what if I did this, what if I did that, you play the "what-if" game. Quite honestly, after Afghanistan and before Iraq, I drank heavily. I was self-medicating, trying to forget a lot of that stuff. To this day, it's still a pretty raw point for me, but it's something that through my therapy through the VA, and through my other counselors, I've learned to deal with and learn from.

I didn't talk about it for the longest time. I was very closed off. Then I realized that after coming home, getting out of the military, my fellow brothers and sisters in combat were being killed. It was the number of people—five more were killed in Afghanistan today, or six more were killed. We're real people, with real families—we're not just some pawn in a political game. We actually bleed red blood, and when we tell these stories to first responders you tell them these are the reasons we ask you to give a little bit more thought to what you are going to do with a veteran in a crisis situation. It's because these are the thoughts and the demons that haunt people.

[Another situation] was pretty similar, typical, almost equal to the 29th. We had an OGA team (meaning "other government agencies") that operated out of Shkin firebase. These were civilians, CIA contractors that were former Navy SEALs, former Green Berets, former Delta Force, Force Recon, you name it. They were training the local Afghan militia forces in guerrilla warfare tactics. They were becoming the Green Berets of the Afghan National Army.

The OGAs were extremely good at intelligence-gathering, helping us with information, and [could] pinpoint where some high value targets were. My platoon became the security element for the team that operated out of firebase Shkin. Any time they went on a long mission they asked us to come along and act as a blocking force for them. So on October 25, 2003, the OGA team was down 50 kilometers south of Shkin, operating in an area near the Pakistani border. They had intel about some bad guys that were crossing the border, so they went down there themselves, trying to find these guys. They wound up getting into a pretty bad ambush. They try to fit in with the local population—they were driving pick-up trucks.

There's a pecking order in the military: in the infantry, 11 bravo is an infantryman, then you have airborne infantry. Then you have airborne rangers, then you have ranger battalion, and you have Green Berets. But the OGA guys didn't care even though a lot of them were former Navy SEALs. "We're all here for the same mission, the same cause."

When that ambush kicked off, one of the OGA guys was killed immediately, a couple of the Afghan security forces were killed, a pretty intense firefight. They called back to the firebase and asked for our platoon to come back them up. We drove the 50 kilometers, we linked up with their leadership, we did a quick assessment, and then we moved on. I was a little shaky after what happened on the 29th. When we were driving down to meet up with the OGA guys, one of their guys, Chris Muller, a former Navy SEAL, heard about this heavy enemy ambush, and he jumped into the patrol with us.

So Chris went with us, walking with me, and then ahead of me to one of the point guys on my squad. Some rifle fire kicked off and I remember seeing Chris lurch backward for a second, and then do this weird cartwheel roll down the hill. I didn't know what was wrong with him, but instinct took over, so without paying attention to enemy or being shot at, I was running to get to him and I rolled him over and there was a dark red stain on his shirt.

You knew immediately he was shot. He was pretty pale. Took his body armor off, cut his shirt off, he had a sucking chest wound. Being an EMT, I was trying to do everything I could, bandaging his wound and doing CPR, I didn't care if I got shot. I kept his pulse for 45 minutes. Unfortunately, the medevac that was supposed to come was late, and because they were late, he wound up dying there. I'll never forget him. And I think one of the hard things for me was his name was Chris. To this day it chokes me up when I think about it.

Probably seven months ago, I had a phone call from Brandon Muller, Chris's brother. [Chris] was a civilian contractor for the CIA, not a lot was put out about what happened. Both of us were crying on the phone. It was a very difficult thing. He just wanted to know who had been the last person with his brother and how it happened and I explained it to him. I eventually am going to go out to Milwaukee and meet him and we're going to have a beer together.

We had a lot of good intentions. Last year, I testified in front of the Senate Committee on Foreign Relations. It was John Kerry who gave a speech in 1971 to the same committee on Vietnam. Once President Obama wanted to refocus all of our efforts on Afghanistan, the Senate Committee on Foreign Relations wanted to get an idea of what people who'd been there felt. It's very easy to watch the news, but it's very different talking to someone who has been on the ground. They wanted to get an idea of what to do moving forward.

One of the things I talked about in the testimony, and one of the things that really frustrated me, was here we are building schools, building hospitals, and digging wells. It's all fine and dandy, it's really good PR, and it's really good photo ops. But when you don't have the money to put teachers in those schools, buy books for those schools, or actually get them up and running and educate a population that has one of the highest illiteracy rates in the world, it doesn't mean anything. You can have all the good intentions in the world, but if we're not actually funding these projects, what are we doing? I can understand the connection to 9/11 and the fact that some of the terrorists trained in Afghanistan, but what I couldn't understand was the blatant [lack of] understanding of what we needed to do to help the Afghan people, a complete lack of making a true effort.

It was difficult for me too, being in Iraq. I believed in the mission in Afghanistan, but I didn't believe in why we were in Iraq. We left Afghanistan prematurely. It's like when you get sick and you have to take antibiotics. You're supposed to take seven days, you take three, you feel better, but your sickness doesn't go away. We just completely dropped the ball, we just went to Iraq.

It's definitely a quagmire. I don't believe you can just shovel Western style democracy into any country and just make it work. Afghanistan is a very tribal culture that doesn't trust the central government. Now, in 2010, seven years later, you're putting troops you've deployed multiple times back into Afghanistan and it doesn't matter anymore that it had legitimate ties to 9/11. Soldiers, sailors, airmen, Marines, you put them on their fifth tour, they don't care anymore, they just want to stay alive and go home. I think the Afghan people are tired of it.

We need to try to achieve some of the goals that we had set forth in the beginning. A lot of the elders still remember what we did to them once the Soviets were defeated. We pulled all funding out of the country and said thanks, see you later. We abandoned them one time, then we abandoned them again after Iraq kicked off. I think we need to do something to try to at least get some of those goals. What these goals are I don't exactly know. I leave that to the policy wonks in Washington.

If we just up and left, the entire Afghan population would just go, "The United States abandoned us once, they abandoned us twice, now they're doing it again—what's the point?" I don't think we would have any credibility with the Afghan people. We don't have the logistics to just pull every US soldier home in a month's time, it's impossible, not to mention the power vacuum that would be created with us leaving. Have small, quantifiable, achievable goals, complete them and then come home. It's going on ten years in this war, and we're in the same place we were when we began. You're not going to get the tribal regions to all sit down and say, I love Afghanistan, I want whatever's best for the country. The people I ran into seemed to care more for what you could do for them than what you could do for Afghanistan. Trying to cater to all the people all the time is just not going to work.

One of the biggest things that causes problems in Afghanistan is corruption. People just don't trust the Karzai government. I think putting some system in place that has complete transparency in the Karzai government, rules and regulations that are actually followed, and getting the people involved. One thing we can do to help them establish a legitimate government is to help create complete transparency where people actually do get to vote and put people in office that they want to be there.

Other than that I don't see a whole lot happening. You're not going to stop the poppy trade in the south—Afghanistan supplies 80 percent of opium. I don't know if I heard this somewhere, or maybe I had an original idea myself, but I don't understand why they don't get the world's pharmaceutical companies into Afghanistan, or bring them into another location, and have a summit to regulate the opium. [The] opium that's used in pain killers, now it's being regulated, it's being monitored, it's being controlled, you're paying farmers to grow a crop that's actually used for benefit as opposed to just trying to burn their crop down. If you burn their crop down and you don't give them a job, what's the next thing that they are going to do? They're going to pick up a weapon because the Taliban is paying them $200 a week to go shoot an American.

You're dealing with a society that has been warring for the last thousand years and you cannot bring in a Western-style democracy and expect it to work. The proverbial you can't put a square peg in a round hole. I don't know if it's self-delusion or just not caring.

IRAQ
Iraq, July of '05 to July of '06, my unit was based out of Camp Liberty, which is Baghdad International Airport (BIA). We patrolled the areas just north, al-Shuala neighborhood and Adhamiya.

The first real bad day we had was September 14, 2005, the day that I heard in the news back here was one of the bloodiest days in Iraq, something like 36 vehicle-borne IEDs, car bombs. We were watching traffic to make sure people weren't putting IEDs into the road. There was a bridge that bridged a Shia and a Sunni neighborhood, and on that bridge Iraqi police and an Iraqi National Guard had a checkpoint. I remember watching the van roll up on top of the bridge. I turned back and looked south along the road, and I heard an explosion.

I was the patrol leader at the time because my platoon sergeant (he was E-7, I was E-6) was sick that day. So I rolled up on the bridge to help them. I remember there was an arm over there, an ear over there—it's no different than Afghanistan. We came off the bridge and we were setting up concertina wire or barbed wire, and put signs in front of it saying "Stop, stay away." While we were setting this wire up my Humvee started taking small arms fire. So I ran back to the Humvee, the door was open, I went to dive in and I hit my head on the door fame. That hurt really bad and it knocked me out for a minute. One of my gunners picked me up and threw me into the truck. We went through the neighborhood and were looking for who was shooting at us.

For a long time our days were 15- to 16-hour mindless patrols. We didn't feel there were any ties to 9/11 there, you didn't feel like there was any reason to be there. Unlike Afghanistan, the people in Iraq really hated us—you could just feel the anger and disdain they had for us. It was very uncomfortable. You just didn't want to be there. Especially after Colin Powell came out and said, yeah, we fabricated some intelligence, it was like, "Why are we here?"

I think you create more terrorists than you train people who actually care about why you are there, or understand why you are there. It creates a hate and it creates lazy attitudes. You don't want to be there. The difference between my generation and Vietnam, it's an all-volunteer army, you aren't dealing with that draft dynamic, but you are to a degree. I worked with some of the most intelligent people I've ever known, very tuned into the political atmosphere, and why we're there. No one believed it, there was no conviction, we didn't care. We were professionals so we did our job, went through the motions.

Some people, this was their third combat tour already. Basically it's like, "Go play in the sand in a giant oven, you're going there just because." It's a recipe for disaster. It's the fact that you have young soldiers who don't care about being there, so they might not necessarily pay attention to what they are doing. They're also not paying attention to how they are speaking and treating people. They're angry, a little more hostile toward the Iraqi public than if they felt they belonged there. From time to time, I acted differently in Iraq than I did in Afghanistan. I would say it was a year of disassociation.

We were [having to] address the growing sectarian violence. I had a really hard time finding, every day, two or three bodies. A place called Adhamiya had a lot of Ba'athist Party members, that's where they used to live. Every day someone would call in and say there was someone lying in the street dead, and it was only because you were Sunni or Shia. I remember one very vividly. We found him lying in the street, probably in his thirties, coming back from the bakery, bread all over the ground. I remember very vividly he was shot six times in the face. Because he was Shia. I just don't understand that. There's not much we can do, it's a visceral hate for one another that's gone on forever.

[We're] being asked to bring a message, we're going to be heard, we're going to give some input, and actually *affect* the national dialogue. We testified [in the Senate Committee on Foreign Relations] and I don't think that very much came of it. You *say* you care about the troops, if you want to support the troops, listen to them. Let our voices be heard. What are our experiences in the area? Unfortunately, without going so far as to say it is some kind of conspiracy theory, the war machine is *status quo*, it's what the American public embraces, the government embraces to a certain degree.

I honestly think that the minute we leave Iraq, the balance of power that was before we got there is the balance of power that's going to be when we leave. I have to word this very delicately because of course it is personal opinion, but it seemed like every facet of society was corrupt. It was who you could bribe, when you get bribed, how much you bribe them. It's a string of corruption. How many times has the Iraqi government been given a chance to set up a viable government over the last three years? The only thing we could do now is begin the troop withdrawal in 2011 and just hope for the best.

I work for the Massachusetts Department of Veteran Services, the SAVE outreach team, a peer-to-peer program. The team works with all generations of veterans, but we try to capture Iraq and Afghanistan veterans as they return home before they slip through the cracks or don't get treatment for PTSD. We'll help any veteran but we focus on high risk, those that have mild to moderate suicide ideation, complex and compounded PTSD, traumatic brain injury, or substance abuse. We try to help veterans by accessing help, the federal and state benefits, reintegrating in normal society as much as possible.

Historically, Vietnam veterans took thirty years to proactively seek out help. My uncle was a Marine, served in Khe Sahn during the Tet offensive. I can't imagine what my uncle witnessed through that night. If it was not for the Vietnam generation, my generation would not have a platform to speak on. I truly thank Vietnam veterans for their service. I went the extra mile for Vietnam veterans because they didn't have it when they came home. If it wasn't for them, I wouldn't be around right now.

In the long run, you ultimately can't force anyone. You can offer the services to veterans, we get a referral from a family member or someone in the community. We'll call the veteran: "My name is Chris McGurk, I'm an Iraq and Afghanistan veteran, I was wounded in Afghanistan, I have a Purple Heart, I know what it's like to come home and be overwhelmed with all the benefits. This is what we do, this is how I can help you, here's my contact information." I want them to take that next step. It's Statewide Advocacy for Veterans' Empowerment (SAVE)—we want to empower them to take charge of their own mental and physical health.

From a description of coming home written by Chris:

It has been a lot harder readjusting to a "normal" life than I thought it would be. I still have the sensation of my arms and face going numb from the crushing weight of my body armor and the restrictiveness of my helmet. I still have moments where I find myself looking for my weapon to be within arm's reach... A part of my soul was left in Iraq and I know I will never be able to get it back. Even if you were never shot at, or had an IED detonate next to you, the sheer sadness and degradation that permeates the streets of Baghdad will change you in a way that cannot be put into words.

Sergeant Woehlke was born in Dorchester, MA in 1983. She served in Afghanistan in 2003 and in Iraq 2009-10 in the Army National Guard, Military Police, first as a specialist and then as a sergeant, 747th Military Police Company out of Pittsfield, MA. Charly graduated from Westfield State University in 2006 in criminal justice. She works at the veterans' service office in Springfield and also with disturbed youth. Charly updated her interview to say that the District Chief of Police where she worked was killed by a bomb, and a policeman she knew "has reverted to kicking in doors and neglecting police steps, very sad to hear that they have taken several steps backwards." In the Veterans' Services office where she works, I watched as Charly greeted veterans of all ages with warmth and empathy.

AFGHANISTAN

I decided to join for college benefits. I'd wanted to be a police officer and they were talking about military police and I thought, National Guard will pay for my college. I signed the papers on February 7, 2001. I went to a semester of college, watched the [9/11] attacks from a college dorm room—Oh my God, I am not going to college anymore. They told us get ready because you're going.

The training at the time for National Guard wasn't as serious, guarding the state and the citizens, flooding, the Red Sox parade. It wasn't as focused on national defense and going to die for your country. The whole focus changed. We got the call to go to Afghanistan in January 2003. There were wills to be written, people with children had to make sure their spouses had daycare set, and tell their jobs that they weren't going to be there for a year.

My first steps in Afghanistan: Oh my God, what did I get myself into! Nineteen years old, I had no clue what I had in store for me. We flew into Bagram airfield and then hopped in the truck and went to Kabul, where I did my tour of duty. We were to back up the Third Group Special Forces, and got to train the first group of military police that went through the Afghan National Army. We did some security with the Special Forces because when they did their raids they needed to bring women with them, [since they] couldn't search Afghan women. The men weren't supposed to touch their clothes at all, even if it was in a box in a corner. It's a sacred type of article, so we'd help with the questioning of the women, sectioning them off, searching them.

They raided a house [where] they had intel that some bad guys were responsible for floating IEDs down the river, and the IEDs were picked up and used to blow up a convoy. The other female and myself were toward the back because we weren't supposed to be up on the front lines of combat. They raided the house, called us and told us that it was safe to go in, and she and I went into the room where they had the women segregated, with children and farm animals. We searched their clothing boxes. They had metal bins they kept their clothing in with locks. [We] searched their person, children, the room that we were in, and ultimately tried to make them feel safe, because the women are so guarded there that a whole bunch of scary army soldiers coming into the house is probably terrifying for them—scary for me. We were there to do the physical searches of the women, because you can't touch women, can't search their clothes, so they would try to hide things in the women's belongings, which stopped working when [our] women joined the military.

We had interpreters with us *always*, local to the area. We had to assume they were telling them what we were telling them: "We have information that your husband, brother, uncle, is responsible for an attack on this party on this date, we're looking for this, do you know where it is?" "No." "Well our job is to search your home, or your belongings for this."

[*Could you spot Taliban?*] You never know. It could be a woman under her burka with a knife or a gun. Most of the older men had beards, so if you were looking for a bomber today, they say look for a clean-cut face because they get themselves ready for the afterlife. But it could be some guy who wanted to shave his beard that day. Some of the kids we saw every day would say, "bomb, bomb, bomb," point to where there was unexploded ordinances, old things from the Soviets even, there were land mines everywhere over there left over from previous wars. The kids would point them out for us because we'd give them water and candy.

But there were some kids [in] the areas [where] they didn't see us as frequently, they'd throw rocks at us, so we'd think they were throwing bombs or hand grenades. One time in my Humvee, a young boy threw big rocks that bounced through our truck and we thought it was a hand grenade, so we're screaming, "Get out, get out, get out!" Our gunner's like, "What?" If it was a hand grenade, he would have no legs right now. The kid was like, "Ha Ha!" and ran away. So it was any age, any place, any gender. There was no definite enemy over there.

In Iraq it was different seven years ago. For quite a while they were using the children because they know in America we won't shoot a kid. The kids would be used with suicide vests, throw things, or even to plant the bomb. They know if you pick the kid up and they planted the bomb, okay, the kid's not going to tell you who made him do it, and you're going to have to let him go. I would say the use of children is a last-ditch effort of terror.

In Afghanistan we'd do presence patrols through the mountains, just to let the locals know where we were, and let the Taliban know we were there, constantly driving through. They can't set them up if we're there. There were always kids bringing their sheep through the mountains or going out to play. Young kids, not in school, you'd recognize the clothing, hand-me-downs, for example, jellies, slip-on shoes, almost everyone had them. Things you bring down to the Salvation Army, they sent them over.

In Afghanistan if we were near a mosque at certain points of the day you could hear the prayers over the loudspeaker. Religion was a big part of the community. But we were not closely involved with the religious aspect. [We'd] stay away from it—something as simple as picking up a Koran by accident can be very disrespectful. If you picked up someone's Bible to move it, or a Torah, it's not considered disrespectful. But that book is a sacred thing. We're trying to make it more personal and political, you can't make it a religious war.

The Afghan men didn't know what the heck to make of us women. I took an old T-shirt, ripped it up and tied it around my hair so they couldn't see it. If I was up in the turret I had my goggles on, I had my face mask, you didn't know if I was a girl or a guy. But when we had an MP on the street, [once] we had a truck that was with us break down, and we had to pull security, 360 [degrees], there was a large group that began to get larger and larger.

I didn't see any weapons but the group was getting closer to us, and I said to the person in charge, I don't like it, and he said, Raise your weapon. So I raised my weapon, a M249, a large weapon, which I thought would intimidate him. I had it inches away from this guy's nose and I was telling him in Afghani, "Get away, go, get back," and he laughed at me. I had a real gun, real bullets, you can see the bullets because they are linked together, and he laughed at me, because I am a woman. Okay!! What do I do now? [*She laughs.*]

You can always tell in the eyes. Not his—mine—because I wasn't in the turret, I didn't have my goggles on in the street. I have a high-pitched voice. I sound like a child. I'm sure he thought some young girl was telling him what to do. I didn't really have cause to shoot him, he didn't have a weapon, he wasn't hurting me. The interpreter started screaming and yelling at them. One of the male MPs started to come over to help me out. I've never had any issue being female in the military; I pull my weight just fine. But at that point I wasn't a military police officer, I was just a girl that guy was not taking seriously.

The little base that we were in was like a fried egg where our area was the smallest area inside the base [of the] Afghan National Army. There were wires that went around the whole thing. We had observation posts, but we were completely surrounded by the Afghan National Army, so there were men everywhere. The Afghans would whistle, shout, or snap their teeth, put up their fingers. It was constant, just part of living over there and you had to have thick skin.

[*Was there harassment from US troops?*] Our guys? Not for me, [or] the other women I was with. It was like having 60 older brothers. They definitely looked out for us. The vests are not shaped for women, there's no arched breast plate, so my vest would sit out a little bit. I used to stand with my thumbs on the side of my vest just to help the weight, and an Afghan national army reached in, and grabbed me before I even had a chance to respond. He was taken into custody, kicked out of the military, and off of me. I thought they were taking very good care of us.

It was explained to the [Afghans] that were going to be working with us directly, they're going to have women in the US military, this is how you're to treat them. I was a woman, but they knew the customs and courtesies of our military. At first, we had to explain because they thought we were prostitutes that just came along with the United States Army. They didn't understand why we had guns, so it had to be clarified for them.

Being a female, try staying clean and maintain your dignity in a group of all men. We would be out for twelve hours a day doing our patrols. I think the worst part of Afghanistan was being a female. If you're a guy and you have to go to the bathroom in the mountains, the world is your urinal. But us, "someone hold this," get out of the truck, it's not easy at all. If we were in the mountains, there were some places that were lined with rocks painted white on the inside and red on the outside. The best you could do was get out of the Humvee and stay on the white side of the rocks, the red side was a minefield so you stay away. A lot of the area we would drive through was abandoned, so you could get out. "Don't turn around, I'll kill you!"

When we went through our training in Fort Dix, they assured us that the Afghans would be stupid, that they would have no education, you had to baby-talk them. That was totally inaccurate. The man that I worked with had the equivalent of my degree. He'd gone through college, he had military training as well, the military academy, I would say he's more educated than I am, especially in what he's seen of the world. Their education levels are much higher than we give them credit for.

I missed my family but I didn't want to go home. You get used to knowing exactly what you're doing the very next day, who's in charge of you, what you're expected to do. It was nice to feel that you were in charge, too. Even though I was a specialist I had some authority.

IRAQ

I got engaged, got married, bought a house, two dogs, got my veterans job here. My unit was activated again. [My husband and I] ended up in the same company, same platoon. We were allowed to live together. The Iraqis got a huge kick out of us. They didn't really know what to do with us at first as a married couple, you usually don't meet a man's wife [and] I was ultimately team leader—I was in charge of troops. Because their women are not in the military as frequently (there are some), they get a kick out of it. "Well, I'm married, this is my husband." They go, "No, No," and the interpreter would [say], "Look at the name tapes, 'Woehlke.' I'm sure they've seen Smith, Jones, and Bennett, but *Woehlke,* to have on two people next to each other, they believed it!

The training officer that I worked with, they exchange a lot of gifts, so I would bring him some candy. I found out he had children, so I would bring him some small toys. Once I brought him make-up for his wife, he opened up. [*She laughs.*] Vitamins were huge, vitamins for 60 days was just $1.99—inexpensive for us but it was relationship-builders. He would tell me how his son wasn't feeling well and he couldn't play with the other children. "I suggest you bring these to your doctor and see if it's okay to take." The doctor said, "That's great, take them." Before I left, I brought him a year's supply of vitamins. It helps them see we were really there to help, we weren't just there for my job.

When the regular police would go out, very few would go out without their face covered. They'd change before they went home. Their identity as police is a danger to their life, especially in the cities where they are really making a difference arresting people. You could have this guy who is a good citizen, honest, not a terrorist, and his brother could be a terrorist. So the police go out and arrest the brother and the good citizen can't be a member of the police because of the family, tribe thing. I'd say that we were safer over there than they were.

Just before we left, [my husband and I] had to go out to the Baghdadi police station and say goodbye to a gentleman. He'd invited us into his home, we'd met his children, I had a picture taken with his wife, which is a big deal. Just before we left he *gave us* his Koran. To us, the highest point of respect that you could ever get because we understand how important is that book—that's what runs their lives. We looked at the interpreter, is it okay for us to take it? It's at home on my mantle, it has its whole separate section. We understand how important it was.

There was a raid, the Navy SEALs (I'm not sure, the 82nd was [also] over there, the CIA, but it was not connected to us), and they killed the mayor's son. He was not the suspect—it wasn't intentional. The police station shut down and wouldn't let us in for a little while. When the army did something, it's the *whole* army. If [Iraqis] hear about a soldier that murdered somebody, that's the *whole* army. They don't see that as an individual person who did that. The Guantanamo Bay issue didn't come up, and even Abu Ghraib they never mentioned, but they were very upset about things that happened across the whole country. [That] directly affected our working and ultimately could set us back a whole month in our own interests and information.

[*Wasn't it July 2010 that was supposed to be the step-down of US combat forces in Iraq?*] It was supposed to be, yes. If you think about it though, MP is not considered combat troops. You can say that all the combat troops are gone, it doesn't mean all the troops are gone, and it doesn't mean we were spending any less over there. We were replaced by a company with the same amount of people to do the same thing, taking over the same amount of space and buildings, the same amount of living quarters—it doesn't seem like there was much of a change when we left.

I think we did help a lot, we did make a difference in a lot of those guys' lives. But we didn't, in my opinion, make enough difference in their world for us to be there. They could have done without us. But with us there they had additional training to help them and they have a little bit more trust in the Americans now because we were there to build relationships with them and ensure that they were doing everything that they needed to be doing over there. It was all report writing, smiling faces, and drinking tea.

[*What will happen?*] I honestly don't know. Because when we left Afghanistan, we thought we were done. Iraq was won years ago, but it's not a stable country yet. I think if America does leave it right now we'll be back there soon. They don't have the same infrastructure that we have where you can put your trash in a barrel outside your house, someone will come and get it. Or you can turn your water on and it's going to work, and if it doesn't work you have a phone number and they will come down and they will fix it for you. It makes a *huge* difference. Now these guys don't have places to pick up their trash, so they have to burn it in the back yard or they dump it and it pollutes the water. Now these people are getting sick and they don't have health care. Now they are mad at the government because there's no health care, there's trash everywhere, and they don't have any water. Something as simple as having trash picked up can affect the whole dynamic of the entire country.

We went on a mission out to one of the remote areas and dropped off school supplies, candy, and coloring books for the kids. This guy came up to us and through my interpreter said, "We don't want this crap, take it back, we want water." We had hundreds of bags of things for the children. "We don't want this, give us water or go away, don't come back." How do you respond to that? "I am sorry, sir, I don't have any ability to give you clean drinking water. You get the brown water out of the river and have a nice day." There's nothing we can do with that, and it's a huge problem.

[Under Saddam] there was a lot more fear, but there was also the knowledge that the food would be coming and they'd be able to provide for their family. That was mentioned quite a bit from the locals. We'd go and ask how are we doing, what's going on, what do you need? It was such a violent time and they still think it was better with Saddam. You could say I don't like Saddam and you could go to jail, they wouldn't have to tell your family where you are.

I took a class in gangs in school, and you can take the gang leader away and there's always someone who will step up. It's not going to change the gang, it's not going to change the dynamics. Like the Mafia, you may be able to take the boss out but somebody's going to step up. Unfortunately, if you can't change the entire group, you can't change the leader.

The Sunni–Shia issue was mostly with the interpreters we had. We'd call them by generic names because they're from this area, from this tribe, from this city, [it] gives away just who you are and what religion you are. It would be dangerous for them if they were from a [different] tribe to be working with us with *this* tribe—I know your family, get out or I'll kill you. They usually settle within areas that have the same religion because it's a neutral area, there's no fighting, everyone related in some way.

There was a shop on the base where they had language books to help you. So if you didn't have an interpreter next to you and someone [was] hurt, you could open up an injury card in your language and in their language, point to where you're hurt, and they'd point to it. What happened to you? Point to that. I found a bomb, this is what it looks like, point to the bomb, point to the color, did it explode yet, how many people are around it, is it in your house? They call them smart cards. "You're under arrest, keep your hands behind your back."

When I left Iraq, I couldn't wait to get home, couldn't get done fast enough. I wanted to go back and be a wife with my husband as opposed to a fellow military police officer. You're wearing the same thing every day. I'd had enough walking down a gravel road to go to the bathroom. As soon as we got home, we put a new roof on, had the driveway redone, did the stairs, ripped the office apart, insulated the area, rewired, sanded the floors in the guest bedroom. The bathroom we retiled, repainted, all the fixtures, I took the first shower only two months ago. [*She laughs.*]

After six years, I reenlisted. There's a big bonus and we bought the house. When my husband reenlisted, he bought my engagement ring and a motorcycle. I would not have the things I have now unless I'd joined the military, a job I love [working with veterans], I wouldn't have gone to Westfield State. I needed the GI Bill. My contract is up in 2013. As far as I know, the National Guard has two years of down time after a deployment, but I still have those six months after. I hope to have kids before then and not go.

You don't have to agree with what was done, but the troop doesn't get to decide where they go, what they do, they're there to serve their country because their country asked. It's not their fault if it is something that you don't agree with. These guys that came home from Vietnam, there were no thank-yous and there was actually the complete opposite where everybody turned their backs on them. It should never happen again. Something as simple as a thank you is a wonderful way to let the troop know that you do care. I appreciate the acknowledgement that I took time out of my life to serve my country, but you don't have to thank me.

[*And if someone is against the war?*] For an American you have a right to say that. That's why there is a military, we fought for the right for people to not want you there. Even the people who hate the troops, well, I don't agree with it, I don't like you for saying it, but you have the right to say it because you're American. You can say that and somebody is not going to pick you up and put you in a deep dark dungeon and torture your family.

We've gotten off track and we need to worry about *our* country and where we're going. We have a caseload of over 260 here [Springfield, MA, population 156,000], it tells you that we're not okay in this country. These benefits in this office are not for millionaires. The caseload is so big it tells you straight out that the economy is not good and our veterans are not all well yet.

As you return, you go through the health checkup—"I'm fine, don't ask me any more questions. I'm not sick, there's nothing wrong with me. No, I don't want to harm myself, no, I'm not going to kill my family, yes, I sleep fine, and no, my dreams aren't scary. Just get me out of here and get me home to my family." We had a lot of troops who came back from Iraq who were not okay, didn't know how to get back into society.

Chris Backlund was born in 1984 and grew up in Eden Prairie, Minnesota. He served in the Marine Corps in Iraq where he fought for five months in the battle of Fallujah 2004–5. In 2006, he was stationed in northern Afghanistan at Camp Blessing. Most of the action he saw was in Fallujah where he first saw the dead and dying, and accepted that as the sacrifice necessary for bringing freedom (and elections) to Iraq. In Afghanistan, he saw little combat action and developed an alternate theory for winning the battle for hearts and minds—not through arms but through education. Chris attended UMass-Amherst in natural sciences and agriculture, studying to be an arborist.

IRAQ

As any warrior, Marine, soldier, will tell you, the rules of engagement can kill an objective. Rules of engagement are the line that you can and cannot cross. Our rules of engagement when we first got [to Fallujah] were: if you see anyone with binoculars or a cell phone you can open fire on them. In April of 2004, American soldiers dropped fliers on Fallujah, saying if you're still here by the time we get here, you're going to be considered an insurgent. By the time we got in there it was understood that if you're still here, you're an insurgent.

The rules of engagement instantly changed once the bullets started flying. It became the actual war that the young men had signed up for. It became zero rules of engagement. It was us versus them, this epic dance, if you will, of survival. On our way there, everyone had been talking about hearts and minds—the big goal, hearts and minds. That transferred into, "Two to the heart and one to the mind." [*He laughs.*] It ended up being a joke, the hearts and minds thing.

The convoy was 130 vehicles. We proceeded to the border of Kuwait and Iraq, and I thought, we are crossing into the worst place on earth. I consider myself a religious man and I remember praying to God for protection. We had to keep dispersion because if you get hit, you want to be the only one, you don't want one bomb to take out two vehicles. As we passed through the border, I'm terrified, my gunner turns on his CD player and on comes "Sweet Home Alabama." He put the speakers right down by the radio, and instantly, the mood changed from "we are going to get killed" to "let's go get some!" My entire attitude changed in a split second. We're on a mission, we're well trained, we're well armed, we know what we are doing, let's go do this and get home. The next 27 hours, I drove to Fallujah. The drive was Red Bull-induced [a power drink with caffeine and other stimulants]—between five guys we finished 80 Red Bulls on the drive.

November 7, 2004, in the middle of the night, we were told to get in our trucks and stage. Five battalions, two of them were army (brigades, they call them), and the objective was to push north to south, like wringing out a wet rag, we were going to push insurgents out of this city. On November 8, the engineers shot something that is called a thick wick. It's a mine-clearing mine charge, a rocket connected to a hose and you shoot this thing out and the rocket pulls the hose behind it and the whole thing drops and when you detonate, it blows up a football field, essentially.

This was 0800 in the morning on November 8. Bravo Company had taken over a mosque. On the loudspeakers, which typically project the prayers, they played "Pleased to Meet You" by the Rolling Stones; that really got us in good spirits. My A-gunner nudges me with his hand and he says, "Hey, Backlund, look at this." I see the back of a vehicle that was blown apart and there were three guys in there. They're suspended in time, completely frozen, charred black. One of the guys had his hands up in the air as if he was trying to get out of the vehicle. It was my first combat dead body. They were insurgents. I was marveling at this horrific display.

I turned to look where I was going and I saw a human brain on the road. I didn't want to hit it with my vehicle (that would have been disgusting), so I straddled it underneath us. I remember hearing someone over the radio, "Did you see that? They tried to take out that tank with an RPG." Our job was to find a mosque that was located around here, the Muj [Mujahereen] Mosque. We got there, we took some fire, we established a bit of a base camp, very temporary.

The colonel had met up with us at this spot. We were told he had gotten intel that one of the key insurgents had been killed, so he wanted to go find him. The vehicle left, the crew returned and in the back of my vehicle was the person we identified to be a key target with a poncho draped over [him]. We wanted to get his body out in the street so we could identify it back in the mosque. We had pictures of this guy.

At any rate, he was sitting in the back of the Humvee. When they were going to pull the poncho out, I positioned myself to his back, because I didn't want to see his face. They pulled the tarp off him and it turns out he was turned backwards, so there I am standing face to face with this guy. I could see through his head. Whoever was the sniper that got him, it was a head shot, pretty impressive. Apparently we identified him and he was the gentleman we were looking for, so that was a bit of good news.

I was instructed to get him out of the truck. He was bleeding on everything. My gunner and I (this guy must have weighed 280 pounds), we pulled the tapestry off the wall inside the mosque, and then we rolled him up in [it], rolled his body all the way to one side of the mosque inside the compound. By then Charlie Company had come inside the compound and a few guys sat down on this dead guy that was rolled up, they just thought it was a big pile of rugs. I said, "Hey, guys, you probably don't want to sit there. It's a rolled-up dead guy."

In Fallujah, on November 10, 2004, we were celebrating the Marine Corps birthday by cutting a piece of pound cake. The tradition is that the eldest and youngest Marines will receive the cake. The colonel decided to play the Marine Corps hymn over the [mosque] speakers. The insurgents had no idea what was going on, so they started shooting. The Marines heard the hymn—they loved it. Our sergeant major [Michael Berg] got mad at the insurgents because they were shooting during the Marine Corps hymn, so he said to us, "Shut those guys up!" So our job was to stop them from shooting during the Marine Corps hymn! [*He laughs.*] [A version of this story is told in Bing West's *No True Glory*, 275–6.]

We were clearing the city for five months. I've heard if you look at the records of World War II veterans, the average World War II veteran was in combat for an hour and forty-five minutes. The invasion of Fallujah was a nonstop firefight for five months. The rules of engagement, as I said, started out to be if they have binoculars, obviously, a weapon, they're shooting at you, cell phone was the other big one, you could shoot at them. That morphed into everyone's insurgents—get rid of them. It was just an unspoken thing. I don't know if it was people who were like, I don't care anymore. It was like, listen, we'll give these guys two seconds, and they're already shooting at us. It turned into just "get them." We'd grown so tired—in my battalion alone, 1st Battalion, 3rd Marines, we lost 52 guys killed. My buddy Richard Slocum, he was the first one killed. That made things so real.

They gave us QID numbers (quick ID numbers), a way to identify an individual. It was a letter, which corresponded [to] your company in the battalion. Delta was weapons' company, what I was in, my QID number was Delta double O7. [*We laugh.*] I know, it was just a coincidence. I was the 7th guy in weapons' company alphabetically. I went around getting the QID numbers from all my good friends before we went into the city of Fallujah. I knew that's what they would be calling over the radios. They were instructed to put it in their pockets, somewhere where you could see it. They'd say standby for QID numbers. There were a few of my friends like Alpha 67, and I remember hearing the numbers and feeling relieved when I didn't hear the ones I was worried about hearing. Either way it's a Marine getting killed.

The engagement afforded the civilians of Fallujah an opportunity they'd never had before. That upcoming election, a record number of civilians voted in Fallujah. That was our shining moment, when we got those people to the ballots [polling places] and the civilians started to return. They were able to vote for the first time in their lives. [Chris is referring to the parliamentary elections on January 30, 2005.] They were invited to come back in, the city had been cleared, so to speak.

It's amazing when you think about all the things that had happened, that was the reward. It was significant in that it was a real vivid expression of why we sacrificed 52 guys. This is why we were there, this is why we were doing what we were doing. We got to see the fruits of our labor, which is unique. A lot of guys, particularly in Vietnam, they'd go in, they'd get shot at for a year, they'd kill everything in sight, and then they'd get pulled out in the middle of nothing and they'd come home. We came, we fought, we established, if only for a moment, we established democracy in that city.

From my standpoint now, I believe that we were over there for the right reasons. We were over there to stop what we had perceived as being a world threat, something that was a great evil, they were preventing people from living their lives. As far as I'm concerned, and as far as a lot of our guys were concerned, that was a no-go, unacceptable. How much of me is just justifying the deaths of those Marines? But I think for the most part what we were doing over there was trying to provide a greater good for those who could not provide for themselves.

In World War I and World War II it was (I hate to use this word) a beautifully-orchestrated event. We saw an enemy, went in there and defeated him—it was gentlemen fighting one another, two sides of the world's greatest going toe-to-toe. The Nazis on one side and the Americans on the other side, it was this perfect combat situation, you had people who fought gentlemanly, who wore uniforms, and were proud of their uniforms.

Hue City, you go back to Vietnam and get yourself in that kind of mindset, there is so much anger and pain involved with Vietnam, and hostility. Everything happened really fast, it was like, "Get that kill." That's what Fallujah was like. It was really violent, so much anger and pain wrapped up in the whole thing, it didn't seem as gentlemanly. It was more like genocide. It was genocide of an insurgency, so in that regard it was good, but it was a slaughterhouse. These people didn't have tanks, didn't have air support, they were for the most part angry youths running around trying to fight the "Great Satan" of the world, which they had been instructed that we were. They were doing what they could to defend what they believed was their religion.

It was bizarre, because it was like if you could just speak with them and say, "Guys, you're not going to win this war, better if you could just come out and we could talk to you, we can instruct you that what you've been told is brainwashing and it's not reality, we're not the way that we're made out to be." But with war you don't get that opportunity. War in itself is the end result of being unable to reach an accord—everything is past reason at that point. Let's just kill everything and sort things out later.

And so they shot at us and we shot at them and we just had more efforts than they did. We just kept it coming. At the end of the day, I heard the casualty numbers for the insurgents were somewhere around 5–7,000. We lost 52 in our battalion. They lost everybody. They never talk about the numbers that they lost [in Vietnam]. If you want to look at who won that war, as far as casualty rates, the real answer is nobody. But if you're looking at the scoreboard, I guess we won that war.

AFGHANISTAN

It was January of 2006. I was there for six months. I had it preset in my mind that I was going to die. We got to Jalalabad, the largest base in Afghanistan in that area. As you moved north, the bases got smaller and less protected. From there, I was told that I was going to go to Asadabad, further north, a higher elevation. That was a good-sized base, we were comfortable there, it had a flight line. Then I was told that I was going to Camp Blessing [Kunar province]. Camp Blessing—that was a red flag right there!

It had been overrun twice, it was in what was called a soup bowl, if you can imagine being at the bottom of a bowl, so 360 degrees around you everyone has the uphill advantage. We had to drive from Asadabad on a road that was probably seven feet wide. On one side there was a straight wall of mountain, and on the other side it was a drop that went down the exact opposite. We're going over terrain that might as well have been some back woods in Kentucky. We're like popcorn kernels in the back of this highback, driving 45 miles an hour down a road that is seven feet wide and our Humvees are seven and a half feet wide. We're bouncing off the wall just to keep from going off the cliff.

It's the middle of the night, can't see, one of the drivers (of course it was the middle driver), the vehicle gets stuck right before what is known as "IED cliff," which is where everyone gets killed in this God-forsaken country. The Taliban had no situational awareness of our passing through, [now] they have full indication, everyone knew we were there. We've lost the cover of darkness, six or seven vehicles. All the citizens started coming out and seeing us in the morning. We were absolutely mortified.

Finally get the vehicle unstuck, it's this big show, like a parade, there are kids sitting on top of their father's shoulders, everyone's watching us. My sergeant turns around to me and he says, "We've lost it, every element of surprise that we had, gentlemen, keep your thumb on your safety, be ready to start shooting." We start driving as hard and as fast as we could up the side of this cliff, vehicles are screaming, they can barely make it up this thing, and the mortar rounds start coming in. It was such a terrible feeling. I flipped my weapon off safe, I see some people in the distance that I am getting ready to shoot at. One of my guys is getting kicked up in front of my muzzle, and I'm thinking, Dear God, one, I'm not going to get a good shot, but two, I'm going to end up hitting one of my guys. So I say, "Put the weapons on safe."

I came unglued. I had a staff sergeant in the truck, and I said, "This is bullshit. There are cowards hiding in the hills" (going back to World War II) "they don't want to fight like gentlemen…" And he says, "They fought the Russians like this for four years and they beat them." I said, "Fuck the Russians and fuck these guys." He grabbed me and said, "Backlund, you better snap out of it." And when he said that, I looked around and saw the guys were all looking at me and they were terrified.

Afghanistan…was the hearts and minds type of thing. They wanted us to go into the villages and ask if there were insurgents nearby, which never worked because when we leave, they come back. It behooves you to stay more true to the insurgents as an Afghan, because after the Americans have left and claimed victory or defeat or whatever they want to say they did, the Taliban are still going to be there. You need to swear allegiance to whomever is going to be there.

I'm trying to think of something similar. When the mafia was rampant and the cops would come by in New York and they'd say, "Hey, where are these guys?" "Well, officer, we don't have that problem here, this is a good neighborhood." You know when the cops left the boys would come back out from the shadows, and say, "Hey, good job. We're not going to kill you now." Essentially, that's how it went down. If you ratted the insurgents out, you're going to get punished for it. So going out to ask people where the insurgents were was kind of silly, because they're not going to tell you anything, they're terrified of the insurgents. When we leave, they're coming back in.

I always love talking to the kids, they are so brutally honest. I'd say, "What do you like better, Afghanistan or America?" "Oh, we love Afghanistan." Ignorantly enough, I'm sitting here acting surprised. "How can you say that, America has got cheeseburgers." They don't want that stuff; for the most part they're happy with what they have. They like the fact that they go into the fields and work all day long. There's something to be said about that. That used to be what made America great.

To understand if this war is winnable, we have to understand the objectives. What's the goal? Are we trying to create another America or are we trying to preserve Afghanistan? If the goal is to preserve Afghanistan, how do you fight that war? Whenever you go to bomb, they just recede back into the hills. You can bomb for centuries, they're just going to come walking back out, nothing has changed other than the landscape because you bombed it. So how do you fight that war? In my opinion, you develop trust with the people. You say, "We're going to be here until you guys are safe from this persecution, the tyranny," being the Taliban, having to live in this state of fear, controlled by the gun.

If I were the general of this war, and I was thinking to win this thing, [there] is a gentleman by the name of Greg Mortensen, most famous for this book, *Three Cups of Tea*. I went and saw him speak, the passion and conviction in which he spoke about education. That helped put some things in perspective for me. Right now our biggest enemy is the Taliban educating their youth in the ways of propaganda and hate—"Americans are evil, we need to fight this terrible enemy." Education is working against us, very effectively.

So the best thing to do is the old saying, "Fight fire with fire." We need to send teachers over there, we need to educate them and say, "Listen, we're not here to take over, this isn't a conquer mission, we don't want your country, all we want is for you guys to have the opportunity to make your own decisions. If you want to continue to live the way you're living now, we want you to be able to say yes, that's what I want. All we want to do is provide you the option to do that, as opposed to, 'This is the only option we have.' Everyone deserves more than one choice in life."

"Women, you can go to school if you want to. Women and men, you can go to college if you want to." Our biggest weapon against the insurgency is going to be education. I think we need to put down our guns and pick up books. You don't need all these cannons and ships, all you need to do is sit down face to face with these women and you talk it out. "Girls, whether you like it or not, you're in charge of this country."

I don't want to be in there forever, I don't think America wants to be in there forever, this war isn't half as popular as it started out to be. In 2001, September 12, everybody was gung-ho. Now it's tired, it's old. The aftermath of combat is setting in, people are seeing their neighbors coming home in wheelchairs. It's depressing. People want to see some sort of resolution. Bullets are not going to win this war.

I wrote in one of my journals that at one point—you remember in Disney's *Pinocchio*, where they all go to Boys' Town, and the kids can smoke cigars, throw bricks through a window, it's a free-for-all? I always thought there were sick parallels there, how Uncle Sam trained us up. "I'll give you a free ride over there," and we went buck-wild crazy. Now they own us. They still own our youth, they own our innocence, who we used to be. Now we are war-hardened.

Peter Duffy was born in 1984 and grew up in Northampton, Massachusetts. He served in the Marine Corps 2002–6 and deployed twice to Iraq: in 2004 in Al-Mahmudiyah, Zaidon, Fallujah, and Al-Karmah and in late 2005–6 in Al-Karmah. He was in the 2nd Battalion, 2nd Marine Regiment, 2nd Marine Division, "The War-lords," first as a nuclear, biological, chemical (NBC) defense specialist, and later as infantry. He was honorably discharged as a sergeant. He graduated from UMass-Amherst with a BS in chemistry in 2010 and is working as a chemist in the field of environmental science.

I wanted to go in the military. I idolized the values that you'd see in movies, books, magazines. It wasn't the uniform and the guns and the fighting and the war, it was about the core values that I saw. These people were honorable; they had traditions and a disciplined style of living that appealed to me. I want to be the best. Who's the best? The Marines. Every Marine goes through Marine combat training, and because everybody's trained to fight, you have a certain idealism. As much tragedy as goes on in war, there's a lot of beneficial things that happen as well. Nobody ever wants war, the soldiers don't, but overall they are usually for purposes of eliminating tyranny or protecting civilians. The job of the military is to help and protect.

    I was a nuclear, biological, chemical defense specialist to train, educate, and protect Marines against chemical threats and advise immediate superiors on issues having to do with chemical and biological defense. Then we deployed to Iraq. Because there weren't any weapons of mass destruction, my job just didn't mean anything. In the Marines you go through basic training, then combat training, *then* you go to your job training. The Marines are known as the first to fight, always ready to go. They send the Marines in first. Marines are very adaptive—if you can't do your job, you have to do another job. In my first deployment, I was a machine gunner on the fourth truck in our convoy.

Between the Americans and the Iraqis, there was a completely different mindset, not easily understandable without being embedded in the culture for a long time. My observations: everybody is very family-oriented. There wasn't a large center of nationalism, now they're coming together as a more national society because they have been forced to. America is a country of individuals but we do have a national affiliation.

In Iraq it's all family-based, your immediate family, outside of that, even within your own town, different families [are like] the Hatfields and the McCoys. You live in the same area, you do the same thing, you're the same people, but your families are just split down the middle. You don't want to associate with them, and if [there] is bad blood between the families, you never deal with them again. It's an amalgam of the clan and the immediate family, your father and your uncles.

The people also fall under your local sheikh or imam. The sheikh's the trusted advisor. How much do you trust your government officials, do you know them personally? Do you trust their word? Not necessarily. If your sheikh tells you to do something, you trust his word. They control a lot of local opinion, as [do] older, wealthier gentlemen in the community because they own businesses, shops, contracting companies, enterprises. In terms of voting, people's sheikhs were like, "Vote for *him*." That's why you have such a large turnout: if the sheikhs say go out and vote—*do it*.

Corruption. Let's say we want to build a school. We have a town council every week, all the sheikhs and imams, all the influential people in the community, and we're talking to them. What do you need? Here's what we're doing to try to help you. Hey, can you try to stop people in your community from blowing us up? The battalion commander says, "We want you to put out the good word, we are in good faith going to help you as much as we can." The Iraqi officials say, "This is what we need. We'd like a school, better water quality, we need you to get off of our streets."

We say, "Well, okay, we can only do so much. When you're on your streets, you need to make sure that people are not putting bombs down, which will not only hurt us, but hurt you." Then we find the money either from the Iraqi government or through our government, and we find people who'll build schools. Everybody over there is very resourceful; you'll find one guy who can do eight jobs. They come and they build the school, and the next day or week it could get blown up. Several times, built a police department and it blew up the next day. Who did it? Sometimes it was the people we'd hired to be the police, sometimes it was local farmers. Sometimes it was external people who were coming through the area.

Why blow up the school or the police department? There are several reasons. Anyone who's not in your immediate family is usually an infidel. The Americans are sometimes seen as invaders, trying to press our ideals on them, even from over here people could say we're going over there and trying to press democracy on them. Our battalion, we never tried to get people to believe in our ideas, we simply went to their town meetings to say, "What do you need to be safe? What do you need to build your community?" That's left out of the media.

We had a pretty large attack on the police station in Karma [10 miles (16 km) from Fallujah] where several armed men ran around a corner and fired at the police station with RPGs, machine guns, and then ran away. Of course, the police all sat inside the police station, shaken. We captured that videotape. They had a videotape of people loading explosives on an oil tanker truck and driving into one of our positions. Almost everything is filmed. Our videotapes are a little different because when the shooting starts, we put our cameras down (we have military reporters who go around with their cameras). Everyone over there is living in dilapidated housing, at best; they have television, a cell phone, probably a video camera.

Blowing up a school or police department? Someone would pay them. They could say here's an artillery shell, take it into the police department, here's 500 dollars. The United States is going to come here tomorrow and build a new police station, and they're probably going to come ask me to help build it. We call them fence-sitters—they really don't care if we are there and they don't care if people who want to fight the US are there. They just need to protect their family and make money. It's not as grandiose as people make it seem, it's really basic, people need to take care of themselves. A lot of people are extremists, they don't like the US, they don't want us there. I can understand that, they want us gone and they are willing to fight us.

I went through a house, the man of the house wasn't home, just the matron of the house. I tried to be as respectful as possible, "Is there another adult here, is there even a younger male here?" But she invited me in, I had a peek around the house, I tried to ask if she knew anything about the explosion earlier in the area. If you bust into somebody's house at two o'clock in the morning and come and take their husband—very frightening. If you're walking around during the day, they *expect* you to come knock on their door.

[*What would you be looking for in a daytime visit?*] Maybe we got some intel that there was someone planting bombs or paying people to plant bombs, we need to question some people. Or somebody actually blew up a bomb that day so we go door to door, looking for him, asking people, Have you seen him? Like a police investigation, did you see anything, do you know anything, can I look around your house? I just talked to a Marine who came back recently and he said they now have a system where everyone has their ID, which tells you where they're from and all sorts of other information.

Things like vehicle-borne IEDs, sometimes you'd see someone with one mortar round in their car and use the car as a battering ram, mortar would explode. Other times we'd find vans with seven artillery shells plus a propane tank, which is immensely destructive. Other times we had a giant oil tanker, a semi, they filled with explosives and just plowed right through the gate and blew it up. I saw that—it was awful. The four Marines at the post got away, thankfully.

What's the point of anyone being a suicide bomber? You've got extremists, they think they're doing the right thing, fighting for a greater cause, or fighting for their family, or being forced into it. Extortion was one of the biggest issues because there wasn't a structure to the judicial and the police system. They say they're going to kill your family, they're going to kill your family. Extortion was one of the main methods used for keeping people from joining the police force, or the military, or working with us at all. Especially interpreters, anyone who came to work on our base, laundry service people, killed, the police chiefs were often killed.

[*How do you view what is happening in Iraq now?*] We're going to be over there for a decade. There's been a large reduction in forces, which I am ecstatic about, they can take over their own government. Fine, they can have it. I hope they can operate their own government, I hope they can provide themselves a secure environment for their people. We don't need to do it, they do. We can go over there and help. Why we are over there in the first place is none of my business. I was just there to do my job. My job was to protect, help.

World War II or World War I, we're trying to protect world stability. We wanted to stay out, we just wanted to supply, then it's gone too far. You've got to protect your own freedom, you've got to protect resources, you're going in to protect other people's freedoms, are you doing it to stop extremism? Usually it's all those ends. People's own political agendas, individuals trying to get their little niche, corporations trying to get their own toe-holds, I want my company to make money because we can manufacture weapons.

You can't have conventional war any more. Just the amount of resources that would be necessary would devastate everything. So war itself now is a war-deterrent. The only kind of war that can be fought is on such a small, archaic scale that it's seemingly inconsequential to the powers. The only efficient kind of warfare anymore is guerrilla warfare, and it's always been the most effective form. Nobody has ever *lost* a guerrilla war, *ever.* The Celts won against the Romans because they fought a guerrilla war; the [American] rebels won against the British because they fought guerrilla-style. Nobody has ever won a fight against guerrillas.

Fighting against a lot of insurgent forces in Afghanistan and Iraq is so incredibly difficult. How do you point a weapon at somebody who could be your friend or could be your enemy? We had a saying for our battalion, "No better friend than a worst enemy," because every day you had to go out and shake their hand and point your gun at them at the same time. It's crazy. Every time you think about pulling the trigger, you have to wonder is this guy really an insurgent? You could go to jail if you pull the trigger in the wrong situation.

I believe that there's a large divide between political agenda and the ability to fight a war and manage the military. I believe they are two separate ways of thinking, and unfortunately when they overlap, everything goes very, very wrong. The military is very good at doing its job. Politics has its place. I think when the two overlap, it's bad. The way you use the military is you go in with your strike, destroy, and eliminate the enemy. Help people for ten years, pick up and leave, and go do it somewhere else if it's ever necessary. You have your strike force, you have your occupation force. The mission of the Marines is that they destroy the enemy.

One of the things that I've gotten from talking to a lot of veterans, although the ideologies of war and the wars themselves have changed throughout the ages, a lot of the fundamentals of being in the military have never changed. Camaraderie and a lot of the principles that people have built upon: if you ask what they have missed the most, it's always the basic stuff, like camaraderie.

Everybody goes through a medical screening when they get back. You fill out a piece of paperwork that says, "Do you have any bad thoughts? How are you feeling?" Based on your answers to that, they might ask you to come down to get further screening or psych evaluation. But honestly, the largest support network you have is either the people in your platoon who've known you for a very long time, or your family. Your family can help just so much. They can't understand what you've been through.

PTSD—look at the demographics of who's getting it. The majority are reservists or people who joined after September 11, people who just weren't prepared mentally for a lot of what was going to happen. Before September 11, I was already okay with a lot of things. Now I meet people who might not have been so prepared, I can see why this has been such a traumatic event in their life. They just didn't expect it.

I get all the time [that] people *think* I already have PTSD. I went to Iraq, so, "How nuts are you?" "I am not crazy at all, actually." "Oh, sure, you're not crazy." Then you tell them something and they look at you like, "How could you be okay with that?" You're crazy for *not* being crazy! I'll tell people stories, they ask how I'm not driven mad by some of that, and I say: "I'm *not*. I understand the situation, I understand the tragedy in it." Nothing of it gives me nightmares. I don't have PTSD.

Victor Nuñez-Ortiz was born in San Salvador, El Salvador, in 1982. He immigrated with his mother to the US when he was seven. He served in the Marine reserves for four years and received his citizenship in November 2008. He served as lance corporal in Iraq for seven months in 2004–5 at Al-Assad Airbase and Al-Qaim FOB. Victor worked in the Massachusetts SAVE program, a statewide outreach program for veterans, and hopes to continue to work in that field.

I got involved in the Marine Corps through my best friend in high school. We made a bet that if he would join, I'd join. By December 2000 he was already a Marine, looking to recruit people. If you re-cruit three, you pick up the next rank, which would normally be either private first class or lance corporal. I remember him coming to my house with a Marine gunnery sergeant, stripes all over his dress blues. My friend was in his dress blues, tried to convince me to join.

I picked the Marine Corps. I felt at that time and I still do to this day, that they instill discipline in you and they show you the real meaning of the warrior, a patriot. I signed my enlistment con-tract on January 4, 2001. It seemed they were ready for me and everything happened within a week. I had my background check, my CORI, my drug test. They saw I was physically able to do the job. I was in Parris Island for boot camp, graduated August 2001. At school I was going for civil engineering, [so] I said "civil engineering, combat engineering." That's why I picked that MOS [Military Occupational Specialty].

I remember getting a phone call from my master sergeant. I was in the dorms sleeping, "Nuñez, are you ready?" "Ready for what?" "Turn on your TV." Turned it on, saw a plane hit, I thought, holy crap, what's this? A practical joke? This was at 11 in the morning. The master sergeant was telling me to get my seabag ready. I remember telling him, "Master Sergeant, I haven't even gone to my basic school. I really don't know what I'm doing." He said, "Did you learn how to shoot your weapon in boot camp?" "Yeah, I'm an expert." "That's all you're going to need." I thought World War III was coming.

Three years later, I was still not at war. We were getting warning orders, we were next in line, [and] then all of a sudden our unit wouldn't make it. The big day came and they handed us orders. January of 2004. They started telling us to write wills, set power of attorney, if you had debt, make sure you have a plan to pay off your debt so you don't come back and find yourself in a worse situation. So I dropped out of school because I didn't want to be in the middle of a semester and get pulled in, [and] all I did was party.

In May 2004 through August we were in Camp Pendleton, getting acclimated to hot weather. Training, doing construction projects, how to deactivate explosives, how to deactivate mines, how to identify mines. Getting our mindset ready, getting ready to go and fight, possibly kill somebody, or possibly die. Once we got to Kuwait, Camp Victory, that's when they warned us, "Devil Dogs, this is the first and last time we're telling you this, you're in a combat zone so keep your eyes open." [The moniker "Devil Dogs" dates from when Germans first applied it to US Marines fighting in 1918.]

They gave us the rules of engagement: "Don't shoot anybody until shot at." Don't do anything unless they were a threat to you, pointing their weapon at you, [then] you have the right to use deadly force. I was in Al-Assad Airbase [west of Baghdad], and I was also in Al-Qaim FOB, AQ for short. When I was in Al-Assad, my job was construction, demolition, surveying, mapping roads, using a prism to know exactly where to site buildings, elevations of ground, the engineer platoon, forty engineers as a team. I was a guardian angel as well, meaning that whenever we were outside the wire I was always the one walking, looking for people, identifying landmines or IEDs. It meant that when the drafters and surveyors went out they didn't hold a gun, so my job was to protect them in case anything happened.

We also had other responsibilities. We cleared the minefield inside our base. According to EOD [explosive ordinance disposal], those mines were deployed in the first Gulf War. They were deployed from planes, just thrown out over the base, British mines (the Brits took over the base during the Gulf War). They were called spider mines, they would shoot out tentacles with a string attached to it, 360 degrees around, and if you stepped on any of those strings you would be within the kill radius of that mine. It took about four days to clear ten square miles. We used a metal probe, which looks similar to a pen, nothing special, you would low-crawl on your stomach, your elbows, and stick the probe in the ground. We did that up and down this field, mapping out the field, plotting the mines. Nothing exploded but we found about three hundred pounds of explosives, right on our base.

When I got sent to AQ we were getting mortared every day. AQ is northern Iraq, next to the Syrian border. We were on an active railroad station where insurgents travel down from Syria to get to other parts of Iraq. Our job was to make sure they didn't get there. At one point they stopped the train and they found over 200 insurgents in the wagons, and that's when they created a prison right in AQ. I wasn't there for that. They brief you.

I couldn't sleep much because Humvees or tanks would be coming back all day and all night and you could hear them 200 yards away. Sometimes our curiosity would lead us to go check it out. Tanks would come back with human debris splattered all over, or Humvees would come back completely demolished. It was really sad to see that. Every time we saw a vehicle come back like that or every time we saw a medevac helicopter leave, we knew that somebody had fallen.

We did get attacked every once in a while. Insurgents we call them, Hajjis, we didn't ask too many questions. We just shot our rifles, or called in air strikes. Air strikes were the most effective. You just give the coordinates and within thirty seconds we'd have a jet shooting them down or you would send out the helicopters to take care of business. We were lucky because we were part of the [air] wing. You had ten million dollar equipment that we could use to our advantage.

When I was in AQ we were eating canned food, tray rats [rations] because we were a forward operating base. The tray is about 8 by 10 [inches]—it would have canned peas, powdered mashed potatoes, canned ham, canned sausages. They had combat cooks do that. After I left the Marine Corps, they started using contractors, like KBR, outsourcing our food. Just to serve you food, they were probably making two times as much as us. These guys were making hundreds of thousands of dollars just by supporting us. We were the ones that were putting our lives out there. That bothered me.

I was there for seven months. The mines that we had put out around the perimeter were all plotted so if someone had to remove them, they could. We also put booby traps, flares, because at night sometimes insurgents would try to get onto our base. Sometimes out of nowhere there was a dog in the desert, dogs would set it off, and everyone's woken up at three in the morning.

My last day there was a Friday. The master sergeant tells us, "You guys aren't going out there today." "What? We're almost done." "No, today you're going to work on the fence." On our way to this fence site a suicide bomber came in and blew up and killed 39 people where we were supposed to be working. We saw it go off. It gave me chills. I came back in mid-February, '05. It felt kind of weird because I left my platoon behind. And sure enough, the day we left they got attacked. When the rest of my platoon came back they reported it: "You were so lucky, we got hit for three days straight."

I started having thoughts of killing myself when I was overseas. I never told anybody because I felt like I was keeping everybody together, for me to show emotions would just make everybody weaker. So I held everything in. I came home, and I seemed to be fine. I was so depressed from seeing all those guys pass away, seeing so many funerals, seeing one of our OEDs got blown up. Seeing Humvees come back bloody, the 39 from the suicide bomber, all that started to eat away at me the first months back.

I thought I was better. Three years after I got back I was working for [a restaurant], their training manager. They let me go because I was "a loose cannon." When you translate that, I got PTSD and it got out of control. I started getting really mad that I was being labeled. I got fired, and I bought a bottle of rum on my way home. I was in a tough situation.

I ended up going to the Puerto Rican Bilingual Veterans Outreach Center, Sergeant Gumersindo Gomez [see pages 220–26]. "Look, I'm a veteran and I just got fired. I have no money, I won't even have money to pay rent, I have one kid, can you help me?" He said, "We can file a claim for you. Were you in Iraq?" He started asking me all these questions, writing down my story. He said, "You are the easiest case I've ever had. All you have to do is call them and say you're still alive and they'll send you a check."

I called the SAVE team [Statewide Advocacy for Veterans' Empowerment, a Massachusetts veterans' program] when the program was starting, and the director and [another staff member] came to visit me at UMass. [They] did an intake, "Are you okay? Are you all right?" I was, "No, I'm fine." But [the staff member] knew something was wrong. "Let's go to the VA because I think you should be screened for PTSD and TBI." Sure enough, I already knew I had PTSD, because that's why the Marine Corps discharged me.

But the TBI part I didn't know. I was whacked in the head by a four by four [wooden beam] in Iraq and it knocked me unconscious. I told the doc that was the only head trauma that I had there, I didn't think about all the explosions that we had done. That's considered a shock wave, especially when you have a wound, it makes it worse. For five months straight I blew something up at least once a month. [They] gave me a booklet of all the services, not that *they* provide, but that are out there. Their service was to refer me to them.

That's how I got involved with SAVE. They asked me why I wanted to do it and I said because I care about the veterans in the Commonwealth. "Why do you care so much?" I said, "Because there's not enough people that care for us." A week later I got a job offer from them. I helped out almost a hundred veterans, helping them made me feel better. It made me feel like I was worth something. [Now] I'm unemployed, so I've been collecting unemployment, working with vocational rehab to finish my school. Finishing college is my next step.

[*How do you look at the war now?*] Do I think it's going to be over soon? I don't think so. I think we're always going to be in

Iraq for our own protection. I don't think the US would spend billions and billions of dollars just to say forget about it. It's not just the money, we've lost so many guys there. I think that should be enough reason for us to stay there and keep protecting our freedom. I don't even know if it's a war any more. I think it's just we're trying to control that country. A political war. Afghanistan has more of a purpose, more of a reason behind it. In Iraq, they never really told us why we were there. We were doing our job because there were bullets and mortars flying around.

Joining the military for college money, I don't buy that. You join because you want to be a soldier. You want to feel bad-ass, you want to do something that not many people do. One percent of our population in the United States has joined, has been overseas. There was a bunch of people in my squadron that got their citizenship while serving overseas, a lot of them joined to get their papers, or residence. I voted in 2008, I voted for Obama. It felt good. I still have the sticker. It was cool. I'd been waiting to vote. Even when I was in the military I didn't have a say.

GOLDIN

Josee Goldin was born in 1979 and grew up in Massachusetts. She was promoted to major in 2010 and when interviewed was based at Joint Base Lewis-McChord in Washington state. She was in Iraq for a total of 41 months, and is planning to retire from the army after ten years' service. She graduated in 2001 from George Washington University in Washington, DC, and was commissioned after completing ROTC. With three tours, she experienced Iraq right after the invasion and before and after the surge. She describes an army that is family to those who serve in it. Her leadership positions have led to an interest in human relations and management, and she also addresses issues relating to women in the armed forces.

How did I join the Army? It's not like Massachusetts is a breeding ground for army service, but somehow I just decided to do ROTC while in college. I really enjoyed the camaraderie, the tough challenge of it, the leadership aspect of it, the firm moral integrity code. It made me feel stronger and more confident.

I got commissioned in 2001, before September 11. The September 11th terrorist attacks occurred while I was in the officer basic course. I was in the field and the battalion commander came out. She said we'd been attacked and asked if anyone had family in the Pentagon or in New York City. If we did, we could contact our family and make sure they were okay. Then we started to watch all the news coverage. The whole army changed overnight—there were guards at the gate and vehicle searches. We all focused on what we may be called upon to do in a very short time.

I had volunteered for Korea as my first duty assignment back in May 2001. At the time, Korea was the most gung-ho and challenging place you could be stationed. I loved being in Korea and it prepared me for being deployed. The 2nd Infantry Division motto was "ready to fight tonight." If we had to go to war, we had everything we needed readily available. I left Korea in October 2002.

Within eight months I deployed for Iraq, mid-June of 2003. This was our chance—the war was going to be over soon, so we had to go. In that first deployment I was in Forward Operating Base Balad, a big logistics hub, and my unit helped repair the airfield in order to receive more equipment, supplies, and personnel. I was there for about ten months. The deployment was extremely rewarding. We were all so full of hope. We were kind of naïve. We didn't have armor and the thing that I remember was how comfortable we all were.

I remember aiding in an effort to supply food to the local populace and taking them boxes of meals ready to eat (no pork of course) to the main street of the closest town and distributing the food. It was a rewarding experience, but maybe, looking at the long-term plan, it may not have been the best idea. We also sent our construction equipment out to reclaim land for farmers that Saddam Hussein had taken for fighting positions. It was amazing to see firsthand what things he'd done to restrict his people (whether in livelihood or lifestyle choices) and impose his will for no reason but to do it. We had all these resources and wanted to help so badly that efforts were not as well coordinated as they were well intentioned.

It was common practice that when the traffic stopped, we'd dismount our vehicles and chat with people. They'd all come up to us, especially me as a woman. They were shocked by a woman in uniform and that she was able to give orders to male soldiers. They all crowded around me. I was thinking that they were going to suffocate me, [but] terrorism didn't enter my mind! It was always amazing when I look back, how much we changed the good things we did in order to become more self-protective and so lost our ability to be more open and available to the Iraqi people.

One of the things I really remember from my first deployment was a trip to a police station. There were three Iraqi women there, I think they were translators. They saw me, and it was like Disney World. They were nine years old and I was Minnie Mouse! They were hugging me and crying and I couldn't understand a word they were saying. They were so warm and proud; it was a wonderful, bizarre experience. I will always remember how thrilled they were to see a woman. I learned Iraq is so much more secular and diverse than what you see on the news.

Between my first and second deployments I was home for 87 days. I volunteered to go so quickly because my husband was deploying and I wanted to make sure our timelines matched. Looking back on the decision, I certainly paid a price in mental resiliency by going so soon. When I returned to Iraq [June 2004], it was a whole different planet. We were still working well with the Iraqi people, [but] there were suddenly concrete barriers everywhere. You didn't roll outside the wire without armor on your vehicle. It was a more restrictive deployment, a much tougher deployment.

The second time we were out by the [Baghdad] airport, beginning of June 2004 to the end of June 2005, close to thirteen months. Muktada al-Sadr's army was starting to gain momentum. You definitely felt the shift between everybody [earlier] being so excited we were going to usher in all these improvements, immediately their lives are going to change, they're going to have electricity, everything that we have in America. It didn't happen as fast as they wanted and people started to get frustrated, one of the many things that contributed to the anger towards the US.

Also, America made a couple of mistakes along the way, and there were obviously some horrific errors like the abuse at Abu Ghraib—almost ruined our reputation. We as Americans sometimes fall short and there are people that decide to do immoral and unethical things. We can't set ourselves on a pedestal like we are perfect. Certain tragedies made it difficult for the local populace to trust us and internationally gave us a very large black eye. It was so terrible to inflict that pain on other human beings. Unfortunately we had people commit crimes that were just as horrific as the people we're fighting against.

The second deployment was much worse than my first or third. We had so many soldiers killed in action. Everyone was trying to do the right thing, but you just couldn't do it all. People were wearing themselves out. You had guys who left looking one way and came back looking literally a shell of themselves because they worked so hard. I felt when I came back from that deployment that it had been three years. It took me so long to get back to a positive state and feeling like myself. Three hundred and ninety days, just exhausting. I was in a support role, there were guys who put their lives on the line day in and day out, and they were not getting any time off either. You want to do your best for them because you almost always feel guilty that you're not doing what they're doing. I still haven't processed a lot of stuff from that deployment. But as I look back, it was amazing to see what I could do, what I could live through.

[On my third deployment], April 2008 to September 2009, we were stationed in Kirkuk, so I got to see firsthand the surge work. There were still quite a few IEDs, suicide bombings, and car-born IEDs when we arrived, but fewer and fewer every week. Before, when route clearance looked for IEDs, they would find eight or nine of them and you'd be there all day because you had to wait for the explosive ordinance guys to come out and blow it. Now it was like you'd find one a week. It was amazing the effect that the surge and the Sunni Awakening had. The surge was effective because the Iraqi people had enough and took charge of their future.

You could drive around and not get hit every time. People shopping, kids in school, playing on the street—people were getting back to their real lives. The army is not really the fixer, the citizens are. We can just help them along. When the Sunni Awakening formed, life became much more positive for all Iraqis and they became a real partner. We did a lot of partnership with the Iraqi Army, teaching them how to conduct route clearance and provide logistics, our system of maintenance, how we check, troubleshoot, fix, track parts, and service our equipment.

Unfortunately, you can't make a new organization mirror a system that has been meticulously improved over decades. We were just trying too hard. Plus there were major cultural differences. In America if something breaks we usually replace the part or the whole piece of equipment. We very rarely put in the intensive effort and time involved to fix something, but that's something Iraqis do brilliantly. It gave them a lot of good ideas and tools for building their systems, but the Iraqis had to figure out how they wanted to do it.

Being a company commander, 99 percent of my energy was with my soldiers, seeing that one hundred people were happy and healthy, contributing, listened to, and feeling like they are being developed. This was the most rewarding time of my life so far, taking care of people, figuring out how people are motivated, how people work, there or back here. In Iraq it takes on an added dimension in that you are worried that a decision you make will hurt somebody or get somebody killed. The responsibility is daunting but it's an amazing and rewarding experience.

Managing all these soldiers from everywhere in the country, with all different ways they were brought up, all different reasons for joining the Army, all different ideas for what they want to do with the rest of their lives, and getting them all to work together. For me, the army is all about the people I've met, the relationships I've formed. The Army for me didn't have anything to do with being in Iraq or being home—it was getting people ready to do the mission, doing what we're supposed to do, for our country, for our families, and for each other.

[*What about other women in the army?*] I've generally worked in male-dominated units. If you're good, work hard, and you're constantly trying to improve, it doesn't matter if you're male or female. Unfortunately, when you're a minority, everything you do is so much more obvious. The most shocking thing in my experience about women in the army is that we don't tend to support each other, and early on I had a lot of very negative experiences. Because of this, I made a huge effort to mentor and support junior female soldiers in my unit. It's a reality of life that some women are going to get pregnant, by accident and not so much by accident, and it's going to look bad for all other women.

[*Don't ask, don't tell?*] On a personal level, people are going to be fine. On a political level, the media is going to stir up feelings and a few military members will go public with their disagreement. The vast majority of us are going to do what our leadership tells us to do. I don't think all these Armageddon-type scenarios are even worth talking about. We talk about being a professional army, we're all going to keep accomplishing our missions, and we're all going to be fine.

In April of 2009, while in Iraq, I took over a brigade headquarters company, 150 soldiers, all senior-ranking people, commanded by a full-bird colonel. I was the company commander of that brigade staff. Because of the climate in the army at the time, I did a lot of developing and implementing the resiliency program, identifying high-risk behavior and mitigating that behavior. Getting into psychology was fascinating—it's amazing what the army has done in the last six years. Unfortunately, it always takes bad things to happen before people start to realize this was not just an isolated incident and they need to systematically tackle it. We had too many soldiers killing themselves, and also committing homicide, so we needed to figure out how to get ahead of this.

You can't just point to the deployments as the reason for the increase in suicide. The most important thing, we're taught to know our soldiers so we can see changes in their behavior. Most suicides occurred when relationships were breaking up. The army is trying so hard. It changed around 2006, 2007. All these surveys, asking about your alcohol use, your depression, your flashbacks, we're going to send you to see a psychologist, they're going to go over your story with you and look you in the eye to make sure you're not going to harm yourself and that you know where help is. They're going to evaluate you and you may come out of it with another appointment, and if you don't make the appointment, you're going to get in trouble. I think it's as close to the best-case scenario as we can do. But, as leaders, I noticed we don't ever take care of ourselves, we're too busy trying to take care of our personnel. I realized I didn't take care of myself, and I'm trying to catch up on that now.

[*Looking back at Iraq?*] I saw it in a bad period, and I saw it get a lot better. When you're deployed you're really in a bubble (confined to your job position and your area of operations). I sometimes learned more about the big picture from watching CNN and reading new non-fiction about Iraq. I think this war will be judged twenty years from now and we'll be able to look back and determine if it was a good idea to invade or not. I never worried about the reasons we went to war and if it was just or not. I was there to support my family (both my immediate and my military family) and do my job. But right now, it's definitely looking successful.

We're starting to transition over to Iraqis who need to be taking the lead, it's their country. We need to take some time and focus on ourselves. The army is deploying the same people over and over again. Not enough people in America join the armed forces [and] certainly not a cross-section of society. We need soldiers from every part of America, every culture, every political and economic position—that's what makes us strong. We need to do a better job of selling service, not necessarily military service, but service that is selfless, to the general public.

I realize how far we've come in a lot of ways. Certainly since Vietnam and Korea, we treat our veterans so much better. When I returned for leave from Iraq in uniform at the many airports, I could barely eat I had so many folks thanking me for my service. There's so much money that goes into training and equipping, we've realized the importance of investing in individuals and that the individual is worth a lot of money, a lot of effort, and a lot of support.

Probably my most amazing moment was when I attended the warrior leader course graduation, a course where junior enlisted soldiers are trained to become noncommissioned officers. I went when some of my soldiers were graduating. I remember sitting and looking at the sea of faces in the graduating class, some female soldiers, every race represented, every kind of last name, every socioeconomic background, soldiers from Georgia, soldiers from Maine, soldiers from California, Alaska, American Samoa, and soldiers from Mexico.

I just sat there and I almost started crying it was so powerful. The army is strong because it's made up of the people that are representative of the best things about this country. No matter what, we're always going to have people that are going to screw up, make a bad name for us. But ultimately, diversity is our strength. It was so powerful to be a part of it.

Sergeant Kenney was born in Springfield, Massachusetts, in 1983. He had two tours in Iraq, 2007–8 in Baghdad, and 2009–10 in Ramadi. He recounts his most important day: two bombs were detonated on the base where he was stationed and he ministered to a badly injured fellow soldier. Sean was in tears telling the story, remembering exactly where he was, what he did, and how he saved his comrade Ken. Surrounded by wounded Iraqis, bullets, chaos, and yet somehow alone on the stage, he summoned up all his personal reserves to salvage a life from this disaster. While back in college at Westfield State he worked to develop more flexible guidelines and support for campus veterans. He decided to leave college, was promoted to staff sergeant, and has plans to become a state policeman.

I joined the military after 9/11, but 9/11 was the main reason. My father was a Vietnam veteran in the Air Force. He didn't see much combat but he transported casualties back and forth from hospitals, and it took a toll on him. It was hard to get his and my mother's support. I ended up joining without their support and it's been an issue of tension in the family ever since. We haven't spoken in a few years but it was something I felt passionate about, and needed to do.

I joined the Massachusetts National Guard, April 19, 2006, 747 MP Company, [but] I volunteered to go on the sister unit, the 972 MPs to Iraq. The National Guard is usually reserved for state or national emergencies; this is the first time the National Guard has been used in such a capacity. [I heard] eighty percent of the forces (boots on the ground) were a reserve or National Guard component. [The 2008 DOD figures for the National Guard component of troops deployed are 7 percent in Iraq and 15 percent in Afghanistan.] I graduated top of my class, the distinguished honor graduate out of 242. Because I did so well in basic training they put me on Warfighter, a grueling competition, one of the best experiences I've had in my military career.

I pushed myself very hard to do as best I could. On my first tour I was married and my wife left me in the middle, which is very hard to deal with. You're young, you're overseas. I still managed to go out every day on missions. This is in Baghdad, in the Green Zone, FOB Freedom, right next to that old [US] embassy, by the 14th of July bridge. The Tigris River was running right next to us. We were doing security for the seven top Iraqi officials in Baghdad, the president, vice president, the minister of the interior. They had their own Iraqi security, like their Secret Service; we did their exterior security.

We took a lot of indirect fire, rockets and mortars going off, a lot of scary close calls. One of the buildings that almost got hit housed half of my company. I was the first one to run through the door to see if anyone had been hit. There was a wall, and if that wall hadn't been there, they probably would have been picking up 60–70 bodies. It was a katyusha rocket—I believe they're Iranian. It was Easter Sunday [March 23, 2008] when it started, it lasted a month and there were over 800 direct hits on the Green Zone. It got to the point where it was safer for us to go outside the wire into the Red Zone [Baghdad outside the Green Zone] than it was to be on our FOB.

I'd gotten home in July of 2008. The little time I did spend in the 474 before I volunteered with the 972, the first sergeant, Michael Domnarski, made a big impression on me. He's that type of leader that you'll never forget. He's got that manner about him, always professional, someone that you idolize as a soldier no matter what rank you are. I did that Warfighter competition with him. Before I left he asked me, "I hope you come with us because you're a great soldier," and that stuck with me from the moment that he said it. And I did.

I'd been home about two and a half months before I decided to go again because I wanted to uphold my promise to him. Transferred back into the 747 from the 972, and got ready to deploy. I left as an E-4, during training I got promoted to sergeant, E-5. I always wanted to be an NCO, be a leader, get a chance to influence somebody, like the first sergeant. I got put into the operations squad as a team leader, I'd been E-5 for maybe ten minutes before I got transferred over there. I'm an E-5 with the responsibility of an E-6, also given the job of an E-7 or a platoon leader [temporarily] reporting directly to the company commander.

We made it to al-Anbar province, the city of Ramadi, Sunni country. I did a little research and realized that Sunnis are the most violent of all the Iraqi population, and the area where we were going was not friendly. Camp Ramadi is the big post, it's the hub. We were approximately four miles away, my squad, the company commander, and a few other personnel on this quarter-mile radius post called the provincial government center. A small little compound within a compound that was the American side, and all the buildings around it were the Iraqi government. We shared the fence-line, we had very low T-walls (cement walls) surrounding our compound. There were four-, five-, six-story civilian buildings peering in at us. You see how vulnerable we were.

It was part of the anti-insurgency, boots on the ground, get in with the people, live with them, show them we are here to help, and be advisers to them. I guess it's to be seen whether it works or not. Al-Anbar province is the size of Texas. The provincial government center, the PCOP, the provincial chief of police, controlled all al-Anbar police departments. We were advisors to the provincial government center and helped them develop their police force into a professional police force. The original mission started at the lowest level, getting Iraqi police officers in, training them, teaching them handcuffing techniques, teaching them how to be police officers.

Our goal was to work with the Iraqi officers, chiefs of police, provincial chiefs of police, the high-ranking people within the Iraqi police system. We were no longer training the lower-ranking guys, we were letting them do that, and we were trying to help them with the administrative part of running a police force so they could secure their own cities. It is to be determined whether it was accomplished or not, I hope it is. I think the most effective thing we did for them was to step back, allowing them to finally take the reins. You've got to let them make their mistakes, let them grow. We were still standing there like the dad holding the seat of the bike, running after them to make sure they didn't fall.

The original provincial chief of police magically disappeared after an attack he organized on his own people. That was the day I'm going to go into most detail about. He was very reluctant to have any kind of US coalition force help. The guy that we brought in to replace him, General Baha, [was] very accepting of US help. Depending on where he needed to go, he would use us as his security instead of his own personnel—inexperience, I guess.

In my time in the provincial government center, my squad did 427 missions. I've done over 600 combat missions in two tours. In my first tour, my squad did more missions than anyone in the company, 150 to 160 missions. My second tour, my company commander started tracking and found out that we did more missions than anybody in the whole country. Any time the generators went down, didn't matter what time of night, day, we had to go get generator mechanics at the nearest base, escort them back to our base, get them to fix it, and take them back. If we ran out of food, we had to go get it and come back. If we ran out of fuel, we had to go get it. The refrigerator systems, we had to go get it fixed. Anything to sustain life, we were spun out. At one point we could get up out of our beds and get out of the gate in seven minutes or less.

Where I lived, that small little compound in the heart of the city, in that mile and a half area was where 80 percent of the attacks happened in al-Anbar province. Car bombings, sniper shots, suicide vests, every 60 to 90 days there was a violent attack on that compound. So to have the EOD team there and have us able to roll out with them at a moment's notice was a huge asset for the compound.

There's also the issue of corruption. Iraqis would seize weapons, explosives they found on raids, and then they would re-sell it into [the] population. When General Baha came in, he utilized our EOD team, anything that came in to that police station, explosives, weapons, he would seal it off and give it to us. We would take it out of circulation and bring it to the US base in Ramadi. EOD teams would dispose of it so that we would never have to worry about that happening again.

December 30th is the day. December 30, 2009. We'd been going every day, balls to the walls, for months since we took over complete control of the mission in October. Our company commander saw how burnt out we were getting. I was already tired—leaders don't go to sleep before the guys, you don't eat before the guys. Our company commander recognized that, and he brought in a few extra personnel so we could have a day where [we] could just rest. Catch up on sleep, clean weapons, do laundry.

So December 30 was the first day I was going to get some sleep and I was so looking forward to it. It's between seven and seven thirty in the morning, just me and my team, Specialist Weyerstrass and Specialist Weaver, my driver and my gunner. I'm sleeping, enjoying it, and all of a sudden, the walls rattle. A car bomb drove right in as far as it could get and detonated. It shook everything—you could hear the crack because you're so close. Anyone who's been shot at or near an explosion understands what it means when you hear the crack.

So I jumped out of bed—there goes my day off. Got dressed, went over to my company talk area which is a little headquarters area, a small office, trying to find out what was going on. Master Sergeant Corcoran said, "Go get one of your guys, you're going to escort Lieutenant Colonel Doran over to the Iraqi headquarters side." We geared up, walked him over, still a decent distance between us and the initial explosion site where it wasn't too dangerous, but we're still on our guard. He's talking to them, we stay outside checking for anything that looks suspicious, anyone that might infiltrate the area. He comes back out and he says that they want to go see the blast site with the Iraqis.

At the time I told him, "Sir, that's not a good idea." He goes, "Just go get eyes on so we have an idea where it is, and then we'll walk back." "Okay, Sir." Weyerstrass, myself, the colonel, a couple of Iraqis, a Navy photographer, walk out about thirty meters away from the initial blast sight, and we have eyes on. The colonel says, "Sergeant Kenney, I want you to go spin up the EOD team, and get them ready to come out." "All right, Sir. Do you want to come back with me?" "No. Leave *him* here (him being Weyerstrass) with us, you go get them, we'll be right behind you." When the lieutenant colonel tells you what to do, you've got to do it.

So I'm walking back to get the EOD team up, I turned around and told Weyerstrass (motioned to him) "make sure you are watching." As I'm walking back, the second explosion happened. I instantly had a bad feeling. You could hear the crack. I ran in and said, "Master sergeant, we still have guys out there." He goes, "Get someone with a radio, go get accountability." So I found someone with the radio. I said, "Sergeant, come with me."

Ran, and as soon as I cleared my wall into the Iraqi side, there was chaos. Bleeding, blown up Iraqi people, running, hundreds of people bleeding from face, from arms, blood-soaked clothes, people screaming, yelling. I told Sergeant Riley to stay within a secure area, he didn't have his body armor on, I was going to go out and try to find our people. I round this corner, and I see the second blast site where the suicide bomber had infiltrated the compound and blown himself up. Still tons of bleeding, blown-up Iraqis, running toward me, and it was something I'll never forget.

[*Sean cries during parts of the following story.*] The first person I saw that was mine, his name's Ken Stevens, an interpreter for us, he was on hundreds of missions with us. When you live in such a small little area you become best friends with everybody. He always had a positive attitude, always making us laugh. I saw Ken lying on the ground. As I was running up to him, Lieutenant Colonel Doran was trying to pick him up. He was covered in blood and bullets were flying everywhere, crack, crack, crack, rounds impacting all over the place. As soon as I get to him, I pick him up and throw him over my shoulder, I grab the colonel by the arm, and I start running back towards our alley. I put Ken down, pull out my knife, cut off his shirt, pull out my first aid kit to see what the damage was because he was pretty messed up.

As soon as I cut off his shirt I saw he had two abdominal wounds, two puncture wounds, and he was bleeding from the neck. I started putting pressure on the neck because that was the wound that was bleeding the worst. I knew that if I had carried him any further, because I had him over my shoulder, I would have killed him because of the trauma to his stomach. So I put him down. The other people had come back, and one of their interpreters was with them, Scott. "Scott, I need you to just focus and get me a truck, get me an Iraqi truck." I started to work on Ken, he's moaning and he just looks at me, and he's telling me,

"Kenney, don't let me die, don't let me die," and I say, "Ken, I'm not going to let you die."

The firefight got bad and started coming back toward us, people were shooting each other left and right. Iraqis are crawling in, bleeding, blown up, missing body parts. I finally got a truck. I picked up Ken, laid him in the back of the truck, I jumped in and we drove into my compound and got Ken into a medevac. We drove him from there to Camp Ramadi. Our medics were gone that day, both of them were out on mission. There was nobody there that was more trained than I was to do first aid. I was covered in Ken's blood, and went right back to work. It was one of the hardest things to just shrug it off and go right back to work.

There were hundreds of people who died that day. [*Many Americans don't focus on that.*] It's a luxury, they don't have to know that. They don't know the price we have to give. They don't understand anything. That's one of the hardest things to come back to, is that you are walking around in the general population, and you see these people living a normal life, so ignorant of anything that has to do with the fact that... [*He cries*]. There are men and women who stand up for something... they don't have a choice. They signed on the dotted line. They don't get to choose where to go, they don't get to choose where to fight.

I've been shot at. People have tried to blow me up. People have tried to kill me. I don't know why I am lucky enough to survive— 4,000 US soldiers have been killed over in Iraq since the beginning of the conflict, almost 2,000 have been killed in Afghanistan. Why am I lucky that I got to come home? [*He cries.*] They awarded me a Bronze Star with Valor for that day. I think back to that day hundreds of times a day. It's never *not* with me. When people find out about my story, and they say something like, "I know what you feel like." They have no clue what it is like to carry one of your best friends and have them beg not to die. I dream about that all the time. [*He cries.*] It's one of the most painful memories, but it's also so rewarding to me. Because of this, I will never, never take for granted anything that I have.

I talk to Ken still, and it took him a long time to recover. He begs me to come out and see him in LA. I want to go out and visit him. I don't know if I could handle it right now, because this happened to me less than a year ago. He's alive. If he had died, I don't think I'd be as okay as I am now. I don't think I'd be able to tell the story.

He got to surgical in Ramadi, they stabilized him and they airlifted him directly to Germany. He lost a kidney, part of his liver, his stomach had collapsed, he eventually needed reconstructive skin surgery. He has a huge scar on his neck. He was bedridden, he didn't walk for a couple of months. He's still in physical therapy, still under doctor's care. It's almost a year later, but spiritually-wise I think he's doing pretty good, considering. Mostly he says, "Thank you," and we try to change the subject. Regardless of that he was my friend, I did my job. I did what I was supposed to do and I did what I was trained to do.

Maybe one day I will talk through it with him, and everything will subside a bit, but for now it's fresh and it's even fresher since I've been home. When it first happened, I literally did have to just shrug it off, I was a leader, I had twelve guys underneath me and they couldn't see the effect it had. They weren't allowed to see me having trouble sleeping, and they weren't allowed to see my hard time dealing with it. I suited up and I went back to work. The mission pace made it so I couldn't have time for myself. I worked straight through until we came home.

Once home it starts to sink in because you go from going a hundred miles an hour, three to eight missions a day. You come home and you are uncomfortable because you are thinking about everything you just went through. It hurts. I don't sleep much, I don't like going out. [*How is it to be a student now?*] Terrible. I registered for classes in April when I was home on leave. If I knew how bad it was going to be when I got home, I never would have.

My battalion is very proud of what I did, and they sent me to WLC [Warrior Leaders Course] to get me to be staff sergeant, E-6. I got home in July, I was in WLC in the second week of September and missed two weeks of school. The school here is not set up to help somebody in that situation. I'm going to try to change that. I'm working with the vice-president of student affairs, trying to put in policies to help students like me. But there's days when I can't come to school because I don't want to leave my house.

I'm not comfortable dealing with, basically, children in college, 18- to 20-year-old children here. They have this useful ignorance: the world isn't bigger than they are. They have their feelings and they think that's it. Good for them. I wish I could do that, but I can't. It's so hard for someone like me to come here, angry being in a class surrounded by people constantly making me uncomfortable. I get asked all the time, "How many people have you killed?" [*Have you learned the way to handle that?*] It's intimidation. I'm not a little guy. I'll tell them it's none of their fucking business. And I'll swell up, and I make sure that they know they are getting intimidated, so that they'll never ask that question to anyone ever again.

I still haven't received my GI Bill benefits for this school year. It's November and they were supposed to start in September. So, being a full-time student, I live on my own, my father moved down to Tennessee, my mother is deceased. [My siblings] are all grown up, they have their lives, my support element around here is not huge. I'm living off what I made over in Iraq. People who had been receiving the Montgomery GI Bill [the pre-August 2009 education benefit bill] had to relinquish that in order to get the Post-9/11 GI Bill. You can't receive both, which is understandable. The Post 9/11 GI Bill is a better bill. I guess it's the perfect storm [of] delayed benefits.

Then I deal with other things as far as the VA. I have three herniated disks in my back from body armor and damage done to me overseas in combat. I lost some of my hearing from explosions, tinnitus, ringing in the ears, typical things. I have nightmares, flashbacks all the time. Going to school, trying to get benefits, trying to get your health right while going to school, the system is not set up to help someone who has my issues. It's a nightmare.

There are 135 veterans on campus, most of them are OIF, OEF whether or not they are combat veterans. We want to make a campus center specifically a hang-out place, a USO-type of place for veterans to come to where they can get all the information they need to go to school. The problem is that veterans are very unapproachable. I don't want to go to support groups and trade war stories. I'm fighting two F's from my previous semester because I had to pull out of school early to deploy. Two professors graded me on my work up to that point, two professors failed me because I couldn't finish the work. I know I'm a smart person. Before I went, my GPA was 3.2, and now I think I am passing one of my five courses. My inability to handle school right now is going to affect my ability to have benefits down the road, tuition fees, waivers.

I've been home for a little over three months. I never got a chance to deal with anything overseas, even if I wanted to, I wouldn't have had time. I sleep two or three hours a night, maybe. I'm at the VA counseling center right now in Springfield. I've always considered myself to be that person you could count on in any kind of emergency or dire-need situation. Everyone who joins the military and does a combat-related job is always so gung-ho about getting into combat, doing their job, and coming out on top. That was me.

I'm more comfortable in my mind in a combat situation than I am in everyday life here. I've considered going back because when you do that job, it's so easy. I've done it, I've succeeded, I'm one of the best. My awards: Combat Action badge, Bronze Star with Valor, Good Conduct medals, graduating at the top of my class. It makes you want to go back over. But you'll never heal. You'll never heal. It pours more cement on an already existing issue that you'd have to chip through eventually.

[*What can you tell readers about the Iraq war?*] The obvious reason why we got sent there was the whole WMD fiasco. We never found anything. Politically, I'm a soldier, I don't get to choose where we get sent. The bad part of Iraq is that those beautiful people don't stand a chance without us being in there and being [their] defender. The interpreters that worked with us were telling us horror stories about how the government officials of the Ba'athist Party would just pick people off of the street, torture them, rape, kill, murder. They said the tribal segregation [was] so that the people would hate each other and there would be an ongoing civil war within the country between the Sunnis and the Shiites. It seemed like everybody wanted to kill everybody else. It was being fed by the government.

Iraq, they have no means of stabilizing themselves, [our] pulling out, taking away all that support, I have a feeling that it's just going to implode. If you don't help them take control of their country, then it's just going to be a war-torn environment for the rest of time. This is just my opinion, but for us to walk away from that situation now does a very big injustice to those over 4,000 soldiers who gave their lives to try to help to stabilize their country and have a life.

Saying all combat troops are out of Iraqi, it's a play on words. For civilians, anyone who doesn't understand what the military is, it seems like a great success on our government's side. But a combat troop is infantry, field artillery, it's those smash and grab people, Marine Corps, they control, they occupy, they hold. That's their job. Well, thousands and thousands and thousands of support elements are there. Military police like myself, explosive ordinance teams, engineers, canine units, advisors, high-ranking US military advisers from four-star generals to lieutenant colonels, captains—there are still thousands of troops in Iraq.

When I was leaving they were still doing hundreds of missions a week. AQI, al-Qaeda of Iraq, the main force that we were fighting against, don't target the United States because they know they're leaving. They target the Iraqis because they want to show instability in the government. They targeted that government building that I lived at, not because we were there, because the government was there. And if that terrorist faction can show instability in the government in that region, then the people of that region will not support the government. If you disrupt that, the terrorists have won.

They would steal ambulances and after detonating something, the first responders would come in, the Iraqi fire department or ambulances, and those hijacked emergency vehicles would come in and blow themselves up. They're trying to disrupt the Iraqi government, not focusing on the Americans. They need the US to still be there as an occupying force, it's what's behind those guys. We have intel, we have communications all over Iraq, we have medical assets, field artillery assets, air support, all of those things lined up behind that one squad that's going out to work.

That's why I think they're going to fail. They need that extra [help]. AQI would be a little more reluctant to attack an Iraqi police force if they knew that an Apache helicopter wasn't too far behind. Can you imagine if somebody broke into your house and was holding a gun to your head, and you couldn't call anyone to help you? That's what they're going through. Somebody comes in the middle of the night and kidnaps a member of your family, and that happens over there all the time, and you couldn't call anyone to help you.

It's like we are a stuck unit. Because we took over this country, we occupied this country, and now we are just tucking tail and are running. They're making everything we have worked for be in vain as far as pulling us out early. There's a high turnover rate when it comes to political officials in Iraq, they either get killed, disappear somehow, get buried out in the desert somewhere. Or they embezzle enough money to get rich and leave. There's a huge Iraqi population living all throughout Europe. When does it come down to saying enough is enough? You have until this time and we're out. That's way above my pay grade!

I get this question a lot: "Do you think we should be policing the world like this?" That's what we are trying to do given the ability we have. It's a responsibility to bring stability to other people, other places. It makes us stable, we have less of a threat. The question Americans ask is why should we have to do that? The answer is if we don't do that, and we don't do our part to secure the world, it's just going to allow events like 9/11 to happen in our country and in other countries, turning a blind eye to the rest of the world.

There's never going to be a storming the beaches at Normandy or a naval battle like you had in World War II. You're not fighting uniformed soldiers. If you don't adapt, you'll fail. They went into it as a traditional war and it wasn't there. They went in, they smashed, they grabbed, airborne guys jumping in, great, everyone is shooting, moving, communicating wonderfully, that's what we are trained to do. And then it ended, and what do we do now? General Petraeus seemed to have the biggest grasp on that. If this ends up being a success, which I hope it does, he's going to be in the history books.

"Steve" Nsaif was born in Iraq in 1987 and asked that I use his last name only. I interviewed him by telephone from his home in the US and have left out material that identifies where he lives, and his family, both in Iraq and the US. Now planning to enlist in the Marine Reserves, he hopes to become a US citizen soon. He was an interpreter for the US forces for periods between 2006 and 2010. He generally refers to the American forces and the United States as "we."

In 2006, right after my first year of college, I was assigned to a Marine unit on the Iraqi–Syrian border, al-Anbar province. I worked right on the Walid port of entry, people coming in from Syria, going to Syria. My main assignment was to train the Iraqi customs police. We had Marines who were trained to do such a mission and we had some federal agents helping them out from the US Customs and Border Protection. [I was] part interpreter, part trainer. I stayed there for three months and I decided to go back to college because summer break was over.

I requested an assignment in Baghdad part time so I could go to college. That's when I started working with the army because the army was controlling Baghdad and south Iraq while the Marine Corps were controlling the western part of Iraq. The new job wasn't what I was expecting. I was attached to a task force unit controlling northeast Baghdad, one of the cities with a lot of killing [from] insurgents. I started going out with them, they worked about eighteen, nineteen hours a day, infantry. Unfortunately, the unit ended up leaving after fifteen or eighteen months with the most number of casualties since the Vietnam War.

They wrote a book about that unit, *They Fought for Each Other: The Triumph and Tragedy of the Hardest Hit Unit in Iraq* by Kelly Kennedy. Task force 1/26, Charlie Company, I was attached to them on November 1, 2006. The city I was in is called Adhamiya, northeast Baghdad. That was the city where most of [Saddam's] loyal people lived, high-ranking officers in the old Iraqi army, where the rich people who used to work for him lived as well.

On November 5, 2006, I was on patrol with the second platoon from Charlie Company. We didn't know it was the day when the court was going to decide to execute Saddam Hussein. The city was calm and quiet in the early morning. Suddenly, we heard shooting nearby, a few minutes later, more shooting, closer this time. We started to see men running around with AK-47 rifles in the alleyways. They shot a couple of rounds on [the] convoy and hid. We called for backup support. Almost all of Charlie Company was outside the base engaged in a large-scale battle, to include the company commander. The firefight took about four to five hours, leaving about 30 to 40 insurgents dead on the streets of Adhamiya. Luckily, no casualties on our side that day. Late 2006 and beginning 2007, that was when we had a lot of casualties including Iraqi military, US military, and civilians as well.

In 2007 there was the bridge that went between Adhamiya and the other side of the river, called Utaifiya. It was blown up by a semi-trailer truck, which was a bomb truck, a big incident. It was right before one of the religious events where people march to the mosque across the river, one of the Shia events. That was a few days before it, so they cut that. It was difficult to see people [killed].

Mainly I was trying to get understood that those [US] soldiers are here to help, if no one helps them out, they're not going to know anything by themselves. Because where they came from is completely different from here. If they don't have somebody who lives here, somebody who knows everything about the culture in Iraq, about how those people think, they're not going to know anything. Even if they were trying to help, they could not do so much, unless they have someone to tell them [because] *you* know what's going on.

The main goal is trying to help [the US troops] and also help our people. On a lot of occasions, soldiers want us to translate the Iraqi, what did he mean? For example I was with one soldier and an Iraqi police officer was praying outside, and the soldier was like, "What's he doing?" "He's praying, it's time for prayer." "Well, he's doing that at the same spot." I was like, "Well, he cannot be praying in just any spot." "Why's he doing it the same way every time?" "You've got to pray facing south where Mecca is." "Wow, I didn't know that." "Well, you know now!"

[The soldiers did not understand] that the religion can control everything. The soldiers are saying why do [Iraqi] people have to say what their religious leader tells them? The religion is a huge part. I would have to say it's the biggest problem in the Middle East, [and] I would say Iraq, right now. People were raised that religion is the first thing, is everything to them. Unfortunately, a lot of people are using this mindset to control people. The religious leaders take advantage of this fact that people would have to listen to them.

That's where the power is coming from. It's more a fight over power than just religion. Right now, all the news about the Iraqi government, it's hard to put a government together because there are so many religious leaders fighting for the chair. The priests [in the US] won't deal with the government, they're not going to have that much power over it. I would say that Iran is the most religious because their government is an Islamic government so they rule everything by Islamic rules.

The problem with Iraq: there are so many types of religion, so many different mixtures of people. You have the Sunnis, you have the Shias, who are also divided into three different kinds of Shias. And you have Christians, Catholics. As far as the nation, not religion, you have the Kurdish and the Arabs. Also, every part of Iraq has a certain type of people. They are not mixed. If someone is from al-Anbar province right away I know he's Sunni, not Shia. Somebody tells me he's from Basra. Right away I assume he's Shia.

If you meet someone, you can tell which part of Iraq he's from. When I was with the Marines in Anbar province, I'd never been in Anbar province in my whole life. I was talking to those guys and they started laughing right away, "You're a pretty boy from Baghdad." They assume that people from Baghdad are rich, they have education. "Pretty boy" is like they have everything, their family's rich. In Baghdad, it's like you live in the capital, like saying you're a New Yorker.

I stayed with Charlie Company from November 2006 until they left in July 2007. I volunteered to stay in the same place with the next unit coming over, a civil affairs unit. The plan and tactics completely changed. I had a hard time dealing with the change because I was on a team for the Sons of Iraq program. The [Sunni] Awakening came up in 2007, that's when the US government started to pay money to people in the city and giving them weapons, so they would control their neighborhoods. [The Sons of Iraq correspond to the Sunni Awakening groups, which, under the leadership of Sunni sheikhs, first started in al-Anbar province in 2005 and spread across the country.]

We told the people, it's your city—you know it better than us. We're going to give you money, weapons, ammunition, and you defend your own city. We're here to help you if you need us, but you deal with your own problems and we're going to pay you for that. That calmed it down, they know better than us, but at the same time there's a lot of stuff that came up, unfortunately, for Adhamiya. When I was in Adhamiya [before], we were looking for those guys, right? We call them high priority targets, insurgents inside the city. We caught a lot of them but a lot of them ran away. When the unit changed, the tactics changed, we're not so aggressive any more. So those same guys that came over to be part of the Awakening, I can recognize them. This guy over here, we were looking for him for four or five months, why would you give him money and weapons right now? This guy was part of killing my guys in my unit, why the hell am I going to give him money right now?

It's more like a political thing. I understand what the main mission is, but still. It's true when we paid those guys money they stopped hitting on us, [but it] doesn't justify the fact that they *did*. What happens if you run out of money or you stop paying them? The way I looked at the Awakening, it's a temporary solution to a permanent problem. I had been there so long I had a good relationship with the Iraqi officers. They talked to me like friends, and I asked, what happens when we stop paying them? They said now we're trying to get them into the Iraqi army and Iraqi police so they have a job. But the Iraqi police are Shia and the [Sons of Iraq] are Sunni—the religious thing also controls the government.

Under Saddam Hussein most jobs went to Sunnis, but to the people who were loyal to him as well. He had the provinces that he was hiring from like his army officers, Tikrit, his hometown, and al-Anbar province. I think they were a big tribe, so they give big support to him, the hiring came from him. One of the things that people still talk about, there are certain families from Anbar province who turned against him, but he pretty much killed everyone in that family.

I would say between 1995 to 2003, the way he ruled the country, there is absolutely *no* room for mistake. You could do anything as long as you're not doing anything related to the government or violating anything, or a possible threat. His translation of a possible threat, you can't give your opinion about something in the government. He'd see it as a possible threat and you'd be executed for it. People start not to trust their own family members, they don't want to say anything in front of anybody. That was only an *opinion*, you didn't *do* anything, you just say what you think. He could take care of you and your family for that. He believed that he could do anything he wants. That's what led to the war with the United States because he was convinced that he could do anything. "I'm strong enough to fight any army in the world"—a huge mistake.

What I think is you should have taken him out during the Gulf War. That's one thing also the Iraqi people blame the United States for because a lot of people got killed during that time. I'm sure you are aware of the Iraqi Shia uprising during the Gulf War. They almost took Saddam out of power. The reason they were moving so fast and the reason they were pushing so fast to Baghdad, because Saddam was not able to fly any of his Air Force. He couldn't fly any fighting jets, he was not authorized by the UN. But once the rising [and] people came close to Baghdad, he *was* authorized to fly fighting jets.

A lot of people look at it like we got screwed over, the Iraqis. So a lot of people blame the US for that, to these days, people lost a lot of family members. They think about it, why didn't they authorize it at the last minute to take him out at the time? After that, nobody ever thought about doing anything like that [uprising]. While at the same time the Kurdish people up north took control of their territory, made their own government, based on a president backed up by the US. It's not part of Iraq any more, just on the map.

Coming from Baghdad, I cannot go by myself unless there is someone Kurdish who lives inside Kurdistan who can escort me inside. That's why I said, their own president, their own government, their own language, their own flag. When you tell them it's part of Iraq—no, it's Kurdistan. I can kind of understand what they did because Kurdistan is the most safe part of Iraq right now. There's only 700 [US] troops in the whole region. They're doing a good job controlling it.

Before Charlie Company left, the company commander, one of the best commanders I have ever seen in my life, was talking to me, the beginning of 2007, six months before they left. "What's your goal?" I said, "I don't know, sir, probably finish college, find a better job." He said, "Do you have any family in the US?" "Yes, I have family member [who] hopefully can help me get a scholarship to go to the US for an education there, hopefully stay there." And he said, "Well, I might be able to help you out. There's a program for interpreters who have served more than one year for the US forces—it's a long shot." "Well, sir, I don't know, you know better." You need letters of recommendation from generals and he was a captain. "I might be able to help you out. How long have you been working for us?" "Six or seven months only." "Well, let's see what we can do for you."

So I came back three or four days later, this company commander had got all the application forms for me. "I'm going to make sure you get out before I leave." He kept his promise. Even though he was moved to the battalion headquarters, he was passing me papers through other officers, getting everything done while he was away, too. I was approved for my visa already two or three days before he was leaving Iraq. It's a two-step process, you've got to get it approved for your case, then they start processing for your visa if you meet all the requirements. He got me a letter from the general and everybody in the chain of command of the unit, all the way up. Once I applied and they said you're approved, it's a matter of time until we process you for a visa, which is a routine process. They got checks, they've got pictures, fingerprints and all that. Okay, it's just a matter of time until I get out of here.

We were moved into a relatively safer area after we had many casualties to include six guys in one day, from my platoon, second platoon of Charlie Company. So after [Charlie Company] left, I was doing the civil affairs thing with the civil affairs team. They tried to make projects to gain the people to be on our side, cleaning the city, a sports complex for them. We were coming up with ideas where we can keep the people occupied doing something useful. The person I was working for did a great job. First time we had a little complications like, "Sir, I am not going to be able to do that job. Those are the guys that killed about fourteen guys in my company. I'm not going to be able to help them out, and just smile in their face every day."

He explained to me, he was a pretty smart officer, "We're not going to be able to do that unless we involve the whole city. It's not going to work out this way because it's going to kill a lot of civilians. The only way to do that is to get more people on our side than on the insurgents' side. Once we get more people on our side, they will feel safer and they will be willing to help us." He went step by step to explain to me because I was 19, 20 years old at the time. I didn't look at the big picture. So I started working with him and he did a great job.

I couldn't believe the city was safe. They were still walking around without body armor. The number of explosions was reduced from four or five times a day, to once every two or three weeks. When Charlie Company was there, we got worn out by getting bombed, like three or four times a day. It came out to be once every three or four weeks or none. Okay, that's the right way to do it then. That was late 2007.

I came to the US in 2008. The main reason I told my company commander, I wanted to join the US army and the only way to do that is to leave Iraq and come to the United States. So they put that in my paperwork why I'm coming to the US. That's part of my recommendation. A few weeks later, the contractor for the Defense Department wanted to hire me as a linguist again. This time, I'm working as a US-hired linguist.

The army already talked to me about enlisting—I didn't even have my social security number. "I just got here, so I'm not going to be able to answer you right now." It's a long process, about five, six months. It took me a long time to get my security clearance because I was born outside, lived outside, so it wasn't easy to go through my background. They asked me if I want to go straight to Iraq, or go on one of the special programs the Marine Corps had at the time to train the Iraqi police forces and the counterterrorism units. They sent me to Camp Pendleton, California, for two, three months training for the mission, to get to know the team I'm going to be working with, train with them before we went to Iraq.

We deployed in January 2009 to al-Anbar province. The team left after six months because Marines only do six-month deployments. Another team came up for two or three months. I got to know pretty much everybody. When the National Guard [came], they pulled all the Marines out of Iraq and sent them to Afghanistan. Two or three months after, there is not even one Marine on Iraqi soil.

My main mission is as an interpreter and an advisor for the leader of the team as well as the Iraqi Police Force. Our mission was to train the Iraqi police forces and the counterterrorism units. They were the main guys on the ground. I was in Asad Airbase, deployed to Iraq late January 2009. I came home June 2010. [*He notes that he is going into Marine Corps reserve.*] My chances of deploying are lower than active-duty members. The reason I joined the Marines is their deployments are always six months. The army can be eighteen months, a minimum of twelve. Even if I get called to deploy to Afghanistan, I'd get back sooner than going in the army. I can read and write Pashtun, but unfortunately I'm not able to understand it. I can know the names of places.

At 23, I still have some time. I can't believe where I am right now, so much stuff that I wasn't planning just happened. I couldn't ask for better. No one over here, including me, knows what's really happening over there. As far as Iraq, I'm talking to my family. They always say it's getting better, then a week later it hits rock bottom again. I believe it's always changing because of the government issues, the political issues, everything changes in minutes.

The way I think about it, and again, it's only my personal

opinion, we kind of messed up in the first place, in 2003, the strategy. The call was right, the decision to remove Saddam from power I believe was right, but the strategy wasn't that good. All the problems started after the invasion. Everybody knows we removed Saddam in less than a month—he was out. But what happened after that? What are we going to do now? Everybody was like, Saddam is out of power. We kind of got lost.

What we should have done at the time was have a government ready, a system ready, then we modify it, instead of taking everything down and trying to rebuild it in the same place. We took the Iraqi army down, we took the Iraqi police down, we took all the government places down, everybody fired. Okay, we're going to start the whole recruiting process, we're going to try to make a new government, elections and all that. But there's no time to do all that because at the moment it's all a mess. Then trying to put everything back they gave a chance for the insurgency to start operating. There's no power, no law enforcement, no army to stop them.

They were trained for conventional warfare but you cannot do that in a city with the people. So we had to stay there, deal with it, and try to fix it for the past seven years. I think what will happen is a federal government. They're going to try to get representatives from each part of Iraq or each group in Iraq represented in the government. Because you have so many types of people within Iraq, you can't just pick one of them to be in charge and screw everybody else because people won't accept it. They had the old regime and they don't want that anymore. Everybody understands that in forming the Iraqi government they have to get a government where everybody accepts it. That's what they are working on right now.

[*Can you tell a story about a humorous situation?*] One of the young soldiers we had, just out of high school, and we were going into a house and they usually cook lamb. Some older people, they cook the total head of the lamb. This soldier walked into the kitchen and he came out running and screaming, "They have a dead guy in there and they are taking hair out of his head!" He was like nineteen years old. "What are you talking about?" "The lady is putting him in hot water and is taking the hair out of his face!" That's a cultural difference, he thought it was a *person's* head. He was so scared he was screaming. Everybody started laughing after that. He had heard all those stories of people being tortured, and finding dead bodies from kidnapping. He didn't know they cook the whole [lamb].

I've been in many situations that people try to make up a story because they think that Americans won't know it. This is where I came in. "Well, this is what he said, but this is what *I think*... This is what he told me, it's up to you, but it doesn't make any sense." The guy will say I came from Basra two years ago, you know his last name or his tribal name, and you know there's no such thing in Basra.

[*Nsaif asks about my book. I explain that I document people's experience in order to educate the public, and that I do it by having veterans talk for themselves.*] One more question, ma'am. Are you going to help out the service members when the book gets published? A lot of people think we're just trying to make a buck, everybody looking to be famous. I don't want to get into that. I would recommend the charities or organizations that support the troops, not for the people in the book, but for people in the military. They would know we are helping them out. The families of the people who got killed, they are the people who deserve something, like the soldiers at Walter Reed Hospital. I guess that's it. Thank you very much, ma'am.

Epilogue

THE RECKONING

One of the pleasures of writing an oral history is listening to something said better than you could ever have said it, offered by someone who speaks from personal experience. Let me draw together a few of those comments that resonate from war to war, a handing off of the torch, from one generation of soldiers to the next.

From the World War II veterans:

Ever since World War II, they've kept some kind of war going, all the time. (Jones)

I believe in my country, they say right or wrong. I believe in my country, right. If it is wrong, I want to make it right! (Cohen)

If everyone has the bomb, good-bye earth. (Kells)

We thought that World War II was going to end all wars and it hasn't. It seems worse now than World War II. (Kostanski)

From Korea veterans:

Unless it is political, why are we sticking our nose into other people's business? It's terrible. (Hart)

From Vietnam veterans:

My conviction is that the reality of war is so obscene, so shockingly terrible, that it's one of the worst things in the world. (Munroe)

I just had a lot of sadness for the little people who are the ones that suffer most from wars. (Rogers)

There is, in my experience, not clear "good guys" or "bad guys." (Rankin)

Americans died in the conflict, you cannot let that go. You spill the blood, now you have to atone for it. (Basye)

They've been to Iraq, they've been to Afghanistan, they've had their houses foreclosed on…their businesses are shut down… These guys have had it tougher than I ever did. (Hartman)

More than anything else, I like to think that all the people that were sacrificed there didn't do nothing out there, because they showed what America is willing to do. (Gregg)

From veterans of Iraq and Afghanistan:

You cannot bring in a Western-style democracy and expect it to work. The proverbial you can't put a square peg in a round hole. I don't know if it's self-delusion or just not caring. (McGurk)

We've gotten off track and we need to worry about our country and where it's going. (Woehlke)

My awards: Combat Action badge, Bronze Star with Valor, Good Conduct medals, graduating top of my class. It makes you want to go back over. But you'll never heal, you'll never heal. It pours more cement on an already existing issue that you'd have to chip through eventually. (Kenney)

In World War II there was a clear road to war and the world watched as it got closer and closer. In Europe, the line was drawn at Poland, and the starter went off on September 1, 1939. The road through war was also clear; it ended in the unconditional surrender of the Axis powers to the Allies, first Germany and then Japan. The goalposts were marked and observed. In Korea, the invasion by North Korea on June 25, 1950 marked the beginning, and a final armistice (not yet a peace treaty) was signed on July 27, 1953. Those goalposts, too, were visible to all. When the Vietnam Veterans Memorial was being constructed in Washington, DC, however, it led to a debate about what years actually bracketed that war. It was decided to list deaths from 1959 to 1975, although those dates stretch the war before its beginning and after its end.

Even more, the current wars are indistinct in duration, purpose, and outcome. Their costs in financial treasure are stupendous and match any previous war, but the cost in fatalities is far lower than in previous and conventional wars. For on-site destruction they match earlier wars, but it is the nature of combatting non-traditional foes that so distinguishes our current endeavors.

We have heard from 55 veterans of foreign wars fought by the United States in the last 70 years. This collection of their personal stories and views on their own and other wars, and on war itself, ends with this question: Of what value to our country are our current wars in Iraq and Afghanistan, and can we even achieve our aims by war? Vietnam raised similar questions earlier. Many, but not all, of the narrators wonder whether America has entered into too many and too poorly selected (and managed) wars since World War II. They say we should consider, before launching into new engagements, what this country can and cannot do and should and should not do. They also weigh whether we can win a given war, and whether it is a just or necessary war.

As civilians and citizens, we also should address these questions. Does US world leadership with its moral, military, and political force, truly depend on a "win" in either or both Afghanistan and Iraq? If it does, then our leadership is very challenged after a decade of sending troops overseas without winning results. Let us consider those two wars, for the sake of argument, lost. Would US global achievements and its democratic traditions be shaken by a "loss" in those countries? Or could these wars be considered major missteps that we recognized and remedied as best we could?

The fear of tarnishing our national and international reputation is rational, and was a major block to resolving the Vietnam War; it is today a barrier to resolving our current wars. We must not operate out of the fear of losing, because losing an improbable or impossible war for hearts and minds in distant and different lands is more than likely, and should be accepted, now that it has happened. We will survive the debacle of retreat, however staged. The pride in being an American, and in being an American soldier, is durable even when war and its conduct—and sometimes its outcome—is self-defeating.

While we are looking to war as a solution, we too often lose track of its measurable cost. We have spent our, and foreign, treasure in Iraq and Afghanistan: both sides have lost men, women, and children, killed, damaged, and bereft. Both sides have siphoned off money that could have been much better spent. The multifaceted cost of what we have done must be acknowledged. There is the constant leakage of the lives of US soldiers from explosives, firepower, and suicide. There is devastation in the lives of local civilians from suicide bombings and explosions in marketplaces, in the lines of police recruits, and among pilgrims of a different sect. These constitute the true cost to be weighed against any benefit from staying on. The tragedy is not only in the persistent killing, but in the cumulative sense of the uselessness of death without lasting gains.

How do we vindicate this cost of treasure and human life? Our role in holding off the "forces of evil" everywhere is not only a very risky adventure but brings further risks when we fail. When the US looks around for rationales in a foreign conflict (both those inflicted on us, as in 9/11, and those we initiate), we are looking inward, because we conceive of war as a solution to our problems. It is interesting that right after we failed to find weapons of mass destruction (WMD) in Iraq because there were none, we immediately spotted the same threat in Iran, although not for the first time. A WMD threat justifies our operations. We will now shift our sights back to nuclear arms in hostile lands or hands (non-state terrorists) just as surely as we did after World War II when first the USSR and then China "got" the bomb.

We need to look outward to where we are going, investigate, and understand local conditions and constraints before resorting to arms. We conceive a war and then busy ourselves with its planning and conduct, its "surges" and draw-downs, even its nomenclature. Most Americans have not noticed that Secretary of Defense Gates wrote a memo to General Petraeus, dated February 17, 2010, changing the name of Operation Iraqi Freedom (OIF) to Operation New Dawn, to reflect an "evolving relationship with the Government of Iraq." As of September 1, 2010, the DOD restarted its casualty statistics on deaths and injuries to our troops in Iraq under a new name. And now we worry about the safety of our soldiers as they leave. But the real point is that we conceive wars that we cannot win.

On Afghanistan, ex-Secretary of Defense Gates concluded that, "Far too much has been accomplished, at far too great a cost, to let the momentum slip away just as the enemy is on his back foot." [June 10, 2011, NATO meeting in Brussels.] While conceding that

Afghanistan and Iraq were wars "of choice" just before he retired, Gates has also reversed the concept of removing combat troops first and support and training troops last, as planned in Iraq. In Afghanistan, the still-lasting war, he wanted to leave combat troops for the last, and have them leave facing backwards, having the last shot—or the last say. That's like maintaining that we didn't lose the war in Vietnam because we had already pulled out when the North Vietnamese invaded South Vietnam and unified the country under communist control. We can lose a war even when we resolve it by being the first to leave the battlefield.

In his speech to the nation after ordering Osama bin Laden killed, President Obama reiterated the American mantra, speaking of our "commitment to stand up for our values abroad, and our sacrifices to make the world a safer place... because of who we are: one nation, under God, indivisible, with liberty and justice for all." We are still married to the tradition of American exceptionalism and the natural supremacy of American and Western values. This has been translated into the belief that there is a democratic (meaning American) solution to civil war and insurgency elsewhere. The soldiers in this volume do not necessarily think so. This, then, is the current American quagmire, the paradox in which we, a great power, again find ourselves.

The reader might review the entire text of the Declaration of Independence of July 4, 1776, proceeding from the first two famous paragraphs to the next and much longer section that excoriates George III as an evil king *forcing* Americans (this is mainly Thomas Jefferson's formulation as moderated for overstatement by Benjamin Franklin) to fight for freedom. America has always had an enemy; there has always been a "bad guy." The period from 1945–89 of the Cold War was a metaphor for our righteousness. We have always as a nation, espoused the "right," as stated in the Declaration of Independence: "appealing to the Supreme Judge of the world for the rectitude of our intentions, do, in the name and by the authority of the good people of these colonies, solemnly publish and declare that these United Colonies are, and of right ought to be, FREE AND INDEPENDENT STATES... We mutually pledge to each other our lives, our fortunes, and our sacred honor."

Such rectitude means that when things go wrong, it has to be someone else's fault, from the Nazis and the Japs to the "Red

Menace," to Ho Chi Minh, Saddam Hussein, Khomeini, and now Ahmadinejad. Or Osama bin Laden, who was (like Hussein) "taken out." I don't believe that most Americans want to follow a God-given destiny to always be right (how then can we correct ourselves and live up to our highest expectations?) or always have to be fighting the bad guys. Yes, we will pull back from these fights, reluctantly, but realistically, as we did in Vietnam, knowing that after war we must strive for peace.

As we are now seeing, misconceived war is harder to end than to start. Our next task—because we must take responsibility for our actions and the devastation in Iraq and Afghanistan—should be to pay for humanitarian aid and rebuilding, using international agencies such as the UN's World Food Program and UNICEF, as well as all available non-government organizations. The challenge is that reconstruction requires peace and security and both are lacking in the wake of our invasions and occupations and local turmoil. We can't blast away these problems with American dollars, using expatriate contractors who are in it for the money. We should be developing a Marshall Plan, headed by the best of Arab and Muslim leadership in and from that area, that has the finite goal of restoring some services and hope to their people in, say, five years. Something can be accomplished in that time. It occurs to me that some veterans who are understanding and empathetic to people in the countries where they fought, might want to help rebuild those countries, not as soldiers, but as graduates of soldiering.

Many problems were entrenched in Iraq and Afghanistan before we came, and we have created further problems by our interventions. Our soldiers have done enough, and should not be the peacemakers, or peacekeepers, even though in both those countries, civilians and in some cases, the government, realistically fear that the departure of US troops will invite chaos. We must stay out of the way as indigenous institutions and methods take over the task of restoring the dignity of the people and authority of domestic leadership. But we cannot let famine, despair, and genocide replace our troops; that would truly be un-American.

So, if US interventions abroad are to be carefully weighed, we should include not only our intentions, but the physical and political impact of our military incursions and the costs to all parties.

At the same time, we have many other demands on us as peace-makers, and we need to shift our focus to honest diplomacy across the Middle East, from working with Arab uprisings, the Arab Spring in Tunisia and Egypt, and "regime change" in Libya, Syria, and Yemen, and other countries poised to alter the nature of Middle Eastern governance in the 21st century. We must seek a new peace for Israel (as we once did) and a new Palestine. We have a role to play, but we cannot determine the outcome. The Middle Eastern and South Asian countries in turmoil must set their own course and elect governments that are accountable in the wake of dictatorial regimes that siphoned off the energies and hopes of their people.

Meanwhile, I believe we should counter terrorism with local and international police action using smaller targeted military methods, not large-scale warfare. Terrorism will be most definitively defeated domestically, not by foreigners. We need intermediate aims, not general goals like spreading democracy and defeating terrorism, which extend too far into the future to be realistic. We can also anticipate that extremism will at some point burn itself out.

Unfortunately, too often we look first for military solutions. For example, the US Army and US Marine Corps keep updating a guide called *Counterinsurgency: Field Manual*, by General David H. Petraeus, USA and General James F. Amos, USMC, most recently in December 2006. General Petraeus is known to the public as the author of the surge and the Sunni Awakening in Iraq, and until recently, was the head of military operations in Afghanistan. As a manual for use by the military, it is informative about insurgencies past and present but it does not offer a political rationale for counterinsurgency; in other words, it cannot guide the US government, just its forces. It does not address the question of why the US fights insurgencies around the globe because counterinsurgency—or COIN—is a military method, the "what" and "how," not the "why." It is not easily combined with aid or diplomacy, and it is unlikely to succeed in any of its forms, as history has shown.

It is believable that we are fighting because of 9/11, the military-industrial complex, a defense system grown huge, or natural resources like oil. While all these reasons play a large role and certainly make the decision to engage in hostilities more politically palatable, I do not believe they are the historical, or even basic, *cause* of our current wars. I think that we fight insurgencies, intervene in wars between religious and political groups, social groups at odds, and in tribal wars despite the fact that the US has no natural ally in such internecine conflicts, because of what we think is our exceptional role in the world.

The US history of war and its foundation in our political exceptionalism make us eager to use combat against insurgencies. If no place is too remote, too alien, too intractable for our troops, we can always wage these wars. As global policemen, it is hard to remember that we are only outsiders in these conflicts. Legitimate local governments can be ineffective as well, so we lend a hand. If we fought in Vietnam against communism for ten years to prove that we were willing to do so, should we replicate that determination against insurgencies now? We can defeat and occupy a country, but how do we defeat terrorist tactics? One veteran of World War II said it's like a war on mosquitos. Another, a veteran of the war in Afghanistan, said it's like the war on drugs, not meant to be won—a process, not a battle.

Well, what's wrong with trying? Is it not a noble and worthwhile cause that befits our country's identity? The problems and challenges of current wars, as well as the Vietnam War, have been identified in these pages by veterans who have faith in the US mission. *They* ask how we can avoid making as many enemies as friends as we seek to impose our vision of freedom on others. *They* wonder, as our (and *their*) military fights terrorism abroad, what will happen if we can't succeed. Do those who have fought in Afghanistan and Iraq think we can win? In fact, *they* ask what is meant by "winning."

No veteran or civilian has to abandon the belief in the United States as a force for good if they are also willing to accept that our intervention may be fruitless. The current wars fought in the hope of removing a bad regime and installing a democratic government in a foreign country are quite simply beyond our own or any outside country's capability. A number of veterans have concluded in these pages that we must learn to accept that while some wars vindicate the best of our purposes, some wars will defeat them.

Veterans are among the most patriotic of Americans, yet while wishing otherwise, they do acknowledge that there are wars that

American forces cannot win. Even if we do some good, or try, the effort may fail. That is not the end of the world as we know it, nor our country as we know it. There must be other, better, ways than major military action to defeat terrorism. The United States of America can work on that.

POSTSCRIPT

What can the reader do to help veterans? There is much to do, and I hope the reader will find a way in his or her community to make things better for veterans of our foreign wars. Some may also want to support humanitarian efforts in those countries that have been devastated by our wars. I plan to do what was suggested to me by the final narrator, an Iraqi now becoming an American citizen. He asked that I provide support not to those who narrated the stories but to those who have been injured, or the families of those injured and killed. I will happily use any proceeds from this book to do so.

GLOSSARY OF MILITARY TERMS

40 and 8	French rail boxcar carrying 40 men or 8 horses (World Wars I, II)
I–IV Corps	Tactical zones in South Vietnam from north to south
Abu Ghraib	Prison where US soldiers abused Iraqi prisoners, made public April 2004
AFB	Air Force base
Agent Orange	"Operation Ranch Hand" in Vietnam 1962–71 used this herbicide to destroy crops and defoliate jungle. A human carcinogen and cause of multiple birth defects in exposed Vietnamese population and US troops
AK-47	Russian-designed assault rifle. *Also* Kalashnikov
AIT	Advanced individual training
ammo	Ammunition
atomic bomb	Hiroshima, August 9, 1945; Nagasaki, August 9, 1945
awards	Medal of Honor, Army Distinguished Cross, Navy/Air Force Cross, Silver Star, Distinguished Flying Cross, Bronze Star
AWOL	Absent without leave
barrage	Balloon protection against low-flying aircraft
bazooka	Short-range rocket launcher, anti-tank
C-4, C-6	Powerful plastic explosives
casualty	Person killed or injured
CH-46	Sea Knight transport helicopter
"Charlie"	Vietcong
CO	Commanding officer

court-martial	Judicial procedure for members of the armed services
Delta Force	Army elite counterterrorism force
DFC	Distinguished Flying Cross medal
DMZ	Demilitarized zone (cf. Korea, Vietnam)
domino theory	If Vietnam fell to communists, neighboring countries would too
EOD	Explosive ordinance disposal (individual or team)
firebase	Secured (often remote) site
FOB	Forward operating base
Force Recon	Marine special operations unit
General Quarters	Announcement for all hands to man battle stations
Green Zone	Protected area of Baghdad, housing US and Iraqi government offices
grenade	Hand-thrown or rocket-propelled (RPG)
HAC	Helicopter aircraft commander
half-track	Vehicle with front truck tires and back tank tracks
HMM-265	Marine medium helicopter, Squadron 265
Ho Chi Minh Trail	Infiltration route from North Vietnam into South Vietnam
howitzer	Movable cannon firing shells
"Huey"	UH-1E turbine powered evacuation and utility helicopter
Humvee	High-mobility multipurpose wheeled vehicle (HMMWV)
IED	Improvised explosive device (often placed by insurgents on roads)
intel	Intelligence information

JAG	Judge advocate general
KIA	Killed in action
klick	Slang for a kilometer
MASH	Mobile army surgical hospital
Medevac	Medical evacuation
M-1	.30-caliber semi-automatic clip-fed rifle, standard in World War II
M-4, M-14, M-16	Assault weapons
MIA	Missing in action
MiG	Russian-made fighter aircraft developed in the 1940s
Montagnards	French term for mountain peoples, including Hmong; mercenaries trained by Special Forces to fight NVA and Vietcong
mortar	short-range high-angled weapon firing shells
MOS	military occupational specialty
MP	military police
MRE	meals ready to eat (field rations)
My Lai	US army massacre of 347 to 504 Vietnamese civilians on March 16, 1968. When made public on November 16, 1969, shocked Americans and fueled anti-war sentiment.
napalm	Highly flammable jellied incendiary
Navy SEAL	Elite Navy operatives
NBC	Nuclear, biological, chemical (potential attacks)
NCO	Noncommissioned officer
NVA	North Vietnamese army
OCS	Officer candidate school
OEF	Operation Enduring Freedom (Afghanistan 2001–)

OIF	Operation Iraqi Freedom (Iraq 2003–)
OTS	Officer training school
PLC	Platoon leaders course
pop a smoke	Verbal request from helicopters to ground troops to use colored smoke to indicate their position
POW	Prisoner of war
PTSD	Post-Traumatic Stress Disorder
Purple Heart	Medal awarded for injuries or death, est. 1782
quonset hut	Building with half-circle corrugated metal roof
radio	UHF (ultrahigh frequency) and FM (frequency modulation)
RAF	Royal Air Force (UK)
rations	C-rations/C-rats, K-rations. *See also* MRE.
recon	Abbreviation for reconnaissance
rocket	Self-propelled projectile
PX	Post-exchange: military store located on base
ROE	Rules of engagement governing permissible action against an enemy
ROTC	Reserve officers' training corps
RPG	Rocket-propelled grenade
SAC	Strategic Air Command (1946–92), US long-range nuclear strike force
SAM	Surface to air missile
ship markings	US ship (USS), name, initials designating type or use, number, e.g. *USS Helena* CL [cruiser, light]-50; *USS Farquhar* DE [destroyer escort]-139
shrapnel	Bomb or shell fragments thrown by an explosion

Special Forces	Elite Army force, often blends into native population, also called Green Berets
Tet offensive	Coordinated attack on South Vietnam by Vietcong and NVA, January 31, 1968
Tomahawk	Cruise missile fired from ship, land, or aircraft
torpedo	Self-propelled underwater or aerial missile
Twentynine Palms	Marine desert training camp in California
USMC	US Marine Corps
USO	United Service Organizations, support and entertainment for troops
VBIED	Vehicle-borne improvised explosive device
VC	Vietcong
V-E Day	Victory in Europe, May 8, 1945
VFW	Veterans of Foreign Wars
V-J Day	Victory in Japan, August 14, 1945
WIA	Wounded in action
XO	Executive officer, second in command

ACKNOWLEDGMENTS

I was raised in Milton, Massachusetts, the second of five children born during the years 1940 to 1947. My parents participated in the war effort, both professionally and personally. They housed Danish pilots on their way to Canada to be trained to fight the Nazis, and were still upset when they told us years later how many of them had died. They took in a teenager who was evacuated from Cambridge, England for three years. My earliest memory is when I was three years old and the grown-ups were dancing and acting silly and building a cairn because it was V-J Day. I also recall my parents telling me that the Korean War was finally over when they picked me up from summer camp.

As a young adult, I lived through every year of the Vietnam War, and it shaped my American identity and what I believed my citizenship entailed: bearing witness to all that was right and all that was wrong with my country's foreign policies. The current wars in Iraq and Afghanistan have inspired me to write this book.

I would like to thank my husband Gordon A. Tripp, MD, for his help, support, and patience. I am also grateful to my two children, Adam Emerson Pachter, a writer and editor, and Gillian Forbes Pachter, a film director and script writer, who were excellent sounding boards throughout.

I have dedicated this book to Leo Parent, a veteran and a Veterans' Services Officer in Franklin County, Massachusetts, who for 25 years has worked tirelessly for veterans of all wars. He helped and supported me in countless ways over the last six years.

I very much appreciate the interest and commitment of my publisher, Michel Moushabeck, of Interlink Publishing Group; my editor Pam Thompson, who guided me thoughtfully and carefully through two books of veterans' narratives; Pam Fontes-May, who did a fine job with the design, Moira Megargee, whose work on publicizing the book has been of great help, and Sara Rauch for her careful copy-editing.

I am most deeply in debt to all the veterans who recorded their stories with me, for what they taught me about America's wars, commitment to country, and our shared American identity.